Axis of Empire

Axis of Empire

A History of Iran-US Relations

Afshin Matin-Asgari

London • New York

To Sofia, Jasamin, Afsaneh and my American compañeros

First published by Verso 2026
© Afshin Matin-Asgari 2026

All rights reserved

The manufacturer's authorized representative in the EU for product safety (GPSR) is LOGOS EUROPE, 9 rue Nicolas Poussin, 17000, La Rochelle, France
Contact@logoseurope.eu

The moral rights of the author have been asserted

3 5 7 9 10 8 6 4 2

Verso
UK: 6 Meard Street, London W1F 0EG
US: 207 East 32nd Street, New York, NY 10016
versobooks.com

Verso is the imprint of New Left Books

ISBN-13: 978-1-83976-226-0
ISBN-13: 978-1-83976-228-4 (US EBK)
ISBN-13: 978-1-83976-227-7 (UK EBK)

British Library Cataloguing in Publication Data
A catalogue record for this book is available from the British Library

Library of Congress Cataloging-in-Publication Data
A catalog record for this book is available from the Library of Congress

Typeset in Minion Pro by MJ & N Gavan, Truro, Cornwall
Printed by Integrated Books International, United States of America

Contents

Acknowledgments

This book owes a great debt to many friends, colleagues and family members who helped me find sources, commented on its chapters, improved my writing, clarified my ideas in conversations, and provided support during its long journey to completion. I am indebted first and foremost to Eskandar Sadeghi-Boroujerdi, who suggested the idea of the book to Verso, read and commented on the entire manuscript, and helped me navigate intellectual detours and pitfalls. Next, I am grateful to Sebastian Budgen for his steady hand and professionalism carrying the book project forward through different stages of writing and editing. Nick Walther and Verso's copy-editors vastly improved my text, as did Melissa Weiss with the book's cover design.

The list of everyone to whom this book is indebted is too long to be fully acknowledged here, but my special gratitude must go to Ervand Abrahamian, Abbas Amanat, Mehrdad Amanat, Maziar Behrooz, Houchang Chehabi, Wai Kit Choi, Sasan Fayazmanesh, Firoozeh Kashani-Sabet, Nasser Mohajer, Mahmoud Monshipouri, Ali Rahnema, Siavush Randjbar-Daemi, Mehrdad Samadzadeh, Vida Samian, Melissa Sanford, Matthew K. Shannon, Angela Vergara, and Scott Wells. I am immensely grateful to my wife and daughter, Jasamin and Sofia, for their intellectual and emotional support, as well as tolerance of my book-writing taking away from our precious time together. The same goes for my sister, Afsaneh, who, through our running discussions, reminds me that everything can be seen from different perspectives.

Afshin Matin-Asgari
September 2025, Los Angeles

Introduction

> *I have seen that we do not intend to free, but to subjugate the people of the Philippines. We have gone there to conquer, not to redeem . . . And so, I am an anti-imperialist. I am opposed to having the eagle put its talons on any other land.*
>
> Mark Twain in the aftermath of the 1898 Spanish-American War[1]

About a year before the outbreak of the COVID-19 pandemic, I received an email from Verso Books asking if I could write a history of Iran-US relations from a left perspective and for nonspecialist readers. Surprised and delighted, I quickly accepted, without thinking much about the enormous challenges the project would entail. First, this had to be a pioneering work, because no single comprehensive narrative covering the entire history of Iran-US relations existed, although different periods and parts of this history were thoroughly studied. Second, the bulk of existing literature consisted of diplomatic and political history, focusing on the post–Second World War period when state actors took center stage. As one scholar of this field notes, "Most recent works do not seriously consider nonstate actors or the transnational flow of ideas."[2] A growing body of new source material, consisting of literary, artistic, and journalistic work, travelogues, memoirs, and migration, gender, anthropological, and cultural studies, probes the hitherto unexplored aspects of America's encounter with Iran. Ideally, these new sources can supplement political

1 Mark Twain, "Mark Twain Home, An Anti-Imperialist," *The New York Herald*, October 16, 1900, p. 4.

2 Matthew Shannon, "Reading Iran: American Academics and the Last Shah," *Iranian Studies* 51, no. 2 (March 2018): 289–316, quoted on 290.

and diplomatic history, making possible an alternative multidimensional narrative, a peoples' history. But this new material remains too small and disjointed, compared to the overwhelming preponderance of diplomatic and political history. This book therefore cannot claim to have overturned the narrative sway of diplomatic history, although I have tried to challenge and go beyond numerous implicit and explicit assumptions of state-centric metanarratives.

While the COVID crisis and my heavy teaching responsibilities slowed the progress of this book, two broad histories of Iranian-American relations were published, providing me with a comparative benchmark. John Ghazvinian, *America and Iran: A History, 1720 to the Present* (2021) and Firoozeh Kashani-Sabet, *Heroes to Hostages: America and Iran, 1800–1988* (2023) are valuable contributions by professional historians, written in quite different styles and scales. I have benefitted from both works, but my book's structure, narration, analysis, and source choices differ from theirs. As its title suggests, Ghazvinian's book is the more ambitious of the two, in fact the most ambitious attempt to date at writing a comprehensive history of the subject, beginning half a century before the United States came into existence. In a readable and engaging style, it delivers an enormous amount of historical information, supplementing familiar political narratives with fitting anecdotes and tidbits of cultural history. More strictly academic, Kashani-Sabet's *Heroes to Hostages* uses a smaller canvas to focus more deeply on the Iranian side of the story, incorporating a good measure of cultural history, culled from Persian primary sources and archival material. The dichotomy in the phrase *Heroes to Hostages* suggests a tragic reversal of American fortunes in Iran, a fall from initial good grace and intentions.[3]

The book you are reading dispenses with the mythologies of good intentions and auspicious beginnings, as well as their implied suggestions about Iran-US history suffering from misperceptions and mistrust.[4]

---

3 James A. Bill, *The Eagle and the Lion: The Tragedy of American-Iranian Relations* (Yale University Press, 1988); Badi Badiozamani, *Iran and America: Rekindling a Love Lost* (Honolulu: East-West Understanding Press, 2005); Barry Rubin, *Paved with Good Intentions: The American Experience in Iran* (Penguin Books, 1981). Matthew K. Shannon, *Mission Manifest: American Evangelicals and Iran in the Twentieth Century* (Cornel University Press, 2024) is a sympathetic but critical study of American Presbyterian missionaries in the twentieth-century Iran.

4 Three new books on US-Iran relations were published in 2025, none dealing with the long-term history of these relations. The first two books are studies in international relations, focusing on how a postrevolutionary Iranian state, the Islamic Republic, was formed and evolved in defiance of a US-dominated international order. The authors share an Iranian nationalist perspective, noting the systematic impositions of the United

Drawing on a massive body of historical evidence, this book shows that, throughout the twentieth century and all the way to the present, American policy toward Iran invariably has been shaped by imperial priorities. The imperialist character of US foreign policy has been amply studied by generations of scholars, ranging from Marxists to theorists of the realist school of international relations.[5] Like all empires throughout history, the American empire was formed through war and military conquest, establishing a formidable base in the North American continent, then extending its sway across South America and the Pacific Ocean, and, after the Second World War, to the entire globe. During the past eight decades, the American empire's global dominance has been enforced

States, while recognizing the Islamic republic's contribution to the impasse of its relations with the global hegemon. As its title suggests, Mohsen Milani's *Iran's Rise and Rivalry with the US in the Middle East* (Oneworld Publications) somewhat exaggerates Iran's challenge to the United States, while Vali Nasr's *Iran's Grand Strategy: A Political History* (Princeton University Press) covers the same ground without delving deeply into its historical background. Both books are sober updates to earlier international relations studies of the same topic such as Mahmood Monshipouri's *In the Shadow of Mistrust: The Geopolitics and Diplomacy of US-Iran Relations* (Oxford University Press, 2022). The third book, Scott Anderson, *King of Kings: The Iranian Revolution: A Study of Hubris, Delusion and Catastrophic Miscalculation* (Doubleday, 2025), is a readable account by a non-specialist. It focuses on the 1970s background of the revolution, showing how major strategic mistakes by the shah and the Carter administration led to the monarchy's revolutionary collapse.

5 For a critical overview of the literature on American imperialism, see Perry Anderson, *American Foreign Policy and its Thinkers* (Verso, 2015); Robert Brenner, "What Is, and What Is Not, Imperialism?" *Historical Materialism* 14, no. 4 (2006); recent works on US imperialism include Daniel Immerwahr, *How to Hide an Empire: A History of the Greater United States* (Farrar, Straus and Giroux, 2019); David Vine, *The United States of War: A Global History of America's Endless Conflicts, From Columbus to the Islamic State* (University of California Press, 2020); Andrew Bacevich, *American Empire* (Harvard University Press, 2002) and *The New American Militarism* (Oxford University Press, 2005); Christopher Layne, *The Peace of Illusions: American Grand Strategy from 1940 to the Present* (Cornell University Press, 2006); David Sanger, *Confront and Conceal: Obama's Secret Wars and Surprising Use of American Power* (Crown, 2012); Odd Arne Westad, *The Global Cold War: Third World Interventions and the Making of Our Times* (Cambridge University Press, 2005); Michael Mann, *Incoherent Empire*, (Verso 2003); Robert Kagan, *Dangerous Nation: America and the World 1600–1900* (Vintage, 2006); Walter Nugent, *Habits of Empire: A History of American Expansion* (Vintage, 2008); and A. G. Hopkins, *American Empire: A Global History* (Princeton University Press, 2018); for outstanding realist international relations studies see E. H. Carr, *The Twenty Years' Crisis, 1919–1939* (Harper Perennial, 1964); Nicholas J. Spykman, *America's Strategy in World Politics* (Harcourt Brace, 1942); John Mearsheimer, *The Tragedy of Great Power Politics* (W. W. Norton, 2001); Hans Morgenthau, *Politics Among Nations* (McGraw Hill, 1992); and most recently Stephen Walt, "America Fueled the Fire in the Middle East," *Foreign Policy*, April 15, 2024; A neoconservative trend embraces the empire concept positively. See, for example, Niall Ferguson, *Colossus: The Rise and Fall of the American Empire* (New York, 2005).

through NATO, a ring of army bases around the world, massive miliary expenditure, initiating and escalating the global nuclear arms race, and waging incessant wars on those resisting its imperial imperatives. Beginning with its mid-twentieth-century nuclear bombing of Japan, the American empire has left its genocidal footprint from Southeast Asia in the 1960s–70s all the way to Iraq, Afghanistan, and Palestine.[6]

While decidedly anti-imperialist, my perspective does not align with historians who "see like a state" and reflexively side with any nationalist government, or with leftists who embrace reactionary "anti-imperialist" regimes like the Islamic Republic of Iran.[7] A brief note on the author's background might help clarify the book's claim that anti-imperialist and antinationalist orientations are not "ideological" blinders undermining rigorous scholarship. My intellectual formation originated in the internationalist New Left milieu of 1970s American and Iranian student-activist circles. It was decisively shaped by my participation in Iran's 1978–79 Revolution, followed by five decades in the academe, studying, teaching, and writing about modern Iranian history. Scholarly training and practice refined but also solidified the critical intellectual orientation of my student activist years. Commitment to internationalism meant identification with anti-imperialist movements and nonstate actors, such as the Iranian student movement, whose history was the subject of my doctoral dissertation and first book.[8] The following chapters show my attempt at combining scholarship with the radical questioning of most mainstream assumptions in both Iranian and American historiography.

Obviously, writing a history of two centuries of Iranian-US relations is a task beyond any single volume or author. The following summary, therefore, is a road map to what this book covers, which admittedly is far from comprehensive in terms of both content and analysis. I survey this history selectively and thematically in six chapters that are organized chronologically but can also be read as individual essays. Chapter 1, "The First Century: The Myth of Auspicious Beginnings," covers roughly one hundred years of early encounters between Americans and Iranians. This is the longest time span surveyed in a single chapter, the other five chapters covering a few decades each. Until the early twentieth century,

---

6 By the time of this writing, even the pro-Zionist *New York Times* features articles admitting to Israel's US-backed genocide of Palestinians. See Omar Bartov, "I'm a Genocide Scholar. I Know It When I See It," *New York Times*, July 15, 2025.

7 James C. Scott, *Seeing Like a State: How Certain Schemes to Improve the Human Condition Have Failed* (Yale University Press, 1999).

8 Afshin Matin-Asgari, *Iranian Student Opposition to the Shah* (Mazda Publishers, 2002).

Iran and the United States had limited interactions, generating a meager amount of primary source material for historians to use. What makes this period different, however, is that relations consisted mainly of interactions among individual Americans and Iranians, rather than between two governments. The Americans in question were mostly two to three generations of Protestant missionaries living and trying to evangelize in Iran. Unsuccessful in religious preaching, these missionaries focused instead on providing what the people of their host country wanted, namely services like modern education and health care. Thus, the missionaries, and a few individuals who championed the cause of Iran's Constitutional Revolution (1906–11), became the harbingers of American goodwill. Significantly, the US government refused to support Iran against the Anglo-Russian imperialist intervention during the Constitutional Revolution and the First World War, primarily backing American business interests pushing for access to Iranian trade and oil concessions in the 1920s–30s. During this entire first century, Iranian presence in the United States was almost negligible, by the 1920s consisting mostly of no more than a few thousand Assyrian Christians, whom American missionaries had helped migrate and settle in the Chicago area of the United States.

Chapter 2, "Defining American Priorities in Iran: Oil and Military-Autocratic Order," begins the book's survey of the second century of American-Iranian encounters. Covering a single decade, it shows how everything drastically changed when the United States joined the Anglo-Soviet occupation of Iran during the Second World War. From that point to the present, relations between Iran and America have been framed within state-to-state interactions, with the rules of engagement generally, but not always, set by the much more powerful American side. Through growing ties to Iran's armed forces, Washington became the Pahlavi monarchy's sustainer during the early Cold War, intervening to restore the shah and overthrow Premier Mohammad Mosaddeq's nationalist government in 1953. Relying on recently declassified US intelligence records and ongoing scholarly debates, the chapter reconstructs this period's history differently, noting a working-class contribution to the oil nationalization campaign and the lack of initiative on part of the Communist (Tudeh) Party and the Soviet Union. It also notes Premier Mosaddeq's strategic mistake in trusting the goodwill of the Truman and Eisenhower administrations, whose real objective was the breakup of the British oil monopoly under the pretext of saving Iran from communism. In a broader perspective, chapter 2 surveys a transition period, during the immediate post–Second World War years, when the US government replaced American missionaries to become a driving force in Iran's economic and educational modernization, a trend that would intensify in the 1950s–60s.

Chapter 3, "Building A Cold War Client State in Iran," begins by tracing America's financing, arming, and training of the shah's military and intelligence organizations for the purpose of crushing political dissent in post-1953 coup Iran. Between 1950 and 1967, Washington provided Iran with about $2 billion in foreign aid, mostly in credit, to purchase armament and cover expenditures strengthening military ties to the United States. In 1955, Iran joined the US-sponsored Baghdad Pact, renamed the Central Treaty Organization (CENTO) when Iraq dropped out in 1958. Meanwhile, US corporations became embedded in the Iranian economy and American "soft power" increasingly shaped the country's cultural and economic development. From Pepsi-Cola to television shows and Hollywood films, US products dominated Iran's emerging consumer markets, while education at all levels adapted to American standards. Beginning with the Kennedy administration, Iran turned into a test case for modernization theory, Washington's blueprint for global socioeconomic transformation under authoritarian rule, precisely the direction of the shah's 1963 White Revolution. Throughout the 1960s, mainstream US news media unanimously praised the shah as an enlightened dictator, while Presidents Kennedy and Johnson ignored occasional congressional or State Department criticism of relations with Iran. Nor did anyone in Washington pay serious attention to growing anti-shah sentiments voiced among thousands of Iranian students in the United States.

Chapter 4, "The Golden Age of Iran-US Relations: Paving the Revolutionary Road," surveys the period of America's most intense political, economic, and cultural involvement with Iran, from the mid-1960s to 1978, ending with President Carter telling the shah to vacate his throne. At the peak of this period, between the shah's 1967 coronation and his 1971 celebration of twenty-five hundred years of monarchy, America's political establishment and mass media continued their adulation of the shah and Iran's progress under his unfolding White Revolution. In particular, the Nixon-Kissinger White House forged a "special relationship" with Tehran, whereby the shah spent billions of dollars of oil revenue on sophisticated US armaments to become the "gendarme of the Gulf" militarily intervening against the Baath regime in Iraq and a revolutionary movement in Oman. Meanwhile, the shah was facing growing opposition at home, spearheaded by Marxist and Islamic leftist guerrillas, backed primarily by radical university students in Iran and abroad. By the 1970s, Iranians were the largest foreign student population in the United States, forming the world's best organized and most effective radical student movement in exile. During the same period, about the same number of Americans, roughly fifty thousand, lived in Iran, mostly as employees of US corporations and the shah's US-made military juggernaut. In the second half of the 1970s, as Iran's worsening economic and political woes coincided with the post-Vietnam crisis of US foreign policy, the media and Congress began questioning the "special relationship" with the shah and his repressive regime. But the Carter administration continued massive US arms sales and support of the shah, oblivious to a brewing revolutionary crisis in Iran until it was forced to accept the monarchy's meltdown and replacement with Ayatollah Khomeini's Islamic Republic. The chapter concludes with a close examination of America's complicated and controversial involvement with the triumphant finale of the Iranian Revolution in fall 1978 to winter 1979.

Chapter 5, "The Empire Strikes Back: The United States and the Islamic Republic of Iran," begins by probing the questions of why and how relations with the United States were crucial to defining the Islamic Republic's character. Dumbfounded by the revolution's anti-imperialist thrust, the Carter administration focused on clandestine diplomacy to rebuild military and security ties with a provisional government out of touch with the revolution's radicalization. In fall 1979, Ayatollah Khomeini used the Iran Hostage Crisis to launch a "second revolution," harnessing pent-up anti-imperialist sentiments to outmaneuver the left, consolidate clerical dictatorship, and crush all dissent. In addition to subverting popular demands for radical social change, Khomeini's brand of anti-imperialism cost the people of Iran eight years of destructive war with Iraq, as well as almost half a century of belligerent relations with the United States. The Iran Hostage Crisis doomed Carter's presidency and served as a major impetus to America's right-wing drift under Ronald Reagan, whose murky dealings with the Islamic Republic, the so-called Iran-Contra affair, almost caused his downfall. Meanwhile, the Iran-Iraq War (1980–88) was prolonged by US intervention; the United States aimed to deny victory to either side while punishing a war-battered Iran through devastating economic sanctions. Nor did Washington's onerous sanctions regime change during the 1990s postwar decade, when the Israel lobby became the decisive factor countering efforts by US corporate interests to roll back the sanctions on Tehran. Khomeini's successors tried to mend fences with the United States, eventually accomplishing a thaw in relations under Iran's President Khatami in the late 1990s, which did not go much beyond relaxing cultural exchange and sports diplomacy.

Chapter 6, "From a Nuclear Deal to War: Iran, the United States, and Israel," traces Iran-US relations during the first quarter of the twenty-first century. In the aftermath of the September 11, 2001, attacks, the Islamic Republic cooperated with the US occupation of Afghanistan and supported Saddam Hussein's overthrow in Iraq. Nevertheless, aligned with the Israel lobby, President George W. Bush's neoconservative foreign policy team intensified the effective state of war with Iran, further tightening the sanctions noose, now accusing Tehran of diverting its nuclear energy program to atomic bomb making. President Obama at first followed the same policy with vengeance, changing course during his second term to enter first secret and then open negotiations with Tehran, leading to a 2015 deal whereby Iran agreed to the strict monitoring of its nuclear program in exchange for significant US sanctions relief. The so-called Obama deal was a major setback for the Israel lobby and its American allies—they managed to reverse it once Donald Trump settled in the White House and escalated the state of war, joining Israel's strikes against Iranian targets and assassinating Iranian military personnel. Under President Joe Biden negotiations with Tehran resumed but stalled while the Islamic Republic became embroiled in crushing unprecedented levels of domestic unrest. Nearly half a century of the most onerous US sanctions had failed to change the behavior of a regime which now stood at the threshold of going nuclear. Instead of changing, the Islamic Republic had grown more defiant in international relations and domestically repressive, blaming American sanctions for its failing economic performance and growing popular discontent. Iran had forged significant economic ties with China and cooperated militarily with Russia, directly backing military resistance to American and Israeli intervention in Palestine, Lebanon, Syria, Yemen, and Iraq. In the end, and as with the shah's regime, US policy toward the Islamic Republic was a massive failure on all counts, effectively waging war on the people of Iran while strengthening the hand of their oppressive rulers. As America's foreign policy spins out of control globally, Iran is yet another country where the prospects of future relations with the United States appear dimmer than ever.

1

The First Century: The Myth of Auspicious Beginnings

The First Americans in Iran: Missionaries and Scholars

> *I do not know why we respect missionaries. Perhaps it is because they have not intruded here from Turkey or China or Polynesia to break our hearts by sapping away our children's faith & winning them to the worship of alien gods.*
>
> Mark Twain[1]

The United States started out with prejudice against Islam and Muslims, an intellectual legacy of both Protestant and Catholic colonizers of the American continent. Beginning with Christopher Columbus, European claims to dominion over the Americas and its "heathen" people involved strong religious overtones, an extension of Catholic Spain's ongoing anti-Islamic crusade. Ironically, what European thinkers ascribed to Muslims (that is, extreme religious fanaticism and the forcible conversion of nonbelievers) was standard practice in Christian Europe and its overseas colonies. The most enlightened architect of the American Republic, Thomas Jefferson, associated Islam with fanatical tyranny and moral corruption, although his presidential policies, including military action against North African Muslim adversaries, were informed by more political considerations. In fact, Jefferson's willingness to extend political toleration to non-Christians, including Muslims, caused him to be seen as "infidel" and even proto-Muslim. Jefferson, however, had no

1 "Missionaries," twainquotes.com.

sympathy for the plight of the young republic's Muslim minority, a considerable portion of its slave population.[2] He saw no irony in waging war to free about a hundred American citizens enslaved in Africa's Barbary Coast while keeping possibly hundreds of thousands of African Muslims in bondage.[3]

During the nineteenth century, the expansion of literacy and the popular press gradually increased and added nuance to American perceptions of the Islamic world, which nevertheless remained largely unsympathetic. Meanwhile, Islam had become less threatening as its formerly powerful champions, India's Mughal rulers and the Ottoman Empire, had fallen prey to Christian powers. As far as Iran was concerned, some awareness of the country appeared in travel literature and within the context of American Orientalism, a literary and artistic trend focused on an imaginary Orient, particularly Egypt and the biblical Holy Lands, stretched via Iran and India to the Far East. American Orientalism paralleled Europe's "Oriental Renaissance," an early nineteenth-century intellectual movement similarly fascinated with Asia, and particularly India, presumed to be the ancient font of human civilization. Iran, known as "Persia," loomed large in the Oriental Renaissance for being the first world empire, perched across three continents from India to Egypt and Greece, and for its Indo-European linguistic and hence presumably "Aryan" cultural roots. In this narrative, Islamic "Persia" had suffered decline while retaining aspects of its former greatness, most notably in the literary masterpieces of the Persian language. Appreciating the medieval poetry of Rumi, Saadi, Hafez, and Khayyam, Orientalist scholars dubbed Iran "a nation of poets," with Ferdowsi's *Book of Kings* (*The Shahnameh*) as its "national epic." Goethe became an enthusiast of Hafiz, the inspiration of his famous *West-Eastern Divan*, while also finding affinity with Shi'ism, which he dubbed "Iranian Islam" due to its purported intellectual flexibility and esotericism.[4] Such positive perception

2 Denise A. Spellberg, *Thomas Jefferson's Qur'an: Islam and the Founders* (Alfred A. Knopf, 2013), 212–13, 236–7.

3 Michael A. Gomez, "Muslims in Early America," *The Journal of Southern History* 60, no. 4 (November 1994): 671–710, 682; Sylviane A. Diouf, *Servants of Allah: African Muslims Enslaved in the Americas* (New York University Press, 2013). An estimated 10 to 20 percent of the slaves brought to colonial America were Muslims, including at least two hundred thousand slaves imported into the United States.

4 Rudi Matthee, "The Imaginary Realm: Europe's Enlightenment Image of Early Modern Iran," *Comparative Studies of South Asia, Africa and the Middle East* 30, no. 3 (2010): 449–62; Raymond Schwab, *Oriental Renaissance: Europe's Rediscovery of India and the East, 1680–1880* trans. Gene Patterson-Black and Victor Reinking (Columbia University Press, 1984).

of Iran influenced American Orientalism, which overlapped with transcendentalism, a homegrown mystical movement espousing humanity's spiritual unity across cultural and religious divides. Thus, for example, transcendentalist poet Ralph Waldo Emerson followed Goethe's interest in the poetry of Hafiz, while hints of affinity with Islam, and occasionally with Iran, appeared in iconic nineteenth-century literature, such as *Moby Dick*.[5] By mid-nineteenth century, scattered attention to Iran trickled down to American popular culture, for example when public entertainer P. T. Barnum built an ostentatious "Oriental villa" in Bridgeport, Connecticut, calling it "Iranistan." Famous for selling exotic hoaxes and circus tricks to large audiences, Barnum supposedly had coined the expression: "There is a sucker born every minute."[6] His Iranistan antics were part of larger American Orientalist tropes circulating via popular classics like *The Arabian Nights* or the contemporary writings of Washington Irving. The most important influence on nineteenth-century American perceptions of the Near East, but not Iran, was Mark Twain's 1869 *The Innocents Abroad*, an account of the celebrated author's visit to the Holy Land. The book was a satirical commentary on American travelers' uninformed arrogance vis-à-vis the rest of the world, a fixture of cultural imperialism. Twain's book also popularized his prejudice against Muslims, whom he called "a people by nature and training filthy, brutish, ignorant, unprogressive, [and] superstitious."[7]

When it came to actual American contact with Iran, the first forays began when Protestant missionaries arrived there during the 1830s, at a time when the ruling Qajar dynasty (1790s–1925) had suffered humiliating defeats and ceded significant territory in two wars with the expanding Russian Empire.[8] American missionary presence in Iran, however,

5 Timothy Marr, *The Cultural Roots of American Islamicism* (Cambridge University Press, 2006); Spellberg, *Thomas Jefferson's Qur'an*; see also John Sweetman, *The Oriental Obsession: Islamic Inspiration in British and American Art and Architecture, 1500–1920* (Cambridge University Press, 1988).

6 Marr, *Cultural Roots*, 265–7.

7 Douglas Little, *American Orientalism, The United States and the Middle East Since 1945* (University of North Carolina Press, 2008), 13.

8 On American missionaries in Iran see Michael P. Zirinsky, "Render therefore unto Caesar the Things which Are Caesar's: American Presbyterian Educators and Reza Shah," *Iranian Studies* 26, no. 3–4 (1993): 337–56; Zirinsky, "A Panacea for the Ills of the Country: American Presbyterian Education in Inter-War Iran," *Iranian Studies* 26, no. 1–2 (1993): 119–37; Zirinsky, "Harbingers of Change: Presbyterian Women in Iran, 1883–1949," *American Presbyterians* 70, no. 3 (fall 1992): 173–86; Jasamin Rostam-Kolayi, "From Evangelizing to Modernizing Iranians: The American Presbyterian Mission and Its Iranian Students," *Iranian Studies* 41, no. 2 (April 2008): 213–40; Firoozeh Kashani-Sabet, "American Crosses, Persian Crescents: Religion and the

remained small, confined mainly to the northwestern province of Azerbaijan, where most of the country's Nestorian, Assyrian, and Armenian Christian population lived. Official Presbyterian records show the Iran mission's modest progress by the end of the century (1893):

> The single station of Oroomieh, which constituted the whole Mission twenty-five years ago, with its little band of missionaries, four clerical and one medical, has been expanded into six well-manned stations . . . including the women, the whole missionary staff has increased from eleven to fifty-nine persons, among whom are four lady physicians.[9]

Given this context, the first Americans who studied Iran were Presbyterians like James Lyman Merrick and the Episcopalian Horatio Southgate. Merrick reached Iran in 1836, hoping to provide medical services to the Nestorian Christian population in Azerbaijan. He naively had thought it possible to directly preach to and convert Muslim Iranians, whom he called "Mohammedans." After a short stay, however, he gained a more sober understanding of Islam, opining:

> Perhaps the general impression in Europe and America respecting Mohammedanism is that it is such a flimsy, frostwork structure, that a few rays of science, a smattering of literature, or a modicum of the arts would annihilate it at once. Whatever may have been the origin of the materials of Mohammedanism, they have been so artfully built on truth, and cemented by excellent sentiments, that the fabric, the more I examine it, appears in every joint and angle a masterpiece of skill and power.

Partly because of his own reports, the Presbyterian Board ordered Merick to preach only to Christians during his decade-long stay in Iran. Southgate, who had arrived in the country at the same time as Merick, recounted a similar experience in the book he published four years later. Islam, according to him, was a formidable belief system, while Iranian Muslims were tough intellectual opponents and "willy antagonists," displaying "subtlety in disputing about essences, substances, and spirits,"

Diplomacy of US-Iranian Relations, 1834–1911," *Iranian Studies* 44, no. 5 (September 2011): 607–25.

9 *1983 Annual Report* (Board of Foreign Missions of the Presbyterian Church, 1983); quoted in Firoozeh Kashani-Sabet, "Before ISIS: What Early America Thought of Islam," *Sociology of Islam* 8 (2020): 17–52, 19, footnote 2.

dragging opponents into "a metaphysical chaos," making further argumentation impossible.[10] Another missionary pioneer was Reverend Justin Perkins, whose 1843 memoir of eight years residence in Azerbaijan was the first major American study of Iran. Perkins must also be credited as the first American who criticized his own country in Iran, since one of his sermons, to the Nestorian mission in Orumieh (or Oroomieh), condemned slavery as "our country's sin, considered especially as an obstacle to the spread and triumph of Christianity abroad." The publication of this particular sermon back home caused a controversy within the American Board of Commissioners for Foreign Missions, which was unwilling to endorse antislavery views. Perkins's abolitionist message, of course, was not meant for Iran, where slavery was legal, though confined largely to the royal court and elite households, where slaves, including those of African descent, were kept as domestic servants.[11] In 1840, American missionaries brought a printing press to Orumieh and began publishing textbooks and religious tracts at the record-setting rate of a half-million pages a year. The publications started with titles such as *Twenty-Two Plain Reasons for Not Being a Roman Catholic*, but also included educational pamphlets on nutrition, hygiene, and home economics. When the printing press finally broke down in 1892, its output approximated thirty million pages, including a full Syriac translation of the New Testament. Perkins and his wife had set up schools for boys and girls, the former evolving into the Orumieh College in 1879, which offered medical as well as theological education. In 1878, Dr. Joseph Cochran and his wife, Catherine, established a modern hospital, serving one hundred patients, and a small college for training physicians in Orumieh.[12]

From the start, Qajar shahs allowed American evangelizing only among Iran's very small Christian population, consisting of Armenians, Nestorians, and Assyrians. Soon, it became clear that converting Iranian Christians was a difficult if not impossible task, mostly because their church leaders opposed Presbyterian evangelizing. A similar pattern was

---

10 Horatio Southgate's book was titled *The Narrative of a Tour through Armenia, Kurdistan, Persia, and Mesopotamia* (London, 1840; reprint Legare Street Press, 2022); Marr, *Cultural Roots*, 120–30, quoted on 123–4, 128; see also Horatio Southgate, *Encouragement to Missionary Effort Among Mohammedans* (New York, 1836), 15.

11 Kashani-Sabet, "Before ISIS," 34, 38; Justin Perkins, A *Residence of Eight Years in Persia Among the Nestorian Christians with Notices of the Muhammedans* (Andover, MA, 1843); and idem, *Our Country's Sin: A Sermon Preached to the Members and Families of the Nestorian Mission at Oroomiah, Persia, July 3, 1853* (New York, 1854).

12 John Ghazvinian, *America and Iran: A History, 1720 to the Present* (Knopf, 2021), 23–4.

evident in the Ottoman Empire, where, after a century of activity, American missionaries failed to make substantial headway in converting local Christians, whose leaders, including Armenian patriarchs, had asked the sultans for the missionaries' dismissal. Thus, as in the Ottoman Empire, during the second half of the nineteenth century, American and other foreign missionaries in Iran redirected their efforts from evangelizing toward pioneering modern secular education.[13] Welcomed by Iranians in their new role, the missionaries still tried to evangelize indirectly by imbuing their secular teaching with principles of "Christian Morality." However, this strategy too proved largely ineffective, since both Muslim and Armenian students saw little difference between Protestant moral percepts and those of their own religion. In the end, American missionaries changed as much as they changed Iranians:

> Thus, the Presbyterians' sojourn in Iran does not conform to the familiar Orientalist plot of missionaries collecting an eager flock of recruits, who in turn act as local agents of imperial domination. Indeed, the Presbyterian evangelization project was met with great disappointment. Consequently, it was seriously modified over time, and it was the missionaries themselves who were changed by the process as much as the Iranians with whom they worked.[14]

American missionaries had reached Iran before their respective governments could establish diplomatic relations. In 1857, the United States and Iran signed a treaty of friendship and commerce, while full diplomatic relations were launched with the arrival of Samuel Green Wheeler Benjamin, the first American envoy, serving in 1882–85. Benjamin was a suitable person for the job, being born in Greece to missionary parents and having lived and worked as a journalist in the Near East. He was sympathetic to Muslims and particularly Turks, an attitude he extended to Iranians during his sojourn among them. His memoir, *Persia and the Persians*, includes vivid descriptions of 1880s Iran, albeit from the point of view of the urban upper classes with whom Benjamin lived and worked. Deliberately picturesque and encyclopedic, he introduced general readers to an exotic land, while providing diplomats, traders, and missionaries with the first "handbook" on Iran. In passing, he mentioned

13 On American Missionaries in the Ottoman Empire, see Karine V. Walther, *Sacred Interests: The United States and the Islamic World, 1821–1921* (University of North Carolina Press, 2018), 2–3.

14 Rostam-Kolayi, "From Evangelizing to Modernizing Iranians," quoted on 214.

Iran's rural and urban lower classes, describing them as hardworking and yet enjoying living standards higher than their counterparts in countries like Italy or Spain. Benjamin painted a particularly dignified picture of Iran's tribal people, comparing their culture and lifestyle to that of Native Americans. His positive mention of tribal people, such as the Bakhtiari, prefigures the first major Iranian-American encounter a generation later, when Merian Cooper's film crew became guests of the Bakhtiari to document their lifestyle and migration (as we shall see later). *Persia and the Persians* also reports of Presbyterian missionaries, numbering them under one hundred and commenting that their uphill effort of preaching to a very small Christian community may not be worth the trouble. In Benjamin's view, American businessmen, offering useful worldly goods, would be better received by Iranians. Finally, and most strategically, Benjamin noted the United States was entering Iran to face the entrenched semicolonial presence of Russia and Great Britain, with France and Germany also maneuvering for influence. Thus, Americans had to assume the role of a faraway power with no colonial ambitions, a benevolent counterweight to the imperialist powers of the Old World. This would be the American diplomatic posture in Iran until after the Second World War.[15]

By the turn of the twentieth century, American knowledge of Iran grew as archeologists and linguists began to visit and study the country, adding scholarly reflections to the firsthand impressions of missionaries and diplomats. By this time, major American universities, including Harvard, Yale, the University of Chicago, University of Pennsylvania, as well as the Hartford and Princeton theological seminaries, had Islamic studies in their curricula. But scholarly attention to Islam, grounded in languages like Arabic and Persian, remained marginal well into the twentieth century. Abraham Valentine Jackson, a pioneering scholar of Iran, visited the country several times between 1903 and 1926, becoming an authority on ancient Iranian religions and languages, as well as the poetry of Khayyam and Ferdowsi. Jackson also noted certain traits henceforth attributed to Iran, such as it being the only country of the ancient Orient having survived independently to the present, while readily adopting foreign cultural influences. Commenting on Iran's adoption of a European-style constitution in the early twentieth century

15 James F. Goode, "A Good Start: The First American Mission to Iran, 1883–1885," *Muslim World* 74 (April 1984): 100–18; see also James F. Goode, "Samuel Benjamin: Unorthodox Observer of the Middle East," *Islam and Christian-Muslim Relations* 9, no. 1 (1998): 23–9.

(see later in this chapter), Jackson repeated Herodotus: "The Persians, of all nations, are the most ready to adopt foreign customs."[16]

The First Iranians in America

The first Iran-born individual in North America was an Armenian from Esfahan named Martin. In 1607, Martin traveled from London to Virginia, serving the colony's governor and settling in Jamestown to become a successful tobacco farmer. He is on official record giving a court testimony in 1619 and apparently brought two more Armenians to Virginia to help him introduce the cultivation of the silkworm in the Americas.[17] The first Iranian report of a visit to the American continent is by Mirza Abul-Hasan Khan Shirazi, an envoy dispatched to London by Fath-Ali Shah. Abul-Hasan's return journey, aboard a British vessel, took a long detour, making a stop at the coast of Brazil, where, after a short stay in Rio, in September 1810, he returned to Iran via India. Abul-Hasan's two-week stay in Brazil can hardly count as a meaningful sojourn, while his explanation of it, as caused by the ship being blown off course, seems rather implausible.[18] The first Iranian to visit the United States was Mar Yohannan, the Assyrian Bishop of Orumieh who, in 1841, was dispatched on a year-long "speaking tour" around the United States by the American Board of Commissioners for Foreign Missions. Thousands flocked to see Yohannan, probably as an exotic curiosity, hearing him speak in "broken English" on topics such as "the evils of drink."[19] Two decades later, we find an Iranian fighting for the Union Army in the American Civil War. Private Mohammed Kahn, known in the United States as John Ammahail, was born in Iran circa 1830 and grew up in Afghanistan, where he gained some military experience. In 1861, he immigrated to the United States and, within a few months, enlisted in the New York Infantry Regiment of the Union Army. After the Battle of Gettysburg in

16 Firoozeh Kashani-Sabet, "The Portals of Persepolis: The Role of Nationalism in Early US-Iran Relations," in *Rethinking Iranian Nationalism and Modernity*, eds. Kamran Scot Aghaie and Afshin Marashi (University of Texas Press, 2014): 137–60, quoted on 141–2.

17 Kamyar Jarahzadeh, "The First 'Iranian-Armenia' in America," Ajam Media Collective, March 23, 2017, ajammc.com.

18 H. Javadi, "Abu'l-Hasan Khan Ilchi," in Encyclopædia Iranica, accessed September 6, 2020, iranicaonline.org; see Hamid Dabashi, *Reversing the Colonial Gaze: Persian Travelers Abroad* (Cambridge University Press, 2020), 89–90.

19 Ghazvinian, *America and Iran*, 25–6.

1863, Khan was separated from his unit and put to work alongside freed slaves, since officers did not believe he was a "white" soldier. Eventually, Khan found and rejoined his unit, taking part in the rest of the war as a sharpshooter, being wounded.[20]

The only Iranian whose extensive travels and stay in the nineteenth-century United States is well-documented is Mirza Mohammad Ali, also known as Hajj Sayyah (Traveler), who is also the first Iranian who became a US citizen. Starting out at age twenty-three, Hajj Sayyah traveled around the globe and met with famous personalities like Pope Pius IX, Russian Tsar Alexander II, Italian nationalist leader Giuseppe Garibaldi, Prussian Prime Minister Otto von Bismarck, US President Ulysses S. Grant, and Pan-Islamist leader Jamal al-Din Al-Afghani. He reportedly spent ten years in the United States, traveling from New York to San Francisco, and became a naturalized American citizen on May 26, 1875. Unfortunately, we know almost nothing of Sayyah's decade in the United States, as his journal recording that trip was lost. Shortly after becoming a US citizen, Sayyah began his long journey home across the Pacific and through Japan, China, and India, eventually visiting Egypt and making the Hajj pilgrimage, thus earning the sobriquet "Hajj." Back in Iran in 1877, he eventually published a memoir (*The Travelogue of Hajj Sayyah*), which became an influential text of Iran's constitutionalist movement (see below) due to its criticism of government and clerical corruption. Fearing persecution due to his involvement with constitutionalist circles, Sayyah took sanctuary at Tehran's US legation in 1893. His five-month long sanctuary, and a potential diplomatic crisis, ended when the American minister resident intervened to secure his safe conduct.[21] By this time, Iran too had official envoys in the United States, beginning with Hossein-qoli Khan Nuri, the so-called Hajj Washington, who served as the first Persian special envoy and minister plenipotentiary to Washington in 1888–89.[22] Hossein-qoli Khan arrived in New York with a small retinue and, according to *The New York Times*, was fluent in French, though speaking only a few words of English. Stationed in Washington, DC, he met with President Grover Cleveland and began sending dispatches to Tehran with detailed information on the United

20 Matthew Schaefer, "Private Mohammed Kahn: Civil War Soldier," *NARAtions* (blog), National Archives, June 23, 2017, narations.blogs.archives.gov.

21 Ali Ferdowsi, "Ḥājj Sayyāh", in Encyclopædia Iranica, accessed September 9, 2020, iranicaonline.org; Dabashi, *Reversing the Colonial Gaze*, chapter 7.

22 *Hajji Washington*, directed by Ali Hatami (1982), on IMVBox; James Goode, "A Good Start: The First American Mission to Iran, 1883–1885," *The Muslim World* 74, no. 2 (1984): 100–18.

States and its political system. In his estimation, Americans were superior to Europeans because they were "alert, intelligent, learned, polite, and wealthy." Moreover, he admired US government officials, who were "servants of the people," as well as American moral values, going as far as claiming, "The essence of the religion of the Prophet [of Islam] is found in the United States." Due to unknown reasons, his mission lasted less than a year and he returned to Iran, taking charge of the ministry of public welfare, later becoming a supporter of the constitutionalist movement.[23] A more descriptive contemporary American travelogue is by Qajar notable Muin al-Saltaneh, who attended the 1893 World's Columbian Exposition in Chicago, featuring a "Persian Pavilion," which was sponsored by an Ottoman Armenian merchant, Hohannes Topakian, and featured carpets and handicraft. Muin al-Saltanah described arriving at the New York Harbor to see the Statue of Liberty, walking in Central Park and visiting the Brooklyn Bridge, then going to Philadelphia and eventually visiting President Cleveland during his weekly public audience.[24] Similar personal observations, including comparisons of Europe and the United States, are also found in the memoir of future diplomat and military leader Hasan Arfa, who, in 1910, spent about two months in the United States visiting New York, Boston, and Washington, DC. Arfa mostly wrote about socializing with rich Americans, concluding that in terms of wealth, opulence, and conspicuous consumption, American millionaires surpass the emperors, sultans, and aristocrats of Eurasia.[25]

Around the turn of the twentieth century, the number of Iranians in the United States was still quite small. During the peak period of worldwide emigration to the United States, from the 1840s to 1903, only 130 Iranians are on record as official immigrants.[26] Assyrian Christians were the largest Iranian immigrant group, arriving in the 1880s–90s in connection with American Presbyterian missionaries who had lived among their communities in Northwestern Iran for half a century. By 1910, about one thousand mostly poor and working-class Iranian Assyrians lived in Chicago, being served by their own Persian Church and Sunday

23 Hossein Kamaly, "Ḥājj Vāšangton" in Encyclopædia Iranica, accessed June 21, 2020, iranicaonline.org.

24 Hajj Mirza Muhammad Ali Mu'in al-Saltanah, *Safarnamah-i Shikagaw: Khatirat-i safar-e Hajj Mirza Muhammad Ali Mu'in al-Saltanah bih Urupa va Amrika, 1310 AH*, edited by Homayun Shahidi (Tehran: Intisharat-i 'Ilmi, 1363/1984).

25 General Hassan Arfa, *Under Five Shahs* (William Morrow, 1965), 449–81.

26 Maboud Ansari, "Iranian Immigrants" in *Multicultural America: An Encyclopedia of the Newest Americans*, ed. Ronald H. Bayor, vol. 1 (Greenwood, 2011): 1069–110, 1076.

school. By the 1920s, Chicago's Iranian Assyrian community had grown to over three thousand, many having fled from massacres inflicted on their coreligionists back home during the First World War. By this time, career diplomats gradually had replaced Ottoman rug merchants and antique dealers as Iran's official representatives in the United States. In 1900, an experienced diplomat, Ishaq Khan Mofakhkham al-Dowleh, arrived to raise the Iranian legation's profile. Still, his activities consisted mostly of marketing Iranian carpets, a lucrative venture hitherto monopolized by Ottoman Armenian merchants like Topakian, who also served as Iranian consuls. The extremely wealthy Topakian had become Iran's most famous cultural representative, regularly entertaining rich New Yorkers at his exotically decorated New Jersey mansion known as the Persian Court. In 1909, Topakian, already famous as "the world's largest importer of costly rugs," was appointed Iran's consul-general in New York and presented President Theodore Roosevelt with a Persian carpet valued $50,000, repeating the same kind of carpet diplomacy with President William Taft the following year. However, the first real Iranian who made a mark on American "high society" and diplomatic circles was Ali Qoli Khan Nabil, whose wealthy family were followers of Iran's new Bahá'í faith. Ali Qoli Khan arrived in the United States in 1901 and three years later married Florence Breed, heiress to a rich Bostonian Bahá'í family. Soon, Ali Qoli Khan and his "Persian princess" wife became a "Persian chic" fixture in New England elite circles, their fame and popularity surpassing Topakian's. Despite belonging to the persecuted Bahá'í religion, in 1910 Ali Qoli Khan was appointed Iran's chargé d'affaires in Washington.[27]

Since the 1890s, Bahá'í missionaries had established a bridgehead in New England, proving more successful than American Presbyterians in transplanting their religion to another continent. Bahá'ís followed a new dispensation beyond Islam whose precise tenets were still unfolding when it reached the United States during the 1890s. The Bahá'í faith was represented at the 1893 World's Parliament of Religions, organized in conjunction with Chicago's Columbian Exposition to bring together representatives of the world's Eastern and Western religions. Interestingly, American Presbyterians, along with the Roman Catholic and Anglican

27 John Ghazvinian, "Flags of Inconvenience: State Failure, Nationhood, and Contested Sovereignty in the Late Qajar Encounter with the United Sates," in *American-Iranian Dialogues: From Constitution to White Revolution, c. 1890s–1960s*, ed. Matthew K. Shannon (Bloomsbury Academic, 2022): 17–32, 20–6; Guity Etemad, "Nabil-al Dawla," in Encyclopædia Iranica, updated January 4, 2014, iranicaonline.org.

churches and the Ottoman Sultan Abdul Hamid, objected to the gathering's equal treatment of all religions. Making a significant breakthrough, the Bahá'í faith received little attention at this gathering, as it seemed to fit somewhere between older Asian religions and modern ecumenical movements such as Spiritualism, Theosophy, and Christian Science. At about the same time, Bahá'í teachings were introduced to Americans by a Syrian convert, Ibrahim Kheirallah, who was preaching in Chicago and New York. Early American coverts apparently found the Bahá'í preaching of human unity and peace attractive, but gradual familiarity with the new religion's emerging doctrine and leadership structure posed problems. Following a dispute with 'Abdu'l-Bahá, the son and successor of the new faith's founder, Kheirallah was replaced by Iranian missionaries who helped the first American Bahá'í leader, Thornton Chase, set up a base in Chicago. Chase was followed by Horace Holley, who, by the 1920s, had established a network of Bahá'í organizations in the United States and Canada. Another early convert, Louise Lua Aurora Getsinger, helped spread the Bahá'í faith beyond Chicago by giving lecture tours across the United States. Getsinger recruited millionaire Phoebe Hearst and together, along with Kheirallah and a dozen "pilgrims," traveled to Ottoman Acre in 1898 to visit 'Abdu'l-Bahá. This was followed by similar parties of pilgrims traveling from the United States and Europe to meet with the living leader of their new faith.[28]

The small American Bahá'í community registered its political presence as early as 1901 by lobbying the US envoy to Tehran, Herbert W. Bowen, to intervene on behalf of their persecuted coreligionists. In 1912, 'Abdu'l-Bahá became the most high-profile Iranian to visit the United States, where he spent eight months speaking and evangelizing in forty cities, from New York to Los Angeles and San Francisco. His visit was facilitated by Ali Qoli Khan, who was promoting stronger Iranian diplomatic and economic ties with the Roosevelt and Taft administrations. 'Abdu'l-Bahá took the same position during his US tour, arguing, for example, in a speech at Washington's Orient-Occident Unity Society:

> For the Persians there is no government better fitted to contribute to the development of their natural resources and helping of their national needs in a reciprocal alliance than the United States of America; and for the Americans there could be no better industrial outlet and market than

28 William S. Hatcher and J. Douglas Martin, *The Baha'i Faith: The Emerging Global Religion* (Harper and Row, 1985), 52–4; see also Robert H. Stockman, *The Bahai Faith in America: Early Expansion, 1900–1912*, vol. 2 (George Ronald, 1995), chapter 28.

> the virgin . . . soil of Persia. The mineral wealth of Persia is still latent and untouched.[29]

To American audiences, 'Abdu'l-Bahá was probably yet another Oriental sage, while early Bahá'í converts, like Phoebe Hearst, considered him the incarnation of Jesus Christ, or indeed the "Messiah" himself.[30] In Maine, he met with Bahá'í convert Sarah Farmer, founder of Green Acre, an adult education facility that became a center for spreading the Bahá'í message. 'Abdu'l-Bahá spoke at churches, universities, trade unions, and social-reform associations. His message of humanity's spiritual unity seemed to challenge America's rigid racial divide, drawing the attention of radical Black intellectual W. E. B. Dubois. The Bahá'í leader met Dubois in New York and spoke at the Fourth Annual Conference of the National Association for the Advancement of Colored People in Chicago. Subsequently, Dubois, whose wife was a convert, would speak at Bahá'í events. After 'Abdu'l-Bahá's death in 1921, Dubois wrote that he was one of the two men who "sit high before the world today," the other being Eugene Debs, America's most prominent socialist leader. By the 1930s, however, Dubois's sympathy for Bahá'ís diminished as he learned their meetings in Southern states remained racially segregated until new converts were fully integrated into the community. American Bahá'í pioneers include social reformer and author Stanwood Cobb; Alain LeRoy Locke, who was a scholar and leader of the 1920s artistic and cultural movement, the Harlem Renaissance; Hollywood golden age actress Carole Lombard; and jazz musician and singer Dizzy Gillespie.[31]

While the Bahá'í faith was making a beachhead in the United States, American Bahá'ís made a notable contribution to modern education in Iran, following the path of Presbyterian missionaries. In 1911, Iranian and American Bahá'ís opened the Tarbiyat Girls' School, whose strong curriculum in science, foreign languages, and the humanities made it popular with Tehran's elite families. The Tarbiyat Girls' School and its counterpart for boys were supported by the Persian American Educational Society, a Washington, DC, Bahá'í institution founded in 1910 to

---

29 Marzieh Gail, *Arches of the Years* (George Ronald, 1991), 42.

30 Hatcher and Martin, *The Baha'i Faith*, 54–8.; see also Howard MacNutt, ed., "The Promulgation of Universal Peace: Talks Delivered by 'Abdu'l-Baha during His Visit to the United States and Canada in 1912," bahai.org.

31 Christopher Buck, "The Interracial 'Baha'i Movement' and the Black Intelligentsia: The Case of W. E. B. Du Bois," *Journal of Religious History* 36, no. 4 (December 2012): 541–62, quote on 547; see also A. Bausani and D. MacEoin, "ABD-AL-BAHĀ," in Encyclopædia Iranica, updated May 4, 2018, iranicaonline.org, and "Bahaism," ibid.

"lobby" diplomatic, business, labor, and peace groups. Dr. Susan Moody was the first American Bahá'í woman arriving in Tehran, where she helped establish the Tarbiyat Girls' School, spending twenty-five years as a physician and educator serving Iranian girls and women. She was joined by Lillian Kappes, a capable administrator who expanded the school's fundraising and enrollment, and like Moody, stayed in Iran for the rest of her life. A few more American women served as Tarbiyat teachers and administrators, but the school was basically staffed by Iranians who followed the Bahá'í leader Shoghi Effendi and brought the school in line with Reza Shah's authoritarian nationalist modernizing agenda.[32]

American Defenders of an Iranian Revolution: Shuster and Baskerville

> *Time with whose passage certain pains abate*
> *But sharpens those of Persia's unjust fate.*
>
> Morgan Shuster, Treasurer-General of Iran, 1911[33]

In the early twentieth century, Iran's transition from a "failed empire" to a modern nation-state reached a turning point through an upheaval in-line with a wave of revolutions sweeping the globe from Russia and the Ottoman Empire to China and Mexico. Iran's Constitutional Revolution of 1906–11 was the culmination of nineteenth-century administrative and political reforms, mainly following those in the Ottoman Empire. Prerevolutionary unrest had included events such as the 1891 country-wide boycott of tobacco, a popular consumer item whose marketing concession the shah had sold to a British subject. During the tobacco boycott, an American envoy in Tehran wrote about "the power of the mollahs" to direct "popular discontent," noting "a parliament seems to have risen from the ground." Iranian reformers saw Britain and Russia as imperialists intervening in Iranian affairs, while the United States was generally considered a distant power and possibly sympathetic to the

32 Jasamin Rostam-Kolayi, "The *Tarbiyat* Girls' School of Tehran: Iranian and American Baha'i Contributions to Modern Education," *Middle East Critique* 22, 1 (Spring 2013): 77–93, 85–90.

33 W. Morgan Shuster, *The Strangulation of Persia: Story of the European Diplomacy an Oriental Intrigue That Resulted in the Denationalization of Twelve Million Mohammedans* (New York, 1912), lxv.

constitutionalist cause. However, when an actual parliamentary system was introduced in 1906, Richmond Pearson, the highest-ranking US diplomat in Iran, would comment: "History does not record a single instance of successful constitutional government in a country where the Mussulman religion is the state religion." By this time, some knowledge of the American political system had appeared in Iran, for example through a 1905 series of newspaper articles covering the life of George Washington, hailed as the champion of American independence.[34]

But the American hailed in Iran as the champion of liberty was not George Washington but a young Nebraskan who sacrificed his life to the cause of Iranian constitutionalism. Twenty-four-year-old Howard Baskerville was a Princeton Seminary graduate teaching English at the Presbyterian Memorial Boys School in Tabriz, capital of the Azerbaijan province. In 1908, a royalist coup had rolled back the fledgling constitutional regime throughout the country, except for the city of Tabriz, whose popular militia was resisting a siege by the shah's army. The Tabriz militia had a small but significant international contingent, consisting of several hundred Georgian, Armenian, and Muslim revolutionaries from Baku with valuable military experience. Inspired by the ordinary people's sacrifices, including the death in battle of a friend and colleague, Baskerville resigned his post and enlisted in the constitutionalist militia. His dramatic intervention in the Iranian Revolution was noted in an April 5, 1909, *New York Times* article titled "American Defends Tabriz." The State Department advised the Board of Foreign Missions to recall Baskerville, and the American consul asked him to surrender his passport. Baskerville thus gave up his American citizenship, choosing to fight and to face death defending the Iranian Revolution. After some basic drilling, he volunteered for a dangerous mission to break the royalist blockade and bring food and provisions to the starving city. On the evening of April 19, 1909, he died after suffering a bullet in the heart while leading a direct charge on the royalist lines. With a mass of the city's people in attendance, he was buried at the American cemetery in Tabriz, alongside Georgian, Armenian, and Iranian revolutionary "martyrs." Baskerville thus became an icon of Iran's Constitutional Revolution, setting a very high benchmark for what individual Americans might offer the people of Iran.[35] His memory lived on particularly strongly in Tabriz, where a

34 Kashani-Sabet, "Portals," 149–50; Pearson quoted in Little, *American Orientalism*, 14.

35 See "Howard Baskerville" in Encyclopædia Iranica, accessed June 2, 2020, iranicaonline.org; Abbas Amanat, *Iran: A Modern History* (Yale University Press, 2017),

school assembly hall bearing his name was built on the site where he had died. Half a century later, another American teaching in Tabriz would observe the emotional commemoration of Baskerville's martyrdom. Curtis Harnack, a Fulbright professor of American literature, records a moving description of people crying at the ceremony, one man telling him: "Some people say this is all over, finished—happened fifty years ago—is all past history. But I tell you, it is not over yet." Harnack reported apprehensively of some Iranians hoping he too might "care" about their country's affairs as much as Baskerville had done, a temptation he was resolved to resist. "It seems likely to me," he wrote,

> Baskerville had been seduced by the activity of teaching itself, for in the process of imparting knowledge a personal relationship forms . . . And so, it must have been for Baskerville; dying from a gunshot wound, he found himself at the end of a process that had started with the simple diagramming of English sentences.[36]

The challenge of deep cultural immersion, and particularly of "going native" politically, as Baskerville had done, would remain a rare feature of Iranian American interactions, its most outstanding example being Peace Corps volunteers teaching in Iran during the 1960s–70s (see chapter 5). Back in early twentieth century, the most widely known American sympathizer of Iran's Constitutional Revolution was William Morgan Shuster, who briefly served as Iran's treasurer-general. Soon after Baskerville's death, the Tabriz militia received the support of similar armed uprising in other provinces, together marching on Tehran and deposing the despotic king. However, the restored constitutional regime could not function with an empty treasury, no taxation system, and no standing army. In 1911, therefore, Iran hired a small team of American experts, headed by Morgan Shuster, to put the country's finances in order. Shuster

---

357; see also Reza Aslan, *An American Martyr in Persia: The Epic Life and Tragic Death of Howard Baskerville* (Norton, 2023). Aslan's book is an engaging account that vividly reconstructs Baskerville's life and death in the unfolding context of Iran's Constitutional Revolution. But even its archival research, for example into the question of whether Baskerville surrendered his American passport, gives us no conclusive new information, 334–5.

36 Curtis Harnack, *Persian Lions, Persian Lambs: An American Odyssey in Iran* (Iowa State University Press, 1981), 66–7; Rezazadeh-Shafaq, "Sattar Khan," in *Mardan-e khodsakhteh*, ed. A. Khajehnuri (Tehran, 1956), 98–101; the Baskerville episode is briefly mentioned by Shafaq who claims he was one of his students with him during the mission that led to his death.

had served as an American colonial administrator in the Philippines but came to Iran as a private citizen. Nevertheless, his mission indirectly involved the United States as a potential counterweight to the blatantly imperialist Anglo-Russian presence in Iran. His brief mission enhanced the positive recognition of Iran and its revolution in the United States, while leaving behind a powerful legacy of trust in American goodwill among the Iranian elite.[37] Iranians, however, would confuse the personal conviction and sacrifice of individual Americans, like Shuster and Baskerville, with the good will of the US government. As we saw in Baskerville's case, Washington refused involvement in the Iranian Revolution, having declared as early as 1907, "This government can take no cognizance of any subversive movement unless it should succeed to actual power." Though the State Department had recommended Shuster, the US government did not oppose the Russian ultimatum for his dismissal nor did it raise any serious objection to the czarist invasion and occupation of Iran. This was despite several direct appeals by the Iranian government for help from Washington, including a 1911 letter in which the head of the Majles (parliament) wrote to US Congress:

> We appeal to the humanitarian sentiment of the United States saying to them: You have tasted the benefits of liberty, would you witness the fall of any people whose only fault was to sympathize with your system to save its future? Would you suffer that Persia should fall for having wished to preserve its national dignity, and for having understood the sentiments so dear to a free people?

Washington's repeated response to such appeals was that it could not interfere in Iran's relations with other powers. Thus, reacting to events leading to the suspension of Iran's constitutional regime, the US government effectively sided with Russian and British imperialism.[38] Shuster was in Iran only from May 1911 to January 1912, being forced to leave after a Russian government ultimatum, backed by the British, demanded his expulsion. His troubled mission and its dramatic termination received press coverage in the United States, particularly by *The New York Times*,

37 Robert A. McDaniel, *The Shuster Mission and the Persian Constitutional Revolution* (Bibliotheca Islamica, 1974); Joan Gaughan, *The Shuster Mission to Iran: Leaving Something Worthwhile Behind* (Real Nice Books, 2021).

38 Kamyar Ghaneabassiri, "US Foreign Policy and Persia, 1856–1921," *Iranian Studies* 35, no. 1–3 (2002): 145–75, 154–60; 1907 State Department quote on 150; letter from the Iranian Majles quoted on 158; and the Majles letter quote on 158.

which already had reported sympathetically on the Constitutional Revolution. A November 1911 *New York Times Sunday Magazine* headline, for example, gave the following summary of the entire Shuster episode:

> How Russia Came to Make War on W. Morgan Schuster: The Thirty-Four-Year Old American Who Defied the Czar—He Went to Persia to Save Her from Financial Ruin and Is Upsetting the International Plot for Her Partition.

The New York Times was portraying Shuster as a Progressive Era anti-imperialist, a white, middle-class icon of American manhood, rushing to rescue revolutionary Iran, cast in the role of the Oriental damsel in distress. The high-profile press coverage of the Shuster mission echoed in the US House of Representatives, where some members called for the Taft administration's armed intervention on his behalf, a proposal that, as noted above, did not go anywhere.[39] Meanwhile, *The New York Times* continued its positive Iran coverage with articles such as "The Boy Shah Likes Americans," quoting young Ahmad Shah to declare:

> Of course I like Americans. They fought for freedom, doing . . . many heroic things. They are inventors of wonderful machines . . . America is the land where everything is done with electricity . . . and where the people are . . . very free.[40]

But it was Shuster himself who created a powerful testimonial causing a minor sensation in the United States and turning it into a primary source of Iran's Constitutional Revolution. Immediately after his forced departure, Shuster published *The Strangling of Persia*, a book whose subtitle, *Story of the European Diplomacy and Oriental Intrigue That Resulted in the Denationalization of Twelve Million Mohammedans*, spelled out its sympathies. Shuster blamed foreign interference for preventing Iran from developing its short five-year (1906–11) experiment of constitutionalism into a "stable and orderly" form of government:

---

39 Kelly J. Shannon, "The Shuster Mission of 1911 and American Perceptions of Iran's First Revolution," in *American-Iranian Dialogues*, ed. Matthew K. Shannon (Bloomsbury Academic, 2021), 33–55, 49, 54.

40 *New York Times*, August 20, 1911, quoted in Ghaneabassiri, "US Foreign Policy and Persia," 150.

> That the Persians were unskillful in the practical politics and in the technique of representative constitutional government no one could deny; but that they had the full right to develop along particular lines of their customs, character, temperament and tendencies, is equally obvious . . . yet after five years of effort, during which the Persian people, with all their difficulties and harassed by the so-called friendly powers, succeeded in thwarting a despot's well-planned effort to wrest from them their hard-earned liberties, the world is told by two European nations that these men were unfit, dangerous and incapable of producing a stable and orderly form of government.

Calling Anglo-Russian intervention in Iran an act of "international brigandage," Shuster could not have anticipated that, within a few decades, the American government too would commit this sort of "brigandage" by overthrowing Iran's nationalist government in 1953. Despite Shuster's departure, a large Russian army moved into northern Iran, while British forces occupied strategic positions in the South.[41] This brazen Anglo-Russian intervention followed the terms of a secret 1907 agreement, whereby the two powers had divided Iran into zones of influence and occupation in case of a European war. Already important, as a buffer state in the nineteenth-century Great Game against Russia, Iran became vital to the British Empire when oil replaced coal as the imperial navy's fuel source. In 1901, an English company had acquired concession rights to southern Iran's oil reserves. The British government soon became the company's majority shareholder, paying the Iranian government a meager 16 percent of its net revenue. Building the world's largest refinery in Abadan, the British were to reap great rewards on their Iranian investment while becoming the hated target of budding Iranian nationalism. During the 1911–21 decade, Iran's new constitutional regime remained in suspension while the country was under occupation, its official neutrality in the First World War violated as Russian, British, and Ottoman armies clashed in its northern and western provinces. As well as undermining Iranian constitutionalism, the 1911–21 decade of imperialist intervention caused economic dislocation and famine, exasperated by pandemics of cholera and Spanish influenza that killed more than 10 percent of Iran's ten million inhabitants. Denying responsibility for these damages, the British government blamed everything on

41 See Abbas Amanat, *Iran: A Modern History* (Yale University Press, 2017), 367–74, quoted on 374.

Iranian "chaos" and "backwardness," a narrative that also justified the need for the kind of military dictatorship that British high command would install before withdrawing their troops in 1921 (see the section below).[42]

Drawing Americans to Iran: Oil, Finances, and Dictatorship (1920s)

The narrative of Iranian history's intrinsic instability, implying the need for a hyper-centralized modern government, appealed to those Iranian nationalists who abandoned constitutionalism to embrace an obscure Cossack commander, Reza Khan, first as Iran's military strongman and then as the founding dictator-monarch of the new Pahlavi dynasty (1926–79). Following a British-engineered military coup, Reza Khan's Cossacks crushed several provincial contenders, the most radical of which had set up a Soviet-backed socialist republic in northern Iran (1920–21). Within a few years, Reza Khan violently quelled all opposition and dissent, becoming Iran's dictator while serving as both prime minister and minister of war. Inspired by Atatürk's authoritarian republicanism, he briefly toyed with the idea of a dictatorial presidency before deciding to become a new dynast, something he would accomplish by 1926.

During the Great War, American missionaries had actively supported Anglo-Russian intervention, with the Presbyterians, in Azerbaijan, helping to organize an "Assyrian-Armenian Army" to fight on behalf of the Allies.[43] At the same time, Americans in Iran had organized the Persian Relief Committee, which, by the end of the war, had raised over $2 million for relief efforts against famine and the war's destruction. Iran's prime minster sent a letter of gratitude to the State Department, showing, once again, that Iranians were confusing the contribution of American citizens with the good offices of their government. In fact, in

42 Influenza epidemic killed about a tenth of Iran's population. Amir Arsalan Afkhami, "Compromised Constitutions: The Iranian Experience with the 1918–1919 Influenza Pandemic," *Bulletin of the History of Medicine* 77, no. 2 (summer 2003): 367–92; Mohammad Gholi Majd, *The Great Famine and Genocide in Persia, 1917–1919* (University Press of America, 2003); on Iranian "chaos" and "backwardness" justifying the 1921 British-backed coup, see Stephanie Cronin, *Soldiers, Shahs and Subalterns in Iran: Opposition, Protest and Revolt, 1921–1941* (Palgrave Macmillan, 2010), 4–5.

43 On the war's highly destructive impact on the areas where American missionaries were stationed see Firoozeh Kashani-Sabet, *Heroes to Hostages: America and Iran, 1800–1988* (Cambridge University Press, 2023), 85–91.

1918, Washington turned down Tehran's official request for a $2 million war-relief loan, arguing such loans were provided only to countries that had fought against Germany.[44]

After the war, American missionaries quickly rallied behind Reza Kahn's emerging dictatorship. Following the launch of his Pahlavi dynasty, American College vice president, Arthur Boyce, described the change as "a brilliant example of what a democratic country Persia is, and how it is possible . . . for a man to rise from the lowest to the highest rank . . . if he only has ability and energy and daring."[45] Unofficial missionary correspondence, however, reflected more sober observations on Reza Kahn's rise. It noted the public's lack of enthusiasm about the change of dynasty, which was considered British inspired and was accomplished with considerable violence, including the murder of dissident journalists. Official missionary sources, however, favorably compared Reza Shah to fascist dictators. Thus, at the peak of his dictatorship, the 1936 centennial commemoration of Presbyterian missions in Iran concluded that Reza Shah was "a strong ruler who is trying to do for Persia what Mussolini is doing for Italy."[46]

At the end of the First World War, the United States had emerged as the world's foremost military and economic power, with President Woodrow Wilson proposing a Fourteen Point agenda for postwar global reconstruction, including the right of national self-determination for colonial peoples. Conceived in competition with the Bolshevik Revolution's aggressive anti-imperialist agenda, the "Wilsonian moment" of American diplomacy appealed to nationalist and anticolonial sentiments, including those in Iran. Unlike the Bolsheviks, however, Wilson, did not oppose the victorious British and French imperialists forcibly repossessing their colonies and expanding them by picking up the pieces of a dismembered Ottoman Empire. Still, during the brief 1919–20 "Wilsonian moment," many Iranian nationalists began to hope that US involvement might counterbalance Anglo-Russian interference in the country.[47] Iran's most experienced diplomat in the United States, Ali Qoli Khan Nabil, personally lobbied Wilson and hosted a dinner for American and Iranian delegations to the Paris Peace Conference. The

44 Ghaneabassiri, "US Foreign Policy and Persia, 1856–1921," 162–3.

45 Zirinsky, "Render therefore unto Caesar," 337–56, quoted on 343.

46 Ibid., 343–4.

47 Erez Manela, *The Wilsonian Moment: Self-Determination and the International Origins of Anticolonial Nationalism* (Oxford University Press, 2007); W. Taylor Fain, *American Ascendance and British Retreat in the Persian Gulf Region* (Palgrave Macmillan, 2008).

Iranians were hoping for US backing in obtaining a seat at the conference, but, despite sympathetic statements by Wilson, received no serious support from Washington.[48] Still, Iranian statesmen and diplomats persistently argued in favor of involving the US government in the country's affairs. In 1921, for instance, prominent constitutionalist leader, Hassan Taqizadeh, wrote:

> In my opinion, to set things on the path of reform, the main point is drawing Americans to Iran and handing them the administration of affairs. We must make great efforts to draw the US into Iran. We should grant American concessions and hire Americans for financial and public projects, agriculture, trade transportation and telegraph, while fully supporting American schools.[49]

Nevertheless, during the 1920s, American business ventures in Iran were limited, consisting of only forty-two companies investing around $6 million, mostly exporting carpets, rugs, and raw materials.[50] A major exception was oil, which had become a key interest of postwar US foreign policy in the Middle East. Right after the war, the American Standard Oil Company began aggressive lobbying for a concession in northern Iran, where the new Bolshevik regime had renounced all czarist privileges and concessions. At the same time, taking advantage of the Soviet pullback, London was trying to impose the so-called 1919 Treaty on Iran, which effectively would have turned the country into a British protectorate. Iranian nationalists, as well as Soviet and French governments, opposed this treaty, which Washington also opposed, marking its first direct intervention in Iran's affairs. The new American position, however, was dictated by interest in Iranian oil, rather than adherence to Wilsonian principles. Had the 1919 agreement gone into effect, all of Iran would have become a British concessionary zone, barring access to American companies like Standard Oil, which had quietly signed a concession for northern oil with Teheran. While Standard Oil Company's concession was soon annulled, the British government was angry with such American moves to cut into its turf even though it had agreed to a joint Anglo-American venture to exploit northern Iranian oil.[51]

---

48 Guity Etemad, "Nabil-Al Dawla," in Encyclopædia Iranica, accessed July 31, 2021, iranicaonline.org; Ghaneabassiri, "US Foreign Policy and Persia," 164–5.

49 Quoted in Jamshid Behnam, *Berlaniha* (Tehran: Farzan, 2000), 54.

50 Kashani-Sabet, "Portals," 153.

51 Ghaneabassiri, "US Foreign Policy and Persia, 1856–1921," 172–3.

In 1922, the Iranian government hired Dr. Arthur C. Millspaugh, a former State Department oil advisor, to continue the Shuster mission and put Iran's finances in order. Coming as a private citizen, Millspaugh nevertheless had a semi-diplomatic function, being involved in negotiations for large American loan- and concession-seeking US oil companies. If successful, such ventures would have broken the British monopoly of Iranian oil, drawing the United States deeply into Iran. Millspaugh's mission coincided with Reza Khan's rise as the country's dictator, something he supported politically and in practice by strengthening the government's revenue collection. In 1924, when Reza Khan's dictatorial ambitions were quite clear, Millspaugh wrote:

> There seems little question that Reza Khan Pahlevi possessed not merely the devotion of his army but also the confidence of the people. He was the natural rallying-point of nationalism; he was the logical leader and therefore marked to bear the symbol of leadership; he was the best hope of the country.[52]

By 1923, Sinclair Oil Corporation was negotiating for a major concession in northern Iran, sweetened by the offer of a $10 million loan to Tehran, a deal backed by Prime Minister Reza Khan. But the anticipated breakthrough in Iran-US economic and political relations did not take place because the British blocked the Standard and Sinclair concessions, while the American loan failed to materialize. Contributing to these setbacks, and causing a crisis in Iran-US relations, was the 1924 murder of an American diplomat working on behalf of the Sinclair oil concession. Major Robert W. Imbrie had recently arrived in Tehran as a special agent of Allen Dulles, then head of the State Department's Near Eastern Affairs, who later would be CIA director during the 1953 overthrow of the Mosaddeq government (see chapter 2). Imbrie had been a spy and soldier of fortune, having served in the Belgian Congo's colonial wars and in the French Army during the First World War, before the American Foreign Service hired and dispatched him, as its special agent, to revolutionary Petrograd in 1917. Expelled for his espionage activities from the Soviet Union, Imbrie landed in Ankara to promote US diplomatic and commercial ties with Turkey's new nationalist government. In 1923, Washington recalled him to answer various charges,

52 Millspaugh in *The American Task in Persia*, quoted in Ali Rahnema, *The Political History of Modern Iran: Revolution, Reaction and Transformation, 1905 to the Present* (I.B. Tauris, 2023), 132.

including telling Turkish officials that American journalist Louise Bryant was a Bolshevik agent. He was cleared and assigned to Iran, tasked with reopening the American consulate in Tabriz and setting up an information gathering post on the Soviet Union. At the same time, Imbrie had connections to Sinclair Oil Corporation's representatives who were seeking an Iranian concession. His convoluted assignment became more complicated when, upon his arrival, he temporarily replaced the American consul on leave from the capital. On July 14, 1924, Imbrie was fatally attacked while visiting a Tehran water fountain that allegedly was performing miracles. Accompanied by a single American bodyguard, Imbrie, who also freelanced for the American National Geographic Society, was taking pictures of the fountain when a local mob, including soldiers and Cossacks, set upon them with rocks and knives. The Americans managed to flee to a government hospital, but the mob followed them, stabbing Imbrie to death while the police watched. Presumably the spontaneous reaction of a fanatical religious mob, Imbrie's murder was linked to Prime Minister Reza Khan, because his Cossacks were part of the murderous mob, and to the British who opposed Imbrie's lobbying against their oil monopoly in Iran. Taking advantage of the crisis, Reza Khan declared martial law, closing the last dissident newspapers and arresting his political opponents. At the same time, he promised to punish the murderers, offering Washington official apologies and financial compensation. The US government demanded the then-huge sum of $60,000 for Imbrie's family and $110,000 to cover the cost of dispatching a navy warship to bring his body home. Reza Khan's government arrested and tried a young Cossack soldier and two boys, fourteen and seventeen, accused of Imbrie's murder. The soldier was promptly executed, and the US consul insisted on the execution of both teenagers, who were then shot in his presence. A State Department memo noted the age of the accused was not an issue because "human life as such is not greatly valued by Orientals." In the aftermath of Imbrie's murder, the US government relented on its oil-concession demands, aligning its Iran policy with Britain's support of Reza Kahn and containment of the Soviet Union.[53] The Imbrie affair had a precedent in the 1829 murder, by a religious mob, of czarist envoy Alexander Griboyedov, along with the entire Russian embassy staff of sixty-nine people. The Griboyedov and Imbrie murders have been compared to the 1979–80 American Hostage Crisis,

53 Michael P. Zirinsky, "Blood, Power, and Hypocrisy: The Murder of Robert Imbrie and American Relations with Pahlavi Iran, 1924," *International Journal of Middle East Studies* 18 (1986): 275–92, quoted 286.

as they link seemingly xenophobic religious reactions against foreign diplomats to Iran's domestic power struggles (see chapter 5).[54]

Millspaugh's mission, however, continued as he imposed heavy taxes on the poorest Iranians to bolster Reza Shah's government and finance its development projects, primarily the Trans-Iranian Railway connecting the Persian Gulf to the Caspian Sea. In 1927, two years into Reza Shah's reign, Millspaugh resigned and left Iran after disagreeing with the monarch's allocation of oil revenue mainly for military expenditure, the largest item of government budgets. Ironically, his mission's failure at opening the country to major US involvement perpetuated the myth of American "neutrality" in Iran, a myth to which Millspaugh contributed by shaping American perceptions of Iran. In 1925, while still on good terms with Reza Khan, he had published *The American Task in Persia*, an account of his mission that was vaguely sympathetic to Iranians and highly critical of their government's incompetence and corruption. This work quickly surpassed Shuster's 1911 account to become the main reference for discussions of Iran in American journals such as *Foreign Affairs*, *Foreign Policy Reports*, and *Time*. Up until the Second World War, Millspaugh remained America's leading Iran expert, commenting, for example, on Reza Shah's unsuccessful 1932–33 attempt at renegotiating the Anglo-Iranian oil concession. In a *Foreign Affairs* article, he criticized Reza Shah's approach while also blaming the British refusal to offer better terms to Iran. This was positioning the United States as an "honest broker," sympathetic to Iranian nationalism and critical of "unreasonable" British impositions, a self-serving narrative that became a fixture in American academic, diplomatic, and journalistic circles all the way to Iran's oil nationalization crisis of the early 1950s (see chapter 2).[55]

Despite the setbacks of 1920, during the next decade, the United States would become Iran's third-largest foreign trading partner. By the early 1930s, Iran was importing fifteen hundred American cars and trucks every year, almost all made by General Motors, while 90 percent of all automobiles in the country were American made. American products, such as agricultural machinery, Singer sewing machines, and Underwood typewriters, dominated the Iranian market, while Iran exported

54 Mohammad Gholi Majd, *Oil and the Killing of the American Consul in Tehran* (University Press of America, 2006); Laurence Kelly, *Diplomacy and Murder in Tehran: Alexander Griboyedov and Imperial Russia's Mission to the Shah of Persia* (I.B. Tauris, 2006).

55 Zirinsky, "Blood, Power, and Hypocrisy"; see also Mansour Bonakdarian, "US-Iranian Relations, 1911–1951," Iran Chamber Society, 14–15, iranchamber.com.

carpets, pistachios, and dates to the United States.[56] Meanwhile, America had become a target of Iran's first modern industrial action when, on May Day 1929, about ten thousand Anglo Persian Oil Company (APOC) workers went on strike for higher wages, better housing, an eight-hour day, and union recognition. Strike leaders had ties to the underground Communist Party, seeking, in addition to labor grievances, the termination of Iran's agreement with the APOC. The government crushed the strike by making hundreds of arrests under martial law, while the British dispatched a gunboat to Abadan. The strike had spread to other cities including the provincial capital Ahwaz where three hundred workers of the American Ulen & Company, building a railway, were also demanding higher wages. Following the APOC, the American company ended the strike by having the governor general arrest its leaders. One year later, a dispute with Reza Shah led to the cancelation of Ulen's railway contract.[57]

America's "Lost Generation" Meets Iran's "Forgotten People"

During the 1920s, a curious US business venture produced a unique documentation of Iranian nomadic lifestyle. In 1924, a three-person American team traveled to Iran to film the annual migration of the Bakhtiari tribe across the country's rugged southwestern mountains. The crew was led by producer Merian Caldwell Cooper, who later would become internationally famous for his 1933 film *King Kong*. Cooper was accompanied by cameraman Ernest Beaumont Schoedsack and Marguerite Elton Harrison, author, journalist, and part-time spy. Their 1925 film, *Grass: A Nation's Battle for Life*, was to be an action-adventure drama featuring people and locations presumably unchanged since time immemorial. Unintentionally, however, *Grass* became a unique portrait of premodern Iran and one of the most authentic renditions of a pastoral-nomadic lifestyle. The film's "forgotten people" were the Bakhtiari people of southwestern Iran, whose armed cavalry had helped restore the constitutional regime and, by the 1920s, was used by the British to control the concession

56 Ghazvinian, *America and Iran*, 122.

57 Stephanie Cronin, "Popular Politics, the New State and the Birth of the Iranian Working Class: The 1929 Abadan Oil Refinery Strike," *Middle Eastern Studies* 46, no. 5 (September 2010): 699–732; Kaveh Ehsani, "The Social History of Labor in the Iranian Oil Industry" (PhD diss., Leiden University, 2004), 379–80.

area of the Anglo-Persian Oil company.[58] Unrelated to the purposes of Cooper's film crew at the time, the Bakhtiari would become an object of US attention in the mid-twentieth century—enlisted among the 1953 CIA coup plan's "assets"—when Washington began to recruit military forces for potential use against communist influence (see chapter 2).

Like Imbrie, whom they would briefly meet in Tehran, Cooper, Harrison, and Schoedsack belonged to the so-called Lost Generation of Americans who had personally experienced Europe's Great War and revolutions and felt ill at ease with routine life back at home. Schoedsack was a professional cameraman and a pioneer of airborne-combat photography during the First World War, later involved in helping refugees escape from Soviet-occupied Poland. Cooper had served in the American military intervention during the Mexican Revolution and later as a flyer in the First World War and in the Polish Army fighting the Bolsheviks. Harrison had lived and traveled widely in Europe and spoke several languages. After serving as a war correspondent, she was hired by the US military to file intelligence reports from postwar Germany and then from the Soviet Union, where she was briefly imprisoned and met Cooper whom she already knew. Back in New York, Harrison teamed up with Cooper to make a "travel film, based on the struggle for existence" and "absolutely authentic in every particular," provided they "could find a people whose daily lives contained all the elements of drama." Harrison put up half of the project's $10,000 budget, becoming one of the first American woman to coproduce a motion picture, appear in it, and be personally involved in every aspect of its making on foreign locations.[59] Given their common experiences abroad, Harrison and Cooper decided to find their "forgotten people" in a remote corner of Asia, initially focusing on Anatolian Kurdish tribes. According to the film's loose story line, Harrison would play a woman alienated from the modern world and searching for her forgotten Asian ancestors. Harrison, Cooper, and Schoedsack reached Turkey in 1924 but were not allowed to film in Kurdistan; hence they began searching for nomads beyond the Taurus Mountains and possibly in Iran. Meanwhile, the enterprising Harrison had managed a brief audience and interview with Mustafa Kemal (the

58 Arash Khazeni, "The Bakhtiari Tribes in the Iranian Constitutional Revolution," *Comparative Studies of South Asia, Africa and the Middle East* 25, no. 2 (2005): 377–98.

59 Bahman Maghsoudlou, *Grass: Untold Stories* (Mazda Publishers, 2009), chapters 1–2, pp. 154, 158; see also Hamid Naficy, "Lured by the East: Ethnographic and Expedition Films about Nomadic Tribes—The Case of Grass," in *Virtual Voyages: Cinema and Travel*, ed. Jeffrey Ruoff (Duke University Press, 2006), 117–38, cited 118–21.

future Atatürk), president of the new Turkish Republic, established that same year. On their way out of Turkey, the American crew filmed "exotic" people and places passing through the former Ottoman provinces that would become Syria and Iraq. In Baghdad, Harrison connected with famous Orientalist and chief of British intelligence in Iraq, Gertrude Bell, who facilitated the filmmakers' taking a few shots of Faisal, the British-imposed king of Iraq. Bell's knowledge of the region led the Americans to focus on Iran's Bakhtiari tribal confederation, whose annual migration across mountainous regions was just about to begin. The trio then rushed to Basra and crossed the border to Iran, arriving at the port of Khorramshahr in late March 1924. There, they contacted the officials of the Anglo-Persian Oil Company, whose concession area crossed Bakhtiari territory. Having influence with Bakhtiari khans, British company officials convinced them to take the Americans along and let them film their migration. Harrison, Schoedsack, and Cooper then spent April and May with the Baba Ahmadi Bakhtiari tribe, accompanying its five thousand members and fifty thousand animals during their sojourn through difficult terrain, the wild rapids of the Karun River, and all the way up to the frozen summit of the formidable Zard-Kuh, on whose eastern slopes lay the tribe's summer pastureland. Schoedsack brilliantly filmed the entire venture, thus producing a unique documentary of the life and migration of Iran's tribal people.[60]

Focused on the journey's dramatic moments, *Grass* nevertheless shows the daily struggles of Bakhtiari men and women to overcome formidable obstacles in the harshest natural environment. Watched closely, the film debunks many Orientalist stereotypes about Middle Eastern and Islamic people and societies.[61] Among other things, it shows how tribal women are neither veiled nor secluded, being responsible for the tribe's livelihood and working alongside men to take care of flocks of animals. A striking scene, for example, captures a young woman carrying a calf on her back all the way up the slopes of Zard-Kuh. Another scene depicts women dancing together to music played by men. Moreover,

---

60 Maghsoudlou, *Grass*, 166–8, 174–86.

61 Anthropologist Amy Malek has criticized *Grass* for its ethnocentric and Orientalist perspective, nevertheless conceding it is a valuable "ethnographic document." See Malek, "'If You're Going to Educate 'Em, You've Got to Entertain 'Em Too': An Examination of Representation and Ethnography in *Grass* and *People of the Wind*." *Iranian Studies* 44, no. 3 (2011): 313–25, 318; similarly, Naficy criticizes the film's deliberate distortions, "racialist" and Orientalist stereotypes and the visual "objectification" of the Bakhtiari people, while acknowledging its considerable merit both artistically and as documentary cinema. Ibid., 129–31.

both Harrison and Cooper reported how Bakhtiari religious beliefs and practice deviated from mainstream Islam. Copper wrote: "They have less superstition and religion than any other people I have ever seen . . . They say they are Mohammedans—but it is only say so." Harrison went further, claiming, "apparently they have no religious beliefs . . . unlike the Arabs who were devout, they never said prayers, did not observe the fast of Ramadan."[62] Copper also noted how his firsthand observation of the Bakhtiari contradicted their depiction, by British Orientalists, as wild and dangerous people.[63] The impression of the Bakhtiari as a hospitable and congenial people was shared by Schoedsack, whose job as cameraman placed him in constant intimate interaction with them. He wrote:

> We had nothing to pay our hosts but I think we gained their liking and respect by trying to be just as tough and humorous as they were—and they were pretty tough—and what we thought was funny, they thought was funny. They enjoyed a good joke, and had a real western sense of humor.[64]

Harrison's view of Bakhtiari culture was less sanguine, particularly when passing judgment on how their women were treated. In a passage that sounds unfairly harsh, given how the tribe had tried to ensure her safety and comfort, she opined:

> They were not a loveable or interesting people—hard, treacherous, thieves and robbers, without any cultural background, living under a remorseless feudal system, crassly material, and devoid of sentiment or spirituality. Their two outstanding qualities are an arrogant pride of race and a contempt for physical weakness.[65]

Soon after the Bakhtiari reached their destination, the Americans left for Tehran. They were almost out of film and eager to warp up a difficult but successful undertaking, although Cooper and Schoedsack thought they only had "half a picture," which they hoped to complete by going

62 Cooper quoted in Maghsoudlou, *Grass*, 195. On the high status of unveiled Bakhtiari women see Khazeni, "Bakhtiari Tribes," 392.

63 Cooper had a copy of archaeologist Austen Henry Layard, *Early Adventures in Persia, Susiana, and Babylonia: Including a Residence among the Bakhtiyari and other Wild Tribes Before the Discovery of Nineveh* (1887). Layard had repeated Henry Rawlinson's highly negative comments about the Bakhtiari people; Maghsoudlou, *Grass*, 196–8.

64 Quoted in Maghsoudlou, *Grass*, 209.

65 Harrison quoted in ibid., 233–4.

back to shoot the tribe's autumn return migration while adding human-interest elements such as aspects of Chief Haidar's family life. In Tehran, they stayed with US Vice Consul Robert Imbrie, who certified a letter by Bakhtiari tribal chiefs testifying to the authenticity of their expedition, which appears at the film's ending.[66] *Grass* did very well in its US screening, and film reviewers ranked it one of the best films of 1925, along with soon-to-be classics like Charlie Chaplin's *The Gold Rush* and Raoul Walsh's *Thief of Bagdad*. It was not shown in Iran until after Reza Shah's fall, possibly because its depiction of the Iranians living a "primitive" tribal lifestyle was not in line with the political and cultural elite's modern nation-state building agenda. Cooper and Schoedsack would continue working together, directing and producing *Chang: A Drama of the Wilderness* (1927), a *Grass*-like silent documentary about ordinary people struggling against natural elements and ferocious animals in the forests of Thailand. In 1933, they released *King Kong*, which became a commercial hit and classic of the horror-fantasy film genre.[67] Back in Tehran, Harrison and Cooper thought of covering their adventurous journey for American newspapers. They managed to write several articles, including Harrison's interview with Prime Minister Reza Khan, published in *The New York Times Magazine*. Titled "Soldierly Dictator of Persia Is a Gracious Host at Tea," the interview features a rare glimpse at Reza Khan relaxing in his garden. Harrison's description of his demeanor and physical appearance conforms to what would soon become Reza Shah's vintage profile:

> His face was heavy, almost sullen—hard-boiled is the American word that best describes it. His skin was tanned as if from exposure to sun and wind in innumerable campaigns; his mouth was set in rigid lines under his close-clipped mustache; but his eyes were his most remarkable feature. They looked straight at you and through you from under thick, level brows, unwavering, appraising, inscrutable.[68]

In an interesting aside, Harrison mentions the "icebreaker" moment of her conversation in Persian with the five-year-old Mohammad Reza, soon to be Iran's crown prince. This little exchange makes Harrison the

66 Naficy, "Lured by the East," 127–8, 136–7. In 1956, Cooper assembled and sent to Iran a crew to remake *Grass* in Technicolor and with sound, producing a forty-minute "demo" film that fell far short of the original version.

67 Ibid., 133–5.

68 Harrison, *New York Times Magazine*, December 6, 1925, quoted in Maghsoudlou, *Grass*, 242.

only non-Iranian journalist who "interviewed" both Reza Khan and his son, the future Mohammad Reza Shah. "You are the first ferengi [Western] lady who could speak our tongue," Reza Khan told her, their conversation warming up over tea, followed by a stroll in his garden, where he told her the names of various flowers and asked about her life and the gardens in America. The exchange quickly switched from Harrison's broken Persian to Russian, which Reza Khan reportedly had picked up while serving under czarist officers in the Cossack Brigade. Harrison provided the following synopsis of Reza Khan's political views while they discussed American financial advisors, the army, and Iran's nomadic people:

> Our chief trouble at the moment in Persia is economic. If we are to be a modern people, we must have a sound financial system. Our American financial advisors are helping us to achieve that end, but it cannot be accomplished without a centralization of government. The townspeople and peasants pay taxes, but they represent only a little over one-half of the population of Persia. The semi-independent tribes, like the Bakhtiari, living under their own princes, who pay taxes when they please, must abolish their feudal system and come under the direct control of Parliament. If they will not do this voluntarily, they must be forced to do it. For this reason, we are compelled for the present to spend much of the revenue in maintaining an army when we should spend it for popular education and improving communications.[69]

This is the gist of a narrative that would become prevalent in Iran and other countries where authoritarian modernization and nation-state building was taking place in the aftermath of the First World War. The narrative prioritized the absolute centralization of political authority, accomplished primarily by military force, and financed by taxing the poor. Harrison finds it perfectly fitting for Reza Khan to be a "dictator" in Iran, where most "people are densely ignorant, a large number are still in the tribal stage of development, there is no articulate public opinion, there are no political parties as we know them."[70] Had she followed Shuster's track, Harrison might have informed her American readers that, when the First World War ended, Iran had a weak but functioning constitutional government, with small but influential political parties

69 Ibid., 242–3.

70 Ibid., 244; on Reza Khan becoming Reza Shah, see Zirinsky, "Imperial Power and Dictatorship."

and a vibrant press that represented public opinion, at least among the educated elite. During the early 1920s, however, it was precisely the rise of Reza Khan's military dictatorship that systematically destroyed the pillars of this fledgling constitutional government. Unlike Shuster, Harrison was sympathetic to such political developments.

A Balance Sheet of the First Century of Iran-US Relations

When *Grass* appeared in movie theaters, the American public's knowledge of Iran was almost nil. By the early 1920s, the most comprehensive popular coverage of Iran had been a 1921 issue of *National Geographic Magazine*, featuring over a hundred photographs along with basic descriptions of the country's climate and physical geography, noting in passing the cultural diversity of its people. The magazine's two photojournalistic articles made scattered references to ancient "Persian" empires, exhibiting pictures of their ruined monuments like Persepolis. But there was no serious discussion of Iran's past or recent history, including what could have been gleaned from American missionary reports or Shuster's account of the country's recent revolutionary upheaval. As one of the authors admitted:

> Persia, for a surprising majority of people in America, is not much more definite than a hazy pink or green spot swimming around India—"Oh, you know, beyond Turkey."
>
> Persia suggests Omar Khayyam, Carpets and rugs, rugs remembered from colorful magazine advertisements or hasty glimpses into Fifth Avenue windows.[71]

During the 1920s–30s, American knowledge of Iran increased through the contributions of scholars, particularly archeologists and art historians, whose cumulative work tended to inform and support the new Pahlavi dynasty's official nationalist ideology. Arthur Upham Pope, a pioneer of such politically inflected scholarship and a self-styled archeologist and art historian, arrived in Tehran in the mid-1920s, coinciding with the launch of the upstart Pahlavi dynasty, which sought legitimation by connecting itself to the glory of ancient Iran's imperial "Aryan"

71 *National Geographic*, April 1921, quoted on 417.

heritage. As in other modernizing countries, reviving Iran's "national heritage" was a state project accomplished through public education and showcased via national museums and monuments. Pope quickly inserted himself in these official projects, becoming the international promoter of Iranian "heritage," consisting of artistic and archeological discoveries. He organized Iran's participation in the 1926 World Fair in Philadelphia, acting as its official curator. Under his direction, the Iran pavilion became a big success, winning the fair's gold medal for architecture by exhibiting a large replica of an Isfahan mosque, complete with actual wooden doors shipped to the United States. In addition, Pope organized a large exhibit of Iranian art at the nearby Pennsylvania Museum. This was America's greatest exposure to Iranian art and architecture, with thousands visiting the Iran exhibit or reading about it in newspapers all over the country. Apparently aware of America's rising global stature, the Iranian government, in 1927, canceled the French monopoly in Iranian archaeology, offering it instead to Americans. Thus, during the 1930s, the University of Pennsylvania and New York's Metropolitan Museum of Art were doing important excavations in different parts of Iran. By the end of the decade, the University of Chicago had completed Iran's first aerial reconnaissance as well as the first major excavation of Persepolis, the oldest imperial capital, going back twenty-five centuries. Thus revamped, Persepolis became the most important monumental representation of Pahlavi-era nationalism, buttressed by American scholarship and technological prowess.[72]

As the 1930s wore on, the United States and Iran had close to a century of relations behind them. The centennial balance sheet of this history coincides with the last years of Reza Shah's reign, before everything changed due to the events of the Second World War. In the mid-1930s, a trivial incident triggered a major crisis between Tehran and Washington. In November 1935, Iran's chargé d'affaires in Washington, Ghaffar Djalal, spent a few hours under arrest after arguing with a police officer who had stopped his car for speeding. Reza Shah became furious when in some press coverage of this incident, he was referred to as a former "stable boy," hired at the British legation. When Washington refused to offer a formal apology, diplomatic relations were broken, taking four years to be fully restored. Ironically, on the day of his arrest, Djalal had been rushing to a meeting with the American Banknote Corporation to close a deal for printing Iran's paper currency, a contract that consequently went

72 Ghazvinian, *America and Iran*, 113–15.

to a German company.[73] When official relations with Washington were resumed in 1939, the Iranian government, looking for modern expertise in framing and animal husbandry, invited Franklin Harris, the president of Utah's Brigham Young University, to spend a year in Iran. Harris then recommended the hiring of two Utah State University professors to teach at the College of Agriculture & Natural Resources in Karaj, near Tehran. Links to Utah State went back to 1912, when Iran's chargé Ali Qoli Khan, who was impressed by the Mormon state's ban on alcohol and smoking, enrolled four of his nephews to study there. Returning to Iran, these students built a bridgehead for institutional relations with Utah, one of them becoming the head of the College of Agriculture & Natural Resources in Karaj and another becoming Reza Shah's advisor on animal husbandry. By the early 1950s, about 150 Iranians, including Ardeshir Zahedi, CIA's key contact in the 1953 coup and later ambassador to the United States (see chapters 2 and 4–5), had graduated from Utah State.[74]

On the Iranian side, throughput an entire century (1830s–1930s), the outstanding feature of American presence and influence was modern education. By the end of the nineteenth century, Presbyterian missionaries had expanded beyond their base in Azerbaijan to open modern primary and secondary schools for boys and girls in Tehran and a few other cities. The crown achievement of such activities was Tehran's American (Alborz) College, a counterpart to Cairo's American University and Istanbul's Robert College. Moving into the twentieth century, the enrollment of American missionary schools had changed from poor religious minority students to urban middle-class Muslim boys and girls. Presbyterian schools stood out as pioneers of girls' modern education, enrolling about one thousand students by the end of the nineteenth century, most famously at Tehran's American Girls' School, or Iran Bethel, which the missionaries administered for sixty-six years, until 1940.[75]

The most famous American educational institution in Iran was Tehran's Presbyterian Boys' School, which came to be known as the American (Alborz) College. With Reverend Samuel Martin Jordan as its head since 1898, the school built its famous campus, complete with dormitories, athletic fields, lecture halls, science labs, and a modern library,

73 Ibid., 120–1; Baqer Aqeli, *Ruzshomar-e tarikh-e Iran: Az mashruteh ta enqelab-e eslami* [The Daily Chronicle of Iranian History: From the Constitutional Revolution to the Islamic Revolution] vol. 1 (Tehran, 1990), 211.

74 Ghazvinian, *America and Iran*, 609; Gail, *Arches of the Years*, 109–10; see also Richard Garlitz, *A Mission for Development: Utah Universities and the Point Four Program in Iran* (Utah State University Press, 2018).

75 Michael P. Zirinsky, "Panacea"; Zirinsky, "Harbingers of Change."

holding twenty thousand volumes. In 1928, the regents of the University of the State of New York chartered Tehran's American College to grant a Bachelor of Art degree. By the time the American College became an Iranian high school in 1940, it had awarded 106 junior college degrees and twenty baccalaureates, including 4 to women. The American College occupies a special place among Iran's modern educational institutions, since its graduates, as well as thousands of its high school students, stood out among twentieth century Iran's cultural, political, and scientific elite. For decades, the illustrious head of Alborz College, respectfully known to Iranians as "Doktor Jordan," was the school's embodiment, leaving behind an enduring legacy even after Alborz became an Iranian high school. Jordan's pedagogy was imbued with the American traits of pragmatism, self-reliance, and respect for science and technology, as well as arrogance of power, rigidity of discipline, and deference to established authority. In his early years, Jordan had described what American educators hoped to bring to their young Iranian students:

> The young Oriental educated in Western lands as a rule gets out of touch with his own country... Too often he discards indiscriminately the good and the bad of the old civilization and fails to assimilate the best of the West... We adapt the best Western methods to the needs of the country while we retain all that is good in their own civilization.[76]

Jordan thus claimed he knew what modern Iranians needed to learn, including what was best in "their own civilization." As American schools, and particularly Alborz College, became established, the social conservatism of missionaries became more evident in their conscious effort at recruiting upper-class students and molding them into future leaders of Iran's authoritarian modernization. Jordan again made this clear when he boasted:

> American schools have been patronized by the leading men of the country. Among the students have been enrolled sons of the princes of the royal family, first and second cousins of former Shahs, the only

76 Y. Armajani, "Alborz College," in *Encyclopædia Iranica*, accessed April 8, 2020, iranicaonline.org; H. E. Chehabi, "Diversity at Alborz," *Iranian Studies* 44, no. 5 (September 2011): 715–29; Thomas M. Ricks, "Alborz College of Tehran, Dr. Samuel Martin Jordan and the American Faculty: Twentieth-Century Presbyterian Mission Education and Modernism in Iran (Persia)." *Iranian Studies* 44, no. 5 (2011): 627–46; Zirinsky, "Inculcate Tehran: Opening a Dialogue of Civilizations in the Shadow of God and the Alborz," *Iranian Studies* 44, no. 5 (2011): 657–69.

> grandson of the present Shah, sons of Prime Ministers and other Cabinet ministers, of members of the Majlis (Congress), of tribal chieftains, of provincial governors, of other influential men . . . Probably no other school in the world has ever enrolled so many of the children of the leading men of any country . . . Our students imbibed liberal ideas, they agitated for reforms, they cooperated with other forward-looking patriots in transforming the medieval despotism of thirty years ago into the modern, progressive democracy of today.

This was written in 1935, at the peak of Reza Shah's dictatorship, which Jordan described as progressive and democratic. Jane Doolittle, the famous principal of Tehran's American Girls' School, echoed similar sentiments: "A great many of our girls were from the upper classes, and they had pull, they had the know-how, and they could get things done for us, both for the clinic and for the school." A partial list of Presbyterian school graduates includes women such as Iran Teymourtash, daughter of Reza Shah's court minister; Moluk Khanom Jalali, daughter of an Esfahan governor; Mehrtaj Rakhshan, educationalist and daughter of influential cleric Agha Imam al-Hokama; and celebrated poet Parvin E'tesami. The most distinguished graduate of the American Girls' School was Sattareh Farman Farmaian, scion of the old Qajar royal family and founder of the professional field of social work in Iran. With the help of her American teachers, Farman Farmaian obtained a visa to study in the United States and arrived at the port of Los Angeles on July 4, 1944, becoming the first Iranian to enroll at the University of Southern California. After receiving a degree in social work, Farman Farmaian stayed in California to gain work experience during Iran's oil nationalization crisis of the early 1950s, when her confidence in the United States was shattered by the news of CIA involvement in Mosaddeq's overthrow (see chapter 2). Later, she returned to Iran and, with the backing of the royal court, opened the Tehran School of Social Work and the country's first family-planning clinic.[77]

Unlike the celebratory accounts of American missionaries and educators, confidential diplomatic reports from Reza Shah's Iran were more realistic and occasionally quite perceptive. For example, in a 1935 report titled "Exile of Iranian Officials," US Minister William Hornibrook wrote to Washington: "Since the ascension of Reza Shah to the throne

77 Sattareh Farman Farmaian and Dona Munker, *Daughter of Persia: A Woman's Journey from Her Father's Harem through the Islamic Revolution* (Anchor Books, 1992), chapter 8, 199–202, 230.

the political history of Iran is clogged with similar incidents. It will not be necessary to mention the long list of sudden deaths, imprisonments or of those who have been exiled from the country." Hornibrook's commentary on Reza Shah era cultural policies was even more prescient:

> My own impression is that the Shah's wholesale introduction of European customs, his hostility to the clergy, his ruthless methods and his success in inculcating into the hearts and minds of his people strong ultra-nationalistic feelings, may possibly result in a bitter anti-foreign feeling in the event of his demise.[78]

As for the overall impact of the missionaries, their role in shaping American public perceptions and government policy toward Iran was as important as their contribution to educating Iranians. Well into the twentieth century, missionary teachers and their students stood out among American academic experts, foreign policy advisors, intelligence officers, and business consultants, especially to the oil industry, dealing with Iran. The most famous of these students included Yahya Armajani who served at the Persian Gulf command during the Second World War and became a history professor at Macalester College, St. Paul, Minnesota. Armajani's relatively balanced scholarly writings on Iran and the Middle East influenced a generation of American scholars and students. Joseph Rasooli was another student and later teacher at mission schools who worked for the Office of War Information in New York and later for the Voice of America. Elgin Groseclose was a teacher in Tabriz who wrote one of the first standard introductions to Iran and worked for *Fortune* magazine and the oil industry. Edwin Wright was borne in Tabriz to missionary parents, serving in Iran during the 1920s–30s. He later worked for the State Department and lectured at Columbia University and the Army and Navy War College, becoming a founding member of the Middle East Institute. Another former missionary teacher was Taylor Gurney, who worked as a cultural officer at the US Embassy in Tehran during the 1940s–50s and later as an advisor to the Iranian Embassy in Washington. Gurney was "an institution in Tehran" and "a man who seemed to know everyone and who had a unique ability to open Iranian doors for Americans." The most outstanding individual influencing mid-century American policy and scholarly perceptions was T. Cuyler Young, who had served as a missionary teacher in Gilan along with his wife and

78 Hornibrook quoted in Kashani-Sabet, *Heroes to Hostages*, 121.

sister during the 1920s–30s. Like other missionary cohorts, Young joined US government service during the Second World War and later had a long academic career, teaching Persian language and Iranian history at Princeton University (1942–69), where he trained a generation of Iran experts. During the war, Young worked for the Office of Strategic Services (OSS) and later for the CIA in Washington and Tehran, where he was engaged in covert operations during Mosaddeq's premiership and later during the Kennedy administration, and as a fellow at the Council on Foreign Relations recommended a reform policy in Iran (see chapters 2 and 3).[79]

A century of American missionary activity in Iran had made a notable but modest contribution to modern education, leaving behind a measure of goodwill toward the United States among elite and upper-class Iranians. Whatever their faults, the missionaries represented an America whose aim appeared not to be Iran's economic exploitation or direct interference in its political affairs. At the same time, American missionaries had aligned themselves with Iran's educational and cultural project of authoritarian modernization and nation-state building. Meanwhile, the missionaries brought back to the United States firsthand knowledge of Iran and educated the first generation of Iranians who forged direct cultural, political, and economic ties between the two countries, often through governments and their darker corridors of intelligence, as well as in the elite halls of the academe and the less intellectually conspicuous business world, particularly in the oil industry. Overall, missionary activity was in-line with the broad agendas of American and Iranian governments and power elites. This was necessary if the missionaries were not prevented from continuing their activities, something that the Iranian government finally did by the end of the 1930s. Ultimately, and despite their positive impact, the missionaries adhered to a conservative ethos, leaving behind little critical reflection on their contribution to the repressive side of Iranian modernity. Still, glimmers of awareness of their host country's political predicaments appear among the missionaries' personal writings. As we saw, high-ranking Presbyterian figures, like Samuel Jordan, publicly endorsed Reza Shah's rule as democratic and progressive. However, as rumors of the king's abdication began to circulate in 1941, Reverend William M. Miler recorded in private

79 Zirinsky, "Render therefore unto Caesar," 354–6; on Cuyler Young see Matthew Shannon, "Reading Iran: American Academics and the Last Shah," *Iranian Studies* 51, no. 2 (March 2018): 289–316; on CIA activities, ibid., 293–4.

correspondence: "I believe everybody in the country would rejoice if that were true." Admitting agreement with his Iranian friends, he noted that the crown prince, Mohammad Reza Pahlavi, could never take his father's place because "the people are so fed up with this family that they can't endure them."[80]

80 Zirinsky, "Render therefore unto Caesar," 345.

2
Defining American Priorities in Iran: Oil and Military-Autocratic Order

America should take the lead in running the world in the way the world ought to be run.

President Truman, 1945[1]

As we saw in chapter 1, Iran had no significant place in US geopolitical considerations during the first century of the two countries' relations (1830s–1930s). In that period, American foreign policy was focused primarily on the Western Hemisphere and the Pacific region. But Iran suddenly became important, as the "bridge of victory," allowing the vital passage to the Soviet Union of American Lend-Lease material during the Second World War. Immediately after the war, Iran was one of the first theaters of the Cold War that shattered the alliance between the United States and the Soviet Union.[2] Consequently, post–Second World War Iran-US relations has been the subject of massive diplomatic, scholarly, archival, and journalistic studies. Hence, while this book's first chapter covered an entire century, the present chapter narrows its focus to a single decade (1942–53), the turning point in the history of Iran-US relations. We begin with the Allied occupation of Iran and then trace American involvement with Iranian oil, Iran's armed forces and monarchy, and the beginning of the Cold War in Iran, ending the chapter with the 1953 CIA coup.

1 Quoted in Ronald Grigor Suny, *The Soviet Experiment: Russia, the USSR, and the Successor States* (Oxford University Press, 1998), 346.

2 Mohammad Gholi Majd, *Iran Under Allied Occupation in World War II: The Bridge to Victory & A Land of Famine* (University Press of America, 2016).

The historiography of mid-twentieth century Iran-US relations can be divided into two broad schools of interpretation. The older school saw American policy during the 1940s–50s, including the 1953 CIA coup, as primarily "defensive," and shaped by the Cold War imperative of pushing back against Soviet aggression. A second and more recent school views Iran-US relations within the broad architecture of America's post–Second World War global dominance, defined by geopolitical and oil interests.[3] These two perspectives need not be mutually exclusive since containing communism required maximizing American access to global economic resources, chief among them oil. Many historians hold the United States responsible for starting the Cold War by taking aggressive steps that forced an incomparably weaker Soviet Union into a defensive posture. "Although at times the Kremlin reacted belligerently," writes one commentator, "the burden of responsibility for the Cold War rested on the United States, the more powerful of the two countries (possessing, among other advantages, a nuclear monopoly), and the one with less to fear from the other."[4] In this perspective, President Harry Truman ended the wartime alliance with the Soviet Union when he used the atomic bomb to force Japan's surrender before the Soviets could join the Pacific War, per the agreement between Franklin Roosevelt and Josef Stalin. The United States then started the nuclear arms race by insisting on its monopoly of nuclear weapons and refusing to place them under UN supervision. Nor did the Cold War start in response to communist aggression. At the 1945 Yalta Conference, Roosevelt and Churchill had agreed that the Red Army's occupation of Eastern Europe involved the setting up of pro-Soviet regimes there, a limited expansion of Moscow's sphere of influence. The war-shattered Soviet Union was incapable of pushing communism beyond Eastern Europe, while an incomparably stronger US was imposing a capitalist order not only on Western Europe and Japan but on the entire planet. Toward the end of the war, government-sponsored studies argued that without free access to global

3 James A. Bill, *The Eagle and the Lion: The Tragedy of American-Iranian Relations* (Yale University Press, 1988); for a strong focus on oil, see Ervand Abrahamian, *The Coup: 1953, the CIA, and the Roots of Modern US-Iranian Relations* (The New Press, 2013); the argument that Cold War anti-communism dictated US policy is best argued by Mark J. Gasiorowski, "The 1953 Coup D'état in Iran," *International Journal of Middle East Studies* 19, no. 3 (August 1987): 261–86.

4 H. W. Brands, *The Devil We Knew: Americans and the Cold War* (Oxford University Press, 1993), 4–23, quoted on vii; on Stalin's Cold War cautiousness, see Suny, *Soviet Experiment*, 338–9; on the politics of ending the war with Japan, see Gar Alperovitz, *The Decision to Use the Atomic Bomb and the Architecture of an America Myth* (Vintage Books, 1996).

markets, the very survival of American capitalism was at risk. The Great Depression of the 1930s had ended only when the US economy began massive wartime production geared toward global-military consumption. After the war, the United States rebuilt the world economy via the Marshall Plan, investment and credit institutions, including the World Bank and the International Monetary Fund, and by making the dollar and US gold reserves the foundation of global finance. Western Europe merged into the American free-trade zone and its governments became US imperial satrapies through the NATO military alliance. This architecture could not be extended to the Soviet Union's planned economy, which was rebuilt almost from scratch, without the investment and loans President Roosevelt had promised.[5] To maintain the newly restructured world economic order, the United States would establish a military grid enmeshing the entire world:

> By the end of World War II, in less than five years' time, the United States would build and occupy some thirty thousand installations at two thousand base sites worldwide. While large numbers of bases would close at war's end, what remained was a global network larger than any in human history. The United States would become a global empire defined to a significant extent by its historically unprecedented collection of bases. These bases would represent a quantitative and qualitative shift in the nature of US power, the US military presence abroad, and the country's relationship with the rest of the world.[6]

Practiced since the Monroe Doctrine of 1823 in Latin America, the "open-door" model of American imperialism, merging private corporate domination and military intervention, went global after WWII.[7] As would be the case in Iran, ties to a country's armed forces were the foundation of US foreign relations, an imperative invariably leading to American sponsorship of autocratic regimes and/or military dictatorships.

---

5 Perry Anderson, *American Foreign Policy and Its Thinkers* (Verso, 2015), 17–18; on Soviet weakness, see Suny, *Soviet Experiment*, 346–51; Melvyn P. Leffler, *A Preponderance of Power: National Security, the Truman Administration, and the Cold War* (Stanford University Press, 1992).

6 David Vine, *The United States of War: A Global History of America's Endless Conflicts, From Columbus to the Islamic State* (University of California Press, 2020), 141.

7 On the continuity of the Cold War with traditional American policy in Latin America, see Justin Hart, *Empire of Ideas: The Origins Public Diplomacy and the Transformation of US Foreign Policy* (Oxford University Press, 2013).

A Superpower Dogfight: The Allies and Iranian Oil

> Like dogs fighting over a bone, the Allied powers—Great Britain, the Soviet Union, and the United States—quickly became locked in frantic competition with one another over Iran's resources. Although the United States was late to the contest, its involvement changed the dynamic almost instantly.[8]

Unprecedented levels of direct American involvement in Iran began when the United States joined the Anglo-Soviet occupation of the country in early 1942. British and Soviet armies had invaded Iran in August 1941, after the head of the newly established Pahlavi dynasty, Reza Shah, was given an ultimatum to expel around one thousand Germans. By the end of the 1930s, Germany was Iran's leading trade partner, and Nazi propaganda had made some headway among the elite, primarily due to Germany's potential role as a counterweight to Russo-British influence in Iran. When Hitler's armies quickly pushed into the Soviet Union in the summer of 1941, Iran suddenly became a strategic game changer. The country's oil fields were vital to the British war effort, while securing a "Persian Corridor" would allow British and Soviet armies to link up through a land bridge. The Trans-Iranian Railway, connecting the Persian Gulf to the Caspian Sea, was thus commandeered by the Allies to send war material in support of the Red Army's life and death struggle on the Eastern Front. Despite accepting the Anglo-Soviet ultimatum, Reza Shah was forced to abdicate and go into exile in September 1941.[9] At that point, both British and Soviet ambassadors wanted to declare Iran a republic, but conservative Iranian politicians convinced them to maintain the Pahlavi monarchy and install the twenty-two-year-old crown prince on the throne.[10] Thus, and more blatantly than his father, Mohammad Reza Shah Pahlavi owed his kingship to foreign intervention, further damaging his dynasty's dubious legitimacy.

---

8 David R. Collier, *Democracy and the Nature of American Influence in Iran, 1941–1979* (Syracuse University Press, 2017), 43.

9 Shaul Bakhash "Britain and the Abdication of Reza Shah," *Middle Eastern Studies* 52, no. 2 (2016): 318–34; Reza Shah's ouster was proposed by the British, to which the Soviets agreed. Nikolay A. Kozhanov, "The USSR and the Allied Occupation of Iran in August 1941: The Untold Story of a Difficult Decision", in *Russians in Iran: Diplomacy and Power in the Qajar Era and Beyond*, ed. Rudi Matthee and Elena Andreeva (I.B. Tauris, 2018): 310–31.

10 Baqer Aqeli, *Zaka al-Molk Foroughi va Shahrivar-e 1320* [Zaka al-Molk Foroughi and August 1941] (Tehran: 1989), 102. Both Soviet and British ambassadors had proposed declaring Iran a republic.

Keeping Mohammad Reza Shah in a largely ceremonial role, the Allies restored Iran's constitutional monarchy, which gave the Majles considerable power. Reviving the parliamentary system served the Allies' interest in holding the country's divergent political factions together. Iran's wartime government was a version of the global antifascist Popular Front, a broad coalition ranging from communists to conservative Anglophiles. Hence began Iran's unique twelve-year experiment with constitutional government and political pluralism, launched under Anglo-Soviet occupation in 1941 and ending with American intervention through the 1953 CIA coup.

In January 1942, the Soviet Union, the United Kingdom, and Iran signed a treaty guaranteeing Iran's independence and the withdrawal of foreign troops no longer than six months after the war's end. Meanwhile, the Allied occupation had revived the old competition of Iran's pro-British and pro-Russian political clans. Traditionally, the British exerted political influence through the royal court, conservative politicians, tribal chieftains, clerics, and Majles deputies. The Soviets made a departure by throwing their full support behind a newly formed political organization, the Tudeh (Masses) Party of Iran, established in fall 1941 as an antifascist front committed to Allied victory, constitutionalism, and socialism. The new party quickly set up grassroots networks, particularly through trade unions, while deftly adapting to the parliamentary system. Soon falling under a Stalinist leadership, the Tudeh Party became Iran's best organized and most popular political organization during the semi-democratic conditions of 1941–53. The party benefitted from its early affiliation with the USSR, seen as the champion of the lower classes that had turned the war's tide against Nazi Germany. While the party benefitted from association with the USSR, its unique success was due to its popular political and economic agenda. Proclaimed in February 1942, and further expanded in 1943, the party's program demanded an eight-hour workday, disability insurance, pensions and subsidized housing for workers, the redistribution of state and crown lands to peasants, the establishment of rural schools and health clinics, equal political rights and equal pay for women, government support of poor mothers and children, and job security, higher pay, and lower taxes for salaried government employees.[11] The Tudeh Party thus presented itself as the only heir to the populist legacy of the Constitutional Revolution (see

11 Afshin Matin-Asgari, *Both Eastern and Western: An Intellectual History of Iranian Modernity* (Cambridge University Press, 2018), 148.

chapter 1), a claim that rang true because no rival emerged to match its appeal among the intelligentsia and working classes.

The 1941 dismantling of Reza Shah's dictatorship opened a floodgate of social upheaval as Iranians suddenly had unprecedented freedom to express discontent and demand political change. With the spread of typhus and famine, bread riots broke out as the occupying armies requisitioned food and basic provisions.[12] In this potentially revolutionary situation, even British officials thought the Tudeh Party might play a positive role in forcing Iran's ruling classes to accept long-overdue social reforms. One seasoned British diplomat noted:

> The present internal situation is so serious that constitutional reform, whether imposed by the Shah from above or by some party from below, seems to be the only alternative to a social upheaval in a few years' time. I do not therefore see why we should strengthen the landowners who compose the majority of the Majlis and from whom we have nothing to hope, against the only party who have succeeded in frightening them to some extent.

In fact, Sir Reader Bullard, the top British minister in Tehran, believed that Tudeh Party's reform proposals were too cautious and "mild in comparison with the conditions of the poor classes." British concern about the urgency of social reform related to widespread perceptions of the United Kingdom as the main defender of a reactionary status quo, whereas the Soviet Union championed the cause of the lower classes.[13] A 1943 report by a British military attaché noted the rise in the popularity of the Soviet Union relative to Britain, connecting it to the possibility of a revolutionary rising:

> There has been recently a very noticeable change in the sentiments of the Persian people towards Russia . . . The generally admirable discipline of Russian troops in Persia, their good behavior towards the people, their professed sympathy with the lower classes, their advertised contentment with their own system, the good relations apparently existing between

12 JAMI, *Gozashteh cheragh-e rah-e ayandeh ast* [The Past is a Beacon to the Future] vol. 1 (Tehran: n.d.), 148. Stephen McFarland, "Anatomy of an Iranian Political Crowd: The Tehran Bread Riot of December 1942," *International Journal of Middle Eastern Studies* 17, no. 1 (1985): 51–65.

13 Quotes in Fakhreddin Azimi, *Iran: The Crisis of Democracy: From the Exile of Reza Shah to the Fall of Musaddiq* (I.B. Tauris, 2009), 82–3.

> officers and men and the obviously magnificent morale of the Russian people have greatly affected preconceived ideas of the Soviet system . . . An increasingly sympathetic interest is being shown in the principles of the Soviet system . . . The less frightful Russia is to masses the more of a bogy does she become to the propertied classes. A situation seems to be developing where the masses may draw closer to Russia and the propertied classes come to be associated more closely than they now are with Great Britain. Indeed, Russia is already beginning to be regarded as the champion of the oppressed and is being looked to by the leaders of the discontented as a possible supporter of a revolution against the present ruling classes.[14]

A major difficulty for the British in Iran was the monarchy's obvious dependence on them. During the early 1940s, the shah met and consulted almost exclusively with British officials, causing Bullard to worry that his unpopularity and preoccupation with military matters would give the impression that the British wanted to revive Reza Shah's "military dictatorship."[15]

This climate of precarious great power rivalry, with the initiative shifting from Britain to the Soviet Union, was the background of America's entrance in Iran as a third foreign power. By the second half of 1942, thirty thousand American military personnel were stationed in Iran, eventually sending, via the Trans-Iranian Railway and dirt roads, 5.5 million tons of tanks, trucks, and aircraft to the USSR. Almost overnight, Iran had become the object of special attention in America's global diplomacy and military strategy. Thinking of the postwar international order, President Franklin Roosevelt pondered the idea of making Iran a test case of a global Pax Americana. Writing to the Secretary of State Cordell Hull, he proposed "the idea of using Iran as an example of what we could do by an unselfish American Policy. We could not take on a more difficult nation than Iran." Responding bluntly, Hull noted, "from a more directly selfish point of view, it is to our interest that no great power be established on the Persian Gulf opposite the important American petroleum development in Saudi Arabia."[16] As Hull hinted, securing access to

14 Military attaché's intelligence summary no. 15 for the period April 7–13, 1943. Quoted in R. M. Burrell, ed., *Iran Political Diaries 1881–1965*, vol. 12 (Oxford Archives Edition, 1997), 3.

15 Azimi, *Iran*, 90.

16 Roosevelt quoted in Roham Alvandi, *Nixon, Kissinger, and the Shah: The United States and Iran in the Cold War* (Oxford University Press, 2016), 8–9; Hull quoted in Bill, *The Eagle and the Lion*, 19.

Middle Eastern oil would be a priority of American foreign policy.[17] The State Department had determined that Saudi Arabian oil was "a stupendous source of strategic power and one of the greatest material prizes in world history."[18] Firmly established in Saudi Arabia during the 1930s, American oil companies were now poised to break the British monopoly on Iranian oil, something they had tried but failed to accomplish in the 1920s (see chapter 1). When the United States joined the Allied occupation, the American oil lobby aggressively resumed its concession-seeking efforts. In 1943, James Byrnes, director of the Office of War Mobilization, recommended to President Roosevelt that Britain should share one-third of its Iranian oil interests as compensation for American support in the war. But the American minister in Tehran, Louis Dreyfus, argued that such moves could cause the "British and the Soviets to suspect our attitude toward Iran is not entirely disinterested and thus weaken our general position here." Secretary Hull insisted, however, that oil concessions were crucial to American war aims, as well as to the "long lasting viewpoint" of the United States in the postwar world.[19]

As Dreyfus had warned, news of secret negotiations with American oil companies seeking concessions in northern Iran caused a political uproar in Tehran. The Soviets renewed their demand for oil concession in northern Iran, their zone of occupation and traditionally Russia's sphere of influence. Thus, both the United States and the Soviet Union were pushing deeper into Iran at Britain's expense. While the Tehran government was considering the occupying powers' demands, radical nationalists entered oil politics by proposing a "negative equilibrium" to rid Iran of all three foreign powers. The respected parliamentarian Mohammad Mosaddeq, argued that granting American oil concessions would lead to the Soviets asking for the same: "When from the other side of the world the American government asks for a concession, why should the Soviet government, which is our neighbor, not do so?" He then spearheaded the passage of parliamentary legislation stipulating

17 Referring to the creation of the "Persian Gulf Command" during WWII, an official US government report explains: "Oil became a military/political concern and other factors made the strategic value of the area more obvious. Soviet and Soviet-sponsored activity in the northern tier immediately after WWII contributed to the Unites States concern and led to the formulation of policies designed to contain the perceived Soviet threat." See *Economic Consequences of the Revolution in Iran: A Compendium of Papers submitted to the Joint Economic Committee, Congress of the United States* (US Government Printing Office: 1980), 6.

18 Quoted in Vine, *The United States of War*, 167.

19 Bill, *Eagle and the Lion*, 80.

that any decision on foreign concessions had to be postponed until after the end of wartime occupation. The 1944 legislation showed Iranian agency, but it left the British oil monopoly intact while denying Soviet and American access to Iranian oil, at least for the war's duration.[20]

Meanwhile, President Roosevelt dispatched a personal envoy, General Patrick J. Hurley, to assess Iran's situation and make recommendations for American policy. Hurley helped draft an Iran Declaration, which Roosevelt, Churchill, and Stalin endorsed at their 1943 Tehran Conference, guaranteeing Iran's "independence, sovereignty, and territorial integrity." His special report to Roosevelt recommended a policy going beyond providing economic and military advisors to "assist in the creation in Iran of a government based upon the consent of the governed and of a system of free enterprise," giving "the Iranian people an opportunity to enjoy the rights of man as set forth in the Constitution of the United States." This American model of capitalist democracy would be an alternative to what British imperialism and Soviet communism offered Iran. Taking issue with this "anti-imperialist" stance, Churchill angrily wrote to Roosevelt: "British imperialism has spread and is spreading democracy more widely than any other system of government since the beginning of time."[21] Hurley's recommendations, however, were related to Britain's deteriorating position in Iran vis-à-vis the Soviet Union:

> For the most part the attitude of the Iranian officials, and indeed of the Iranian people, who are in a position to appraise conditions, is one of intense bitterness toward Great Britain . . . Toward Russia there is less bitterness . . . The Iranians openly charge and believe that Britain has been guilty of conduct akin to that of Nazis in Europe. If the Iranians had to decide today between Britain and Russia, they would in my opinion unquestionably choose the Russians.[22]

As Allied victory became more certain, Roosevelt "enjoyed thinking aloud on the changes he saw ahead—the end of colonial empires and the rise of independent nations across the sweep of Africa and Asia." But the

---

20 Ibid., 28–9.

21 Collier, *Democracy and the Nature of American Influence*, 34–6. Quoted on 41.

22 General Patrick Hurley, "Memorandum to the President, State Department," quoted in Abrahamian, *The Coup*, 31; On Hurley as an advocate of American-style democracy in Iran see Collier, *Democracy and the Nature of American Influence*, 10–11.

application of this "idealistic" policy to Iran, recommended by Hurley and Dreyfus, was soon dismissed in Washington. The State Department called Hurley's ideas "innocent indulgence in messianic globaloney," while Dreyfus, who had hoped to serve as the first US ambassador to Iran, was removed from his post in 1944 and "put on ice" as ambassador to Iceland. The same year, the American Office of Strategic Services (OSS), precursor to the CIA, warned: "The apparent clumsiness and lack of unified policy among the American group is leading an increasing number of thoughtful Iranians to believe that they eventually will have to look to the Soviet Union for aid."[23] But, to successfully intervene in Iran, the United States had to first deal with the negative impression it had made during the occupation years.

The most recurrent Iranian complaint against Americans involved traffic accidents, whereby pedestrians, who were not used to fast-moving motorized vehicles, were run over by reckless GIs. Iranian authorities filed complaints about hundreds of such accidents to Minister Dreyfus who, in turn, reported to General Connolly, the American commander in chief, who did nothing more than issuing cautionary memos to his men. Although the United States had no occupation treaty with Iran, its personnel enjoyed extraterritorial rights making them immune to Iranian laws. Not only ordinary people, but government officials felt that this extraterritoriality violated Iran's sovereignty, a grievance that originated during the occupation years and lingered for decades.[24] For example, in a famous 1964 speech, Ayatollah Khomeini inveighed that American drivers could run over anyone, including the shah, while enjoying immunity from Iranian laws (see chapter 3). The grievance also appeared in a popular postwar novel, Jalal Al-e-Ahmad's *The School Principal*, which includes an episode whereby an American driver runs over an elementary school teacher.[25] The school principal then laments: "Didn't you know that streets and traffic lights and civilization and pavement all belong to those who, in cars built in their own country, trample the rest of the world?"[26] When the principal files a report with the police and the Education Ministry, the American sends word asking if the injured teacher wants a job with the US Point Four Program of technical

23 Bill, *Eagle and the Lion*, 20–3, Quoted on 22, 23.

24 Ibid., 47.

25 Jalal Al-Ahmad, *Modir-e madreseh* (Tehran: 1966), 86.

26 Quoted in M. R. Ghanoonparvar, *In a Persian Mirror: Images of the West and Westerners in Iranian Fiction* (University of Texas Press, 1993), 74.

assistance to Iran. Understanding that his complaint would go nowhere, the principal concludes: "Damn this country."[27]

The perception of American and British soldiers being more reckless and abusive than Red Army troops was, in part, related to the different logistics and deployment of the three occupying armies. American and British troops were more closely associated with the outbreak of famine, deadly pandemics, and general disregard for civilian populations. A January–February 1943 British intelligence report noted: "The food situation in almost all parts of Persia, except the Soviet occupied zone, is causing the greatest anxiety. In Tehran the bread is so adulterated as to be almost uneatable and no bread at all is obtainable in the suburbs. The temper of the poor is approaching an outbreak."[28] According to another report: "Tehran is on the verge of starvation. The daily death rates have trebled. A complete breakdown of bread supplies has been averted more by luck than management, and the bread issued is almost uneatable." Throughout the country, there were reports of the "influx to the towns of hungry villagers" and "disorder" related to bread supplies.[29] All three occupying armies requisitioned food; but, whereas the Soviets confiscated grain wholesale and tightly regulated its distribution to their troops, American personnel used cash stipends to buy food on the black market, driving up prices, further aggravating starving Iranians. Moreover, American GIs stood out as consumers of contraband alcohol and prostitution, a behavior that did not endear them to the hungry and destitute local population.[30] In numerous memos to the State Department, Dreyfus complained of the GIs bad behavior, particularly drunkenness and a lack of respect toward women, noting how this was reported in the Iranian press. On June 26, 1943, for example, he wrote to the Secretary of State,

> Inform the Department fully as to the conduct of American forces in Iran. The situation is, in my opinion, wholly unsatisfactory, an opinion which is shared by the Foreign Minister and other high-ranking officials, as well as by the average Iranian citizen. The fire is still smoldering but may at any time break out into full flame.[31]

27 Ghanoonparvar, *In a Persian Mirror*, 95–8, quoted on 96, 98.

28 "Military attaché's intelligence summary for the period of January 7 to February 2, 1943," in *Iran Political Diaries (1881–1965)*, ed. R. M. Burrell, vol. 12 (Archives Edition, 1997), 15.

29 "Military attaché's intelligence summary for the period February 17–23, 1943," ibid., 22–3.

30 John Ghazvinian, *America and Iran: A History, 1720 to the Present* (Knopf, 2021), 138–9.

31 "The Minister in Iran (Dreyfus) to the Secretary of State," Office of the Historian, June 26, 1943, history.state.gov.

In a September 1943 report to the US Secretary of State, Dreyfus summed up the situation:

> The American troops here have now thoroughly established a reputation for drunkenness, rowdyism (sic) and for a complete lack of respect for the sensibilities and customs of the local population. The cases of misconduct towards women are particularly offensive . . . I am convinced that this situation is unnecessary and that it could be easily corrected if the military authorities had any inclination in that direction. The crux of the matter would appear to be the fact that the troops being thoroughly unhappy in Iran are given a free rein by General Connolly in disciplinary matters . . . The War Department might be willing to instruct General Connolly to pay more attention to this important matter.[32]

The careless behavior of the American Armed Forces stood in sharp contrast to the Red Army's discipline. Reporting on his travels in Iran, the ardently anti-communist US Supreme Court Justice William Orville Douglas observed:

> Russian occupation armies are notoriously brutal. But the Russian Army that occupied Azerbaijan was a model of rectitude. Everyone told me the same story; even the most bitter critics of the Soviets conceded it. The Soviets put on an act which left a deep imprint on the people. Russian Troops were dealt with summarily if they showed any discourtesy or offense to the civilian population. They toed the line of propriety in all respects. A Russian soldier would be shot for laying hands on a woman in Azerbaijan.[33]

Trying to better mobilize its citizens, including millions of Muslims, for the war effort, the Soviet Union had become significantly more tolerant of religious practices. At the same time, to counter Nazi appeals to the Muslim world, Soviet propaganda systematically targeted Muslim populations in neighboring countries including Iran. In June 1945, at the invitation of a Majles deputy, the Soviet government sent three Shi'i Muslim clerics to visit Iran and explain how Muslims enjoyed freedom in the USSR. The delegation's appeal to their Iranian coreligionists was broadcast over Moscow radio, which also noted at least fifty Soviet

32 Ibid.

33 William Orville Douglas, *Strange Lands and Friendly People* (Harper and Brothers, 1951), 40–1.

citizens were studying in the Shi'i seminaries of Iran and Iraq.[34] Such propaganda aimed to counter assumptions of immoral Soviet atheism compared to American religiosity, clearly not a major contrast given the behavior of American GIs in Iran.

From the start, therefore, Iranians could see that, individual exceptions notwithstanding, Americans could behave as selfishly as other foreigners. Meanwhile, at higher diplomatic levels, "self-interested" American behavior showed in the special relationship Washington was forging with the shah. Initially, President Roosevelt had snubbed the young king by denying him an official visit while in Tehran for the 1943 Allied conference. By contrast, Stalin, who had hosted the conference at the Soviet embassy, had made a point of paying the shah an official visit. But the wartime US aloofness toward the shah quickly changed with the 1946 arrival of Ambassador George Allen who would regularly meet with the shah in private, in addition to playing tennis and having weekly family dinners with him. Thus, "the United States began a long and special relationship with the Shah that consistently bypassed the formal governmental apparatus in Iran . . . As Ambassador Allen tightened his relationship with the Shah, American policy slowly moved in support of autocracy in Iran." An early cold warrior, Allen quickly joined the advisory position hitherto monopolized by the British, recommending to the shah the dismissal or even imprisonment of prime ministers.[35]

Even more important was America's deepening ties to the Iranian military. Beginning with Reza Shah, the army had been the Pahlavi monarchy's main pillar, receiving the lion's share of the state budget and dominating all branches of government. While in name a constitutional monarchy, Reza Shah's regime gradually had evolved into an open military dictatorship. Emulating his father, the young Mohammad Reza Pahlavi aspired to be the head of the executive branch and the commander in chief of the armed forces. He exercised control through the office of the chief of general staff, personally appointing its members and bypassing the war ministry.[36] As early as 1943, the American OSS was reporting on the shah's increasingly strong ties with the top-military brass. It noted the shah was successfully taking control of the armed

34 Jeff Eden, *God Save the USSR: Soviet Muslims and the Second World War* (Oxford University Press, 2021), 9–12. See "Address from the leaders of the Spiritual Administration of the Muslim Transcaucasia (DUMZAK) to the Muslims of Iran (June 13, 1945)," 172–5; on Nazi propaganda in Muslim countries, including Iran, see David Motadel, *Islam and Nazi Germany's War* (Harvard University Press, 2014).

35 Azimi, *Iran*, 64, 74–5.

36 Ibid., 18–20.

forces, violating constitutional provisions making the general staff subordinate to war ministry and hence under the control of the prime minister.[37] Predictably, therefore, the armed forces, and the shah as their commander-in-chief, would become the institutional foundation of US influence in Iran. Upon the arrival of American occupation forces in 1942, Wallace Murray, then chief of the Bureau of Near Eastern Affairs and later ambassador to Iran, predicted, "We shall soon be in a position of actually 'running' Iran through our impressive body of American advisors eagerly sought by the Iranian Government and urgently recommended by the British Government."[38] An American general was put in charge of reorganizing Iran's collapsed armed forces, and Norman Schwarzkopf, formerly head of the New Jersey Police Department, brought an advisory team to train Iran's gendarmerie, or rural police, while the urban police force was also placed under American advisors. Within a few years, the initially small US army-advisory team had turned into a major military mission, known as the US Army Mission in Iran (ARMISH), joined by the US Air Force and the Military Assistance Advisory Group (MAAG). The ARMISH-MAAG mission would remain pivotal to Iran-US relations until the shah's overthrow in 1979. With US logistical support and training, the Iranian Army quickly was rebuilt, its size increasing from 65,000 in 1941 to 102,000 in 1946 and 120,000 by 1949.[39] It was clear that strengthening the armed forces meant supporting the shah's authoritarian ambitions, the two becoming intertwined pillars of American policy in Iran. Ultimately, however, critical events such as the 1953 coup and the 1978–79 Revolution would show that US ties to Iran's armed forces were more important than those to the shah (as we will see below and in chapters 3–4).

From the outset, the American agenda prioritized the Iranian Army's use against domestic insurrectionary "threats." This imperative was summed up by John C. Wiley, US ambassador to Iran from 1948 to 1950: "Iran needs an army capable primarily of maintaining order within the country, an army capable of putting down any insurrection—no matter where or by whom inspired or abetted."[40] Thus, and despite occasional secondary considerations, US policy toward Iran was fundamentally and

---

37 Habib Ladjevardi, "The Origins of US Support for an Autocratic Iran," *International Journal of Middle East Studies* 15, no. 2 (May 1983): 225–39, 227.

38 Quoted in Thomas M. Ricks, "US Military Missions to Iran, 1943–1978: The Political Economy of Military Assistance," *Iranian Studies*, 12, no. 3/4 (summer–autumn 1979): 163–93, 165.

39 Collier, *Democracy*, 56, 61; Bill, *Eagle and the Lion*, 19–20.

40 Bill, *Eagle and the Lion*, 41.

systematically antidemocratic from the 1940s onward. According to a 1949 State Department "Policy Statement on Iran," the primary American objective was "to prevent [Iran's] domination . . . by the USSR," while secondary concerns were strengthening the central government, internal security, and economic development. Last on the list were measures to "improve democratic institutions and processes in Iran."[41]

Moreover, American assistance in Iran's economic development was always subordinate to concerns about oil and political control. Upon the arrival of American forces in 1942, Arthur Millspaugh returned to take charge of Iran's finances, repeating his 1920s assignment (see chapter 1), only now with the full backing of the State Department. This time, however, his mission was immediately opposed by nationalist politicians such as Mosaddeq, who argued that Iranians were fully capable of managing their country's finances. Arrogantly firing the head of Iran's national bank, Millspaugh was soon rebuked by the Majles and found only pro-British Iranians on his side. Moreover, Millspaugh's second mission was burdened by the presence of his son, who apparently had come along to avoid serving in the front, but whose "drunken rowdy behavior scandalized many Iranians." Eventually, the US government withdrew its support of Millspaugh, who left in February 1945, after the Majles stripped him of his powers. In 1946, Millspaugh published *Americans in Persia*, a work that went beyond his first book (see chapter 1) to blame his mission's failure on alleged Iranian character flaws, which made them incapable of self-government.[42]

Throughout the 1940s, Washington would turn down Tehran's loan requests, providing a major package of financial assistance only to the government it would bring to power after the 1953 CIA coup. Nonmilitary US aid came through Truman's Point Four program, providing assistance for projects such as water purification, spraying against malaria, improving livestock, and vocational education mainly in rural areas. Iran became the first country to receive Point Four aid when prime minister Ali Razmara signed a pilot agreement with the US Technical Cooperation Administration in October 1950. Taking office the following year, Mosaddeq negotiated for an increase in Point Four assistance, and by January 1952, the program had a budget of $23.5 million and 138 "technicians" working in rural health, agriculture, and educational projects. The Point Four's mission was to counter Soviet influence by providing

41 Quoted in Collier, *Democracy*, 62.

42 Bill, *Eagle and the Lion*, 48; James F. Goode, *The United States and Iran: In the Shadow of Musaddiq* (St. Martin's Press, 1997), 4.

development aid, while it also provided cover for US intelligence activities. Ardeshir Zahedi, who played an important role in the 1953 CIA coup (see later in this chapter), was the principal assistant and interpreter for the Point Four director in Iran.[43] Clarence Hendershot, the head of Point Four in the early 1960s, admitted the program served primary US Cold War objectives, namely "to keep Iranian oil out of the hands of the Russians," while helping the shah's regime contain "grave Communist threats from within and without."[44]

American involvement with Iran's economic development began with a preliminary 1946 study by the Morrison-Knudsen Company, followed by a larger contract with Overseas Consultants, to draw up a seven-year economic-development plan for the country. The lead person in both cases was Max Weston Thornburg, an influential oil executive and a consultant to the State Department. Overseas Consultants was a lobby of American oil interests with the future head of the CIA Allen Dulles as its representative. Diverging from the British position in Iran, the Overseas Consultant plan proposed "the formation of a government petroleum company to develop the oil resources outside the Anglo-Iranian Oil Company concession." Later, during Iran's confrontation with the Anglo-Iranian Oil Company, Thornburg would advise Mosaddeq's government to hold out for a better deal from the US. Overseas Consultants also hired Kermit (Kim) Roosevelt Jr., whose Iranian connection proved invaluable when he became the chief of the CIA's Near East and Africa Division in 1949 and later the operational director of the 1953 CIA coup.[45] The grandson of former US President Teddy Roosevelt, Kermit was the textbook American spy coming from the old East Coast elite and enjoying personal ties to the highest echelons of the political establishment. The quintessential British double agent, Kim Philby, described Roosevelt as a "soft-spoken Easterner with impeccable social connections, well-educated rather than intellectual, pleasant, and unassuming . . . In fact, the last person you would expect to be up to the neck in dirty tricks." Philby claimed to have nicknamed Kim Roosevelt "the Quiet American,"

43 Richard Garlitz, *A Mission for Development: Utah Universities and the Point Four Program in Iran* (Utah State University Press, 2018), 36, 84; Jacob Shively, "'Good Deeds Aren't Enough': Point Four in Iran, 1949–1953," *Diplomacy and Statecraft* 29, no. 3 (2018): 413–31, 421.

44 Clarence Hendershot, *Politics, Polemics, and Pedagogues* (Vantage Press, 1975), 302, xvi.

45 Information and quotes on Overseas Consultant are in Stephen Dorril, *MI6: Inside the Covert World of Her Majesty's Secret Intelligence Service* (Free Press, 2000), 266–7.

which became a generic term for CIA operatives after Philby's friend, author Graham Greene, used it the title of his famous 1955 novel.[46]

The Cold War in Iran: The Devil and the Bear

> *The major problem in Iran today, as everywhere else in the world, results from rivalry between two major ideologies . . . One of those ideologies, supported by Soviet Russia, promises the hungry peasants and workers of Iran a Utopia under communism. The other, supported by the United States and other Western powers, offers an opportunity for gradual improvement under democracy.*[47]
>
> US Ambassador George Allen, 1948

President Roosevelt had envisioned Allied cooperation in Iran to continue into the postwar period. In a major concession to Stalin at the 1943 Tehran Conference, he had suggested that the Trans-Iranian Railway be placed under international control, providing the USSR with direct access to a Persian Gulf port.[48] All such arrangements, however, quickly fell apart as the Cold War began under the Truman administration in 1946, with Iran being one of the first countries where the US-Soviet alliance turned into a confrontation. The Allies had agreed to end their military occupation of Iran within six months after the war's end, but the Soviet Union refused to meet this deadline, leaving its troops to back up autonomy-seeking movements in the northern Iranian provinces of Azerbaijan and Kurdistan.[49] The people of these regions had long faced economic, political, and cultural discrimination, including the imposition of Persian as the national language. When Reza Shah fell from power, autonomy-seeking movements sprung up across the country, particularly in non-Persian speaking regions and among tribal populations. These movements sometimes appealed to Iran's constitution,

---

46 Hugh Wilford, *America's Great Game: The CIA's Secret Arabists and the Shaping of the Modern Middle East* (Basic Books, 2013), 114.

47 Allen quoted in George Lenczowski, *Russia and the West in Iran, 1918–1948* (Cornell University Press, 1949), vii; on Allen, see Hart, *Empire of Ideas*, 124–34, 136.

48 Mark Gasiorowski, *US Foreign Policy and the Shah: Building a Client State in Iran* (Cornell University Press, 1991), 51.

49 A "revisionist" academic trend revives traditional Cold War perspectives without much attention to contemporary Iranian sources. See, for example, Louise Fawcett, "Revisiting the Iranian Crisis of 1946: How Much More Do We Know?," *Iranian Studies* 47, no. 3, (May 2014): 379–99.

which allowed for potential decentralization through the setting up of locally elected provincial councils. However, like other democratic provisions of the 1906 Constitution, provincial council elections were never put into practice. Autonomy-seeking movements had a class component as well, particularly in Azerbaijan where peasants were seizing land and clashing with landlord militias. Given this situation, in the late summer of 1945, the Tudeh Party's powerful Azerbaijan branch split off to form a new organization called the Democratic Party of Azerbaijan. Led by veteran communist Ja'far Pishevari and protected by the Red Army, the new party called for Azerbaijan's autonomy within a democratic Iran, the use of the Azeri Turkish language alongside Persian, progressive labor laws, agrarian reform, and women's enfranchisement.[50] The Azerbaijan government claimed to spearhead Iran's democratization by challenging a corrupt and repressive central government, thus repeating a historical precedent when, during the Constitutional Revolution, Azerbaijan's armed uprising had saved the constitutional regime. Contemporary Iranian and foreign sources agreed that Azerbaijan's autonomous government enjoyed significant grassroots support because it addressed popular grievances. According to the British consul in Tabriz, for example:

> While it is of course inconceivable that the movement could have succeeded without Russian support, and while the Russians no doubt gave their support for their own ends, I cannot help observing that there is among the workers and peasants of this province what has always seemed to me genuine exasperation with the incompetence and corruption of the Iranian government, and that there exists real miseries and injustices which in any other country would be enough to produce a spontaneous revolt. I do not believe that the Russians have fabricated the whole movement: it seems to me rather that they are exploiting a genuine revolutionary situation.[51]

While denying it wanted to secede from Iran, the Azerbaijan government was effectively independent, even appealing to the 1941 Anglo-American Atlantic Charter that promised self-government to countries occupied during the war. The Democratic Party's December 1945 Congress declared itself a "constituent assembly," establishing a "national government,"

50 Douglas, *Strange Lands and Friendly People*, 44.

51 Ervand Abrahamian, *Iran Between Two Revolutions* (Princeton University Press,1982), 218.

presumably still within Iran's constitutional frame.[52] The Azerbaijan government also formed a militia while the Red Army prevented the advance of Iranian military columns into the province. Trying to avoid open confrontation with the Soviet Union, the British and American governments advised Tehran to take its case to the United Nations Security Council.[53] London and Washington also proposed a "tripartite commission" to defuse the crisis with Moscow's cooperation, a proposal that was rejected by Iran's nationalist politicians, including Mosaddeq. A common concern of all three powers was the question of access to northern Iranian oil, something that British Foreign Secretary Ernest Bevin admitted, saying it was "no use disguising the fact that amidst all these troubles, there were the very vital interests of the United States, ourselves and the Soviet Russia in regard to oil."[54]

Alongside the Azerbaijan government, a smaller Soviet-backed regime had declared a republic in Iranian Kurdistan, with its capital at the town of Mahabad and backed by the battle-seasoned Kurdish Barzani militia crossing over from Iraq. As in Azerbaijan, autonomy-seeking Kurdish leaders justified their demand by appealing to Iran's Constitution while also tying their cause to the struggle for democracy across the country.[55] Matters were further complicated by overlapping territorial claims between the two autonomous regimes, with the Soviets expecting the Kurdish Republic to defer to the much larger and more populous Azerbaijan government.[56] But the Kurdish government refused to do this, underscoring the fact that it was no puppet of the Soviet Union, in defiance of which the republic was declared in the first place. Moreover, while negotiating with Tehran, the Kurdish leader, Qazi Muhammad, sought British and American recognition of

52 JAMI, *Gozashteh cheragh-e rah-e ayandeh ast*, vol. 2 (Tehran: n.d.) 281–2.

53 James A. Thorpe, "Truman's Ultimatum to Stalin on the 1946 Azerbaijan Crisis: The Making of a Myth," *The Journal of Politics* 40, no. 1 (1978): 188–95.

54 Azimi, *Iran*, 140–2, quoted on 140, 142. The British Foreign Office insisted on a tripartite commission, which initially seemed agreeable to Stalin as well.

55 Abbas Vali, *The Forgotten Years of Kurdish Nationalism in Iran* (Palgrave Macmillan, 2019), 91. Kurdistan Democratic Party's program in William Eagleton Jr., *The Kurdish Republic of 1946* (Oxford University Press, 1963), 57; on grassroots Kurdish peasant movements, see Amir Hasanpour, *Shuresh-e dehqanan-e Mokrian* [The Peasant Uprising of Mokrian] (Iran Namag Books, 2022).

56 Vali, *The Forgotten Years of Kurdish Nationalism in Iran*, 159, 161. The population of the Mahabad Republic was around half a million, with the city of Mahabad counting some sixteen thousand people. In comparison, Azerbaijan had about four million inhabitants. According to Iran's provincial divisions, most of Mahabad Republic's small territory lay in Eastern and Western Azerbaijan. This was a source of tension between the two autonomous regimes, as the Kurdish entity was inside Azeri territory.

his government.[57] As with the Azerbaijan regime, the Kurdish Republic had genuine popular support, something attested to by an American consular team invited to visit its capital. Among the four-member team was Archie Roosevelt Jr., a US military attaché in Iran and later CIA agent, who in 1947 published an article giving a sympathetic firsthand account of the republic's rise and fall, concluding:

> This latest attempt to found a Kurdish state ended with the Iranian occupation of Mahabad. Like previous attempts, it failed because of disunity among the Kurds themselves . . . The principal immediate reason for the collapse of the republic was the failure of Soviet support to materialize. A young and strong nationalist party which might have united a majority of educated Kurds was infiltrated by foreigners who used it for their own purpose and then let it be destroyed . . . The whole episode was a serious blow to the development of Kurdish nationalism . . . Yet this does not mean that Kurdish nationalism is finished.[58]

Before leaving Iran, Archie Roosevelt had asked Ambassador Allen to intercede with the shah to not execute Kurdish leader Qazi Muhammad and his brother. Promising Allen not to shoot the Kurdish leaders, the shah ordered them to be hanged.[59] Roosevelt had rightly blamed the Soviet Union for its initial encouragement and eventual abandonment of autonomous governments in Azerbaijan and Kurdistan. But his claim, soon a staple of Cold War propaganda, that the Soviets intended these governments to secede from Iran was not true. Nor was it true that the Soviets evacuated Iran because of American pressure, including an ultimatum from Truman.[60] In the end, it was a wily Iranian premier, Ahmad Qavam, who made a deal with Stalin, arranging for the Red

57 Vali, *The Forgotten Years of Kurdish Nationalism in Iran*, 53–7.

58 Archie Roosevelt Jr. "The Kurdish Republic of Mahabad." *Middle East Journal* 1, no. 3 (1947): 247–69, quoted 268–9.

59 Wilford, *America's Great Game*, 53. See chapter 4 on Archie Roosevelt's intelligence career, including his brief stint in Iran; for a new Marxist interpretation of the Kurdish Republic, see Kamran Matin and Jahangir Mahmoudi, "The Kurdish Janus: The Intersectional Construction of Nations," *Nations and Nationalism* 29, no. 2 (2023): 718–33.

60 Thorpe, "Truman's Ultimatum to Stalin on the 1946 Azerbaijan Crisis: The Making of a Myth." Loy Henderson too denied there was a Truman ultimatum. See "Oral History Interview with Loy W. Henderson" in Harry S. Truman National Archives, trumanlibrary.gov; for the argument that Soviet behavior in 1945–46 was "defensive," see Richard Cottam, *Iran and The Unites States: A Cold War Case Study* (University of Pittsburgh Press, 1988), 80–1.

Army's evacuation and abandonment of its client regimes in northern Iran. In return, Qavam promised Stalin an oil concession in northern Iran, contingent on its approval by the Majles. Consequently, in fall 1946, the Iranian military invaded Azerbaijan and Kurdistan, violently crushing their autonomous governments, which had surrendered without fighting. Official casualties included about 2,500 executions, while various sources estimated close to twenty thousand civilians killed by the army and right-wing militias in Azerbaijan alone.[61] Retaliations against the Kurdish regime were proportionately smaller, but, as we saw, its top leaders were hanged, whereas Azerbaijani government leaders and thousands of their followers fled to the Soviet Union.[62] US Supreme Court Justice William Douglas, whose travels in Iran included a stay in Azerbaijan, wrote the following description of government repression:

> When the Persian Army returned to Azerbaijan it came with a roar. Soldiers ran riot, looting and plundering, taking what they wanted. The Russian army had been on its best behavior. The Persian Army—the army of emancipation—was a savage army of occupation. It left a brutal mark on the people. The beards of peasants were burned, their wives and daughters were raped. Houses were plundered; livestock were stolen. The Army was out of control. Its mission was liberation; but it preyed on the civilians, leaving death and destruction behind.[63]

Douglas had visited Iran as part of a political fact-finding tour of Greece, the Middle East, and India. His travels in Iran were facilitated by General Ali Razmara, army chief of staff in 1949 and prime minister in 1950. Douglas came to believe the only way to stop the spread of communism in Iran and all of Asia was radical land reform, following the example of Azerbaijan. While in Iran, he drew the attention of Radio Moscow's Persian broadcast, which dubbed him the Big Devil. Noting the Persian word for *devil* is *shaytan*, one scholar has suggested the moniker Great Satan for the United States, which was later widely used by Ayatollah Khomeini (see chapter 5) and probably originated in such Soviet propaganda, thus reaching politicized Iranians in the early days of the Cold War.[64] Douglas

61 JAMI, *Gozashteh cheragh-e rah-e ayandeh ast*, 422, 429.

62 Following the news of the Iranian military's massacres in Azerbaijan, plans of resistance in the Kurdish Republic collapsed. Vali, *The Forgotten Years of Kurdish Nationalism in Iran*, 110–12.

63 Douglas, *Strange Lands and Friendly People*, 45.

64 Ibid., xi–xii; Abbas Amanat, *Apocalyptic Islam and Iranian Shi'ism* (I.B. Tauris: 209), 213–15.

also reported of another Iranian catastrophe, caused by the government's negligence and incompetence in the wake of the Azerbaijan-Kurdistan crisis. This was a famine that hit parts of Iran, particularly Azerbaijan, during the exceptionally harsh winters of 1948 and 1949, when livestock perished and landlords hoarded grain, causing food prices to soar. Contrasting the Tehran government's neglect of Azerbaijan to the policies of Pishevari's Democratic Party, he wrote:

> Pishevari's program was so popular—especially land reform, severe punishment of public officials who took bribes, and price control—that if there had been a free election in Azerbaijan during the summer of 1950, Pishevari would have been restored to power by the vote of 90 percent of the people.[65]

As Douglas had noted, the short-lived Azerbaijan autonomous government left behind an important political legacy. To compete with its popularity, Prime Minister Qavam had brought three Tudeh Party ministers to his cabinet and launched a rival "Democrat Party," advocating agrarian reform and women's franchise throughout Iran. Qavam soon abandoned his leftist posturing, but the reform agenda copied from the Tudeh Party and Azerbaijan government later became the core of the shah's White Revolution in the early 1960s (see chapter 3).[66] The shah too would occasionally borrow leftist rhetoric and speak of the need for land reform. For example, during his first visit to the United States in 1949, he declared:

> We must strive to provide peasants and other deprived classes with a good life. In Iran, a small minority lives a luxurious life, while the majority is deprived of basic necessities, as if that small group does not want the others to count. My real struggle must be against those opposing reforms . . . I am not opposed to capitalists or to wealth, but I do oppose capital's concentration in a few hands, preventing its use by others. I don't want a few individuals becoming rich capitalists at the expense of most Iranians living in misery and poverty, the former becoming fortunate by destroying others.[67]

---

65 Douglas, *Strange Lands and Friendly People*, 49–50. On the great 1948–50 famine see Mohammad Maljoo, *Kuch dar pey-e kar va nan* [Migration in Search of Work and Bread] (Tehran: Akhtaran, 2021).

66 Matin-Asgari, *Both Eastern and Western*, 149.

67 Mohamad Reza Pahlavi, *Safarnameh shahanshah beh keshvar-e Amrika* [The Shahanshah's US Travelogue] (Tehran: 1950), 89.

Though popularizing the left's social-reform agenda, the impact of the Azerbaijan and Kurdistan crisis on the Iranian left was, on balance, negative. In the fall of 1947, the Majles overwhelmingly rejected the oil concession Prime Minister Qavam had discussed with the Soviet Union. By fomenting and then abandoning rebellion in Azerbaijan and Kurdistan, Stalin had inflicted irreparable damage to the Soviet Union's standing in Iran and to Iranian leftists. The Tudeh Party suffered a split by a large faction, objecting to its servile Stalinism. Even hard-line communists would later complain about Stalin imposing the Azerbaijan fiasco on Tudeh Party leaders:

> The Soviet comrades, and perhaps Stalin himself, did not properly understand the Azerbaijan situation and particularly the national question there . . . Unfortunately, our party's leadership was not involved in the matter . . . How can the matter of Iran's revolution be handled without its internal revolutionary forces being involved?[68]

Stalin's blunder was a major Soviet setback, causing a defensive Russian posture in Iran through the second half of the 1940s and up to the Anglo-American overthrow of Mosaddeq (see later in this chapter). After consulting declassified Soviet archives, one expert has concluded:

> For the next seven years, Soviet policy would be guided by a belief that the Soviets had nothing to gain in Iran . . . Moscow's policy between 1947 and 1952 was focused primarily on protecting its (limited) economic interests and keeping a watchful eye on the British and American presence in Iran.[69]

Soviet and British setbacks allowed more aggressive American moves in Iran as the global Cold War went into high gear. In 1947, London's Labour government agreed to India's independence, while informing Washington that Britain could no longer sustain its client regimes in Greece and Turkey. Suddenly, Europe's southern flank, the Middle East and India, seemed more vulnerable to communist advances as the Chinese communists were on the verge of coming to power. Truman's chief foreign political advisor, Dean Acheson, argued leftist gains in

---

68 Ardeshir Avanesian, *Khaterat-e Ardeshir Avanesian* [Memoir of Ardeshir Avanesian] (Tehran: *Negareh*, 1995), 368, 370.

69 Artemy M. Kalinovsky, "The Soviet Union and Mosaddeq: A Research Note," *Iranian Studies* 47, no. 3 (May 2014): 401–18, quoted on 404.

Greece could "open three continents to Soviet penetration. Like apples in a barrel infected by one rotten one, the corruption of Greece would affect Iran and all to the East." Washington's response was the "Truman Doctrine," declaring political, economic, and military support of Greece and Turkey, as well as "free peoples who are resisting subjugation by armed minorities or outside pressure" anywhere in the world.[70] A key architect of the Truman Doctrine, overseeing its implementation in Greece and Turkey, was the seasoned anti-communist diplomat Loy Henderson, ambassador to Iran during Mosaddeq's premiership.[71] Iran and the Middle East were already important to American foreign policy, but now the stakes were raised much higher. In 1947, Washington and Tehran signed an agreement whereby the wartime ARMISH became an official training and advisory mission to the Iranian army, while the Iranian government agreed to consult with Washington before hiring military personnel from any other country.[72]

The US and Iran's Oil Nationalization: A Dishonest Broker

> *In 1953 the United States played a significant role in orchestrating the overthrow of Iran's popular Prime Minister, Mohammed Mossadegh. The Eisenhower Administration believed its actions were justified for strategic reasons; but the coup was clearly a setback for Iran's political development. And it is easy to see now why many Iranians continue to resent this intervention by America in their internal affairs.*
>
> US Secretary of State Madeleine Albright, 2000[73]

The twisted tale of American involvement in Iran's oil nationalization crisis is one of duplicitous diplomacy and espionage more intricate and tragic than John le Carré's spy novels or Graham Greene's political fiction. The oil nationalization movement fused together all the

---

70 Quotes in Oliver Stone and Peter Kuznick, *The Untold History of the United States* (Gallery Books, 2012), 206–7.

71 H. W. Brands, *Inside the Cold War: Loy Henderson and the Rise of the American Empire, 1918–1961* (Oxford University Press, 1991), chapter 11.

72 Thomas M. Ricks, "US Military Missions to Iran, 1943–1978: The Political Economy of Military Assistance," *Iranian Studies* 12, no. 3/4 (summer–autumn, 1979): 163–93, 173.

73 US Secretary of State Madeleine Albright's remarks before the American-Iranian Council, March 17, 2000, Washington, DC, Office of the Spokesman US Department of State, state.gov.

challenges Iran faced in the mid-twentieth century, those of sustaining national sovereignty, constitutional government, and social and economic reform, as well as balancing relations with the United Kingdom, the United States, and the USSR. Consequently, the outcome of this crisis (that is, the overthrow of Mosaddeq's nationalist government) shaped the course of Iranian history during the second half of the century. The CIA's participation in Mosaddeq's overthrow was the culmination of an American policy that prioritized oil interests and ties to the shah and the armed forces. Contrary to its rhetoric of democracy promotion, America's involvement in Iran during 1943–53 systematically undermined the country's semi-democratic constitutional government. Had Washington been interested in promoting Iranian democracy, it would have supported, not overthrown, Mosaddeq. But the failure of Iran's democratic experiment cannot be blamed on the United States alone. The 1953 coup's razor-thin margin of victory (see below) implies a different resolution of the oil nationalization crisis was possible if the Iranian side, and particularly Mosaddeq himself, had acted differently.[74]

74 The literature on the 1953 coup, including scholarly studies, memoirs, and declassified British Foreign Office and US State Department and CIA documents, is massive. The most relevant academic studies are Ervand Abrahamian, "The CIA Coup in Iran," *Science and Society* 56, no. 2 (summer 2001): 182–215; Abrahamian, *Coup: 1953*; Mark J. Gasiorowski and Malcolm Byrne, eds., *Mohammad Mosaddeq and the 1953 Coup in Iran* (Syracuse University press, 2004); Gasiorowski, *US Foreign Policy and the Shah: Building A Client State in Iran* (Cornell University Press, 1991); Siavush Randjbar-Daemi, "'Down with the Monarchy,' Iran's Republican Moment of August 1953," *Iranian Studies* 50, no. 2 (2017): 293–313; Ali Rahnema, *Behind the 1953 Coup in Iran: Thugs, Turncoats, Soldiers, and Spooks* (Cambridge University Press, 2015); Gasiorowski, "The 1953 coup d'état in Iran," *International Journal of Middle Eastern Studies* 19, no.3 (1987): 261–86; Kermit Roosevelt, *Countercoup: The Struggle for the Control of Iran* (McGraw Hill, 1979); Ali Rahnema, "Overthrowing Mosaddeq in Iran: 28 Mordad/19 August 1953," *Iranian Studies* 45, no. 5 (September 2012): 661–8; Gasiorowski, "The Causes of Iran's 1953 Coup: A Critique of Darioush Bayandor's Iran and the CIA," *Iranian Studies* 45, no. 5 (September 2012): 669–78; Darioush Bayandor, "The Fall of Mosaddeq, August 1953: Institutional Narratives, Professor Mark Gasiorowski and My Study," *Iranian Studies* 45, no. 5 (September 2012): 679–91; Fakherddin Azimi, "The Overthrow of the Government of Mosaddeq Reconsidered," *Iranian Studies* 45, no. 5 (September 201): 693–712; Darioush Bayandor, *Iran and the CIA: The Fall of Mosaddeq Revisited* (Palgrave Macmillan, 2010); Christopher M. Woodhouse, *Something Ventured* (Granada, 1982); Artemy M. Kalinovsky, "The Soviet Union and Mosaddeq: A Research Note," *Iranian Studies* 47, no. 3 (May 2014): 401–18; Dorril, *MI6*, chapter 28.

For declassified US government and CIA accounts see James C. Van Hook, ed., *Foreign Relations of the United States, 1952–1954: Iran, 1951–1954* (US Government Publishing Office, 2017); *Donald Wilbur, Regime Change in Iran: Overthrow of Premier Mosaddeq of Iran, November 1952–August 1953* (Russell Press, 2006); links to many useful archival sources and documents are found at The Mossadegh Project, mohammad mossadegh.com.

Narratives of Iran's oil nationalization movement often begin with the 1949 establishment of the National Front, an incongruous coalition of nationalist parties following Mosaddeq's charismatic leadership. Initially formed to uphold free Majles elections, the National Front quickly became the vociferous champion of nationalizing the British-owned oil industry. The Front's social base encompassed "various urban middle class strata: the intelligentsia, the politicized merchants, shopkeepers and artisans of the bazaar, and certain guilds."[75] Like Mosaddeq himself, the National Front's secular wing was parliamentarian, fiercely anti-British, fearful of communism, and optimistic about American intentions. Most accounts of this period focus on Mosaddeq's leadership and the National Front's middle-class politics, missing the point that the oil nationalization movement had originated earlier and among the working class. As discussed in chapter 1, twenty years before the emergence of the National Front, the 1929 Abadan oil workers' strike was the first grassroots movement demanding an end to Britain's control of the oil industry.[76] The same kind of working-class intervention in national politics was repeated a few years before the National Front's formation in the more massive 1946 oil workers' strike. During the war years, the Tudeh Party had organized Iran's small but strategically placed industrial workers in a centralized trade union network. Supporting the Allied war effort, communist unions maintained industrial discipline in the operation of the Anglo-Iranian Oil Company (AIOC). When the Anglo-American alliance with the Soviet Union unraveled in 1945–46, Tudeh-afflicted unions unleashed a wave of militant strikes, first in the Soviet occupied northern provinces and then across the country. "The strikes in the oil industry were used by the leftist press in their relentless campaign against the AIOC . . . Indeed, the actions of the labor movement in the southern oil industry were depicted in the leftist press as a struggle for national liberation against imperialism." The Tudeh Party exercised almost total control of Abadan's labor force, having organized a women's labor union and enjoying strong support among small bazaar merchants, traders, and artisans. Even Abadan's ice-making plant was unionized and no one in the boiling hot city could have access to ice without the written permission of Tudeh operatives. In June 1946, British Foreign Office sources were reporting the Tudeh Party's clout in the oil industry could translate into success in

75 Azimi, *Iran*, 220.

76 Kaveh Ehsani, *The Social History of Labor in the Iranian Oil Industry* (PhD diss., Leiden University, 2004), 379–80.

Majles elections, eventually leading to the cancellation of the AIOC's oil concession.[77]

The Abadan strike peaked in July 1946, when at least fifty thousand Iranian AIOC workers and technicians staged a walkout, "by far the largest industrial action seen in the Middle East." The company's underpaid workers toiled and lived in horrible conditions, while the AIOC treated its Iranian workers and technical staff like colonial subjects. As a general strike spread from Abadan throughout the Khuzestan province, the AIOC brought in army troops and a tribal militia to violently break up the worker's resistance. Forty-six people were killed and one hundred seventy injured before the strike ended with mass arrests under martial law. At the same time, the Iranian government asked the AIOC to accept the strikers' demand for minimum wage raises and paid Fridays.[78] Mass arrests of Tudeh Party members and union leaders finally broke the strike by the end of the year, but the 1946 Abadan strike became a defining moment in "the ethos of the labor movement," cementing its attachment to the Tudeh Party. The strike further focused national attention on the AIOC, as press reports increasingly linked the company's treatment of Iranian workers to the need for the oil industry's nationalization.[79] Beyond its immediate demands, the 1946 strike showed how anti-British sentiments were linked to the Tudeh Party's growing national clout. A US Senate Committee Report summed up the strike's national significance:

> July 1946 saw 50,000 Iranian employees of the Anglo-Iranian Oil Company in Abadan leave their work in the greatest strike in Iran's history. It seemed on the surface to be a dispute between a foreign company and its workers, but it was a grave power conflict involving oil, and, for a time, the very future of Iran itself. This strike climaxed a campaign to organize the AIOC employees into Tudeh-controlled labor unions . . . By the time of the Abadan strike, Tudeh has managed to secure effective control over the AIOC employees and Iranian organized labor in general.[80]

By all accounts, Iran received a meager share of the AIOC's lucrative income, an annual royalty lower than the taxes the company paid at home. Grievances against Britain's exploitation of Iranian oil had existed

77 Nimrod Zagagi, "An Oasis of Radicalism: The Labor Movement in Abadan in the 1940s," *Iranian Studies* 53, no. 5–6 (September–December 2020): 847–72, 859–60, quoted on 859.

78 Abrahamian, *Coup*, 19–22, quoted on 19.

79 Zagagi, "An Oasis of Radicalism," 867–9.

80 Abrahamian, *Coup*, 22.

for decades, but by the second half of the 1940s, the issue had become a truly national concern as the AIOC appeared to be trampling upon Iran's sovereignty. As Britain's position in Iran quickly deteriorated, the United States moved more aggressively to fill its place. By 1946, Ambassador Allen would regularly advise the shah in his appointment or dismissal of prime ministers, formerly a prerogative of British diplomats. When Premier Qavam appeared too close to the Soviet Union, Allen blatantly told the shah that he "should force Qavam out and should make him leave the country or put him in jail if he caused trouble." The shah then dismissed Qavam and, with full Anglo-American backing, began pushing to bend the constitution in an autocratic direction.[81] In 1948, he pushed through the Majles a bill authorizing the US military advisory mission to work directly with the Iranian war ministry. The bill formalized and expanded an unpublicized 1943 agreement, giving American personnel immunity from Iranian laws and allowing the United States to veto Iran's hiring of military advisors from other countries. At the same time, another 1943 agreement was renewed for the American supervision of the Iranian Gendarmerie. Hence, by the end of the 1940s, the United States had successfully pursued a two-pronged Iran policy: It had steadily strengthened ties to the shah and his armed forces while putting in place a seven-year development plan which would open the Iranian economy to US private companies.[82] As a US National Security Council policy statement put it:

> Over the long term, the most effective instrument for maintaining Iran's orientation toward the West is the monarch, which in turn has the Army as its only real source of power. US military aid serves to improve Army morale, cement Army loyalty to the Shah, and thus consolidate the present regime and provide some assurance that Iran's current orientation toward the West will be perpetuated.[83]

The US-backed drift toward royal autocracy went into high gear after a January 1949 assassination attempt on the shah during his visit to Tehran University. Firing at close range, the would-be assassin slightly wounded the shah and immediately surrendered. He was then shot and killed by the chief of police, giving rise to speculations about a conspiracy. Dubious

81 Azimi, *Iran*, 232–4. Allen quoted on 232.

82 Ibid., 166, 187–9.

83 "United States Policy toward Iran," US National Security Council, Washington, January 2, 1954; Van Hook, *Foreign Relations of the United States*, 868–74, cited on 871.

evidence pinned the assassination plot on the Tudeh Party, which was declared illegal, while the government imposed a major crackdown on press freedom.[84] Under these conditions, and with US encouragement, the shah went on political offensive, convening a constituent assembly that gave him the power to dissolve the Majles and to appoint half of the deputies to a newly created Senate chamber. The new US ambassador, John C. Wiley, approvingly noted that henceforth "the shah will rule and not merely reign."[85]

Despite expanding his constitutional powers, the shah lost the political initiative as the oil nationalization campaign, led by the National Front, gained momentum in 1950. By the end of that year, Iran was in the throes of unrest and popular agitation demanding the nationalization of the AIOC. In March 1951, Prime Minister Ali Razmara, seen as an obstacle to oil nationalization, was murdered by an Islamic terrorist tied to National Front leader Ayatollah Kashani. At the same time, another strike by tens of thousands of AIOC workers was shutting down the Abadan refinery and spreading to several cities, threatening to become nationwide. In addition to better wages and working conditions, the strikers were asking for oil nationalization. In response, the British sent three warships to the Abadan Harbor and prepared to land troops, while the Iranian government dispatched twenty thousand soldiers with tanks and armored vehicles to the region. British residents fled Abadan and three of them were killed in scuffles. A dozen Iranians were also killed and many more were injured as troops fired and tanks and armored vehicles drove into crowds. The strike ended when the AIOC agreed to raise the minimum wage and restore the workers' housing allowances it had cut.[86] Two weeks after Prime Minister Razmara's assassination, the Majles and the Senate passed the oil nationalization bill and Mosaddeq became prime minister in late April 1951. A US embassy analysis attested to Mosaddeq's phenomenal popularity at this time:

> For many months after oil nationalization the Prime Minister's popularity mounted. To the common people Musaddiq was looked upon as a demi-god . . . In a country where political corruption had been the accepted norm, there now appeared a man whose patriotism and financial honesty were unassailable.[87]

84 JAMI, *Gozashteh cheragh-e rah-e ayandeh ast*, 480–4.
85 Ladjevardi, "The Origins of US Support," Wiley quoted on 235.
86 Abrahamian, *Coup*, 67–71.
87 Quoted in ibid., 76–7.

Mosaddeq combined personal integrity with impeccable nationalistic credentials, but he paid little attention to the need for political organization or a comprehensive social-reform agenda.[88] His organized political support, the National Front, was a fragile parliamentary coalition of small secular nationalist parties, Ayatollah Kashani's right-wing Islamic nationalists, and a small socialist party that had splintered from the Tudeh. The country's only real mass political organization, the Tudeh Party, initially opposed Mosaddeq before coming around to half-heartedly supporting him in 1953 (see below). During Mosaddeq's second year in office, National Front and Tudeh forces would join together in street rallies and demonstrations. But the leadership on both sides failed to form a strategic alliance, which could have saved the day during the final showdown with the shah and his Anglo-American backers. Mosaddeq unrealistically believed he could manage not only the British and the Americans, but also the Tudeh Party, the shah, the army, and right-wing nationalists. To his close confidants, he boasted of being able to "ride" the Tudeh Party, while he occasionally talked of the "communist threat" to scare the Americans into backing his government.[89] He should have known better, since the threat of communism standing behind his government was precisely the American excuse for overthrowing him. In fact, the Tudeh Party had no plans for coming to power, while, after its debacle in Azerbaijan and Kurdistan, the Soviet Union had retreated into a cautious Iran policy. During the oil nationalization crisis, Moscow initially dismissed Mosaddeq as an American puppet, before giving him lukewarm support in 1953. Giving up on an oil concession, the Soviets now backed the nationalization of Iran's resources, including oil, to counter Anglo-American gains. Accordingly, they agreed to the nationalization of a Soviet-Iranian Caspian Sea fishery, while negotiating to pay $21 million owed to Iran for the Red Army's wartime procurements. But Moscow procrastinated on its debt payment until after Mosaddeq's overthrow, while the Soviet Union and its Eastern European allies failed to help Mosaddeq by purchasing Iranian oil during its boycott by the British government.[90]

88 Karim Sanjabi, *Omidha va naomidiha* [Hopes and Despairs] (London: JEBHE, 1990), 167–8. According to Azimi: "Later in life Musaddiq attributed Iran's backwardness to the absence of political and social organizations . . . Perhaps this was where he failed at the time, since at one level he understood usefulness of political parties but at a deeper level he did not fully appreciate the need for proper organization"; Azimi, *Iran*, 336. Azimi also notes that Mosaddeq "constructed no coherent ideological framework and no organizational structure." to overcome the structural obstacles posed by Iran's parliamentary government; ibid., 337.

89 Sanjabi, *Omidha va naomidiha*, 193–4.

90 JAMI, *Gozashteh cheragh-e rah-e ayandeh ast*, 534–7, 600–1.

The British government immediately had rejected oil nationalization in principle even though Iran had offered to negotiate terms and pay compensation. Iranian oil was a great financial asset to Britain's battered postwar economy and compromising with Iranian nationalism was another political humiliation in the British Empire's waning hours. At the same time, having nationalized its own coal and railroad industries, London's Labour government was hard pressed to reject resource nationalization in other countries. Even before Iran nationalized the AIOC, British Foreign Secretary Ernest Bevin had rhetorically asked: "What argument can I advance against anyone claiming the right to nationalize the resources of their country? . . . We are doing the same thing with our power in the shape of coal, electricity, railways, transport and steel."[91] Despite such reservations, Britain's initial response was the July 1951 launch of Operation Buccaneer, which assembled an armada near Abadan, threatening to seize oil installations by force. But an actual military operation against Iran did not happen due to American intervention. The Truman administration had two good reasons for opposing London's military adventurism. First, the breakup of Britain's monopoly of Iranian oil served American oil interests. Second, Iran's 1921 treaty with the Soviet Union allowed Moscow to militarily intervene against a third-party threat. Opposing a military confrontation, the United States offered to mediate between the two parties, a posture whose hypocrisy was clear to the British side, but not to Mosaddeq. Consequently, in mid-July 1951, Truman sent his personal envoy, Averell Harriman, a millionaire banker, former US ambassador and cabinet secretary, to help resume British-Iranian negotiations in Tehran. Harriman was greeted by a massive Tudeh demonstration, which the army crushed by firing into crowds, killing at least twenty and injuring hundreds. Taking the British side, Harriman concluded that no compromise was possible with Mosaddeq and Iranians could not run the oil industry themselves. As negotiations failed and British personnel refused to work, Mosaddeq asked them to vacate the Abadan refinery, which continued to function properly under Iranian management. Britain then declared an embargo on Iranian oil, while newly independent India's prime minister, Jawaharlal Nehru, and Mexico's president, Lazaro Cardenas, who had recently nationalized his country's oil industry, sent congratulatory messages to Iran. Gleefully commenting on Britain's painful setbacks, Secretary of

91 Bevin quoted in Jack Straw, *The English Job: Understanding Iran and Why It Distrusts Britain* (Biteback Publishing, 2019), 119.

State Dean Acheson put a twist on Churchill's famous adage, saying that never "had so few lost so much so stupidly and so fast."[92]

The Harriman mission showed that less than six months into Mosaddeq's premiership, the Americans were openly siding with the British, who had already started planning Mosaddeq's overthrow. In the fall of 1951, Britain's Conservative Party, headed by Churchill, returned to power, escalating the diplomatic and economic war against Mosaddeq while drawing up a plan to topple him through covert action. The anti-Mosaddeq hard line was pushed by Churchill's Foreign Secretary Anthony Eden, an old Iran hand who had been involved with the 1933 renewal of the Anglo-Persian oil concession. Eden had studied Persian at Oxford and once claimed he recited classical Persian poetry before going to bed at night. As with many British and American academics and diplomats, familiarity with Iranian history and culture did not make Eden sympathetic to Iranian nationalism.[93] In fact, the plan of combining covert action with diplomatic pressure against Mosaddeq was initially conceived by Britain's foremost Iran scholar, Ann Lambton, reader in Persian at London's School of Oriental and African Studies and former British press attaché in Tehran. From the outset, Lambton was emphatic that, while continuing to negotiate, Britain should not compromise with Mosaddeq, thus letting domestic and international pressure build up against him, leading to a crisis point when covert British intervention could remove him from office. She chose an academic colleague, Robert Zaehner, lecturer in Persian at Oxford, to direct covert operations in Tehran. In fall 1951, Lambton endorsed the British government's hard line with Mosaddeq: "Our own unofficial efforts to undermine him are making good progress. If we agree to discuss and compromise with him, the effort will strengthen him." A year later, she still argued that her plan was working but needed more time: "If only we keep steady, Dr. Mosaddeq will fall. There may be a period of chaos, but ultimately a government with which we can deal will come back."[94] Lambton's blueprint was developed into a two-tiered plan for Mosaddeq's overthrow, one pursued openly by the Foreign and Commonwealth Office and the other covertly by the British Secret Intelligence Service (SIS, or MI-6). Code-named Operation Boot, the plan was for the British government to negotiate but not compromise with Mosaddeq while applying maximum

92 Acheson quoted in Collier, *Democracy and the Nature of American Influence*, 92, 88; *Coup*, 79.

93 Dorril, *MI6*, 560–2; Goode, *The United States and Iran*, 55, 58–60.

94 Dorril, *MI6*, 561–4, 570–1; Lambton quoted in Abrahamian, *Coup*, 90.

economic and diplomatic pressure to undermine his popularity and legitimacy. The plan's covert part called for British intelligence to recruit the shah, while its network of Iranian agents bought the services of influential Majles deputies, clerics, journalists, and military men. In addition, Mosaddeq was to be smeared by "black operations," whereby SIS-paid agents, posing as communists or Mosaddeq supporters, engaged in street violence, fomenting political disorder and instability. At the right time, Mosaddeq would be dismissed by the shah or forced to resign, being replaced by a prime minister chosen by the UK. A budget of £1.5 million was allocated for payment to Iranian agents, and the entire operation was to be supplemented by a massive campaign of propaganda and misinformation, saturating Iranian and international press and news outlets, including the BBC. The propaganda campaign would convince the public that Mosaddeq's premiership led to chaos, inevitably followed by a communist takeover, something that British intelligence knew was unlikely. A 1951–52 British intelligence report on the Tudeh Party, for instance, noted that "a most significant feature of the Tudeh activity is the nonappearance of para-military organization and training," concluding the party had no plans for "seizing power."[95]

While Britain's Iran experts and diplomats had decided to bring down Mosaddeq only a few months into his premiership, the US government came to that decision in 1953. The Americans had their own agenda for dealing with both the British and the Iranians, following a game plan that did not change with the transition from Democratic to Republican administrations. Basically, the United States was maneuvering to replace the UK as the dominant power in Iran and both administrations welcomed the end of Britain's monopoly of Iranian oil.[96] While Mosaddeq was steadily undermined by Truman, his overthrow would be Eisenhower's decision, implemented under the watch of John and Allen Dulles, US secretary of state and CIA director. The Dulles brothers were fanatical cold warriors, as well as corporate lobbyists, working for the Wall Street

95 "The Tudeh Party of Persia, 'A Test Case for Communist Planning in the Middle East,'" 1951–52, UK National Archives, 12–15, quoted on 13.

96 Ervand Abrahamian, "US Concerns: Oil or Communism?," in *Oil Crisis in Iran: From Nationalism to the Coup d'Etat* (Cambridge University Press, 2021). Based on extensive research in primary and secondary sources, including CIA and State Department documents declassified in 2017, Ervand Abrahamian, the leading scholar of the 1953 coup, argues access to oil, rather than the fear of communism, was the main reason for American involvement in overthrowing Mosaddeq's government. He also shows the American decision to carry out the coup was independent of negotiations to settle the oil dispute, including the last offer made to Mosaddeq in 1953.

law firm Sullivan & Cromwell that represented international oil companies including the AIOC.

In October 1951, Mosaddeq traveled to the United States to present Iran's case at the UN and to secure the Truman administration's support of his government. He would succeed in his first goal and fail in the second. After extensive meetings with American officials, including President Truman, a new compromise resolution to the oil crisis was drafted and presented to the incoming Conservative British government, headed by Churchill, which promptly rejected it. The proposal had called for the marketing of Iran's nationalized oil through an international consortium, in which US companies would have a large share. Churchill was angry with the US attempt at cutting into Britain's Iranian oil monopoly, an arrangement that he eventually would accept after the 1953 coup. Mosaddeq too was disappointed, facing another setback when Truman refused to bail out his government with a loan until the oil issue was resolved. Though Mosaddeq refused to see it, the American hard line against his government was already drawn during this visit. As one of Mosaddeq's closest allies concluded in retrospect: "America's Democratic administration showed mild support of Iran, although this was rather formalistic, with no real effects whatsoever, since the main US goal was access to Iranian oil." The same source also noted:

> He [Mosaddeq] wanted to convince the Americans of the righteousness of Iran's cause, proving to them that Iran's standing firm behind its legitimate demand was in the best interest of the UK, the US, and the entire world. He was very interested in having friendly relations with the US, being particularly optimistic during the Democratic administration, when he considered President Truman, [Secretary of State] Dean Acheson and [Undersecretary] George McGhee his friends.[97]

In fact, these American officials were hiding their true intentions behind friendly facades. Acheson, for example, later would describe Mosaddeq as a "self-defeating leader" and a "reactionary, feudal-minded Persian."[98] Highly disappointed at the end of his visit, Mosaddeq wrote a long letter to Truman warning that, without American financial assistance, his government would collapse, paving the way for a communist takeover. Truman was not moved, watching Mosaddeq echo the rhetoric of his

97 Sanjabi, *Omidha va naomidiha*, 112, 192.
98 Abrahamian, *Coup*, 129.

enemies, chief among them the new US ambassador, Loy Henderson, a veteran diplomat and ardent cold warrior. Systematically sending exaggerated reports of communist threats from Tehran, Henderson publicly pretended neutrality toward Mosaddeq, while privately backing the British "to the hilt."[99] Mosaddeq's only ally of some influence in Washington was Justice Douglas, who was a strong advocate of his government in 1951–53 and would continue to lobby for the National Front into the Kennedy administration (see chapter 3).[100]

Failing to move the Truman administration, Mosaddeq's US visit proved successful from an international publicity perspective. In New York, he presented his government's case at the UN, where the British had lodged their complaint against Iran's oil nationalization. After hearing Mosaddeq, the UN Security Council effectively handed him a victory, deciding to wait out the verdict of the International Court of Justice at The Hague, where the same British complaint was pending. Meanwhile, Mosaddeq was receiving sympathetic coverage in the international press, *The Times of India*, for instance, declaring him a champion of his people and "a leader that could not be bought." On his way back, Mosaddeq stopped in Cairo to receive a hero's welcome, with Egypt's leading daily, *Al-Ahram*, calling him "the vital and alert spirit of the East and its will to smash the iron fetters of politics and economics." *Al-Ahram* declared that in their joint struggle against British imperialism, Iran and Egypt would "close down the oil fields and fill in the Suez Canal, if necessary."[101] A few weeks later, Cairo was burning in riots after British tanks had crushed fifty Egyptians. Within six months, Gamal Abdel Nasser and other Free Officers would take over to end British control, and in a few years, the Suez Canal would be nationalized, as Iran's oil had been.[102]

Contrary to his heroic image in countries like Egypt and India, Mosaddeq's image in the United States was tarnished by a largely dismissive and hostile press coverage. Ironically, Mosaddeq beat Truman, Eisenhower, and Churchill to appear as "Man of the Year" on the January 1952 cover of *Time* magazine. But *Time*'s cover article called him an "obstinate opportunist" as well as "the most world-renowned man his ancient race had produced for centuries."[103] Mocking his leadership, the

---

99 Brands, *Inside the Cold War*, 260.

100 Matthew K. Shannon, *Losing Hearts and Minds: American-Iranian Relations and International Education during the Cold War* (Cornell University Press, 2017), 47–8.

101 Goode, *United States and Iran*, 67, 64.

102 Straw, *The English Job*, 154–5.

103 Stephen Kinzer, *Overthrow: America's Century of Regime Change from Hawaii to Iraq* (Times Books, 2006), 120.

article turned Mosaddeq into a ludicrous character from the tales of *One Thousand and One Nights*:

> Once upon a time in a mountainous land between Baghdad and the Sea of Caviar, there lived a nobleman—and the nobleman turned out, as in Burton's beloved version of the tales, to be cunning and to revel, sprite-like, in his own irresponsibility . . . His weapon was the threat of his own political suicide, as a willful little boy might say, "If you don't give me what I want I'll hold my breath until I'm blue in the face. Then you'll be sorry." The nobleman had the whole world hanging on his words and deeds, his jokes, his tears, his tantrums.[104]

Like *Time* magazine, major American news outlets, including *The New York Times*, *The Washington Post*, and *The Wall Street Journal*, treated Mosaddeq only slightly better than the British press. *The Times* of London, for example, was calling him "Mossy Dick," while London's *Observer* described him as an "elderly Robespierre" and a "tragic Frankenstein."[105] Beyond typical racist and Orientalist biases, Mosaddeq's negative coverage in the supposedly independent British and American press was linked to a smear campaign covertly waged by both countries' intelligence organizations.[106]

Back home, Mosaddeq's problems would multiply in 1952. As the British embargo decimated its oil revenue, Iran plunged into an economic and political crisis, undercutting Mosaddeq's popularity and emboldening his opponents, just as London had planned. In that year's Majles election, the National Front bloc found itself outnumbered by pro-British and pro-shah deputies who rejected Mosaddeq's request for special powers to deal with the British boycott and economic crisis.[107] At the same time, the Tudeh Party was gaining ground, adding support of oil nationalization to its already popular social reform and anti-imperialist agenda. An exceptionally candid early-1952 *New York Times* report from Tehran noted:

---

104 Christopher de Bellaigue, *Patriot of Persia: Muhammad Mossadegh and a Tragic Anglo-American Coup* (Harper, 2012), 162.

105 Goode, *The United States and Iran*, 67; Abrahamian, *Coup*, 101–2; for a documentary coverage of the Mosaddeq years in US press, see "Mossadegh Media Archive," updated August 6, 2025, mohammadmossadegh.com.

106 William Dorman and Mansour Farhang, *The US Press and Iran: Foreign Policy and the Journalism of Deference* (University of California Press, 1988).

107 Abrahamian, *Iran Between Two Revolutions*, 268–9.

> The communist election manifesto, which was being distributed all over Tehran, demanded the expulsion of the United States military advisory mission from Iran, the rejection of the United States Point Four aid, the closing of the British bank in Iran, the distribution of private landholdings among the peasants, universal obligatory education, and of course uncompromising nationalization of oil . . . It was again strikingly apparent that the Communist Party was the only one with a genuine program an ideology that went beyond the nationalization of oil and nationalistic enthusiasm.[108]

Throughout winter and spring 1952, Iran unsuccessfully negotiated with the World Bank to find a way out of its financial dispute with the UK. Meanwhile, London and Washington were proven wrong to assume that Iran could not manage the oil industry and that its economy would quickly collapse under their joint embargo. As noted above, the United States paid only for its Point Four Program in Iran, providing technical assistance for projects such as water purification, spraying against malaria, and improving livestock.[109] Mosaddeq had allowed Point Four, and the much more important American military missions, to continue despite being suspicious of their intentions. Ironically, or perhaps revealingly, the Point Four headquarters in Tehran was a building owned by Mosaddeq, located across from his residence where he held cabinet meetings. At one point, he had told his ministers to expect "to be hit" from that direction, a prediction that literally came true when, on August 19, 1953, bullets began raining on his residence from the Point Four headquarters.[110] More disastrous was Mosaddeq's neglect of the US military mission's obvious political role. By 1953, the three military missions (army, gendarmerie, and air force) enlisted 123 American advisors led by General Robert McClure, an expert in psychological warfare, who was transferred to Iran from Korea. McClure would be directly involved in the coup's operational phase by keeping close contact with Iranian generals working with the CIA. Particularly significant was the American advisors' link to the army's tank division, staffed by US-trained officers.

108 Albion Ross, "Reds in Iran Press Election Campaign," *New York Times*, January 9, 1952.

109 Goode, *The United States and Iran*, 63, 74; Azimi, *Iran*, 281.

110 Karim Sanjabi, *Omidha va naomidiha*, 183–4. The Point Four headquarters was occupied and used by army units to attack Mosaddeq's house and was later looted by the CIA-hired mobs. Earlier, in April 1953, when a mob attacked his residence, Mosaddeq took refuge at the Point Four compound, whence an employee drove him away to safety. Garlitz, *A Mission for Development*, 73–6, 68.

While the Tudeh Party loudly demanded the American military mission's termination, Mosaddeq saw no problem with its continuation, once jokingly telling an American colonel he hoped America's strengthening of Iran's armed forces would not lead to his overthrow.[111]

In May 1952, British and American Iran experts, including ambassador Henderson and the CIA's Donald Wilber, met in Washington to choose a replacement for Mosaddeq, deciding on Ahmad Qavam. Contrary to its public declarations, the Truman administration was quietly working with the British for Mosaddeq's removal. In July, facing mounting political pressure, Mosaddeq resigned when the shah refused to let him choose the war minister and the army chief of staff. With Anglo-American endorsement, the shah quickly called on Qavam to form a government, and the new premier declared he'd violently crush all opposition. On July 16, countywide protests and strikes broke out as National Front deputies asked the people to come out demanding Mosaddeq's restoration. With Ayatollah Kashani's followers and Tudeh militants joining the fray, the protests turned into a landslide of popular support for Mosaddeq. After inflicting significant casualties, the troops in Tehran refused to shoot further, leaving the capital in the hands of the demonstrators. Fortuitously for Mosaddeq, the same evening, the International Court of Justice at The Hague handed him a major victory, declaring its lack of jurisdiction in the Iran-UK dispute. The next day, massive demonstrations in support of Mosaddeq continued with Tehran fully under popular control, as police and army stayed in their stations. Qavam then resigned and the shah asked Mosaddeq to return to premiership. Back in office, Mossadegh was now in charge of the war ministry and the army chief of staff, while receiving six months of extra-parliamentary powers to deal with the oil embargo and other crises. With the events of July 16–17, 1952, Mosaddeq's second term began with an unprecedented popular mandate, made in the streets. Significantly, the protests had anti-monarchist tones, delivering a serious blow to the shah's standing. In a conciliatory move, Mosaddeq made a public pledge of loyalty to constitutional monarchy, promising he would not seek the presidency even if Iran were to become a republic. Mosaddeq thus started his second term with great confidence, but still without a clear plan for ending the oil crisis and organizing political support to counter powerful domestic and international enemies. The seemingly spontaneous July 1952

111 Abrahamian, *The Coup*, 157–8, 163; for McClure's direct involvement in 1953 events, see "Factors Involved in the Overthrow of Mossadeq, Washington, April 16, 1953; in Van Hook, *Foreign Relations of the United States*, 730–1.

uprising was the result of an ad hoc alliance between the Tudeh Party and the National Front, including the followers of Ayatollah Kashani. Soon, however, Kashani and other right-wing nationalists would turn against Mosaddeq, who could then rely only on the small liberal and leftist factions of the National Front, and potentially on the Tudeh Party. Being in charge of the war ministry, he began to purge the armed forces but failed to clear its highest echelons of Anglo-American ties.[112] Meeting with Henderson in late July, Mosaddeq complained of US-UK complicity against his government and yet continued to hope for Washington's support. Keeping up the facade of neutrality, Henderson privately agreed with the CIA and British intelligence that Mosaddeq had to be removed by any means, including a military coup. Predicting the course of events that would take place a year later, the CIA Tehran station concluded that, if Mosaddeq could not be removed legally, it would be necessary for "military leaders to carry out a coup in the shah's name; even if they do not have his authority."[113]

Mosaddeq's extraordinary powers amounted to ruling by decree, which allowed him to bypass the Majles and initiate progressive legislation, such as worker's social insurance and agrarian laws favorable to peasants. But his government was overthrown before these laws could go into effect. He also introduced a national security law expanding government surveillance and power to suppress strikes and demonstrations. These new security ordinances, and the imposition of martial law during most of his second term, enabled Mosaddeq to legally root out the conspiracies openly brewing against him. Ironically, while enemies accused him of accumulating dictatorial powers, Mosaddeq hesitated to use his enhanced powers against them.[114] In August 1952, early in Mosaddeq's second term, Truman and Churchill issued a joint communiqué making it clear that Washington backed London in its oil dispute with Iran. This development was "deeply damaging" to Mosaddeq who could no longer claim he was using the Americans against the British.[115] Nevertheless, Mosaddeq continued to act on the assumption of American goodwill all the way to his downfall. Hailed as the champion of constitutionalism

112 Azimi, *Iran*, 303–4. Ervand Abrahamian, *Oil Crisis in Iran: From Nationalism to Coup d' Etat* (Cambridge University Press, 2021), 29, 32–6.

113 Abrahamian, *Oil Crisis in Iran*, 39–41, quoted on 41.

114 JAMI, *Gozashteh cheragh-e rah-e ayandeh ast*, 559–83.

115 Azimi, "Unseating Mosaddeq: The Configuration and Role of Domestic Forces," in *Mohammad Mosaddeq and the 1953 Coup*, eds. Gasiorowski and Byrne, 27–101, cited on 74.

and free elections, Mosaddeq was now bending the electoral process for what he considered a higher purpose. His interpretation of the constitution vastly empowered the prime minister, assigning the shah a mere ceremonial role and claiming that the monarch "must reign, and not rule." According to the constitution, however, the shah was "the head of the executive power" and able to initiate legislation, while recent constitutional amendments allowed the shah to choose and dismiss prime ministers and dissolve both the Majles and the Senate. Underestimating the institution of monarchy, Mosaddeq ignored the fact that the shah was the pivot of the powerful coalition formed by his domestic enemies, the United States, and the UK. Meanwhile, suspecting the shah of involvement in an attempt on his life, Mosaddeq's personal relationship with the monarch deteriorated, his attitude toward the shah becoming more dismissive and humiliating. As a scholar sympathetic to Mosaddeq has argued, "had he been less stubborn (or even paranoid) toward the Shah, he might have been able to prevent the hesitant Shah from entering into the covenant that brought the about the coup against him."[116] In February 1953, Henderson was informed that the shah had "lost his nerve" and was about to leave the country, while a CIA brief concluded the shah had politically "capitulated," having lost "control to the prime minister."[117] In a dress rehearsal of August 1953 events, a small monarchist mob formed in front of the royal palace asking the shah not to leave, before converging on Mosaddeq's house and trying to break in. Fearing for his life, Mosaddeq climbed over the wall to the adjacent building, which he had rented to the Point Four, and was driven away to safety by an American employee.[118] Behind the scenes, Henderson was feverishly active to prevent the shah from leaving, telling Mosaddeq that the United States opposed his departure. A few months later, the shah privately acknowledged Henderson's crucial role, saying, "If it had not been for the actions of the Ambassador at that time the institution of monarchy would have been overthrown."[119] Mosaddeq, however, remained ambivalent toward the shah and without a plan of action in case the shah abdicated or left the country.[120] As discussed below, he would remain nominally loyal to the throne even after the shah fled abroad in August 1953 when a

116 Rahnema, *Behind the 1953 Coup in Iran*, 261.

117 Abrahamian, *Oil Crisis in Iran*, 42–3.

118 Garlitz, *Mission for Development*, 68.

119 The shah, NSC memorandum, May 14, 1953, quoted in Abrahamian, *Oil Crisis in Iran*, 46.

120 Azimi, *Iran*, 344.

resolute break with the monarchy might have thwarted the coup unfolding against him.[121]

By the end of 1952, diplomatic relations with the UK were broken as oil negotiations were deadlocked. The apparent obstacle was the amount of compensation claimed by the AIOC, which the British deliberately had set too high to be acceptable to Mosaddeq. Some of his supporters have argued that accepting a less than perfect compromise could have saved the government. Whether this were possible or not, Mosaddeq clearly had no alternative plan to reverse his setbacks with no resolution to the oil dispute.[122] The National Front's right-wing faction had defected after Mosaddeq refused to give them more government posts. Ayatollah Kashani now joined the anti-Mosaddeq conspirators, whose military wing was operating from Tehran's retired army officers club, linked to the British and led by the shah's brother and General Fazlollah Zahedi. When Tudeh Party newspapers reported the details of a military-coup plan, the government admitted the existence of a "conspiracy on behalf of a foreign embassy" and issued arrest warrants for General Zahedi and his coconspirators, who nevertheless remained free and continued their activities.[123] This was a fatal mistake because Zahedi's political and military leadership was central to the Anglo-American coup plan. Originally recruited by British intelligence, Zahedi's network was placed at the CIA's disposal after Iran severed relations with the UK. In November 1952, the SIS chief of Iran station, Christopher Montague Woodhouse, traveled to Washington to discuss the coup plan with State Department and CIA officials. Woodhouse told the Americans the gist of the SIS plan was for British agents "to seize control of Tehran with the support of the Shah but if necessary, without it, and to arrest Mosaddeq and his ministers." As noted above, the CIA was already on board with this plan, although official US government decision to implement it was reached in early 1953. In February 1953, Zahedi told American officials that, backed by Ayatollah Kashani and army commanders, he was ready to "take over power" as prime minister, with or without the shah's approval. He also emphasized the need for careful preparation to prevent another popular uprising in Mosaddeq's support, as had happened in July 1952. Admitting that American support of the coup was vital, Zahedi had told Ambassador

121 See Azimi, "The Overthrow of the Government of Mosaddeq Reconsidered," 702–3. Azimi notes this point, without blaming Mosaddeq.

122 Azimi, *Iran*, 300.

123 JAMI, *Gozashteh cheragh-e rah-e ayandeh ast*, 583.

Henderson that it would be "impossible for Iranians to remove the present Government by their own efforts."[124]

By this time, the British and the Americans had also agreed that after Mosaddeq's overthrow, US companies would have a 40 percent share in the marketing of Iranian oil. Churchill, however, was still upset that the Americans were using the bogus claim of fighting communism to break up Britain's oil monopoly in Iran. His own office had found "no signs that Persia was nearer to communism," while the Foreign Office had reported, "little Soviet activity in the Middle East recently."[125] Similarly, as late as July 1953, the CIA saw no threat of an imminent communist takeover in Iran, though it predicted the growth of Tudeh Party influence, including the possibility of its coming to power legally, if existing conditions did not change.[126]

Implementing the Coup

I had already made contingency plans with the help of my American friends, who in those days included Kermit Roosevelt of the CIA and the US ambassador in Tehran, Lloyd [sic] *Henderson.*

The shah, 1979[127]

British involvement with the coup plan continued indirectly through 1953 as the SIS kept close contact with the network of Iranian agents it had left behind, merging its activities with a parallel CIA network. Joining the two espionage grids proved easy, though it meant British assets had to be under CIA control. Code-named (BE)DAMN, American covert operations in Iran had begun in 1947, aiming primarily to counter Soviet and Tudeh Party influence. By 1951, the CIA's Iran station

124 See Top Secret British Foreign Office Report, no. 3342 (February 23, 1953), UK National Archives; on Woodhouse visiting the United States, see Dorril, *MI6*, 578–9; Zahedi's message to Henderson in Brands, *Inside the Cold War*, 279.

125 Quoted in Dorril, *MI6*, 582–3. Top Secret British Foreign Office Report, no. 23 (March 3, 1953), UK National Archives.

126 "Tudeh may succeed in coming to power by parliamentary means. Although Tudeh is unlikely to secure a large representation in any Majlis election which might be held in 1953, continued failure to check its growth and provide some alternate vehicle for popular sentiment might enable it to secure a dominant position or even a clear majority in some later Majlis." Quoted in "Draft National Intelligence Estimate," Washington, August 12, 1953, in Van Hook, *Foreign Relations of the United States*, 656–62.

127 Mohammad Reza Pahlavi, *Answer to History* (Stein and Day, 1980), 89.

received $1 million a year, a significant portion of the total budget for its international activities. The money was spent on paying Iranian politicians, journalists, and clerics, as well as on publishing anti-communist articles in the Iranian and international press. The CIA also hired street gangs to break up Tudeh demonstrations, or to pose as communists and attack religious and political figures, the same kind of "black operations" organized by the SIS. Crucial to CIA operations was an international campaign of misinformation, using major news outlets in Iran; the US *New York Times* coverage of Iran, for instance, was systematically distorted by the CIA through special reports from Tehran by its undercover agent, Kenneth Love. At the US embassy in Tehran, CIA propaganda was directed by future scholar of Iranian nationalism, Richard Cottam, who wrote articles, filled with false accusations against Mosaddeq and the Tudeh Party, for publication in the Iranian press.[128] The CIA's saturation-propaganda campaign, advocating US intervention to save Iran from communism, trickled down from the most influential American and international media to popular-culture outlets. By 1952, for example, cartoonish versions of the CIA's master narrative were appearing in a comic book series whose hero, T-Man, was dispatched to Tehran, where he single-handedly broke up a communist plot against the government.[129]

Contrary to Anglo-American propaganda, the Soviets had no master plan for direct intervention in Iran, via the Tudeh Party or otherwise. This was known to the SIS-CIA coup makers and was a key factor in their planning. An April 1953 CIA planning memorandum, titled "Factors Involved in the Overthrow of Mossadeq," noted that Soviet reaction to an American-induced "forced change" in Iran would not be a major concern.[130] Commenting on Soviet passivity in 1953, Iran scholar James Bill has concluded: "If the Soviets had chosen to get involved, the outcome might have differed greatly."[131] Former Tehran CIA staffer Richard Cottam is even more emphatic:

128 Collier, *Democracy and the Nature of American Influence in Iran*, 93–5, 140; Dorril, *MI6*, 588.

129 Paul S. Hirsch, *Pulp Empire: The Secret History of Comic Book Imperialism* (University of Chicago Press, 2021), 218–19.

130 "Memorandum From the Chief of the Iran Branch, Near East and Africa Division (Waller) to the Chief of the Near East and Africa Division, Directorate of Plans, Central Intelligence Agency (Roosevelt)," Office of the Historian, April 16, 1953, in Van Hook, *Foreign Relations of the United States*, 523–37, quoted on 526–7.

131 Bill, *Eagle and the Lion*, 91.

> We [the United States] were politically dominant in that area. We were politically dominant because they [the Soviets] did not resist. Take, for instance, the overthrow of Mosaddeq: We overthrew that regime and put in its place one that was essentially a puppet of US policy.[132]

Probably tipped off by Tudeh Party sources, Moscow was aware of the American coup plan and even issued warnings about it. About a month before the coup, the official Soviet daily, *Pravda*, published an article under the headline: "The State Department Is Preparing a Military Coup in Iran." But the dramatic Iranian events were unfolding just a few months after Stalin's death, when the Soviet Union was preoccupied with an intense power struggle for his succession. At the same time, the Soviets were trying to end the war in Korea, where an armistice was signed a month before Mosaddeq's overthrow. In such challenging times, a clash with the United States and Britain over Iran was hardly on the agenda of a shaky and divided Soviet leadership. Later, in 1957, the Soviets officially admitted to having missed "enormous opportunities" with Mosaddeq, blaming it on the then Foreign Minister Vyacheslav Molotov, who was already purged from leadership:

> Enormous opportunities appeared for Soviet diplomacy to influence Iran and the Mosaddegh government. But because of the rigid and un-Leninist policy pursued by Comrade Molotov, who was then minister of foreign affairs, in relation to Iran, these opportunities were not exploited.[133]

On the Iranian side, keeping the Soviets uninvolved was essential to Mosaddeq's foreign policy of "negative equilibrium," which sought to end British hegemony in Iran while denying a similar position to any other power. But Mosaddeq applied this principle to the Soviet Union and not to the United States, whose uniquely privileged position, particularly ties to Iran's armed forces, he left intact. A more prudent application of "negative equilibrium" would have been better relations with the Soviet Union, while ending or at least reducing military links to the United States. Improving relations with Moscow, Mosaddeq could have drawn the Tudeh Party into an informal alliance—without making undue

132 Alirza Tajvidi, "An Interview with Richard Cottam," *Critique: Journal of Critical Studies of the Middle East* 11 (fall 1997): 5–20, cited on 6.

133 Kalinovsky, "The Soviet Union and Mosaddeq: A Research Note," quoted on 414 and 416.

concessions to communism. Premier Qavam had successfully done this during the 1945–46 crisis, something Mosaddeq could have tried in dire circumstances. But he remained cool to Moscow, even when an Anglo-American coup appeared imminent and the Soviets kept sending positive signals, offering to settle all border disputes and pay their financial debt.[134] At the same time, there were rumors of the Tudeh Party being made legal to more actively support Mosaddeq. A July 1953 CIA memorandum noted these developments with alarm:

> The Soviet Union and the Tudeh would benefit by the return of the gold. Soviet action in making about $21,000,000 available lends itself as a contrast to American failure to grant financial aid.
>
> The Tudeh can be expected to use the development as a major propaganda theme to win popular support and whip up enthusiasm for the cause of Iranian-Soviet friendship. The last two demonstrations by the Tudeh, permitted by Mossadeq although the party is illegal, indicate a marked increase in Tudeh capabilities. On 22 June, an anti-American Communist demonstration turned out about 12,000 well-disciplined participants. On 21 July, an estimated 50,000 well-organized Communist sympathizers demonstrated against Point IV and the American military missions. In both cases the Communists outnumbered the nationalist demonstrators by two or three to one.[135]

Coming a month after this observation, the August coup preempted a possible breakthrough in Mosaddeq's relations with the Soviet Union, providing his government with direct Tudeh Party backing. The CIA had predicted such a development if its coup attempt were not successful:

> Should Zahedi fail in his effort to replace Mossadeq when Agency assets had been involved in this effort, the result would be that these assets would be compromised and possibly destroyed. In addition, such a failure would fan National Front and public antipathy to such an extent that the Point Four and Military Missions might be expelled from Iran. The reaction might include a swing to closer relations with the USSR on the part of the Mossadeq Government.[136]

---

134 On the Soviet Union's warming up to Mosaddeq, traced in Radio Moscow's summer 1953 Persian broadcasts, see Mervyn Roberts, "Analysis of Radio Propaganda in the 1953 Iran Coup," *Iranian Studies* 45, no. 6 (November 2012): 759–77.

135 "Soviet Union Offers to Settle Iranian Financial Claims," Central Intelligence Agency, Washington, July 22, 1953, in Van Hook, *Foreign Relations of the United States*, 633–4.

136 "Memorandum from the Chief of the Iran Branch, Near East and Africa

Counterfactual narratives notwithstanding, what took place was the methodical implementation of a carefully laid out Anglo-American plan for Mosaddeq's overthrow. By spring 1953, the coup's operational phase was on track, directed from a CIA station at the US embassy in Tehran and an SIS station in Nicosia, Cyprus, under the supervision of SIS agent Norman Darbyshire and Donald Wilber, a CIA agent who worked in Iran undercover as an architect and archeologist. Ayatollah Kashani and some of Mosaddeq's other influential former supporters were recruited and paid, standing ready for SIS-CIA instructions. Most importantly, SIS-CIA agents had enlisted Iran's commander of the imperial guard, chief of the air force, chief of the gendarmerie, the head of army intelligence, commanders of provincial armored and motorized divisions, and Tehran's tank-division commanders. The Iranian military network recruited by SIS-CIA would act under the direction of General McClure, commander of US military advisory mission in Iran.[137] The impeccable planning of the coup's military operations would prove decisive during the fateful August days. As the director of the US Office of Security Assistance would later testify about preparing the Iranian military personnel for the coup:

> The guns they had in their hands, the trucks they rode in, the armored cars that they drove through the streets, and the radio communications that permitted their control, were all furnished through the military defense assistance program . . . had it not been for this program a government unfriendly to the United States probably would now be in power.[138]

In April, under SIS-CIA supervision, Tehran's chief of police was kidnapped and tortured to death on the day he was to provide Mosaddeq with a list of military commanders conspiring with foreigners. A bold preemptive move, this act also meant the conspirators were on the offensive and willing to terrorize Mosaddeq and his supporters.[139] Once again,

---

Division (Waller) to the Chief of the Near East and Africa Division, Directorate of Plans, Central Intelligence Agency (Roosevelt)," in Van Hook, *Foreign Relations of the United States*, 523–37, quoted on 526.

137 On the CIA's link to the Iranian military, see Rahnema, *Behind the 1953 Coup in Iran*, 87–94; see also Dorril, *MI6*, 584–5, and Mark Gasiorowski, "The 1953 Coup d'état Against Mosaddeq" in Gasiorowski and Byrne, *Mohammad Mosaddeq and the 1953 Coup*, 227–60, 241–2.

138 Director of the US Office of Military Assistance, testifying on the 1953 Iran coup before the House Committee on Foreign Affairs, quoted in Ricks, "US Military Missions to Iran, 1943–1978," 181.

139 Rahnema, *Behind the 1953 Coup in Iran*, 40–5.

the government failed to respond decisively against known conspirators, including Zahedi, who eluded arrest and continued their operations from CIA safe houses. By early summer, political tensions had reached a fever pitch, giving the coup planners the opportunity to strike. Already ruling by decree and acting under martial law, Mosaddeq now dissolved the Majles via a national referendum, a move that even some of his advisers deemed unwise and unconstitutional.[140] According to Karim Sanjabi, one of Mosaddeq's closest allies and most competent legal and constitutional advisor:

> Mosaddeq was extremely angry and agitated, saying we must shut down the Majles. When I asked how, he said the Majles opposes us and interferes with our work, therefore we must close it with a referendum. Respectfully disagreeing, I said . . . all governments are sustained by three powers: force, public opinion, and legality. You don't have military force because the army is mostly siding with the Shah. You can rely on public opinion, but this has changed during the past two years, being much abused and damaged. Our ranks are splintered, the oil issue remains unresolved, you are clashing with the Shah, the Tudeh Party is growing more powerful, and all of this causes public confusion . . . Closing the Majles is not in your best interest . . . Without the Majles you have two alternatives: Either the Shah dismisses you, or you face a coup. What would you do then? Mosaddeq said: the Shah would not order my dismissal, nor would I obey, if he does. As for a coup, I hold governmental power and can prevent it . . . Mosaddeq said the Shah cannot dismiss me because the Majles has voted for me and the nation is behind me, installing me in power through its July 1952 uprising.[141]

As Sanjabi implies, Mosaddeq had reached a political, as well as legal-constitutional, impasse. Faced with faltering public support, he still hoped to manage foreign conspiracies, domestic opposition, the Tudeh Party, the military, and the shah. By this time, the government's organized support had dwindled down to Sanjabi's small social democratic Iran Party and Khalil Maleki's anti-Soviet socialist party. The loyal but outspoken Maleki had openly criticized Mosaddeq for having no party organization and no plan for resolving the oil issue. He also opposed dissolving the Majles, arguing it would give the shah an excuse to dismiss

140 Azimi, *Iran*, 323–4.
141 Sanjabi, *Omidha va naomidiha*, 134–6.

Mosaddeq. When the coup appeared imminent, Maleki proposed the formation of a citizens' militia to defend the government against the violence of the army and hired mobs. Though the prime minster ignored all his recommendations, Maleki remined loyal to the very last, bluntly telling Mosaddeq: "Your path leads to hell, but we will follow you even to the very gates of hell."[142]

In July, after Eisenhower's authorization, the coup plan, codenamed Operation AJAX, went into its final implementation phase. Eisenhower had already informed Mosaddeq that, without a settlement with London, the United States would not buy Iranian oil, provide financial aid, or increase its military assistance. This came in response to a confidential letter from Mosaddeq asking for US financial assistance to protect his government from the threat of communism. Thus, up to a few months before his overthrow, Mosaddeq still hoped to bring the United States to his side, oblivious to the fact that raising the specter of communism would further undermine him.[143] By this time, the US embassy in Tehran had turned into a veritable "den of spies"—the moniker Iranians would give it after the shah's overthrow (see chapter 5). Ambassador Henderson was doubling down on his efforts, sending Washington reports of communist threats and claiming Mosaddeq wanted to depose the shah. Henderson had an important role in the June 25 meeting when top CIA and State Department officials decided on going ahead with the coup plan. According to Kermit Roosevelt:

> Loy was, without question, a key person in the meeting. He rushed to Washington from his post in Tehran for the express purpose of offering his recommendations. JFD [John Foster Dulles] might decide, but Loy would be most influential in that decision.[144]

Henderson told Dulles precisely what he wanted to hear:

> Mr. Secretary, I don't like this business at all. You know that. But we are confronted by a dangerous situation and a madman who would ally himself with the Russians. We have no choice but to proceed with this undertaking. May God grant US success.[145]

142 Abrahamian, *The Coup*, 16. Abrahamian quotes the second half of Maleki's famous sentence.

143 Kristen Blake, *The US-Soviet Confrontation in Iran, 1945–1962: A Case in the Annals of the Cold War* (University Press of America, 2009), 83–4.

144 Brands, *Inside the Cold War*, 281.

145 Quoted in Bill, *Eagle and the Lion*, 88.

On July 19, using an alias, Kermit Roosevelt crossed the Iraqi border into Iran to hide in a CIA safe house in Tehran. Aided by CIA paramilitary-warfare expert, George Carroll, Roosevelt was to direct Operation AJAX from the US Embassy, while Henderson had left the country to keep up the pretense of noninvolvement in the coup.[146] Before leaving Tehran, Henderson had warned the shah that his hesitation in replacing Mosaddeq with Zahedi would lead to "disastrous" consequences.[147] Roosevelt's first task was to overcome the shah's hesitation by assuring him of strong Anglo-American backing. The shah had lost confidence in British support and could not make up his mind to trust the Americans. As far back as August 1952, British chargé, George Middleton, who had recruited Zahedi, reported:

> I did my best to instill some courage into the Shah, who was full of reproaches for our deposing his father in 1941 and our alleged lack of support for the throne since then. His general theme was "nobody loves me" and he refused to be comforted.
>
> It is abundantly clear that the shah is likely to bow his head before any political storm, even though it means his abdication.[148]

The shah continued to ponder abdication, thinking the British had given up on him. A May 1953 State Department memo to the British Foreign Office noted:

> He [the shah] is reported to be harping on the theme that the British had thrown out the Qajar Dynasty, had brought in his father and had thrown his father out. Now they could keep him in power or remove him in turn as they saw fit. If they desired that he should stay and that the crown should retain the powers given to it by the Constitution, he should be informed. If on the other hand they wished him to go he should be told immediately so that he could leave quietly.[149]

Henderson too lacked confidence in the shah's resolve, predicting he would "take flight at the very idea of a coup."[150] To help overcome his fears, a CIA-SIS team recruited the shah's twin sister, Princess Ashraf,

146 Dorril, *MI6*, 586–7.

147 Top Secret British Foreign Office Report, "From Washington to Foreign Office," No. 1085 (May 21, 1953), UK, National Archives.

148 Azimi, *Iran*, 302.

149 Top Secret British Foreign Office Report, no. 474 (June 4, 1953), UK, National Archives.

150 Brands, *Inside the Cold War*, 268.

who was spending time in the French Riviera, effectively exiled there by Mosaddeq. The princess was won over with Derbyshire's bundle of cash and the '"irresistible" charm of CIA colonel Stephen Meade, a "tough-looking, muscular, 'James Bond kind of character.'" Returning to Tehran in disguise, however, her assurances of British and American support failed to convince her brother.[151] Next, General Norman Schwarzkopf, former American advisor to the gendarmerie, was flown to Tehran to assure the shah, but he too failed. The task was finally accomplished by Kermit Roosevelt after several midnight meetings with the shah, who was told Mosaddeq's overthrow would happen with or without his cooperation. Additional assurance was provided through coded messages from Washington and London. President Eisenhower sent the shah a secret message by ending a radio broadcast—about his determination to stop Soviet advances in Iran—with the phrase "that's what we are trying to do." The British message was more subtle. The BBC's nightly Persian-language broadcast invariably began with the sentence: "It is now midnight in London." Messaging the shah, the sentence turned into, "It is now *exactly* midnight in London."[152]

Once the shah agreed to cooperate, events moved quickly, though their outcome would remain uncertain until the very last day on August 19, 1953. As per the SIS-CIA plan, on the early morning of August 16, the commander of the Imperial Guard arrived at Mosaddeq's house to deliver the shah's decree removing him from premiership. But he was arrested on the spot by military units loyal to Mosaddeq, who rejected the decree's authenticity. Mosaddeq was forewarned by the Tudeh Party, whose clandestine military network had learned of the coup plan.[153] Army units loyal to Mosaddeq then began to sweep Tehran, searching for Zahedi and the coup's other leaders, who were hiding in the US Embassy or CIA safe houses. The "quasi-constitutional" phase of the coup having failed, the shah fled the country, flying first to Baghdad where he asked US ambassador Burton Berry "whether he should now oppose Musaddeq openly or not, and what he should do."[154] According to Berry, the

151 Wilford, *America's Great Game*, 99, 165; Dorril, *MI6*, 588–9. Though giving a somewhat different version of her meeting with British and American intelligence agents, Ashraf admits to having acted as their courier, taking their secret message to the shah. See Gholam Reza Afkhami, *The Life and Times of the Shah* (University of California Press, 2009), 165.

152 Dorril, *MI6*, 589.

153 Maziar Behrooz, "The 1953 Coup in Iran and Legacy of the Tudeh," in Gasiorowski and Byrne, *Mohammad Mosaddeq and the 1953 Coup*, 102–25, quoted on 105.

154 Top Secret British Foreign Office Report, dispatched to London from the

shah was in a defeatist mood, planning to go to Europe and eventually settle in the United States. He also worried about finances, telling Berry that he "would be looking for work shortly as he has a large family and very small means outside of Iran."[155] After consultation with Berry, the shah flew to Rome, waiting for further US instructions. Following the coup's backup option, on August 18 the American ambassador in Rome instructed the shah to issue a statement emphasizing three points: Mosaddeq's dismissal was within "his constitutional rights"; he had left the country "to avoid bloodshed"; and he was "the victim of a coup." These three points would become the core of the official narrative of events after the shah's restoration.[156]

In Tehran, the news of the shah's flight led to jubilant demonstrations, separately held by the Tudeh Party and the National Front. Tudeh newspapers asked for the immediate formation of a constituent assembly to replace the monarchy with a "democratic republic." Radical National Front leader and foreign minister, Hossein Fatemi, also proposed the declaration of a republic. Mosaddeq, however, vacillated, proposing a telegram to the shah asking if he had abdicated and offering assurance that he could return to his throne.[157] Two days of confusion and disarray in Mosaddeq's camp allowed Roosevelt and his team to shift gears and implement their backup plan for a military takeover by General Zahedi.[158] Even sources sympathetic to Mosaddeq admit his leadership flaw at this decisive moment:

> The indecision, uncertainty and inertia of Mosaddeq's popular base were exacerbated by the Prime Minister's silence after the first coup attempt . . . Mosaddeq fell silent when he should have spoken . . . The success of the coup was partially attributable to the political and military shortcomings of those forces that could have prevented the coup, including Mosaddeq and the Tudeh Party. Yet Mosaddeq's burden of responsibility is more significant as he was in power and therefore legally responsible.[159]

British Embassy in Baghdad, no. 149 (August 19, 1953), EP 1015/218, UK, National Archives.

155 Roberts, "Analysis of Radio Propaganda in the 1953 Iran Coup," 777.

156 Top Secret British Foreign Office Report, "From Washington to Foreign Office," no. 1790 (August 18, 1953), UK, National Archives.

157 Sanjabi, *Omidha va naomidiha*, 148; JAMI, *Gozashteh cheragh-e rah-e ayandeh ast*, 612–13.

158 Gasiorowski, "The Causes of Iran's 1953 Coup: A Critique of Darioush Bayandor's Iran and the CIA," 677.

159 Rahnema, *Behind the 1953 Coup in Iran*, 255, 261. During its fourth plenum, held in Moscow in 1957, the Tudeh Party officially criticized its insufficient support of

The failure of the coup's "quasi-constitutional" phase had caused "depression and despair" at the CIA headquarters, which sent a cable telling Roosevelt to terminate the entire operation and flee Tehran. The SIS-CIA station in Cypress deliberately delayed the cable's dispatch, which Roosevelt ignored anyway, instead telling Henderson, who had rushed back to Tehran, that their mission could be accomplished within a few days. The CIA contingency plan called for creating chaos in Tehran, which would justify a military takeover to restore the shah. Thus, from August 17 to 18, CIA's hired mobs, posing as communists, went on a rampage of violent anti-shah and anti-Islamic demonstrations. On August 18, Henderson met with Mosaddeq, telling him the United States supported the shah, and asked him to stop anti-monarchist and anti-American demonstrations. According to Henderson's notes, during their tense meeting, Mosaddeq denied the authenticity of the shah's decree removing him as prime minister, adding that, even if authentic, such an order was invalid under existing circumstances. Moreover,

> the Ambassador was inclined to believe that Mossadeq was suspicious that the United States Government or at least United States officials were either implicated in the effort to oust him or were sympathetically aware of such an effort in advance . . . In general, the jibes hinted that the United States was conniving with the British to remove him as Prime Minister.[160]

Some sources, including Henderson himself, have implied that his threats compelled Mosaddeq to ban street demonstrations, the decisive factor in the success of the military takeover the next day. Henderson's detailed notes, however, show only that he asked for the protection of Americans in Iran, which Mosaddeq promised to do. Moreover, Henderson could not have dictated terms to an angry Mosaddeq who was accusing the United States of colluding with the British to overthrow his government. In a 1973 interview, Henderson said that, during their August 18 meeting,

---

Mosaddeq and the National Front in 1951–53, as well as for confusion and inaction during the decisive August 1953 days. But, even with the best policy line, the Tudeh Party's ability to change the course of events was limited. The party's rank and file were not armed and its military branch, most of whose approximately five hundred members were petty officers in noncombat positions, was no match for the bulk of the army under the command of generals tied to the CIA. See Behrooz, "The 1953 Coup in Iran and Legacy of the Tudeh," 121–3.

160 "Memorandum for the Record," Tehran, August 19, 1953," in Van Hook, *Foreign Relations of the United States*, 689–90.

Mosaddeq told him that "there could be no doubt that the United States was responsible for the Shah's action, and it would now be held responsible for their aftermath." He also claims that, after his request for ensuring the safety of Americans, Mosaddeq ordered the police to clear the streets of protesters.[161] At any rate, Mosaddeq's order banning street demonstrations was issued before his meeting with Henderson, already published in that afternoon's newspapers. Therefore, following Mosaddeq's orders, on August 18, army troops violently cleared the streets, arresting about six hundred Tudeh Party members. The ban on demonstrations would keep not only Tudeh militants but Mosaddeq's National Front supporters off the streets the next day.[162] Making matters worse, on August 18, Mosaddeq had appointed his nephew—whose links to coup makers were known—chief of police. The next day, the new chief would order Tehran's police to fraternize with pro-shah crowds and military columns.[163]

On the morning of August 19, a CIA-hired pro-shah mob, initially numbering no more than a few hundred and soon backed by the police, came out in central Tehran. This was the signal for the CIA's military network to go into operation, deploying soldiers and tanks to occupy Tehran's radio station, the central telephone and telegraph building, various ministries, and barracks loyal to Mosaddeq. When a Tudeh Party leader telephoned Mosaddeq to request orders for resistance, the prime minster responded that everything was under control and bloodshed had to be avoided. When the Tudeh contact called again later in the afternoon, Mosaddeq said it was too late to do anything.[164] By evening, Mosaddeq's house was under attack by tanks, which forced him to flee and later surrender to Zahedi. At least sixty and up to three hundred people were reported killed that day. A British embassy report later noted that Mosaddeq's "order to break up demonstrations was instrumental in his downfall," while a sympathetic scholar admitted: "In the final showdown Mosaddeq's refusal to mobilize his supporters and appeal to the public facilitated the success of the coup."[165] Mosaddeq's main ally Sanjabi

161 In this interview, Henderson is very circumspect, denying his deep involvement in the coup plan. "Oral History Interview with Loy W. Henderson, Washington, DC June 14, 1973," Sections 193–230, at trumanlibrary.gov.

162 Siavush Randjbar-Daemi, "'Down with the Monarchy': Iran's Republican Movement of August 1953," *Iranian Studies* 50, 2, (2017): 293–313, 305. According to Behrooz, around 600 Tudeh militants were arrested. "The 1953 Coup in Iran and Legacy of the Tudeh," 121.

163 Sanjabi, *Omidha va naomidiha*, 140–1.

164 Nureddin Kianuri, *Khaterat Nureddin Kianuri* [Memoir of Nureddin Kianuri] (Tehran: *Ettela'at*, 1992), 276–7.

165 The British embassy source is quoted in Abrahamian, "The 1953 Coup in

also blames the coup's success on "the negligence and shortcomings of Mosaddeq's governmental system," concluding:

> On that day [August 19], the crowd that was paid by the agents of [ayatollahs] Kashani and Behbehani, to come out in Shah's support, was initially small and insignificant. Had we previously called on the people to counteract, or [deployed] sufficient military force and a few tanks, the disorderly (pro-Shah) crowd could be crushed at the outset. Zahedi and his cohorts made no appearance until that afternoon, when they were emboldened to come out of their holes and show themselves.[166]

On August 22, the shah flew back to Tehran and promptly met with Henderson and with Roosevelt, to whom he said, "I owe my throne to God, my people, my army, and to you!" Roosevelt then flew home, stopping in London to give a report of the coup to the Foreign Office and privately to Churchill. Lying in bed, recovering from a stroke, Churchill admiringly told Roosevelt: "Young man, if I had been but a few years younger, I would have loved nothing better than to have served under your command in this great venture." Back in Washington, Roosevelt recounted the story to Eisenhower and the Dulles brothers. He later wrote that John Foster Dulles listened joyously, "purring like a giant cat."[167] Eisenhower, who would decorate Roosevelt with a National Security Medal of Honor, wrote in his journal entry for October 8, 1953:

> Another recent development that we helped bring about was the restoration of the Shah to power in Iran and the elimination of Mossadegh. The things we did were 'covert.' If knowledge of them became public,

---

Iran," 290. The sympathetic source is Azimi, "The 1953 Coup in Iran and Legacy of the Tudeh," 704. In another study Azimi concludes:

> The Mosadeqqists' reaction to the coup was characterized by a remarkable lack of agility and decisiveness . . . The Mosaddeqists might have succeeded in averting collapse in August, but in the face of overwhelming odds, they could only hope to maintain their hold on power by adopting a revolutionary cast of mind and course of action, for which they were fundamentally ill-equipped.

Azimi, "Unseating Mosaddeq: The Configuration and Role of Domestic Forces," 88, 89; for an overall analysis of how American, British, and Iranian actors contributed the events leading up to and including the coup, see Mark Gasiorowski, "Conclusion: Why Did Mosaddeq Fall?," 261–77, in Gasiorowski and Byrne, *Mohammad Mosaddeq and the 1953 Coup*.

166 Sanjabi, *Omidha va naomidiha*, 147.

167 Dorril, *MI6*, 594; The shah quoted in Wilford, *America's Great Game*, 166; Churchill and Dulles quoted in ibid., 173.

> we would not only be embarrassed in that region, but our chances to do anything of like nature in the future would almost totally disappear. Nevertheless, our agent there, a member of the CIA, worked intelligently, courageously and tirelessly. I listened to his detailed report, and it seemed more like a dime novel than an historical fact. When we realize that in the first hours of the attempted coup, all element of surprise disappeared through betrayal, the Shah fled to Baghdad, and Mossadegh seemed to be more firmly entrenched in power than ever before, then we can understand exactly how courageous our agent was in staying right on the job and continuing to work until he reversed the entire situation.[168]

Roosevelt's special connection to Iran continued for many years. His public relations firm would represent the shah in the United States, while he visited Tehran several times a year during the 1960s, enjoying closer access to the shah than any American diplomat. The shah too paid Roosevelt personal visits when he came to the United States. In 1955, for example, while in Washington to discuss joining the Baghdad Pact, the shah and Queen Soraya took leisure time off with Roosevelt and his wife, staying at the mansion of their wealthy oil executive friend in Palm Beach, Florida. The royal couple took the Roosevelts water skiing and together went shopping for "costly trinkets" at expensive stores. On their last day of visit, "the Shah drove everyone to Miami in his blue Rolls Royce, discussing politics with Kim, while the queen fussed over her lapdog." That evening, the couples dined at Miami's posh Maxim's restaurant and listened to Louis Armstrong perform at an exclusive nightclub.[169] While Richard Nixon would be the US president most intimately linked to the shah (see chapter 3), Kim Roosevelt probably was the American with the closest personal ties to Mohammad Reza Pahlavi, and for good reason.

This chapter focused on a single decade (1943–53) that was pivotal in shaping Iran-US relations in the following quarter century, all the way to the fall of the monarchy in 1979. In most accounts of this period, American involvement with Iran starts with "good intentions" before tragically going wrong, due to Cold War paranoia or misunderstanding of Iranian nationalism. Drawing on the consensus of the most reliable

168 Eisenhower quoted in "Editorial Note" in Hook, *Foreign Relations of the United States*, 780–1.

169 Bill, *Eagle and the Lion*, 95; on the shah's 1955 US visit, see Wilford, *America's Great Game*, 277.

sources, this chapter came to a different conclusion, namely that the myth of "good intentions" does not hold up in the light of harsh reality. From the aftermath of the First World War, American policy in Iran was driven primarily by an interest in oil, and, following the Second World War, by the imperatives of US geopolitical dominance, which called for building an autocratic Iranian state relying first and foremost on military links to the United States.

The second part of the chapter was a case study of US intervention in crucial events that culminated in the overthrow of Premier Mosaddeq's nationalist government. The coup that toppled him was engineered by the SIS-CIA, but Mosaddeq's own strategic mistakes (that is, his trust in American "good intentions" and his inability to settle the oil dispute) contributed to his downfall.[170] Though decisive in shaping the course of Iran-US relations, the 1953 coup's historical significance can also be overstated. Some observers tend to draw a straight line from 1953 to 1978–79, seeing the Iranian Revolution as an inevitable "blowback" against the CIA coup. Such interpretations exaggerate the import of American intervention at a crucial historical moment, while underestimating the agency and responsibility of Iranians in shaping their own history. To the extent that the 1978–79 revolution was as an American "blowback," this was a reaction to almost four decades of US involvement with the Pahlavi dynasty, an entanglement that did not inexorably dictate the shah's downfall. As a leading scholar of Iran-US relations concluded,

> the American intervention of 1951–1953 did not determine the revolutionary events of 1978–79. Although the American image was tarnished severely by its actions against Musaddiq, the United States had numerous opportunities to rethink and revise its policy toward the Shah's Iran in the quarter century before the revolution. Instead, however, America slowly tightened its relationship with the Pahlavi regime.[171]

170 The most comprehensive Iranian study of the oil nationalization crisis concludes that Mosaddeq's rejection of the final US-UK offer for settling the oil dispute (February 1953) was a mistake. Other scholars, best represented by Ervand Abrahamian, insist that all Anglo-American offers, including the last one, were designed to be unacceptable to Mosaddeq. This is true, but Mosaddeq's government might have survived had he accepted a bad compromise. See Mohammad-Ali Movahhed, *Khab-e Ashofte-ye naft: Doktor Mosaddeq va nehzat-e melli-ye Iran* [The Disturbed Slumber of Oil: Dr. Mosaddeq and Iran's National Movement] vol. 2 (Tehran: 2000), 678–9; Ervand Abrahamian, *Oil Crisis in Iran*, 56–62.

171 Bill, *Eagle and the Lion*, 97.

The following two chapters detail how the shah's regime was undermined by a quarter century of postcoup US intervention, concluding his regime ultimately was responsible for its own collapse. The 1950s–70s "golden age" of Iran-US relations did not follow a path paved with good intentions, but its hellish termination would be a joint Iranian-American venture.[172]

172 Barry Rubin, *Paved with Good Intentions: The American Experience and Iran* (Penguin Books, 1980).

3

Building A Cold War Client State in Iran

Underdeveloped countries with rich resources now have an object lesson in the heavy cost that must be paid by one of their number which goes berserk with fanatical nationalism.

New York Times editorial, commenting on the first anniversary of Mosaddeq's overthrow[1]

This chapter covers what a leading scholar of Iran-US relation has called the building of an American client state in Iran in the period between the CIA's restoration of the Pahlavi monarchy in 1953 to the US-backed stabilization of the shah's regime in the wake of the White Revolution in the mid-1960s. During this period, US involvement in Iran deepened primarily through growing ties to the armed forces and by drawing Tehran into Cold War alliances (the Baghdad Pact and CENTO). The US also provided Iran with financial aid, which served to steer the country toward American-style modernization and economic development. Last, but not least, Washington waged a vigorous campaign of cultural diplomacy in Iran, mainly via sponsoring educational programs and promoting the commercialization of an emerging mass culture. The bulk of scholarly and archival sources for the study of this period are political and diplomatic, inevitably imposing a "state-centric" perspective and forcing us to "see like a state."[2] But we will also rely on more recent studies to view this period through the lens of cultural history.

1 *New York Times*, editorial, August 6, 1954, quoted in Noam Chomsky, "A View from Below," in *The End of the Cold War: Its Meaning and Implications*, ed. Michael J. Hogan (Cambridge University Press, 1992), 137–50, 139.

2 Cyrus Schayegh, "'Seeing Like a State': An Essay on the Historiography of Modern Iran," *International Journal of Middle Eastern Studies* 42 (2010): 37–61; Afshin Matin-Asgari, *Iranian Student Opposition to the Shah: 1960s–1970s* (Mazda Publishers, 2002).

The United States and the Shaky Postcoup Settlement

> *I fought the fascists and Nazis . . . my lesson was that we were becoming just like them.*
>
> CIA Officer, reflecting on his role in training the SAVAK[3]

Six months after the coup, British intelligence sources in Tehran were reporting that "the majority of the people still favour Dr. Mussadiq," while the regime installed through the CIA coup "lacks any popular support."[4] As we saw in chapter 2, British and American coup makers had invented a cover story according to which the shah was restored by a popular uprising against Mosaddeq's irresponsible government that had pushed Iran to the verge of a communist takeover, a narrative which soon became official in Iran. However, the basic facts of Anglo-American involvement in Mosaddeq's overthrow were known to informed Iranians and appeared in contemporary international press, for example in a series of articles published in *The Times of India* in September 1953. But the Western "free press" remained complicit in covering up the CIA coup story, as did the Anglo-American scholarly community, most of whose luminaries twisted their narratives in favor of the coup regime. The list of such scholars includes George Lenczowski of University of California, Berkeley; Peter Avery of University of Cambridge; J. C. Hurewitz of Columbia University; and Roger Savory of University of Toronto. Those like Ann Lambton, Richard Cottam, Donald Wilber, and Cuyler Young, who had directly worked with the coup makers, of course remained silent, though Cottam and Young later became critics of US policy toward the shah, and Wilber expressed misgivings, mainly because his contribution to the CIA coup was not sufficiently acknowledged.[5] The political complicity of American and British academics of course confirmed Iranian suspicions that all foreigners, including supposedly objective scholars, were agents or spies of their governments.

Meanwhile, the success of the 1953 Iran coup made it a template for future CIA operations, beginning with Guatemala in 1954 and all the way to Chile in 1973. The basic formula used in Iran called for buying

3 Stephen Dorril, *MI6: Inside the Covert World of Her Majesty's Secret Intelligence Service* (Free Press, 2000), 596.

4 David R. Collier, *Democracy and the Nature of American Influence in Iran, 1941–1979* (Syracuse University Press, 2017), 142.

5 Ervand Abrahamian, *The Coup: 1953, the CIA, and the Roots of Modern US-Iranian Relations* (The New Press, 2013), 199–203.

local politicians, journalists, clerics, and labor leaders to destabilize an unfriendly government, justifying the intervention of the armed forces, invariably tied to the United States. As we saw in chapter 2, though it became a routine CIA script, the Iran coup was originally conceived by the British intelligence, which continued to keep its role in the shadows. The CIA, on the other hand, almost flaunted its clandestine role in overthrowing governments, albeit in distorted narratives implying its own omnipotence. In 1954, for example, Allen Dulles ordered the agency's cooperation with the publication, in the popular *Saturday Evening Post*, of a series of articles titled "The Mysterious Doings of the CIA." Among numerous accomplishments, it was mentioned how the CIA had helped rescue Iran "from the closing clutches of Moscow." Still, some in the CIA, including Kermit Roosevelt, cautioned against the universal applicability of the Iran script. He criticized, for example, the CIA's methods in Guatemala, whose left-leaning president was forced to step down when the United States became overtly involved against him. According to Roosevelt, regime change under the open threat of US military force, as in Guatemala, was different from the kind of clandestine operation he had led in Iran, whereby the CIA used the army to "tip the balance" in favor of friendly domestic forces. In 1957, Roosevelt left the CIA to work first with Gulf Oil and then at his own consultancy firm, using insider information and personal contacts with American and Middle Eastern governments to make lucrative business deals. With the 1979 fall of the shah, he published *Countercoup: The Struggle for the Control of Iran*, a celebratory account of his own role in the CIA's 1953 Iran operation. Lacking new revelations or critical reflection, *Countercoup* failed to put a positive spin on the kind of American intervention whose disastrous consequences were obvious in the Iranian Revolution.[6]

In the aftermath of the 1953 coup, American involvement in shaping Iran's political, economic, and cultural development escalated dramatically. As we see in this chapter, the 1950s–70s were an unprecedented period of cultural interaction between Iranians and Americans, whose positive results hardly compensate for the US government's support of the shah's dictatorship. Washington's propping up of an undemocratic Iranian government began immediately after the 1953 coup. Having refused to provide Mosaddeq with badly needed financial assistance, the United States rushed a $35 million aid package to the coup makers, raising

6 Hugh Wilford, *America's Great Game: The CIA's Secret Arabists and the Shaping of the Modern Middle East* (Basic Books, 2013), 224, 293–4; Kermit Roosevelt, *Countercoup: The Struggle for the Control of Iran* (McGraw Hill, 1979).

it to $400 million by 1956. The CIA allocated $1 million of its unspent coup budget to the crackdown on the Tudeh Party and the National Front, while ambassador Henderson assured the shah of US support of "an undemocratic independent Iran," unencumbered by real elections or opposition. Thus, the postcoup regime launched a severe political crackdown, supervised by CIA Colonel Stephen Meade, the agent tasked with enlisting the shah's sister, Princess Ashraf, in the CIA coup plan (see chapter 2).[7] Meade worked closely with Tehran's military governor, General Teymur Bakhtiar, until 1955 when a five-man CIA team arrived to train Iran's National Intelligence and Security Organization (SAVAK). Launched in 1957, SAVAK was headed by General Bakhtiar, who had spent a year in the United States studying the CIA's and the FBI's methods of intelligence and espionage. The CIA team in Tehran trained the first generation of SAVAK operatives, some receiving additional training in the United States, Britain, France, and West Germany. When the CIA team left in the early 1960s, it was replaced by instructors from Mossad, the Israeli foreign-intelligence service, whose links to SAVAK became particularly strong. By the mid-1960s, SAVAK could train its own personnel, while its agents continued to receive specialized instructions from American, Israeli, French, and West German instructors visiting Iran. As SAVAK grew stronger, its relationship with the CIA became more complex, the two organizations closely cooperating in sensitive areas. The CIA station chief in Tehran was in regular contact with the shah, while SAVAK's director worked with the CIA and its chief representative in the United States was a CIA agent. Using clandestine electronic listening posts in northern Iran, the CIA gathered information on the Soviet Union, selectively sharing them only with the shah.[8]

The United States also played an important role in training Iran's police force. After the coup, J. J. Leonard, a Chicago police captain and counterintelligence expert arrived in Tehran to help General Bakhtiar and his staff. In 1954, a select group of the gendarmerie (rural police) were sent to the United States, on Point Four grants, to receive police and intelligence training. They studied detective techniques at the New York Police Academy and took courses in police administration, interrogation, and penology at New York University. These trainees, whose total number reached 218 over the next two decades, played an important

7 Collier, *Democracy,* 154–5; Meade is named in Wilford, *America's Great Game,* 168.

8 Mark J. Gasiorowski, *US Foreign Policy and the Shah: Building A Client State in Iran* (Cornell University Press, 1991), 117–20.

role in strengthening Iranian police according to American standards. Political policing was the job of SAVAK, whose chiefs were appointed by the shah and answerable only to him. To deflect the shah's responsibility for dirty business, such as torturing political prisoners, SAVAK functioned under the prime minister's office. Its special operatives were trained by the CIA in modern techniques of espionage, surveillance, and interrogation, including torture. Higher echelon SAVAK agents were typically "smooth, well-educated young men who dressed . . . in designer suits with wide ties and heavy gold cufflinks." Despite their polished image, these "western-educated professionals were the most ruthless members of SAVAK." When allegations of SAVAK torture became widespread in the European and American press in the mid-1970s, the shah at some point retorted: "We have learned sophisticated methods of torture from you."[9]

Back in the months immediately after the coup, Mosaddeq was tried in military court and sentenced to three years imprisonment, followed by house arrest that lasted until his death in 1967. Despite the charge of high treason, he was spared more severe punishment due to his popularity. Mosaddeq's trial, in November and December 1953, became an ultimate career performance, as he skillfully defended himself, turning political defeat into moral victory:

> He wept, laughed, shouted, went on hunger strike, and—once or twice-fainted . . . Musaddiq had lost some popular support before the coup . . . But his unfair and illegal trial, and, especially his conduct both at the trial and in the appeal tribunal won him more support and admiration than he had ever enjoyed.[10]

Mosaddeq's radical foreign minister, Hossein Fatemi, who had denounced the shah and called for a republic, was executed, despite Justice William Douglass's appeal to the shah to commute his death sentence.[11]

Other National Front leaders were treated less harshly, none sentenced to more than a few years and most released after serving shorter terms. On American recommendation, the Tudeh Party bore the brunt of the repression, with thirty-one members executed, a dozen tortured

9 Matthew K. Shannon, *Losing Hearts and Minds: American-Iranian Relations and International Education during the Cold War* (Cornell University Press, 2017), 26–7.

10 Homa Katouzian quoted in James A. Bill, *The Eagle and the Lion: The Tragedy of American-Iranian Relations* (Yale University Press, 1988), 101.

11 Shannon, *Losing Hearts and Minds*, 49.

to death, fifty-two members receiving death sentences—later commuted to life—and another ninety-two serving life. More than two thousand regular party members were rounded up in the months after the coup and hundreds received prison sentences from one to fifteen years.[12] With the discovery and destruction of its clandestine military network in 1954, the Tudeh Party was effectively decimated, most of its leaders taking refuge in the Soviet Union and Eastern Europe. The relatively easy dismantling of the party, and its clandestine military organization, showed it was not prepared for defending itself, let alone taking over the government. With roughly five hundred members, about one hundred twenty joining after the coup, the party's military organization counted for one percent of the officer corps. Almost all members were junior officers and cadets, serving in medical, engineering, and teaching corps, many in distant the provinces. Moreover, precoup purges by the military intelligence had made sure no leftist officers remained in the Tehran garrison and in any armored division. Only two communist officers commanded tanks in Tehran, one of them defending Mosaddeq's house during the coup. Ironically, a few Tudeh officers had escaped detection in highly sensitive posts, being responsible for the personal safety of the shah, coup commander General Zahedi, and Vice President Nixon during his 1953 visit. These party members could have changed the course of events by decapitating the regime at its highest level. But they did not, showing, once again, that the party was not up to taking radical measures.[13]

The postcoup regime's violent repression quickly reached ordinary citizens, most famously in a US-related case. During Mosaddeq's trial in fall 1953, Tehran University was the site of demonstrations in his support and against the coup government. In early December, student protests intensified when it was announced that US Vice President Richard Nixon was arriving in Tehran for an official visit. On December 7, one day before Nixon's arrival to receive an honorary doctorate from Tehran University, troops dispatched to the campus entered classroom and opened fire, killing three students. Henceforth, December 7 was to be Iran's "Student Day," commemorated annually with student protests and demonstrations.[14] Meanwhile, negotiations for the settlement of the oil dispute continued throughout 1954 and finally led to an official agreement later that year. The principle of nationalization remained in effect,

12 Abrahamian, *Coup*, 213.

13 Ibid., 212–15.

14 Matin-Asgari, *Iranian Student Opposition*, 28.

but the production and marketing of oil was given to an international consortium, based on fifty-fifty profit sharing with Iran. Forty percent of this consortium's shares were held by the AIOC, renamed British Petroleum, 40 percent by American companies, and the remaining 20 percent divided between Dutch and French companies. The United States had emerged as the major winner at the end of Iran's oil nationalization, getting a share equal to the UK in the oil's production and marketing. At the same time, Washington had replaced London as the predominant foreign hegemon in Tehran. Iran's oil revenue rapidly increased, starting at $10 million in 1954, reaching $91 million in 1955, and $285 million by 1960. American financial aid to Iran also multiplied, reaching $400 million by 1956.[15] The same year, a US congressional investigation found serious faults with economic aid to Iran, concluding it was not possible to say if ordinary Iranians had benefited by it. According to one estimate, between 1950 and 1967, the United States gave Iran $1.9 billion in foreign aid, the largest portion of which (45 percent) was military grants, surpassing economic aid by more than $100 million.[16] Most of the aid package was credit for purchasing US military hardware and other expenditures to strengthen the army's ties to the United States. In keeping with a foundation established in 1943 (see chapter 2), military ties would remain the basis of Iran-US relations, a pattern that lasted all the way to the shah's downfall in 1979. The relationship had proven crucial in 1953, when over three hundred US-trained officers, including General Abbas Farzanegan, liaison between the Iranian army and the CIA's Tehran station, took the shah's side. As the director of the US Army's Office of Military Assistance testified in Congress in 1954, "The results we have gotten and are getting out of training officers of the Iranian armed forces in the United States" was a key factor in strengthening the "loyal armed forces who sustained the shah and remained loyal to him." As early as 1956, Iran hosted the largest US military aid mission in the world, which, according to Eisenhower's National Security Council (NSC), served to "improve Army morale, cement Army loyalty to the shah, and thus consolidate the present regime and provide some assurance that Iran's current orientation toward the West will be perpetuated."[17]

As with the military, US involvement in Iran's economic development escalated after the coup. In the 1950s, the Iranian economy became more

15 Collier, *Democracy*, 156–7.

16 Richard Garlitz, *A Mission for Development: Utah State and the Point Four Program in Iran* (Utah University Press, 2018), 136–8.

17 Shannon, *Losing Hearts and Minds*, 24, 25.

dependent on oil revenue, which increased fivefold, from $35 million, during the anti-Mosaddeq Anglo-American boycott, to $91 million in 1955, climbing to $285 million in 1960 and nearly $500 million in 1963. During the first half of the 1950s, oil income was close to 40 percent of government revenue; by the mid-1960s, it would rise to about 70 percent, steadily increasing in percentage until the shah's overthrow. Oil revenue provided the postcoup regime with growing political clout, according to a theory proposed by economist Hossein Mahdavi, turning Iran into a rentier state, whereby the state relies on monopolistic "rent," such as oil income, to develop substantial economic, and hence political, autonomy from tax-paying citizens.[18] In the Iranian case, since the state came to synonymous with the shah, the "rentier state" theory would explain the shah's autocratic rule, seemingly hovering above social classes. At the same time, and at least until the late 1960s, the shah's regime was also an American "client state" because of its fundamental political dependence on the United States.[19]

The decisive impact of rising oil prices on Iran's economic and political development, however, would not become obvious until the 1960s. Back in the 1950s, economic development remained haphazard and sluggish, failing to provide political stability to the postcoup regime. Following the guidelines proposed by the American firm Overseas Consultants (see chapter 2), Iran's first seven-year economic development plan (1949–56) did not produce impressive results, nor did the second plan (1956–62) fare much better. Despite the steady rise of oil income, the government faced chronic budget deficits and out-of-control inflation. The US-sponsored "open door" economic policy of the 1950s brought some investment from abroad and by the end of the decade over a thousand foreign companies were active in Iran, taking advantage of new laws allowing the free movement of their investment and profit in and out of the country. Of these, 285 were British, 230 American, 160 French, 150 West German, and the rest from other European countries and Japan. The 1950s also saw an explosion of banking and credit, with many new banks mixing Iranian assets with Japanese, Dutch, and British capital. Nevertheless, neither growing oil income nor foreign credit, investment, and loans from the World Bank were enough to bring about the kind of economic development that could "trickle down" to the lower strata,

18 Abbas Amanat, *Iran: A Modern History* (Yale University Press, 2017), 564; for a critique of Rentier State Theory, see Kevan Harris, *A Social Revolution: Politics and the Welfare State in Iran* (University of California Press, 2017), 27–30.

19 Gasiorowski, *US Foreign Policy and the Shah.*

reducing social tension and political frustration. As many critics would argue, the shah's obsession with expanding military expenditures was the main drain on funds available for economic development. Military expenditure would remain the largest item in the government budget, soon climbing to 40 percent, the same proportion it had been under Reza Shah.[20]

Iran's militarization was in line with Eisenhower's New Look foreign policy, which called for reducing the US defense budget by relying on covert operations and building regional military alliance around the Soviet Union. Thus, in 1955, Iran joined the US-sponsored Baghdad Pact, and remained in its replacement, the Central Treaty Organization (CENTO), after Iraq dropped out of the pact in 1958. Meanwhile, the shah was expanding his political clout under the facade of a two-party system, whereby the ruling party was headed by a prime minister who called himself "His Majesty's self-sacrificing servant," while the "opposition" party's leader proudly referred to himself as the king's "house-born slave." Clearly, the days when a prime minister, like Mosaddeq, could tell the shah to reign, and not rule, were over.[21] American officials of course were aware of Iran's real political situation, through their own sources, as well as reports by their Iranian confidants. In 1956, for example, a Majles deputy had told the US embassy that if any parliamentarian dared to be more than the monarch's "loyal servant and bootlicker," he would be dismissed. Early that year, Ambassador Sheldon Chapin noted that "not since the time of Reza Shah has it been evident to most Iranians that government policy was being made and administered under the personal direction of the monarch." Still, in December 1956, *The New York Times* confidently reported that Iran was "the calmest country in the troubled Middle East today." In private, however, the CIA and ambassador Sheldon knew all was not well and worried that the shah's personal rule could in fact lead to further instability.[22] During the second half of the 1950s, American concerns about Iran's stability grew as the Arab nationalist regimes of Egypt and Syria titled away from Anglo-American alliances and the Baghdad Pact was dismantled after the overthrow of the

20 Mojtaba Maqsudi, ed., *Tahavvolat-e siasi-ejetema'i-ye Iran 1320–57* [Iran's socio-political Developments, 1941–1979] (Tehran: 2001), 163–5.

21 Some years later, the shah referred to this period saying, "We were blindly mimicking the delicate political game played in the West under the rubric of ruling and opposition parties." Quoted in press interview, published in *Khandaniha* 36, April 1978, 2.

22 Collier, *Democracy and the Nature of American Influence in Iran, 1941–1979*, 162–5. Quoted on 162, 163, 154.

Iraqi monarchy in 1958. By this time, the CIA was predicting that, without meaningful reforms, the shah was likely to be overthrown "within a year or so," while National Security directives recommended that the United States look for his successor regime. In February 1958, the shah was shaken when he learned that Washington had been quietly aware of a coup plan hatched against him. The coup leader, commander of army intelligence General Valiollah Qarani, had informed the US Embassy and American officials visiting Iran, including John Foster Dulles, of his plan, but Washington had not shared this information with shah. Qarani's plan was for the shah to either abdicate or accept an army-backed government headed by Ali Amini, then ambassador to Washington.[23] After the plot was foiled, the shah sought assurance of Eisenhower's support during his third visit to the United States in late June–July 1958. Meeting with over forty leading businessmen, the shah told them that Iran provided lucrative and safe investment opportunities and further impressed the US capital's upper crust by hosting "a dinner at the Mayflower Hotel, in which twenty pounds of caviar was served on gold" and princess Ashraf's "diamonds knocked everybody's eyes out." Fortuitously for the shah, his visit coincided with the overthrow of the Iraqi monarchy, strengthening his pleas to Eisenhower for more military support. A few months after his return, US secretaries of defense and treasury visited Tehran, and in March 1959, Iran and the United States signed a bilateral defense treaty. Still, and despite Eisenhower's brief visit to the Tehran in April, the shah remained insecure.[24]

American Cultural Diplomacy, Cold War Modernization and Education

With the intensification of the Cold War during the 1950s, culture and education became the "fourth dimension" of American global hegemony, already cemented in military, economic, and political arenas. This feature of US hegemony was later called "soft power," defined as "the ability to get what you want through attraction rather than coercion."[25]

---

23 Collier, *Democracy*, 169–70; Mark J. Gasiorowski, "The Qarani Affair and Iranian Politics," *International Journal of Middle East Studies* 25 (1993): 625–44.

24 Bill, *Eagle and the Lion*, 118–19.

25 Shannon, *Losing Hearts and Minds*, 2–3. Shannon cites Phillip Coombs, *The Fourth Dimension of Foreign Policy: Educational and Cultural Affairs* (New York, 1964), and Joseph S. Nye Jr., *Soft Power: The Means to Success in World Politics* (New York, 2004), 165.

The idea that political and economic domination worked through cultural legitimation was familiar in the Marxist tradition going back to Antonio Gramsci, while sociologists, like Karl Polanyi and Max Weber, had argued that modern capitalism was predicated on fundamental cultural transformations. These insights found their non-Marxist iteration in American Modernization theory, articulated in works such as *The Stages of Economic Growth: A Non-Communist Manifesto*, by Walt Whitman Rostow, advisor to President John Kennedy. Rostow, along with a host of other modernization theorists, proposed a universal historical pattern whereby all societies would transition from "traditional" agrarian formations after "taking off" into "modernity," a condition characterized by the rise of market relations and the political dominance of the "middle classes." Modernization theory became pervasive first in midcentury American social science and then spread worldwide thanks largely to US hegemony in international higher education. Some of its advocates, for example Rostow and Samuel Huntington, admitted to obstacles in the path of modernization, requiring the need for its forced implementation, thus rationalizing US support of repressive "modernizing" regimes such as those in Vietnam, Brazil, and Iran. Huntington in fact noted the case of Iran, referring to the shah as a "modernizing monarch" initiating a "royal revolution from above."[26]

America's use of higher education as "an instrument of official policy" had begun earlier. In 1936, Secretary of State Cordell Hull inaugurated a US government–funded scholarship program for the Americas, followed, within two years, by the establishment, within the State Department, of the Division of Cultural Relations, integrating international education into the frame of US national security. In 1946, Truman signed into law the Fulbright Scholarship program to globally promote American education and within three years Iran became the first Middle Eastern country signing a Fulbright agreement with the United States. America's politically motivated global educational agenda expanded with Eisenhower's International Student Exchange Program, and more so with the launch of the Agency for International Development, the Peace Corps, and the Alliance for Progress under Kennedy in the early 1960s.[27] Within this global frame, Iran-US relations grew beyond military and political ties to

26 Michael E. Latham, *Modernization as Ideology: American Social Science and "Nation Building" in the Kennedy Era* (University of North Carolina Press, 2000); Samuel P. Huntington, *Political Order in Changing Societies* (Yale University Press, 1968); Huntington quoted in Shannon, *Losing Hearts and Minds*, 67.

27 Shannon, *Losing Hearts and Minds*, 7–8.

include the acculturation of both elites and the public to American-style modernization. This was to be accomplished via US government-sponsored programs in higher education, journalism, book publishing, and various fields of technical training. In the early 1950s, education, along with rural development and public health, had been the three focus areas of the American Point Four program, officially called the US Technical Cooperation Administration, which became part of the US Agency for International Development (USAID) under Kennedy in 1961.

The Point Four budget jumped from $23 million under Mosaddeq to $85 million immediately after his overthrow in 1954. Soon, the number of "technical advisors" at the US embassy rose from ten in 1952 to more than two hundred in 1956. US technical aid was divided between educational programs, building Tehran's water and sewage systems, fighting malaria, and improving mule and chicken breeding. Point Four was also involved in the construction of the Karaj dam near Tehran, 1950s Iran's pioneering modernization project, with considerable political significance. Tehran's population of one million in 1950 would double by 1960, posing an urgent demand for clean water and electrical power. The inauguration of the Karaj Dam in 1961 doubled the output of the country's electricity, until then provided by private generators and French and American power stations set up during the second half of the 1950s. Politically, electrical power built the infrastructure for transition to the market-oriented consumer society advocated by modernization theorists. By the late 1950s, utopian samples of American-style consumerism could be seen at Tehran's first department store and a Pepsi-Cola factory, appropriately located on Eisenhower Avenue, displaying its assembly line through glass windows. Soon, mass advertising for all kinds of foreign and domestic products would inundate the pages of magazines and newspaper, then the airwaves with the advent of a privately owned television station in the early 1960s.[28]

As we saw in chapter 2, Point Four's director in Tehran during the early 1960s, Clarence Hendershot, had acknowledged the program, and particularly its educational mission, served Cold War anti-communist policies. As the head of Point Four's education division explained, teacher training was its priority because "eighty percent of the teachers were communists . . . We felt that if we could meet face to face with these

28 Cyrus Schayegh, "Iran's Karaj Dam Affair: Emerging Mass Consumerism, the Politics of Promise, and the Cold War in the Third World," *Comparative Studies in Society and History* (2012) 54, no. 3: 612–43, cited on 621–2, 625–6; see also Pamela Karimi, *Domesticity and Consumer Culture in Iran* (Routledge, 2012).

teachers that we could eventually change their attitude which proved to be correct."[29] In tandem with teacher training, Point Four quickly became involved in the provision of books, magazines, pamphlets, and visual aids to support the curriculum in the "demonstration" schools. Meanwhile, institutional educational links between Iran and the United States were built on the existing connections of Pennsylvania's Lafayette College to Tehran's American (Alborz) College. By the late 1950s, a few experts from Lafayette College had helped establish the Abadan Institute of Technology and, in 1960, the shah invited the University of Pennsylvania's president to launch the Pahlavi University of Shiraz, which would offer a fully American-style curriculum. Iran's second oldest American academic connection was to Utah State University, whose links to the Agricultural College of Karaj, near Tehran, were established under Reza Shah (see chapter 1). By the early 1950s, Utah State had graduated about one hundred fifty Iranians, including Ardeshir Zahedi, who would work as assistant to the Point Four director in Tehran while acting as liaison between the CIA and his father General Zahedi during the 1953 coup. During the 1950s, Utah State University faculty were in Iran teaching agricultural development, while those from Utah's Brigham Young University taught liberal arts, and educators from the University of Utah taught public health. The Utah faculty who brought their families to Iran were almost all Mormon and lived at "Utahville" in north Tehran's rich neighborhood, in comfortable houses with tennis courts and swimming pools. As early as 1951, Tehran's Mormon church had seventy-three members, some considering their presence as a kind of missionary activity, which was against Point Four guidelines.[30]

Meanwhile, the State Department's Leader Grants dispatched members of the political elite to spend time in the United States to become familiar with American culture. The most outstanding leader grant recipient was Manouchehr Eghbal, the shah's "house-born slave" prime minister (1957–60). A year before his premiership, Eghbal, who was then Tehran University chancellor, had returned from a Leader Grant Tour of the United States to advocate switching the country's higher education from the French to the American model.[31] As we shall

29 Clarence Hendershot, *Politics, Polemics, and Pedagogues* (Vantage Press, 1975), 302, xvi, quoted on 21.

30 Richard Garlitz, *A Mission for Development: Utah Universities and the Point Four Program in Iran* (Utah State University Press, 2018), 39, 45–7.

31 John Ghazvinian, *America and Iran: A History, 1720 to the Present* (Knopf, 2021), 213–14.

see in chapter 4, Eghbal's vision became a reality during the 1960s–70s when the expansion of higher education in Iran was guided by American experts and US-educated Iranians, following an American template in campus structuring, administration, and curriculum. Back in the 1950s, the Americanization of higher education, through the promotion of modern "social sciences" such as business and public administration, was deemed a politically useful "weapon against red infiltration." A few months after the 1953 coup, the Public Administration Division of the US Operations Mission in Tehran arranged for a contract with the University of Southern California (USC) to establish Tehran University's Institute for Public and Business Administration. At the same time, thirty students received scholarships to study public administration at USC. Completing their education, they were to return and teach at the new institute or go into government service. In a broader sense, it was hoped that the Tehran University USC graduates would "contribute to re-examination of all educational attitudes and institutions in their home country." Meanwhile, the project's political objectives were openly addressed in contemporary sources, such as a 1955 *Los Angeles Times* headline declaring: "SC Aids Iran in Resistance to Communism."[32] As we saw in chapter 2, the first USC Iranian student, Sattareh Farmanfarmaian, had graduated with a master's degree in social work and became the pioneer of modern social work in Iran.

The most important early US educational impact was the training of academic experts who, during the 1950–60s, would chart and manage the course of Iran's economic development through the Plan Organization. Borrowing a page from its rival Marxist paradigm, modernization theory advocated central economic planning in "underdeveloped" countries, but for the purpose of guiding their transition to American-style capitalism. As we saw in chapter 2, during the 1940s, Iran's first comprehensive economic development plan was drawn up by the American firms Morrison-Knudsen and Overseas Consultants. With the help of Point Four technical staff, this early blueprint evolved into a seven-year plan, whose implementation was left to Iran's Plan Organization, established in 1949. The United States became directly involved with the Plan and Budget Organization, which closely worked with the World Bank, the Ford Foundation, and a team of twenty experts from Harvard University, selected by Edward S. Mason, an economics professor and

32 Shannon, *Losing Hearts and Minds*, 27–8; *Los Angeles Times* headline in note 76, 173.

dean of the graduate school of public administration at Harvard. The Harvard group stayed four years until the Plan Organization's top management posts could be filled by Iranians who returned after studying economics and public administration in the United States on Ford Foundation grants. Ostensibly a private philanthropic organization, the Ford Foundation was closely aligned with US foreign policy and linked to the CIA, whose famous international front organization, the Congress for Cultural Freedom, it funded.[33] During its early years, the Plan Organization was a "state within the state," ordering government ministries to implement its directives. When the Second Plan (1956–62) began under banker-economist Abolhassan Ebtehaj (1956–62), Iran obtained a loan from the World Bank and signed a contract with the Development and Resources Corporation of New York to build a massive irrigation system in the oil-rich Khuzestan province. The New York company's representative in Iran was David Lilienthal, who had managed the Tennessee Valley Authority, a project that in the 1930s had brought hydroelectric and agricultural development to areas hard hit by the Great Depression. Lilienthal became a fixture among early 1960s Iran's modernizing technocratic elite and a vociferous advocate for the shah in the United States. But his showcase 1960s modernization and development project for the Khuzestan province became a "debacle" by the 1970s.[34] Meanwhile, Ebtehaj, who wanted the bulk of oil revenue for economic-development projects, was running into trouble with the shah's prioritization of military expenditures. Before resigning in 1959, Ebtehaj also had criticized military ties to the United States during a meeting attended by American officials, including a former chief of staff who was in Tehran on a fact-finding tour of US military aid to Middle Eastern countries.[35] After Ebtehaj's departure, the Plan Organization lost its relative autonomy and its American-educated staff fell in line with implementing the shah's White Revolution during the 1960s. Ebtehaj, however, remained an outspoken critic of the shah's relationship with Washington, even though his own politics were aligned with the United States. In a 1961 speech in San Francisco, for example, Ebtehaj had said:

33 Khodadad Farmanfarmaian, ed., *Towse'eh dar Iran 1320–1357* [Development in Iran, 1941–1979] (Gam-e no, 2000), 51–2, 175–8; on the Ford Foundation's CIA links see Frances Stoner Saunders, *The Cultural Cold War: The CIA and the World of Arts and Letters* (The News Press, 1999), 141–3.

34 Garlitz, *A Mission for Development*, 145.

35 Farmanfarmaian, *Towse'eh dar Iran*, 207–8, 300.

> Not so very many years ago in Iran, the United States was loved and respected as no other country and without having given a penny of aid. Now, after more than $1 billion of loans and grants, America is neither loved, nor respected; she is distrusted by most people, and hated by many.[36]

Returning to Tehran, Ebtehaj faced trumped up corruption charges and spent some time in prison but was released after officials in the Kennedy Administration campaigned in his support. In 1963, US embassy officials quietly asked if he was interested in becoming prime minister. He agreed to take the job only if the shah stopped interfering with government affairs, the size of the military was reduced, and Iran withdrew from the US-sponsored CENTO. The United States, of course, would not accept these conditions and Ebtehaj became more bitter in his criticism of Washington's support of the shah, telling a State Department liaison in 1965 that the United States "would lose 'everything' in Iran when the regime met its inevitable doom."[37]

Meanwhile, United States "soft power" was spreading through institutions such as Iran-America Society, established in 1925 and later linked to the US Information Agency (USIA). By the 1960s, the Iran-America Society had opened branches in Esfahan, Mashhad, and Shiraz, offering English-language classes and cultural programs, such as films and lectures. In 1970, the Society had 1,280 members, and most (886) were Iranians. The same year, four to five thousand students were enrolled in English-language courses offered by the society. About seven thousand students visited the academic center every month. These were mostly youth from Tehran's middle-class families interested in learning English and curious about American culture. The society was run by a mixed Iranian-American board that followed US foreign policy line discreetly and that of the shah's regime more blatantly.[38]

Another organization, the American Friends of the Middle East (AFME), helped Iranian students get acceptance to American universities. Established in 1951, the AFME ostensibly was a nongovernment organization dedicated to international peace and cultural understanding between the United States and the Middle East. In fact, it was a CIA front run by Allen Dulles and Kermit Roosevelt. In August 1953, the

36 Quoted in Bill, *Eagle and the Lion*, 130.

37 Geoffrey Jones, "Ebtehaj, Abolhassan," in Encyclopædia Iranica, accessed August 3, 2021, iranicaonline.org; Shannon, *Losing Hearts and Minds*, 29–33, last quote on 33.

38 Bill, *Eagle and the Lion*, 398–9.

AFME opened its first overseas office in Tehran, using the existing educational network built by Presbyterian missionaries. Its Tehran office was headed by Charles R. Hulac, a former Presbyterian minister and international student director at Lafayette College, Pennsylvania. During the 1940s, Hulac had spent five years in Iran on behalf of the Presbyterian Board of Foreign Missions before joining the CIA. The AFME's connection to American missionary networks extended beyond Iran to the entire Middle East. Pursuing its objective of political and ideological conversion of young Middle Easterners, the AFME followed the Presbyterian approach of emphasizing religious affinities and shared moral values between Muslims and Christians. Given its duplicitous agenda, the AFME in fact did major damage to the cause of building intellectual trust and goodwill between Americans and Middle Easterners. Its Tehran office focused on getting student to American universities through a careful screening process. In its first year of full operation in Iran (1955), the AFME chose and helped the acceptance of 375 students out of 6,795 applicants. By 1959, the AFME Tehran office was placing 694 students in the United States, more than half of its totals for the Middle East. By the mid-1950s, around 2,800 Iranians were studying abroad, the United States being their first destination, with slightly over a thousand students, and Germany following as a close second. The actual numbers were higher because many were studying abroad without student visas.[39]

The AFME was actively involved with the monitoring and political manipulation of the students it was sending to the United States. It helped set up the first Iranian student organizations in American universities, including on the Lafayette campus with Hulac as its advisor. In 1952, the AFME and Iranian embassy brought together a few student organizations to form the Iranian Student Association in the United States (ISAUS), at a meeting in Madison, Wisconsin. The next ISAUS conference was a four-day event in September 1953 at University of Denver, Colorado, with eighty-five Iranian students as well as Iranian and American officials. This meeting took place right after the 1953 coup, and some students criticized US involvement with Mosaddeq's overthrow, but AFME and the embassy remained in control. The next (1954) ISAUS meeting in Berkley, California, was attended by seventy students and a minority faction proposed a resolution condemning the government's new agreement with the oil consortium. But pressure from the AFME

39 Wilford, *America's Great Game*, 122–3; Shannon, *Losing Hearts and Minds*, 34–6.

and a progovernment faction forced the congress to reject the resolution. The ISAUS was controlled by the AFME and the Iranian embassy until the late 1950s, electing the shah as its honorary chairman during his 1958 visit to the United States. But the opposition was gaining ground, voicing its views in independent student journals *Iran Nameh* and *Pendar*, published in New York and Cambridge, Massachusetts, to rival *Daneshjoo*, the official organ of ISAUS.

By the end of the decade, the ISAUS had about twelve hundred members, many of whom would occupy important academic and government posts in 1960s–70s Iran. Dissent within the ISUAS grew stronger until students opposed to the shah and US policies took over the organization in 1960 and ended its ties with the AFME.[40] While the AFME may have steered a good number of highly educated Iranians toward pro-shah and pro-American politics during the 1950s, it lost control of the ISAUS, which would, as we shall see, recruit tens of thousands of Iranian students in one of the most effective anti-imperialist organization of 1960s–70s America.

Another institution launched in the early 1950s to prompt American soft power in Iran and the Middle East during the Cold War was the Franklin Book Programs (1952–77), a title alluding to Benjamin Franklin, America's first famous publisher and printer. Officially, Franklin Publishers was a private corporation established to support book publishing in developing countries, focused on the translation and publication of American books. It started with a half million-dollar grant from the US State Department's International Information Administration, and later by funds from the USAID. Most of Franklin's budget, however, came from its host country's governments and private donors. In addition to translations, Franklin published textbooks and weekly readers' magazines, developed dictionaries and encyclopedias, helped train publishers, textbook writers, and booksellers. Despite its claims of autonomy from the US government, Franklin Publishers was an arm of America's Cold War cultural diplomacy. Commenting on the program's launch, a 1952 *New York Times Book Review* writer noted, "No one pretends that you can shoot books out of cannons, but there is a passionate hope that if you make ideas work for democracy you won't have to shoot the cannons at all." Put another way, the idea behind Franklin Publishers was for American cultural diplomacy to wage intellectual warfare, "bombing" the Third

40 Shannon, *Losing Hearts and Minds*, 36–9; Matin-Asgari, *Iranian Student Opposition to the Shah*, 36–8.

World with books. According to the guidelines established by its first president, Datus C. Smith, Franklin translations were chosen by the influential elite of each host country from a list provided or approved by the US Information Agency. The actual translation and publication of these titles was to be done by host country private individuals or government organizations, with support and training provided by Franklin's local offices, also to be managed by local professionals.[41]

Thus, the manager of Franklin's Tehran branch enlisted the president of the Senate, who was a patron of the country's conservative intellectual elite, to help launch Franklin's publications with a "prestigious" book with the unprecedented print run of twenty thousand copies. Half of this volume consisted of Persian translations of chapters from Sarah K. Bolton's *Lives of Poor Boys Who Became Famous*, featuring rags to riches biographies of famous Americans like Benjamin Franklin, Abraham Lincoln, Henry Ford, and Thomas Edison. The other chapters featured biographies of Iranian "great men," written in Persian, including a biography of Reza Shah, penned by his son, the shah, who also donated $10,000 to support the book's publication. Franklin's Tehran office also arranged for the publication in Persian of Benjamin Spock's best-seller *The Common Sense Book of Baby and Child Care*, whose translation was credited to the shah's sister, Ashraf Pahlavi.[42] In keeping with a familiar US Cultural Cold War policy, Franklin hired noncommunist leftists, such as writer and essayist Jalal Al-e Ahmad, and even former Tudeh Party members like leading translator Najaf Daryabandari, who served as its chief editor in Tehran. Al-e Ahmad, who had written a biography of Gandhi for the Persian edition of *Lives of Poor Boys Who Became Famous*, later regretted his association with Franklin Publishers, which he criticized as a tool of American cultural imperialism.[43]

Opened in 1954, a few months after the CIA coup, Franklin's Tehran office was its second, after Cairo (1953), and the organization's largest branch in terms of the volume and diversity of the material produced.

41 Louise S. Robbins, "Publishing American Values: The Franklin Book Programs as Cold War Cultural Diplomacy," *Library Trends* 55, no. 3 (winter 2007): 638–50, 640–2; for an extensive study of the Franklin Book Programs, see also Mahdi Ganjavi, *Education and the Cultural Cold War in the Middle East: The Franklin Book Programs in Iran* (I.B. Tauris, 2023), 24–5.

42 E. Khajehnuri, ed. *Mardan-e khod-sakhteh* [Self-made Men] (Tehran: 1956). Ganjavi, *Education and the Cultural Cold War in the Middle East*, 80.

43 Jalal Al-Ahmad, *Yek chah va do chaleh* [A Well and Two Hollows] (Tehran: 1964), 15. See also Ganjavi, *Education and the Cultural Cold War in the Middle East*, 131–2; Abdol-Hossein Azarang and Ali Dehbashi, *Tarikh-e shafahi-ye nashr Iran* [The Oral History of Print in Iran] (Tehran: 2013), 340–4.

Most of the eight hundred fifty books published with Franklin's assistance were translations of American works, with some British and French, and about fifty originally Persian titles. The most outstanding translations were literary works, such as *The Call of the Wild*, *Gone with the Wind*, *The Great Gatsby*, *Adventures of Huckleberry Finn*, *The House of the Seven Gables*, *Moby Dick*, *A Tale of Two Cities*, and *The Adventures of Tom Sawyer*, as well as historical and philosophical works like *A History of Civilization*, *The Story of Civilization*, *The History of the Decline and Fall of the Roman Empire*, *The Age of Enlightenment*, *Democracy and Education*, *The Varieties of Religious Experience*, and *The Public Philosophy*. As per Franklin's stated mission, these books cumulatively promoted a sophisticated liberal-democratic worldview rather than crude anti-communist propaganda. In addition to translation, Franklin's Tehran branch sponsored other projects. In 1958, it helped set up the Offset Printing, the largest printing house in the Middle East, and in the 1960s it assisted with the launch of the Pocket Books company, publishing small books at low prices for sale in unconventional settings such as markets and bus stops. Franklin also sent managers of Iranian publishing companies to professional workshops in the United States, England, and France, and provided loans and technical advice for importing paper and the establishment of a major papermaking company in 1968. Franklin also sponsored the translation and publication of a major encyclopedia, dictionaries, atlases, and historical reference works for general readers and schoolchildren. Finally, Franklin's Tehran office collaborated with the Ministry of Education to publish school textbooks for the first four grades and millions of copies of educational "support material" in the form of *Payk* (*Courier*) magazine series. With a circulation of 7.5 million copies every two weeks, *Payk* was formatted for different readers, primary-school students, children, kindergarteners, and teachers and parents.[44] Thus, Franklin became a major influence during the launch of the mass production, publication, and circulation of books geared toward all levels of readers in Iran. Moreover, Franklin's success in Iran became the foundation for its entry into Afghanistan and Pakistan, where Franklin similarly helped in establishing a modern print culture and produced millions of textbooks. The Franklin program dissolved itself in 1978–77, partly due to the lack of funding, partly because Iran and other countries had developed their own printing and publishing industries and also because the mid-century campaign of promoting

44 Ganjavi, *Education and the Cultural Cold War*, 117–19.

American cultural values through book publishing seemed to have lost its purpose and urgency.[45] By the 1970s, hundreds of millions all over the world, including in Iran, were drawn into the ambit of American popular culture through the much more powerful media of film and television. At the same time, as we will see in chapter 4, the first generation of mass-educated Iranians had not exactly turned out pro-American.

The Kennedy Years: A US-backed White Revolution

> *Do you know what the head of the Iranian Army told one of our people. He said the Army was in good shape, thanks to US aid—it was now capable of coping with the civilian population. That Army isn't going to fight the Russians. It's planning to fight the Iranian people.*
>
> Senator Hubert Humphrey, Senate Foreign Relations Committee, 1961[46]

By the end of the 1950s, the shah's relation with the United States remained tense. Between 1953 and 1960, the United States had given Iran $567 million in economic assistance and $450 in military aid. As Ebtehaj had noted, in less than a decade, the United States had spent over $1billion, supporting a regime that was neither popular nor one that had achieved political stability or economic development.[47] This was noted by several observers on the American side. In a January 1962 *Foreign Affairs* article, Princeton University Iran expert and former CIA consultant, T. Cuyler Young, summed up the situation:

> During the last decade . . . the United States has furnished Iran with more than a billion dollars in economic and military aid. Like it or not, justly or unjustly, this has served to identify the United States with the Shah's regime, together with responsibility for what that regime has done, or failed to do . . . For this reason, the United States is distrusted, if not thoroughly disliked, by all those who have come to distrust the Shah and oppose his policies.[48]

---

45 Datus C. Smith, "Franklin Book Program," in Encyclopædia Iranica, accessed July 14, 2023, iranicaonline.org.

46 Humphrey quoted in *Newsweek*, May 22, 1961.

47 Bill, *Eagle and the Lion*, 114.

48 Ibid., 129.

Cuyler Young's assessment reflected the crisis mode of US relations with the shah, developing after John Kennedy's victory in the presidential election of 1960. The shah had preferred Kennedy's Republican opponent, Richard Nixon—he had reportedly contributed financially to his campaign. What made the shah more insecure was Kennedy's New Frontier rhetoric, hinting at a foreign policy change from Eisenhower's seemingly unconditional military support of repressive regimes like Iran. Tensions mounted when, a few months after Kennedy's inauguration, Soviet Premier Nikita Khrushchev openly declared what US officials murmured in private, that even without communist interference, Iran was ripe for a revolution. This open Soviet challenge is often noted as an impetus to Kennedy's push for reform in Iran. But Khrushchev had only frankly stated the obvious, namely that instead of pushing for revolution, Moscow would wait to exploit inevitable American blunders in Iran. Starting with Stalin, this basic Soviet strategy would remain unchanged to the end of the shah's rule and even after his overthrow. In 1961, however, Khrushchev was expressing frustration with the shah's recent defense treaty with Washington, which was a setback to recently improved Soviet-Iranian relations, initiated with the shah's 1956 visit to Moscow. In Washington, liberal senators seized upon Khrushchev's statement to harshly criticize US support for the shah. At a June 1961 Senate Foreign Relations Committee hearing, Senator Frank Church blatantly asserted: "Khrushchev is right. I just think it is going to be a miracle if we save the shah of Iran . . . And when he goes down, boom, we go with him." Senator Hubert Humphrey's view of the shah and his entourage was the same: "They are dead . . . They just don't know it. I don't care what kind of revolution it is. Somebody is going to get those fellows. They are out. It is just a matter of time."[49]

Khrushchev's threats notwithstanding, the American foreign policy establishment knew that the shah's regime was unstable and might fall without some meaningful change of course. Kennedy and liberal cold warriors thus advocated moderate reform from above to forestall radical revolution from below. This rhetoric had appeared in Kennedy's inaugural address on January 20, 1961:

> To those people in the huts and villages of half the globe struggling to break the bonds of mass misery, we pledge our best efforts to help them help themselves, for whatever period is required—not because

49 Church and Humphrey quoted in Ghazvinian, *America and Iran*, 223.

> the communists may be doing it, not because we seek their votes, but because it is right. If a free society cannot help that many who are poor, it cannot save the few who are rich.[50]

Soon after taking office, and largely in response to the Cuban Revolution, Kennedy launched his hemispheric reform program, the Alliance for Progress, aiming to promote land reform and improve health, education, and labor conditions across Latin America. As the examples of Cuba and Vietnam showed, however, Kennedy remained fully committed to Third World regime change through covert operations and military intervention. As we will see in the case of Iran below, US foreign policy under Kennedy had more continuity than rupture with those of Eisenhower and Johnson after him.

Under Kennedy, Iran became one of the "developing" world's laboratories for the application of modernization theory, represented in Washington by its avatar, Walt Rostow, serving as Kennedy's foreign policy advisor. Iran's 1963 White Revolution, the shah's signature reform and development project, was an example of modernization theory's application. Often associated with the Kennedy administration, the idea of a "White Revolution," to forestall a Red one, was proposed in the late 1950s by members of Iran's political elite, shrewdly borrowing from the left's agenda. Its first articulation was by Asadollah Alam, a rich landowner, the shah's loyal confidant and leader of the "opposition" People (Mardom) Party. Alam's party had copied the Tudeh (Masses) Party's name, while also enlisting former communist intellectuals to draft a "leftist" program, including land reform and women's enfranchisement. Following the Iraqi monarchy's overthrow in 1958, Alam had a confidential meeting with British diplomats, reminding them of their old idea of a preemptive revolution from above to save the shah (see chapter 2). According to this meeting's transcript:

> Asadullah Alam went on to explain that what he had in mind was in fact a "*white revolution*," which he hoped to bring about under the auspices of the Shah . . . Asadullah hoped to prevail upon the Shah to be rid of the present "establishment," the existing ruling classes must give place to new and younger men. The old gang were not of course to be hurt; this was white not a red revolution; but the Shah must sack them all . . . The

50 John F. Kennedy, "Inaugural Address," January 20, 1961, National Archives, archives.gov.

> Mardom Party was to be the instrument of this new order . . . The Shah was wary . . . He was afraid also that popular and nationalistic policies, however well controlled, might endanger stability.[51]

The core agenda of the White Revolution (that is, land reform, women's enfranchisement, literacy corps, and the nationalization of forests and pasture lands) was copied from the program of the Tudeh Party and its splinter fractions, including Azerbaijan's autonomous government that had carried out Iran's first agrarian reform and enfranchised women in 1946. As we saw in chapter 2, during the 1940s, British diplomats had suggested implementing a watered-down version of the communist agenda, particularly land reform, in order to shake up Iran's reactionary status quo and placate the masses' revolutionary impulse. Kennedy's advisors came up with similar reform proposals, responding to growing popular unrest and the revival of open opposition in Iran during 1960–61. In March 1961, and prior to Khrushchev's declaration in April, Iran expert John W. Bowling wrote an analysis of the political situation in Iran, making a set of specific recommendations for the shah to initiate some token land reform, make defiant declarations against the oil consortium, assume a posture of neutrality in international relations, and trim the size of the military while increasing its capability to handle internal security and guerrilla activities; remove US advisors except in health, education, and public welfare, bring moderate oppositionists into nonessential government posts, and curb the royal family's ostentatious life style. These points then became the Kennedy administration's blueprint for reform in Iran. Clearly, the package included neither serious political liberalization nor radical social and economic reform. Bowling himself admitted as much, saying "many of them would be demagogic in nature and would be hard for the West to swallow. But it is still possible that the shah could turn the trick. He has the brains, the personality, and the cunning to do it."[52]

Young, probably the country's most astute Iran expert, was more concerned about the nature of the US relation with the shah. A week before Khrushchev's warning, he wrote a letter to Kennedy's foreign policy advisor, Walt Rostow, predicting a similar turn of events if the current US identification with the shah's regime continued:

---

51 Ali M. Ansari, "The Myth of the White Revolution: Mohammad Reza Shah, 'Modernization' and the Consolidation of Power," *Middle Eastern Studies* 37, no. 3 (July 2001): 1–24, quoted on 5–6.

52 Bill, *Eagle and the Lion*, 134–5.

> This regime is considered by most aware and articulated Iranians as reactionary, corrupt, and a tool of Western (and especially Anglo-American) imperialism. The fact that the US economic and military aid has been used to buttress the current regime is ample evidence for the people that the US generally approves and supports the regime.
>
> Moreover, since the regime has ruthlessly eliminated almost all genuine opposition, even of a fairly conservative nature, and increasing number of Iranians are beginning to think of communism as the only means to effect basic change in Iran.

Young then made a set of policy recommendations, almost identical to those suggested by Bowling.[53] These debates in Washington coincided with an upsurge of opposition activities in Iran, spearheaded by a younger generation of urban middle classes, particularly university students, precisely as modernization theorists and observers like Blowing and Young had anticipated. Between 1957 and 1960, the government faced a steep budget deficit, cost of living rose by about 35 percent, and labor unrest broke out in a wave of strikes across the country, some broken up with casualties. The largest labor protest was by tens of thousands of Tehran bricklayers who repeatedly went on strike in 1960 and 1961. Prime Minster Eghbal became the opposition's target, and the shah replaced him, promising 1960 Majles elections would be free. Sensing an opening, Mosaddeq's closest allies declared the formation of a Second National Front in the summer of 1960. Tehran University students led the second National Front's most militant faction, organizing its first public meeting, followed by more strikes and protests that would spread from the university campus into the capital. Enrolling about two-thirds of the country's twelve thousand total student population in 1959–60, University of Tehran was also the epicenter of radical student politics. Formerly a stronghold of the Tudeh Party, by the 1960s, University of Tehran saw the emergence of a more diverse leftist generation of activists. On December 7, 1960, the newly formed Organization of Tehran University Students (OTUS) held the first open commemoration of "Student Day," when three students were killed during Nixon's 1953 visit. The arrest of OTUS leadership led to a sit-in strike by four thousand students in January 1961. Condemning Majles election fraud, protests then spilled into the streets and continued for two weeks, joined by student strikes in other cities and the closure of the Tehran bazaar. By spring,

53 Ibid., 135.

high school students and teachers had joined the protests and when the police killed a striking teacher, the shah's caretaker prime minister was forced to step down and, by early May, Ali Amini, who was widely seen as a US choice, became prime minister with extraordinary powers to rule without the Majles.[54] On May 18, 1961, the Second National Front held its largest gathering since the early 1950s, where its leader Karim Sanjabi spoke to eighty thousand people, acknowledging the university students' leading role in the opposition, while attacking Amini as a "servant" of foreigners, saying, "We emphatically declare that Iran is not a chessboard for players to move around their chosen pieces."[55]

On December 7, 1961, nearly fifteen thousand protested against Amini's government during the commemoration of "Student Day" on University of Tehran's campus, while similar protests took place at the universities of Tabriz, Shiraz, Esfahan, Abadan, and Mashhad. By January 1962, unrest had spread to high schools and, on January 21, police and paratroopers stormed the University of Tehran. Hundreds of students were seriously injured and about two hundred were hospitalized. Violence against peaceful protests, however, continued unabated, with the police firing on high school students and killing one of them. Meanwhile, Kennedy's task force "Review of Problems in Iran" argued against holding elections because "Iran simply was not ready for a democratic consensus."[56] The three-sided political tussle between the Second National Front, Amini's government, and the shah continued into 1962. It was clear that the Kennedy administration supported a reform package implemented from above, rather than political liberalization and free elections, which the Second National Front was asking for. The shah's April 1962 visit to Washington marked the turning point when Kennedy agreed to let him take personal charge of the reform agenda. Meeting with Kennedy and his high officials, the shah persistently asked for more US military aid, complaining that "America treats Turkey as a wife and Iran as a concubine." Kennedy gave in to the shah's demand of keeping the Iranian army at two hundred thousand strong, suggesting a token cut of ten thousand. According to one study, Kennedy's remark, "the Shah is the keystone of the arch in Iran," signaled the fact that "American

54 Matin-Asgari, *Iranian Student Opposition to the Shah*, 41, 44–6; on Amini's imposition by Kennedy, see also *Kayhan* airmail edition, November 9, 1977 and *Ettela'at*, October 23, 1977; the shah too admitted he was "pressed" by the United States to appoint Amini. See Mohammad Reza Pahlavi, *Answer to History*, 146.

55 Sanjabi's speech is in *Kayhan*, May 20, 1961, 13.

56 Matin-Asgari, *Iranian Student Opposition to the Shah*, 56–7; Kennedy Task Force quoted in Collier, *Democracy*, 205–6.

interests in Iran had turned into virtually unequivocal support for the Shah through the use of continuing military and economic assistance, with little emphasis on political development."[57] Thus, despite initial hesitations, Kennedy's Iran policy was pivoted on the shah, consistent with the pattern that was established with Truman and Eisenhower and would continue with Johnson, Nixon, Ford, and Carter.

The shah's 1962 US visit had proven successful. He was received by Kennedy at Washington airport, invited to address a joint session of Congress, reached five million Americans via a CBS television interview, watched the launch of NASA rockets at Cape Canaveral, Florida, and along with his new wife, Empress Farah, mingled with the Kennedy family on the White House lawn. Mainstream American media heaped praise on him, and he picked up an honorary doctorate at the University of Pennsylvania in Philadelphia.[58] The visit, however, was marred by the emergence of vocal Iranian opposition to the shah in America, a phenomenon that would grow stronger in the years ahead. Kennedy's election had coincided with National Front supporters taking over the ISAUS, at its September 1960 conference in Ypsilanti, Michigan. Claiming to represent about four thousand students in twenty-five states, the ISAUS cut its ties with the Iranian embassy and the AFME, forging ahead to become the voice of Iranian opposition in the United States, and soon a major participant in the global student upheavals of the 1960s–70s. In the early 1960s, however, the ISAUS was a liberal organization, aligned with the Second National Front in Iran. It launched a campaign of open letters and telegrams asking Kennedy and other American officials not to support the shah's "unpopular regime." Kennedy was addressed as "the leader of the Free World" and asked to stand against repression in Iran, particularly when another ideology (communism) was "competing to attract the trust of the Iranian people." ISAUS leaders had access to the White House through personal contacts with Supreme Court Justice William Douglas (see chapter 2) and the president's brother, Attorney General Robert Kennedy, who met Iranian student leaders in his office. Though rather small, compared to what they would become by the 1970s, ISAUS demonstrations and protest actions were effective in embarrassing the shah, chasing him everywhere during his 1962 US visit. The irritated shah began pressing Washington to deport about thirty student activists. This caused some tension between the State Department and the

57 Ben Offiler, *US Foreign Policy and the Modernization of Iran: Kennedy, Johnson, Nixon, and the Shah* (Palgrave, 2015), 43–4.

58 Ghazvinian, *America and Iran*, 224–5.

Justice Department, where Robert Kennedy, who personally knew a few ISAUS leaders, blocked their deportation. When the State Department launched an investigation into these students' alleged communist links, Justice Douglas told Robert Kennedy that "the Shah was making up lists for the firing squad when they got back." Convinced that "not a bloody one of these kids is a communist," Robert Kennedy told Secretary of State Dean Rusk "to go chase himself." Eventually no student was deported, while Robert Kennedy canceled an official visit to Tehran.[59]

At the same time, the shah kept pressing Washington to let him to dump Amini and personally implement the reforms Amini had called the "White Revolution." By mid-1962, the US embassy in Tehran informed the shah that the United States wanted him to personally "enforce discipline and order." Realizing he had lost American support, Amini resigned and was replaced by Asadollah Alam, the shah's "house-born slave" whose obeisance was so blatant that a CIA report concluded that "for all practical purposes it is the Shah himself who will be prime minister."[60] In fall 1962, while Kennedy was preoccupied with removing Soviet nuclear missiles from Cuba, the shah announced that he would not allow missile bases threatening the Soviet Union in Iran. Though significantly improving Soviet Iranian relations, this policy accorded with the resolution of the Cuban Missile Crisis, whereby Kennedy quietly agreed to remove US nuclear warheads from Turkey. Assuming a posture of independence from the United States, the shah was ready to launch his White Revolution, which now would receive Soviet as well as American support. In January 1963, the six proposals of the White Revolution passed in a national referendum with the requisite 99 percent approval rating. The centerpiece of this package, land reform, had already begun under Amini, whose agricultural minister, Hasan Arsanjani, wanted to establish genuine support for the regime by creating a class of peasant proprietors. With the White Revolution, the shah blatantly had copied the left's agenda of land reform, women's enfranchisement, natural resource nationalization, and universal literacy, presenting them as his own progressive "antifeudal" revolution. In the end, rather than dictating terms, Washington had used its considerable leverage to persistently steer the shah in a certain direction. In the words of one scholar, Kennedy's advisors had adopted a "massage policy," gently nudging and encouraging the shah toward shared goals. American leverage consisted of loans and

59 Shannon, *Losing Hearts and Minds*, 57–60; Matin-Asgari, *Iranian Student Opposition to the Shah*, 47–9.

60 Collier, *Democracy*, 212–13.

military aid, but Kennedy began to "massage" the shah's ego by treating him as a regional ally, asking him, for example, to meditate in a border dispute between Pakistan and Afghanistan.[61] While the shah was not a "puppet," merely dancing to Washington's every tune, he always acted within the ambit of US strategic interests.

To the extent that the White Revolution implemented the left's reform agenda, it brought progressive transformation to Iranian society, something that was denied by the shah's right-wing opponents as well as leftists who claimed the whole thing was an American imperialist ploy. The White Revolution's fundamental flaw, and the structural weakness that ultimately brought down the shah's regime, was the systematic exclusion of political participation. Here, again, the merger of the White Revolution with royal dictatorship was the shah's choice, backed but not dictated by the United States. With the successful launch of the White Revolution, the shah could have reconciled many liberal and left opponents. In 1963, the National Front, the Tudeh Party, other leftist factions, and the incipient clerical opposition led by Khomeini all converged on demanding the restoration of constitutional monarchy.[62] Acceding to such demands would have strengthened the shah by neutralizing political opposition and broadening his social base of support. Instead, he chose the exact opposite route of barring political participation and violently repressing dissent. This fateful strategic choice became the regime's fatal fault line, contained during the 1960s but showing up in the 1970s when real developmental achievements proved insufficient to sustain a regime of personal dictatorship. Therefore, the shah, and the crony elite who actively supported his dictatorship, were responsible for the revolutionary meltdown of the whole system. The United States also shares a direct burden of responsibility because of its systematic aiding and abetting of the shah's dictatorship. Ultimately, a quarter century of American support and encouragement of the shah's dictatorship (1953–78) would be much more politically damaging to Iran than the CIA's overthrow of Mosaddeq in 1953.

As the shah had hoped, his White Revolution caused confusion and disarray within the ranks of the opposition, which had to react to its own demands being appropriated by the shah. Whether they thought the reforms were real or not, the National Front and the left remained firmly opposed to the shah's personal rule. The secular opposition's response

61 Offiler, *US Foreign Policy and the Modernization of Iran*, see chapter 3 and 58–61.

62 Siavush Randjbar-Daemi, "The Tudeh Party of Iran and the Land Reform Initiatives of the Pahlavi State, 1958–1964," *Middle Eastern Studies* 58, 4 (2020): 617–35.

was summed up in a phrase posted at the main gates of the University of Tehran on the eve of the referendum: "Reforms Yes, Dictatorship, No!"[63] A very different response to the White Revolution, however, came from a newly emerging militant Islamic opposition, led by Ayatollah Ruhollah Khomeini. Iran's clerical establishment traditionally had avoided direct engagement with politics, thus effectively supporting the conservative status quo. Nor had clerics, including Khomeini, ever opposed the principle of monarchy, not even during Reza Shah's dictatorship. As we saw in chapter 2, during Mosaddeq's premiership, the National Front had a right-wing Islamic faction, led by Ayatollah Kashani, who eventually cooperated with the CIA coup. But Khomeini's sudden appearance on the scene marked a new departure in opposition politics. Khomeini already had some recognition as a contender for the clerical establishment's top leadership position, vacated with the 1961 passing of the politically circumspect Ayatollah Boroujerdi. In 1962, Khomeini and other clerical leaders opposed changes in electoral laws allowing women to vote and dropping the oath of allegiance to the Koran. When the government backed down, Khomeini and other senior ayatollahs boycotted the 1963 referendum on the White Revolution, arguing women's franchise and tampering with land ownership were un-Islamic. But Khomeini broke with conservative clerics when he began to openly criticize the shah and US interference in Iran. In March 1963, security forces broke up pro-Khomeini protests in the Shi'i shrine city of Qom, killing some seminarians. In early June, Khomeini gave a sermon calling the White Revolution a fraud and holding the shah responsible for selling Iran to foreigners. When he was arrested on June 5, violent protests broke out in Tehran and other cities. Government troops put down the uprising by firing into the crowds, inflicting hundreds—or thousands, according to pro-Khomeini sources—of casualties. Thus, the uprising on June 5, 1963, became a watershed event whereby the shah's regime established the position that its response to public protest would be massive and naked violence. Written in blood, the message registered with the entire spectrum of the opposition. The National Front leaders were in prison, refusing the regime's offer of limited political participation in exchange for unconditional endorsement of the White Revolution. The June 1963 massacre made compromise more difficult, and hence, after serving short prison terms, National Front leaders adopted the so-called

63 Matin-Asgari, *Iranian Student Opposition to the Shah*, 64; Mohammad Baheri, the minister of justice, reported seeing this slogan. Transcript of interview with Mohammad Baheri, tape no. 8, 14, fas.harvard.edu.

politics of patience and anticipation, waiting for more opportune times. A younger and more militant generation, mostly university students politicized during the early 1960s, began discussing, and some preparing for, armed struggle against the regime. Six months after the June 5 massacre, the Confederation of Iranian Students, formed in 1963 as the national union of university students in Iran and abroad, passed a resolution including the declaration: "The Shah speaks the language of bullets, one must speak to him in his own language!" About a year later, during his trial, National Front leader Mehdi Bazargan declared the end of peaceful constitutional struggle. "We are the last group," he said, "to have struggled politically through constitutional means. We expect the judge to convey this point to his superiors."[64] The same warning echoed in the pages of mainstream American journal *Foreign Affairs*, where an article by Iranian graduate student Hossein Mahdavi concluded: "Opposition forces are moving toward accepting violence as the only way to bring about solutions to Iran's ills."[65]

American media and government reactions to the events of 1963, including the June massacre, converged on categorical support for the shah. In May, the Kennedy task force reported that the "Shah had substantially satisfied US pressure for reform by his unilateral program of January 1963." A month later, a National Security study concurred, saying that the shah's White Revolution "promises to achieve some of our fundamental policy objectives . . . [so] we have been using and will continue to use every opportunity to reiterate our confidence in him." The US press dismissed the June 1963 event as a reactionary uprising, a *New York Times* headline, for instance, declared "No Casualties Are Reported," while mentioning official Iranian government reports of eighty-four killed and close to two hundred injured. Secretary of State Dean Rusk wrote to the shah saying nothing about the massacre, except that "such manifestations will gradually disappear as your people realize the importance of the measures you are taking to establish social justice and equal opportunity for all Iranians." A confidential US embassy report, however, warned that "Khomeini is now the most important figure with whom the regime has to deal with" as well as "the outstanding opposition leader against the Shah, the government and the reform program."[66]

64 Afshin Matin-Asgari, *Both Eastern and Western: An Intellectual History of Iranian Modernity* (Cambridge University Press, 2018), 173–4.

65 Hossein Mahdavi, "The Coming Crisis in Iran," *Foreign Affairs* (October 1965): 134–46, quoted on 146.

66 Collier, *Democracy*, 218, 220–1; "Tanks Disperse Tehran Crowds, No Casualties are Reported," *New York Times*, June 9, 1963, 18.

The Modern Iran Party, American Residents, and Khomeini

After a few months in detention, Khomeini was placed under house arrest, being spared harsher treatment, possibly a death sentence, due to influential ayatollahs interceding on his behalf. In fall 1963, Majles convened again, after a two-year hiatus, filled with prescreened deputies, whose composition had changed from mainly big landlords to mostly modern-educated technocrats. The US embassy praised the election results, and *The New York Times* called them "the fairest and most representative election Iran has ever had."[67] During the 1960s, a new bureaucratic-technocratic elite would emerge to manage and implement the White Revolution at the shah's behest. Totally subservient to the shah, this new managerial elite was the enabler and beneficiary of royal despotism, their collective contribution to its functioning, and ultimate failure, often ignored as the shah alone took credit, and later was blamed, for everything. The arrival of the new elite was marked by the shah's appointment, in March 1964, of Hassan Ali Mansur, to premiership. Mansur was the head of the newly formed Modern Iran (Iran Novin) Party, whose top cadres were mostly US-educated or had close American ties. Mansur's tenure, however, coincided with another crisis, caused by Washington pressing the shah for a Status of Forces Agreement, giving US advisors and their dependents diplomatic immunity from Iranian laws. Reminiscent of colonial-era capitulatory treaties, the agreement violated Iranian sovereignty and barely passed when put before the rubber-stamp Majles. The shah's acceding to this humiliating arrangement shows he was still a few years away from the arrogant posturing of independence he would assume vis-à-vis the United States by the 1970s. But he was handsomely rewarded for the service rendered. Less than two weeks after the passage of the new agreement, the US government authorized a $200 million loan to Iran for the purchase of new military hardware. The largest "aid" package of its kind thus far, the loan was obviously a payment for the shah's shielding of Americans from Iranian jurisdiction.[68] Widespread public resentment was most forcefully articulated in an October 1964 speech by Khomeini who personally attacked the shah and US President Lyndon Johnson. In the most remembered part of his sermon, Khomeini declared:

---

67 Collier, *Democracy*, 222.

68 On Iran-e Novin Party, see Ghoalm-Reza Afkhami, *The Life and Times of the Shah* (University of California Press, 2009), 423–6.

> They have reduced the Iranian People to a level lower than an American dog. If someone runs over a dog belonging to an American, he will be prosecuted. Even if the Shah himself were to run over a dog belonging to an American, he would be prosecuted. But if an American cook runs over the Shah, the head of state, no one will have the right to interfere with him.
>
> Why? Because they wanted a loan and America demanded this in return.
>
> Let the American President know that in the eyes of the Iranian people, he is the most repulsive member of the human race today . . . Let the American government know that its name has been ruined and disgraced in Iran.[69]

No one in Iran had dared speak about the shah in this manner since the early 1950s; nor would anyone dare do so until the very last year of the shah's rule in 1978. Its boldness notwithstanding, this sermon marked a transitional phase in the trajectory of Khomeini's rise as a leading figure of the opposition. First, and despite his uncompromising stand against the shah, Khomeini did not question the principle of monarchy, something he would do within a few years. Second, Khomeini's social conservatism and class position were clear as his sermon addressed the army, politicians, clerics, merchants, scholars, and university students. This too would change by the 1970s, when, influenced by the left, Khomeini's vocabulary would include references to workers, peasants, class exploitation, and revolution. The regime's response to Khomeini was swift and decisive. He was arrested and, within a few days, sent into exile in Turkey. There was no popular uprising in his support, possibly because the memory of the previous year's massive crackdown repression was too fresh. But a major response soon followed, showing the opposition's drift toward violence. Only a few months after Khomeini's exile, on January 21, 1965, Prime Minster Mansur was assassinated by a young man linked to an underground group called the Islamic Nations Party, an offshoot of the Islamic terrorist group that in 1951 had murdered Prime Minster Razmara.

While the Johnson administration's official position continued to be full support of the shah, confidential US diplomatic and intelligence reports showed awareness that all was not well in Iran. An astute commentary on the political culture of the Modern (New) Iran Party and its

69 Full text translated in Algar, 181–8, quoted on 182, 186.

American ties was recorded in a 1964 dispatch to the State Department by Martin J. Herz, the political secretary at the US embassy in Tehran. According to Herz, despite the successful launch of the White Revolution, the regime lacked popular support, suffering to its very core from a deep crisis of confidence:

> Evidence of this is to be found at every turn: prominent members of the New Iran party who express the belief, privately and quietly, that their party is a sham and a fraud and that no political party can be expected to do useful work as long as the Shah's heavy hand rests on the decision-making process; hand-picked Majlis members who deplore "American support" for a regime which they call a travesty of democracy.

Herz's roster of the politically discontented included the shah's "most devoted supporters," "prominent judges," "military officers," and "foreign ministry officials" who were in touch with the Americans:

> These are not members of the opposition. They are members of the Establishment who, even when loyal to the Shah, are suffering from a profound malaise, from lack of conviction in what they are doing, from doubts about whether the regime deserves to endure.

The report concluded that "the Shah's regime is a highly unpopular dictatorship," considered so "not only by its opponents, but far more significantly, by its proponents as well."[70] Neither this kind of critical intelligence assessment, nor the increasingly vocal protests and demonstrations by thousands of Iranian students in the United States, made the slightest difference in the Johnson administration's policy toward the shah. With the post-1963 crushing of all dissent inside the country, the Confederation of Iranian Students, National Union (CISNU) remained Iran's only opposition organization, active in Europe and the United States. The CISNU's claim to be Iran's National Union of students was related to the fact that, by the mid-1960s, about half of the country's fifty-to-sixty thousand university-student population was enrolled in European and American campuses, where the CISNU had recruited roughly 10 percent as members and a larger percentage as supporters and sympathizers. Initially in line with the legal-constitutionalist politics of the Second National Front, the CISNU quickly radicalized after the 1963

70 Herz quoted in Matin-Asgari, *Both Eastern and Western*, 229.

events, emerging in the forefront of the 1960s–70s global student movement and playing a major role in the international protest campaign against repression and dictatorship in Iran.[71] Building alliances with student, leftist, labor, and human rights organizations, the CISNU effectively showed its new militancy during the shah's 1964 visits to Europe and the United States. In January, faced with aggressive CISNU protests in Austria, the shah canceled his trips to Switzerland and Germany, stopping in Italy to meet with even larger and more embarrassing demonstrations. The shah's second encounter with the CISNU that year, during his June 1964 visit to the United States, must have affected him deeply because he bitterly remembers it in his last book. He was received at Washington airport by noisy student protesters before being officially greeted by Johnson as the "reformist twentieth century monarch." He then picked up an honorary doctorate in law from New York University, in recognition of his "building the future of Iran on social justice and democratic ideals," while student demonstrators were shouting "Down with the Shah." After receiving a second honorary degree, from the American University in Washington, the shah flew to Los Angles to be commencement speaker and recognized as doctor of humane letters at the University of California in Los Angeles. CISNU protests received backing from the faculty and students at the university's Berkeley and Los Angeles campuses, but the UCLA chancellor announced, "The university stands without apology and without reservation behind its invitation to the shah." Over two hundred Iranian and American students picketed the ceremony, distributing petitions and asking UCLA to cancel its invitation of the shah, including a letter by the International Federation of Narcotic Education accusing him of involvement with heroin smuggling into the United States. The ceremony was disrupted when a small plane, with a banner saying "Need a Fix? See the Shah" appeared to circle above the crowd before being chased away by a police helicopter.[72]

Finally, looking back at the 1960s, mention must be made of the US Peace Corps program which promised a new departure in Iran-US relations via direct "people-to-people" interactions. The launch of the White Revolution in 1963 coincided with the arrival in Tehran of the first group of US Peace Corps volunteers, representing a program that, despite its limitations and short duration, is generally considered the most positive

71 Matin-Asgari, *Iranian Student Opposition to the Shah*, 101.

72 Ibid., 74–5; the shah mentions the "Need a Fix, See the Shah" incident, but mistakes the year and the UC campus. Mohammad Reza Pahlavi, *Answer to History* (Stein and Day, 1980), 146.

American "mission" to Iran.[73] The idea of the Peace Corps was proposed in the late 1950s by liberal cold warriors who thought sending young Americans abroad to help with development projects could win ordinary peoples' hearts and minds in the newly emerging Third World bloc of countries. Kennedy embraced the idea during his 1960 presidential campaign and launched the Peace Corps with an executive order in 1961, making his brother-in-law, Robert Sargent Shriver, its director. The Peace Corps Act passed by US Congress called for the program to provide aid to developing countries while making Americans better understood around the world and promoting better American understanding of the world. Iran was one of the first countries to receive the Peace Corps and had its largest and longest-lasting contingent in the Middle East with eighteen hundred volunteers serving from 1962 to 1976.[74]

Though the Peace Corps built on existing American aid projects, primarily Point Four, its initial dispatch was rather experimental and haphazard. The first group of about three dozen volunteers were mostly young college-educated white men who had two months of intensive training, mostly in Persian language, at Utah State University in Logan. Their motives seem to have been a mixture of altruistic desire to help people in "developing" countries, curiosity about the world, and in some cases, the evasion or postponement of being drafted for the Vietnam war. The volunteers' work in Iran included English instruction, vocational education, community development, and city planning, though in time most of them became English teachers to high school students and adults. Since 1952, English had replaced French as the foreign language taught in Iranian secondary schools, and by the 1960s, it was the language of Iran's development and modernization. The overlap of the Peace Corps with the White Revolution, which included a literacy corps as one its main principles, created confusion about how the two projects and their implementation were related. Like land reform and women's enfranchisement, the literacy corps was first proposed by Iranian leftist parties and incorporated into the shah's conception of the White Revolution. The Kennedy administration did not initiate reformist measures but supported them primarily as an alternative to a possible revolutionary upheaval in Iran. What was different about the Peace Corps was its

73 James Bill, for example, notes that Peace Corps Iran made "a strong, positive impact" and US volunteers were "the antithesis of the 'ugly American,'" quoted in Jasamin Rostam-Kolayi, "The New Frontier Meets the White Revolution: The Peace Corps in Iran, 1962–76," *Iranian Studies* 51, no. 4 (July 2018): 587–612, quoted on 589.

74 Rostam-Kolayi, "New Frontier Meets the White Revolution," 588–91.

reach to practically every corner of the country, including small towns and rural areas, where its volunteers lived among and had daily interactions with Iranians of all social backgrounds. At its peak during the mid-1960s, the Peace Corps had around four hundred volunteers, their activities ranging from teaching English in Kurdish-speaking regions to serving as faculty at the elite Pahlavi University in Shiraz to helping build a library and sports club in a small town in the Khorasan province. Though Iranians could be suspicious about the Peace Corps volunteers possibly acting as American spies, the State Department and the CIA had agreed to keep the Peace Corps uninvolved in intelligence operations. The Iranian opposition did not pay much attention to the Peace Corps, but there were exceptions, such as the influential Islamist cultural critic Ali Shariati befriending Peace Corps volunteer Michael Hillman as his colleague at the University of Mashhad in 1965–67.[75]

The Iran Peace Corps had a generally positive impact on the small number of Iranians who came into direct contact with its volunteers. But this was not enough to change the perspective of the vast majority who inevitably saw Americans and their government standing behind the shah's repressive regime. The exception of a uniquely benign program only proved the general rule of America's imperial presence in Iran. If the Peace Corps failed to change Iranian perceptions of the United States, it was a transformative experience for its volunteers, though not in ways that the Kennedy administration had intended. A good number of volunteers developed strong ties to Iran, many forming lasting friendship and some marrying Iranians. Former Peace Corps volunteers stood out among late-twentieth-century American academic experts on Iranian or Middle Eastern politics, history, literature, and anthropology. Most prominent among them would be Eric Hooglund, Richard Eaton, Mary Hegland, Thomas Ricks, Michael Hillman, John Limbert, John Lorentz, and Jerome Clinton.[76] A few volunteers went into diplomatic service, and three of them were among the fifty-two Americans taken hostage at the US embassy in 1979. Significantly, in contrast to the previous generation of Anglo-American Iran scholars, who almost invariably were involved

75 Jasamin Rostam-Kolayi, "'We Learned How to Be Friends': What Oral History Tells Us about the American Peace Corps in Iran'" in Shannon, *Losing Hearts and Minds*, 149–65, 151, 157–60; the idea of a literacy corps was proposed in 1961 in the student opposition journal *Name-ye Pasri*; see Matin-Asgari, *Iranian Student Opposition to the Shah*, 44.

76 Thomas M. Ricks, "US Military Missions to Iran, 1943–1978: The Political Economy of Military Assistance," *Iranian Studies*, 12, no. 3/4 (summer–autumn, 1979): 163–93, 182.

in covert intelligence, there is no evidence of former Peace Corps academics, or even those going into government or diplomatic service, were involved in espionage against Iran. But the deeper knowledge and critical perspective of these men and women had little to no impact on changing US policy toward Iran. By the early 1970s, many Peace Corps volunteers were becoming cynical of the White Revolution and its ties to the shah's authoritarian rule. Here is a vivid account of the situation by a US consular official in Iran in 1972–74:

> The director of the Peace Corps in Iran asked me, as political counselor, if I would be willing to come down and talk to the Peace Corps volunteers. I said, "Sure." And I did. I learned more from them than they learned from me. They kept referring to a fellow named George. "George has built the greatest society on earth, health corps, literacy corps, villages are being rebuilt, fresh water, pure water." They were talking about George Bernard Shaw—Shah. They referred to the Shah as George. They told me that the so-called literacy corps and health corps that were much touted in the media and in the PR pronouncements by the government of Iran, were simply not happening at all; they were just words. There was nothing but poverty and misery out in the villages, that the government wasn't doing anything. Subsequently, I traveled to every corner of Iran by road. The truth of what the volunteers said was evident.[77]

The Iran Peace Corps mission lasted longer than those in Turkey, Afghanistan, Pakistan, and Oman but by the 1970s, it was facing a crisis that led to its 1976 closure, a decision made by the vote of its volunteers. Both Iranian and American political and cultural context had rapidly changed within the Peace Corps' first decade of operation in the early 1960s to the early 1970s. With its significantly rising oil income, Iran was no longer a recipient of American aid, while the shah was more independently charting the course of the country's modernization and development. At the same time, escalating military and economic entanglement with the United States had flooded Iran with thousands of American technical advisors, entrepreneurs, and military personnel. The high demand for teaching English, the Peace Corps main job, was now met by Iranian instructors and American professionals fetching hefty salaries. Colonies of American miliary personnel and their families lived in Tehran and Esfahan, and some of their members treated Iranians with attitudes

77 Rostam-Kolayi, "New Frontier Meets the White Revolution," 600–2.

diametrically opposed to that of the Peace Corps volunteers. A Peace Corps staff member and longtime resident in Iran remembered how in Esfahan "American youths were . . . helling around the city—calling the Isfahanis 'niggers' . . . There were times when I tried, by speaking only in Persian, to hide the fact that I was an American."[78]

In 1975, a bomb exploded at the Tehran Peace Corps office without causing casualties. Although not a decisive event, this seemed like a clear signal that even this relatively benign American presence was no longer welcome.[79] Under such conditions, there was not much the Peace Corps could do to positively contribute to Iran's "development," something that many volunteers had realized from the start. A decade of Peace Corps interaction with Iranians had generated tangible goodwill, but this could not stem the growing tide of anti-American sentiments tied to the US support of the shah's unpopular rule.

78 Ibid., 601.
79 Ibid., 599.

4
The Golden Age of Iran-US Relations: Paving the Revolutionary Road

From Iran's tumultuous postrevolutionary perspective, the mid-1960s to the mid-1970s decade might appear like a golden age of peace and prosperity, sustained by a close relationship with the United States. But those who lament the passing of this imaginary golden age are at a loss to explain why it suddenly imploded in an obviously popular revolution. Monarchists see the revolution as a conspiracy hatched by Iran's foreign enemies seeking to undermine the shah's great accomplishments. The shah pioneered this narrative in *Answer to History*, a small book he completed in exile, shortly before his death. He explained:

> I launched the series of reforms known as "The White Revolution," and for ten years the West muted its agitation against me. However, it erupted in full force again after the 1973 oil embargo and my decision to raise world oil prices. Throughout the seventies opposition mounted and, in the end, created a strange confluence of interests—the international oil consortium, the British and American governments, the international media, reactionary religious circles in my own country, and the relentless drive of the Communists.[1]

This narrative's problems are obvious: First, the shah cannot explain why such an improbable coalition of enemies, joining British and American governments to communists, suddenly formed against him in the late 1970s. Second, blaming everything on a foreign conspiracy, the shah

1 Mohammad Reza Pahlavi, *Answer to History* (Stein and Day, 1980), 23.

refuses to admit his regime's responsibility for major failures leading to its downfall. This chapter, on the contrary, presents the prerevolutionary decade as a time of fateful choices made by the shah and his statesmen, and backed by the United States, particularly during the Nixon administration. By the mid-1970s, these choices had brought about a multifaceted crisis, whose mishandling, by the shah and the Carter administration, led to the monarchy's collapse. Though the shah exercised personal dictatorship, his regime functioned with the active participation of numerous civilian and military officials with various kinds and degrees of input and agency. As one scholar put it, "The Shah's autocracy knew certain systemic constraints. A principle one was officials shaping everyday administration and long-term policymaking. Iran was much too complex, certainly by the 1960s, to be run by an all-powerful, all-knowing monarch."[2] Recognizing the collective agency of the shah and his regime's high officials means that they could have acted differently, thus altering the course of events, and possibly averting the regime's revolutionary overthrow. In the end, and conforming to the familiar pattern of mass revolutions, Iran's ancien régime carries the main burden of responsibility for its own downfall.

Taking Off into American-Style Modernization (1960s)

> *What is going on in Iran is about the best thing going on anywhere in the world.*
>
> President Lyndon Johnson, 1964[3]

By the mid-1960s, the Johnson administration had decided the White Revolution was an unqualified success and the shah's autocratic rule was necessary to ensure Iran's stability. During Johnson's presidential tenure (1964–68), his administration routinely ignored criticism of the shah by diplomatic and intelligence sources, Iranian and American experts, and an ever-louder chorus of Iranian student protests in the United States. As early as 1965, for instance, a State Department Bureau of Intelligence and Research report had noted:

2 Cyrus Schayegh, "Mohammad Reza Shah Pahlavi's Autocracy: Government Constraints, 1960s–1970s," *Iranian Studies* 51, no. 6 (November 2018): 889–904, quoted on 899.

3 Quoted in James A. Bill, *The Eagle and the Lion: The Tragedy of American-Iranian Relations* (Yale University Press, 1988), 178.

> The present Shah is not only king; he is de facto Prime Minister and in operational command of the armed forces. He determines, or approves, all important government actions. No appointment to an important position in the bureaucracy is made without his approval. He personally directs the work of the internal security apparatus and controls the conduct of foreign affairs, including diplomatic assignments. No promotion in the armed forces from the rank of lieutenant up can be made without his explicit approval. Economic development proposals —whether to accept foreign credit or where to locate a particular factory—are referred to the shah for decision. He determines how the universities are administered, who is to be prosecuted for corruption, the selection of parliamentary deputies, the degree to which opposition will be permitted, and what bills will pass the parliament.[4]

Another 1965 report, again by the State Department's Bureau of Intelligence and Research, offered a pessimistic long-term prognosis:

> On the political side, the Shah has alienated the landlords and the clergy without winning the bulk of the reform-minded intellectuals and members of the middle-class . . . Eventually, the various opposition factions may be driven together by a common desire to limit the Shah's power. Should the Shah fail to follow through on the reforms he has begun, the opposition will have an immediate cause and may eventually also acquire the necessary popular support to unseat him.[5]

All such warnings were ignored in the Johnson White House, which was increasingly attuned to an aggressive pro-shah lobby led by Iran's Foreign Minister Ardeshir Zahedi (1966–71) and ambassador to Washington Hushang Ansary (1967–69), aided and abetted by CIA and diplomat lobbyists Kermit Roosevelt and Averell Harriman, modernization guru and Assistant National Security Advisor Walt Rostow, US Ambassador to Iran Armin Meyer (1965–69), and Iran-connected banker-businessmen David Rockefeller and David Lilienthal. By 1966, the shah was sending private messages to Washington, via Kermit Roosevelt, saying he was

4 Bureau of Intelligence and Research, US Department of State, "Studies in Political Dynamics in Iran," Secret Intelligence Report, no. 13, NSA, no. 603, quoted in Abbas Milani, *The Persian Sphinx: Amir Abbas Hoveyda and the Riddle of the Iranian Revolution* (Mage Publishers, 2000), 178–9.

5 Director of Intelligence and Research, US Department of State, "Land Reform in Iran: Implications for the Shah's 'White Revolution,'" February 8, 1965, NSA, no. 548, quoted in Milani, *The Persian Sphinx*, 169.

"tired of being treated as a schoolboy," emphasizing Iran's position as a buffer against the Soviet Union, its support of the US war in Vietnam and of Israel vis-à-vis its Arab neighbors, and its readiness to fill the military vacuum when Britain would end its military presence in the Persian Gulf. What the shah wanted was more American arms, which he could now pay for in cash, thanks to Iran's growing oil income. The Johnson administration was more than happy to oblige, while the shah would flaunt improved relations with the Soviet Union as a scare tactic to silence liberal American critics. In 1966, Tehran and Moscow signed an agreement to build a steel mill and natural gas pipelines, plus a deal for the purchase of $110 million worth of Soviet military trucks and light arms. About a year later, in 1967–68, the United States sold Iran close to $100 million worth of armaments, a figure that would triple in 1969–70. About $250 million of the latter package consisted of F-4 Phantoms, the most advanced American fighter jet, plus hundreds of air-to-air missiles, forty Iroquois helicopters, and five naval fighters and gunboats. When William Fulbright, chair of the Senate Foreign Relations Committee, raised objections to these sales, Rostow retorted they helped with the Middle East balance of power as well as the US balance of payments. In 1967 Johnson's Defense Secretary Robert McNamara wrote that foreign-arms sales to countries like Iran "have created about 1.4 million man-years of employment in the United States and over $1 billion in profits to American industry over the last five years."[6]

Meanwhile, largely fueled by growing oil revenue, Iran's Gross National Product had risen at the rate of 7 percent per year between 1963 and 1968. American-style modernization (that is, market-oriented industrialization and economic growth without political democratization) was indeed taking place. In 1968, Rostow observed that Iran had reached "that point on the development ladder where the 'take off' is just about finished and the nation is beginning to diffuse its resources and technology into broad range of new industries." The shah was on the exact same page, telling an American interviewer in 1969 that Iran no longer needed nonmilitary American aid because it "had passed the stage of countries that still need it." Echoing Rostow's language and analysis, he too pointed out that Iran had "taken off."[7] Equating economic development with urban-based industrialization, the shah would

6 Bill, *Eagle and the Lion*, 169–72, McNamara quoted on 173.

7 Rostow quoted in David R. Collier, *Democracy and the Nature of American Influence in Iran, 1941–1979* (Syracuse University Press, 2017), 241; The shah quoted in *US News and World Report*, January 27, 1969.

soon abandon the White Revolution's initial goal of rural development backed by a land-owning peasantry. In a few years, he would tell the last American ambassador: "I don't want those villages to survive. I want them to disappear. We can buy food cheaper than they can produce it. I need the people from these villages in our industrial labor force. They must come into the cities and work in industry."[8] A massive rural-urban exodus indeed took place during the 1960s–70s, but the former villagers, some of whom joined the industrial labor force, became a restless and dissatisfied urban underclass, many turning into the 1978–79 revolution's shock troops.

In 1967, with Iran no longer considered a "developing" country, the US Agency for International Development closed its Tehran office and Washington ended technical and economic assistance to Iran. Meanwhile, the shah's relationship with the United States was changing from the Kennedy-era "concubinage" to a "marriage" with the Iranian bride now endowed with an impressive oil dowry. The pillar of the new relationship was Iran's unprecedented purchase of America's most expensive and sophisticated armaments with the shah seemingly in a position to make demands on Washington. In fact, the shah's recycling of petrodollars into the coffers of American arms manufacturers was a "demand" that successive US administration would welcome and encourage. Eventually, Nixon and Kissinger would push arms-sale escalation to its logical conclusion of allowing the shah to buy anything in the American arsenal short of nuclear weapons.

Meanwhile, mainstream American media was cheerleading the White House, promoting the shah's image as a glamorous and benevolent modernizing dictator. In 1967, the year of the shah's coronation gala, *The New York Times* opined: "The Shah has been instrumental in leading the country into the modern era through land reform and other progressive programs."[9] The same year, *Time* magazine featured laudatory coverage of the shah's reforms and coronation, mentioning his dictatorship in passing and without criticism:

> The Shah's attempts at political reform have been less thorough. He reopened Parliament in 1963, but uses it mostly for window dressing. All candidates must be approved by SAVAK, his powerful security police,

8 William H. Sullivan, *Obbligato, 1939–1979: Notes on a Foreign Service Career* (W.W. Norton, 1984), 266.

9 John Ghazvinian, *America and Iran: A History, 1720 to the Present* (Knopf, 2021), 241–4, quotes on 244.

> and elections are so arranged as to give the Shah's Iran Novin (New Iran) Party an overwhelming majority of the seats. The Shah, in fact, makes little pretense of being a democrat. "For 2,500 years," he says, "we have had a monarchical system, which implies a certain amount of imposed authority." His word is law, and he keeps his Prime Minister, Amirabass Hoveida, 48, working 15 hours a day making sure that his orders are carried out. The press is controlled, and all public criticism of the Shah is forbidden by law.[10]

The US media continued its misrepresentation of the next big Iran story after the royal coronation. In 1968 Tehran hosted the United Nation's first International Conference on Human Rights, commemorating the twentieth anniversary of the 1948 Universal Declaration of Human Rights. The conference was presided over by the shah's sister Princess Ashraf, and opened with the shah's remarks, boasting of Tehran being the perfect site for such an event. This was because, he claimed, "the ancestor of the documents recognizing the rights of man was promulgated in this very country by Cyrus the Great about two thousand years ago." During the conference, families of political prisoners presented a petition to the head of the UN delegation, naming prisoners tortured in SAVAK detention centers, including one adjacent to the conference site. While the American press continued with laudatory nods to the humanitarian endeavors of the shah and his sister, other voices were pointing out the irony of the shah's regime posing as the champion of human rights. Informed by Iranian dissidents, particularly the student opposition, British philosopher Bertrand Russell noted, "The new wave of repression that has swept the country, culminating absurdly, in the world conference of human rights, held in Teheran," concluding that "after Saigon and Athens, Teheran was the least appropriate choice for such a celebration." Princess Ashraf's service at the UN, and her connection to its human rights commission, were crucial to the humanitarian image the shah liked to project internationally. But, when Ashraf began lobbying for the position of United Nations Secretary General in 1970, even the shah was embarrassed, ordering her to return from New York. Within a few

---

10 "Iran: Revolution from the Throne," *Time*, October 6, 1967. Leading newspapers, like *The New York Times*, and magazines, such as *Newsweek* and *Time*, set the tone for mainstream American media's uncritical coverage of Iran. However, serious commentary occasionally appeared in *The Washington Post* and *The Christian Science Monitor*; see William A. Dorman and Mansur Farhang, *The US Press and Iran: Foreign Policy and the Journalism of Deference* (University of California Press, 1987).

years, and mainly due to growing student opposition abroad, international public opinion would see the Iranian regime as a leading violator of human rights.[11]

While no criticism of the shah was allowed inside Iran, public indifference and official cynicism were visible beneath the official narrative spun by Prime Minister Hoveyda and his New Iran Party. The private diary of the shah's court minister and confidant Asadollah Alam reveals a loyal insider's growing anxiety about the country's drift into corruption and autocracy. In an August 1969 entry, for instance, Alam wrote:

> This afternoon, I was at the Senate, celebrating the sixty-fourth anniversary of the Constitution's inauguration. The event looked more like a funeral than a celebration. Returning home, I kept thinking how I belonged to a corrupt money-worshiping ruling class, under whose rule Iran has almost no chance of salvation.[12]

Alam was noting a malaise afflicting Iran's rapidly modernizing but politically stifling culture, acutely felt among the country's intellectuals and growing university student population. A famous expression of this malaise was the 1962 booklet titled *Plagued by the West*, whose author, Jalal Al-e-Ahmad, bemoaned the destruction of authentic Iranian identity by Western, and especially American, cultural colonialism. As we saw in chapter 3, Al-e-Ahmad had been involved, and later disillusioned, with American cultural projects such as Franklin Books. Still, he accepted an invitation to attend Harvard University's summer seminars, a program organized by Henry Kissinger for intellectual exchange among scholars, writers, and artists from Europe, Asia, and Africa. Following his wife, the writer and scholar Simin Daneshvar, Al-e-Ahmad attended the Harvard Seminar in 1965. There he presented a summary of his *Plagued by the West*, took part in discussions about American popular culture, met with civil rights activists, and came to appreciate writer Ralph Ellison's ideas on the American race problem. Though no more than a superficial exposure to American culture, this brief interaction helped broaden

11 Golnar Nikpour, "Claiming Human Rights: Iranian Political Prisoners and the Making of a Transnational Movement, 1963–1979," *Humanity: An International Journal of Human Rights, Humanitarianism, and Development* 9, no. 3 (Winter 2018): 363–88, 365–8; for the shah's 1970 outburst against his sister, see Alinaqi Alikhani, ed., *The Shah and I: The Confidential Diary of Iran's Royal Court*, 1969–77, trans. Nicholas Vincent (I.B. Tauris, 2007), 174–5.

12 Abdolreza Hushing Mahdavi, *Goftoguha-ye man ba shah: Khaterat-e mahramane-ye Amir Asdaollah Alam*, vol. 1 (Tehran: 1993), 121.

Al-e-Ahmad's intellectual horizons, as it did in the case of other Harvard visitors, such as writer and scholar Mohammad-Ali Eslami Nodushan, who attended the Harvard seminar in 1967. Meeting with Kissinger, Defense Secretary McNamara, and Senator Robert Kennedy, Nodushan would write positively of the American ability of self-reflection, while criticizing the country's race relations and intervention in Vietnam, the role of money in US politics, its media's provincialism, and the American public's lack of knowledge about the world.[13]

During the 1960s, the "Western plague" Al-e-Ahmad and other intellectuals had diagnosed was spreading through Iran's Americanized newspapers, popular magazines, and radio programs, and, increasingly, in television and the cinema. A 1971 study published by New York's Columbia University observed,

> Radio has had a formidable effect upon popular culture, where its impetus has been toward the acceleration of westernization—and more specifically Americanization—of the more superficial aspects of the life-style in urban society. In the late 1950s and early 1960s, a significant portion of the entertainment programs of Radio Iran was made up of translations of American radio detective series and "soap operas." In this area, however, television has already surpassed the radio.
>
> The commercial TVI is closely patterned after American commercial operations. Much of its program content is popular American TV series dubbed in Persian. Its locally produced programs are also largely modeled on American quiz shows and variety programs. It is essentially conceived as an entertainment medium and seems to follow the general assumption that to be entertaining it must be banal and vulgar.[14]

Television was introduced to Iran in 1958 via a private commercial station owned by businessman Habib Sabet, who also had exclusive franchise contracts with American companies, including Pepsi-Cola, General Tire, Philips (razors), Magic Chef (cookers), Kelvinator Commercial (refrigerators), Studebaker (cars), Duo-Therm (heaters), and Esso/ExxonMobil (motor oil). An indirect subsidiary of the Radio Corporation of America

---

13 Afshin Matin-Asgari, *Both Eastern and Western: An Intellectual History of Iranian Modernity* (Cambridge University Press, 2018), 182; Firoozeh Kashani-Sabet, *Heroes to Hostages: America and Iran, 1800–1988* (Cambridge University Press, 2023), 316–19.

14 Amin Banani, "The Role of the Mass Media," in *Iran Faces the Seventies*, ed. Ehsan Yarshater (Prager Publishers, 1971): 321–40, quoted on 328–9.

(RCA), Sabet's network (TVI) established a distinctly American-style television culture before being replaced by Iran's state-owned National Television in the late 1960s. It ran popular serials produced by US television networks and copied their game shows, punctured by long segments of dubbed American commercials, or their Iranian imitations, featuring Sabet-licensed and other US-made consumer items. The iconic product introduced by Sabet Enterprises was Pepsi-Cola, whose popularity also proved the success of American-style marketing as the franchise was managed and promoted by Sabet's son, who had an MBA from Harvard University.[15] By the 1960s, American-style consumer culture and marketing were already so pervasive that guerrilla opposition theorist Bijan Jazani worked as the co-owner of a company that made commercials for television and movie theaters.[16] Even Iran's proud culinary tradition was changing under the influence of American fast food, with Tehran's first pizzeria opening in 1969 by a US-educated entrepreneur who also obtained the franchise for Kentucky Fried Chicken, staffing its showcase store with the teenage children of US military personnel. Soon, hamburger, pizza, and hot dog shops were proliferating across the country, a trend that continued after the revolution, though American brand names would be replaced by close Persian imitations—McDonald's, for example, turning into MashDonalds.[17]

Nixon, Kissinger, and the Shah: Illusions of Power (1969–74)

We will give investors ample opportunity to get wealthy.

Iran's Minister of the Economy, American-Investment Conference, Tehran, 1970[18]

The 1970s marked a decade of Iran-US relations that began with a major gathering of American investors in Tehran, an event that *Time* magazine called "A Welcome for Capitalists." Between 1965 and 1970, US companies

15 Moojan Momen, "Habib Sabet," in Encyclopædia Iranica, accessed August 6, 2023, iranicaonline.org.

16 Ali Rahnema, *Call to Arms: Iran's Marxist Revolutionaries: Formation and Evolution of the Fada'is, 1964–1976* (Oneworld Academic, 2021), 131; film showings took off in the 1940s, with about four hundred movies screened annually, dominated by the United States (three hundred films). The first film magazine, published in 1943, was named *Hollywood*, Hamidreza Sadr, *Tarikh-e Siasi-ye sinema-ye Iran* (Tehran: 2002), 54–5.

17 Houchang E. Chehabi, "The Westernization of Iranian Culinary Culture," *Iranian Studies* 36. no. 1 (March 2003): 43–61, 57–8, 60.

18 Quoted in *Time*, May 25, 1970.

had invested more than $150 million in Iran—in addition to their dealings with the oil sector. In May 1970, on the shah's personal invitation, representatives of the thirty-two largest American corporations gathered in Tehran for a week-long conference looking into investment opportunities. This was the largest US private investment conference ever held in a developing country. The companies included Allied Corporation, BFGoodrich Tires, Reynolds Metals, Standard Oil of Indiana, Caterpillar Inc., Pepsi-Cola, Westinghouse, and Pan American World Airways. The main conference organizers were Time Inc. and Chase Manhattan Bank, whose president, David Rockefeller, had close personal ties to the shah and would be his banker in the United States. Borrowing leftist language and rhetoric, Ayatollah Khomeini issued a statement saying: "Any agreement that is concluded with these American capitalists and other imperialists is contrary to the will of the people and the ordinances of Islam." When a devoted student of Khomeini, a cleric named Sa'idi, openly denounced the American investors' conference, he was arrested and killed under SAVAK torture.[19]

On the political side, Washington's unconditional support of the shah was evolving into a special relationship in line with the Nixon Doctrine, which called for reliance on the military power of regional surrogates, such as Iran, to protect US strategic interests. The shah had already signaled his willingness for Iran to fill the power vacuum created by British military withdrawal from the Persian Gulf in the late 1960s. Nixon's close advisors, including CIA Director Richard Helms, had told him that a "special relationship" with Iran based on massively arming the shah as a regional hegemon served strategic US interests. Helms's connections to Iran went back to the 1950s when he had secured the shah's permission to put two clandestine American electronic posts in northern Iran to monitor Soviet missile activities.[20] But Nixon was not sure if the shah was up to the task, whether he had "got the stuff" to "fill that—the role out there, you know, in the whole darn Gulf area." In 1971, he told his advisors: "If he could do it, it'd be wonderful. Because he is our friend . . . I like him, and I like the country. And some of those other bastards out there I don't like." The shah, however, was fully in line with the Nixon Doctrine, insisting that Kissinger's "geo-political ideas coincided perfectly" with his own. Kissinger, who served as Nixon's national security advisor and later as secretary of state, returned the sentiment,

19 Bill, *Eagle and the Lion*, 180–2.

20 Roham Alvandi, *Nixon, Kissinger, and the Shah: The United State and Iran in the Cold War* (Oxford University Press, 2014), 49.

writing that "the shah's views of the realities of the world paralleled our own. Iran's influence was always on our side."[21] One scholar has recently argued that during the Nixon years, "the US-Iran patron-client relationship" changed into a relationship whereby "the Shah would remake Iran as a partner of the United States," thus becoming "the confident and independent international figure of the 1970s."[22] This argument is hard to sustain given the sudden rise and rapid fall of the shah's international standing, including his growing problems with the United States following Nixon's demise. Moreover, the shah's military interventions in Iraq and Oman (see below), though in line with the Nixon Doctrine, destabilized the region without making the shah more secure at home. Finally, as we shall see, when a revolutionary crisis hit Iran in 1978, the shah proved incapable of decisive action, instead asking Washington what to do and eventually leaving his throne on Carter's advice. This was not the behavior of a "confident and independent international figure."

The shah's most egregious intervention in a neighboring country took place against Iraq's Baath regime, which by the late 1960s had drawn close to the Soviet Union, a development that the CIA saw as no threat to Iran. Still, throughout the 1960s, the shah and Israel had been funding and providing military support to a Kurdish rebellion against the Iraqi government. In addition to the shah's flagrant intervention in Iraq, an old border dispute almost flared up into an Iran-Iraq war in the late 1960s, while in 1969–71, Iran was involved in coups attempts against the Baghdad regime. Following Nixon's 1972 visit to Tehran, the United States joined the shah's intervention in Iraq with the CIA covertly sending funds and weapons to the Kurds through Iran. Helms's role in coordinating the CIA-Iran-Israel intervention in Iraq continued when he became ambassador to Tehran in 1973. The operation's objective was to arm and support Kurdish rebels to pin down the Iraqi army without allowing them a decisive military victory. This cynical policy was seen by some CIA analysists as contrary to American, Iranian, and Kurdish interests and later was criticized during the 1976 congressional hearings on the Nixon administration's covert operations. In the end, Iraq's military power stiffened with its growing oil income, and, by 1975, Baghdad and Tehran signed an agreement resolving their border dispute and the

---

21 Nixon, the shah, and Kissinger quoted in ibid., 58–9.

22 Ibid., 26–7. The scholarly consensus remains on the side of earlier studies, such as Bill's *The Eagle and the Lion*, that see the shah's relationship with Nixon and Kissinger making Iran more dependent on the United States.

shah ceased support of the Kurdish uprising.[23] Historians rarely note how the shah's military adventurism in Iraq, his attempts at overthrowing its government, and the 1975 treaty he imposed on Baghdad shaped the background to the hostilities that would lead to the Iran-Iraq War of the 1980s. Following his Iraqi adventure, the shah's direct military intervention, per the Nixon Doctrine, occurred in defense of the Sultanate of Oman against an insurgency in 1972–76. The shah sent naval detachments, helicopter gunships and several thousand troops to put down leftist guerrillas fighting in Oman's Dhofar province. Iran admitted to having lost twenty-five officers and close to two hundred troops before crushing the Dhofar rebellion after which it continued to keep bases in Oman and to patrol its air and sea borders.[24]

Arriving as US ambassador in 1973, Helms made sure no critical reports of the shah's foreign or domestic policies emerged from the embassy or CIA sources. According to Henry Precht, the embassy's chief political officer, "Henry Kissinger and Nixon didn't want to know that the Shah had any problems domestically . . . it was assumed that the country people loved the Shah." Consequently, instead of independent intelligence gathering, the CIA began to rely on the SAVAK for information on Iran. As one State Department official put it, one did not "report on an ally once he's become 'The Chosen Instrument.'"[25] The occasionally critical reports emerging from the Tehran embassy or CIA headquarters were suppressed or ignored. In 1976 a press officer at the embassy resigned after his report on SAVAK torture was suppressed, while CIA analysts in Langley, Virginia, were told not to write about torture.[26] Thus, if there was a US intelligence failure in Iran, it was due to a deliberately blindsided policy, which, particularly under Nixon, placed constraints even on the CIA. Shortly after the shah's fall, a State Department analysis concluded, "We were unprepared for the collapse of the Pahlavi regime because we did not want to know the truth."[27] The CIA's intelligence failure in Iran was matched by the KGB's, whose sources operated within the similar framework of the Soviet Union's positive relations with the shah. Though unhappy with the shah's role

23 Fred Halliday, *Iran: Dictatorship and Development* (Penguin Books, 1979), 274–6; Alvandi, *Nixon, Kissinger, and the Shah*, 72, 84–91.

24 Halliday, *Iran: Dictatorship and Development*, 271.

25 Collier, *Democracy*, 251, 253.

26 Transcript of "60 Minutes," vol. XII, no. 25, a broadcast over the CBS Television Network (March 2, 1980), 3–5.

27 Charles Kurzman, *The Unthinkable Revolution in Iran* (Harvard University Press, 2004), 4

as the "policeman" of the Persian Gulf, per the Nixon Doctrine, the Soviets had steered clear of interference in Iran's domestic affairs. Like the Americans, they were surprised by the sudden emergence of a revolutionary situation in 1978 Iran. Nor did the Soviets play any role in the events leading to shah's overthrow, their major response being Secretary General Leonid Brezhnev's official statement on November 19, 1978, warning against foreign intervention in Iran, a message obviously addressing the United States.[28]

One scholarly study has argued that the shah's fall and the Iranian Revolution were "unthinkable" before they happened and remain inexplicable afterward. This is true as far as all revolutions, and their precise outcomes, are unpredictable. On the other hand, an Iranian revolution was in fact widely anticipated in the decade that preceded it.[29] During the 1970s, growing opposition to the shah was visible on the ground in Iran and loudly broadcast in the United States, mainly by thousands of Iranians studying there. A small but tenacious revolutionary guerrilla movement shook the shah's regime, while thousands of student militants in Iran and abroad aspired to Russian, Cuban, or Chinese-style revolution. Meanwhile, by the mid-1970s, not only mainstream news media but US Congress were concerned about the stability of the shah's repressive one-man rule. Washington's official myth of Iranian tranquility reinforced the shah's illusion of power, which, by the early 1970s, bordered on a disconnect to reality. The shah's delusional mindset was on display in interviews with foreign reporters, such as his declarations in a 1973 conversation with Italian journalist Oriana Fallaci.

> I believe in God, in the fact of having been chosen by God to accomplish a mission. My visions and miracles have saved the country. My reign has saved the country and it's saved it because God was beside me . . . If you're asking me who I consider our best friend, the answer is the United States . . . I get along with Nixon . . . only if I'm sure that he's treating me as a friend. In fact, as a friend who within a few years will represent a world power . . .[30]

---

28 Dmitry Asinovskiy, "'A Priest does not consider the toppling of the Shah as an option'; the KGB and the revolution in Iran," *Iranian Studies* 55 (2022): 929–51; Brezhnev's declaration, 938.

29 Kurzman, *Unthinkable Revolution in Iran.*

30 The shah quoted in Oriana Fallaci, *Interview with History*, trans. John Shepley (Houghton Mifflin, 1976), 268, 280.

Fallaci, who liked to psychoanalyze her interviewees, diagnosed the shah as "a highly dangerous megalomaniac" who believed himself "the reincarnation of Darius and Xerxes, sent to earth to rebuild their lost empire."[31] The shah's neo-imperial self-perception was globally showcased during the 1971 gala celebrations of twenty-five hundred years of Iranian monarchy, attended by heads of states from dozens of countries and recorded in the *Guinness World Records* as the most lavish official banquet in modern history. During the ceremony's peak moment, the shah stood by the tomb of Cyrus and delivered a pompous speech, whose punchline "Rest in Peace, Cyrus, We Are Awake" quickly became the target of popular jokes about his megalomania.[32] The celebration was so embarrassing and wasteful that even *Newsweek* would comment that "more serious critics found it staggering that the shah would spend $11 million of his country's money on food and liquor for some of the wealthiest people in the world when poverty and starvation still exist in Iran."[33]

In the aftermath of Iran's exploding post-1973 oil income, the shah gained such confidence that he even considered defying Nixon's request for consultation before further raising oil prices in OPEC. "Nixon," he said to his confidant Alam, "has the audacity to tell me to do nothing in the interest of my country until he dictates where that interest lies . . . I say to hell with such special relations . . . We shall accept no further advice from friend or foe."[34] A summer 1973 visit to the United States, however, restored the shah's faith in Nixon and he assured Alam: "The Americans gave me whatever I asked for." Still, tensions with Washington concerning the price of oil would flare up under the new administration of Gerald Ford with whom the shah maintained a collaborative relationship, believing the "devil Kissinger" continued to run US foreign policy. In private, however, the shah was arrogantly contemptuous of Ford, calling him "a hopeless old donkey."[35] After Nixon's fall, however, tensions with the United States grew more serious. By 1975 Defense

31 Ibid., 264.

32 Historians consider the 1971 celebrations a major indication of the regime's wastefulness and disconnect to reality. See, for example, Abbas Amanat, *Iran: A Modern History* (Yale University Press, 2017), 664–6. For an unconvincing attempt at finding positive silver linings in the 1971 celebrations, see Robert Steetle, *The Shah's Imperial Celebrations of 1971: Nationalism, Culture and Politics in Late Pahlavi Iran* (I.B. Tauris, 2022).

33 "Iran's Birthday Party," *Newsweek*, October 25, 1971.

34 Alikhani, *Shah and I*, 277.

35 The shah quoted in ibid., 308, 442.

Secretary James Schlesinger would ask President Ford to review the arms sales policy to Iran, questioning whether supporting the shah's open-ended military buildup served long-term US interests. But, as the shah had correctly predicted, Kissinger managed to contain the criticism of America's shah-centric Iran policy.[36]

The major impetus behind growing international criticism of the shah during the 1970s was the Iranian student opposition in Europe and the United States. As we saw in chapter 3, a significant minority of the student population abroad was politically active against the shah's dictatorship, closely aligning itself with growing unrest on Iranian university campuses. A 1971–72 official survey of seventy-seven thousand students in Iranian universities reflected their critical stance toward the United States. Most respondents complained about the lack of freedom, while believing that living conditions for all classes had improved. Asked which foreign country they would choose for studying, an overwhelming majority named the United States, mainly because of its scientific accomplishments, while only a small minority reported attraction to American social life and cultural values.[37] The same year, a US embassy report noted young Iranians were highly critical of the United States, particularly because they linked government repression and SAVAK activities to the United States and the CIA.[38] Political protest on Iranian university campuses intensified during the 1960s and surged with the start of guerrilla armed actions in the early 1970s. By this time, even the American-style, elite Pahlavi University in Shiraz was experiencing strikes, described by an American visiting professor:

> At present, most Iranian universities are on strike, a fact unnoticed in the Western press, because the news from Iran is so effectively controlled... In late May of 1970, for example, a strike occurred at Pahlavi University ... Subsequently, the army was called in to restore order; students were beaten indiscriminately, and more than seventy-five were arrested.

Ironically, this strike was witnessed by thirty American exchange students from Kent State University in Ohio where, earlier the same month,

36 Gary Sick, *All Fall Down: America's Tragic Encounter with Iran* (Random House, 1985), 17–18.

37 Moretza Nasfat, *Sanjesh-e afkar-e daneshjuyan-e keshvar* (University of Tehran Publishers, 1975), 7, 99, 126, 212, 221, 320.

38 "Youth in Iran: Assessment by Embassy Youth Committee," from the Embassy in Iran to the United States, February 22, 1971, cited in Kashani-Sabet, *America and Iran*, 324–5.

the US National Guard had fired on anti-Vietnam war protesters, killing four and injuring nine students.[39]

By the end of the decade, Iran had at least sixty-seven thousand university students abroad, ranking first in the world. The bulk of this population, between fifty thousand to fifty-four thousand, studied in the United States where they formed the largest foreign student body. According to various estimates, including those by the Iranian government, roughly ten percent of students abroad were members or supporters of the Confederation of Iranian Students, National Union (see chapter 3). This was an exceptionally strong degree of affiliation with a student organization declared illegal in 1971, its members facing prison terms of three to ten years.[40] Active in the United States and about a dozen European countries, and at times even in Eastern Europe, organized Iranian student opposition grew both in size and political clout through the 1960s–70s. During nearly two decades of increasingly militant activism, and working with international student groups, media outlets, and human rights organizations, the Iranian student opposition led a global campaign exposing and delegitimizing the shah's dictatorship.[41] The student opposition in the United States also produced a scholarly spinoff, namely the Society for Iranian Studies, formed in 1967 by young American and Iranians academics, the latter including several student-movement veterans. Avoiding direct political engagement, this organization launched the quarterly journal *Iranian Studies* and went on to become the leading international association dedicated to the scholarly study of Iran.[42]

The mainstream American academic establishment, however, had a largely uncritical and at times servile attitude toward the shah's regime and its relations with the United States. Throughout the 1960s–70s, the Iranian government provided leading American universities, including Harvard, MIT, Princeton, University of Southern California, and Georgetown, with large grants and lucrative contracts that only a few institutions,

39 G. H. Muller, "Shah vs. Bureaucrats," *Nation*, February 22, 1971, 240–4.

40 *Amar-e Amuzesh-e ali –e Iran* [Statistics of Higher Education in Iran] (Institute of Research and Planning for Higher Education, 1975), 1, 3; Afshin Matin-Asgari, *Iranian Student Opposition to the Shah* (Mazda Publishers, 2002), 131.

41 Matin-Asgari, *Iranian Student Opposition to the Shah*, 163–4.

42 Matthew K. Shannon, "Reading Iran: American Academics and the Last Shah," *Iranian Studies* 51 no. 2 (March 2018): 289–316, 298–300; Ali Banuazizi, "Forty Years on: A Note by the Founding Editor," *Iranian Studies* 40, no. 1 (February 2007): 1–4; Naghmeh Sohrabi, "MERIP's First Decade of Iran Coverage from Political Challenge to Revolution," *MERIP* 300 (fall 2021), merip.org.

such as the University of Chicago, turned down. In return the grantee universities bestowed honorary degrees on the shah and Queen Farah and produced scholarly studies of Iran that were by and large favorable. The 1970s, for example, opened with *Iran Faces the Seventies*, the proceedings of an international scholarly conference at Columbia University offering uncritical surveys of economic and cultural trends without a single chapter on Iran-US relations. In 1975 the Pahlavi Foundation gave a $750,000 grant to the Aspen Institute for Humanistic Studies to organize another international conference on Iran's development, this time at Persepolis outside of Shiraz. The result was *Iran: Past, Present and Future* (1976), another uncritical tome published just as Iran was sliding into an acute economic and political crisis. On the eve of the revolution in 1978, the conservative Hoover Institution Press published *Iran under the Pahlavis*, another uncritical collection of articles edited by cold warrior Iran expert George Lenczowski.[43]

Meanwhile, the coverage of the shah's regime in the US news media was becoming gradually less laudatory and, by the mid-1970s, serious criticism appeared even in the mainstream press. With Nixon's fall, the no-questions-asked "special relationship" he and Kissinger had forged with the shah came under congressional scrutiny, as Iran's push for higher oil prices and stockpiling of US armaments appeared destabilizing to the Middle East and a potential threat to American security. In November 1974, *Harper's Magazine* ran Frances FitzGerald's article, "Giving the Shah Everything He Wants," warning against the kind of entanglement with Iran she had covered in her Pulitzer Prize–winning *Fire in the Lake: The Vietnamese and the Americans in Vietnam*. In December, *New York* magazine published "The Coming Oil War: How the Shah Will Win the World," imagining an unhinged shah using his US military hardware to seize all the oil in the Middle East, causing the collapse of the world economy. The writer Paul Erdman then developed the same plot into a 1976 bestselling novel, *The Crash of '79*. For his part, up until the mid-1970s, the shah arrogantly dismissed all unfavorable foreign media coverage. For instance, responding to a critical 1974 *Washington Post* article, he told Alam: "Whether they are for or against us, it makes not a blind bit of difference to our conduct of policy. Who do you suppose brought Iran to its current state of grandeur: foreign

43 Bill, *Eagle and the Lion*, 352–3, 373–4; Ehsan Yarshater, ed., *Iran Faces the Seventies* (Prager Publishers, 1971); Jane W. Jacqz, *Iran: Past, Present, and Future* (Aspen Institute for Humanistic Studies, 1976); George Lenczowski, *Iran Under the Pahlavis* (Hoover Institution publication, 1978).

journalists or myself?" And he was amused while reading Erdman's fictional account of Iran's takeover of all Middle East oil.[44] The shah even tried to control the US news media. Believing, for example, that popular television interviewer Mike Wallace had lured him into giving incriminatory answers, he asked the US ambassador to stop the interview's broadcast on CBS television.[45]

Soon, however, the shah was forced to change tactics as the critical scrutiny of Iran policy moved beyond the press to US Congress. By 1975, and in the aftermath of the Watergate scandal, Congress was trying to regain the constitutional powers Nixon had usurped during his "imperial presidency." It launched an investigation into the criminal activities of the FBI and the CIA while asserting legislative oversight of foreign policy in matters such as arms sales to Iran. These developments coincided with growing international attention to human rights abuses in Iran. As a recent study has shown, the case of Iran, brought to international attention largely by the dissident student movement abroad, played a major role in the emerging prominence of the global human rights movement during the 1960s–70s.[46] Amnesty International's 1974–75 report ranked the shah's regime among the world's most repressive governments, its secretary general declaring: "No country in the world has a worse record in human rights than Iran." From this point onward, the shah would face tough questions about his regime's torture and human rights violations in almost every American press or television interview.[47] Famous American artists, novelists, playwrights, poets, scholars, and civil rights activists were now speaking out against torture and repression in Iran in publications like *The New York Review of Books* and *The Village Voice*.[48]

44 The shah in Alikhani, *Shah and I*, 373, 400. The same year, another fictional account, *A Bullet for the Shah*, by Allan Williams, was published by Popular Library in the United States.

45 Document 31, February 19, 1974 in Abbas Milani, ed., *A Window into Modern Iran: The Ardeshir Zahedi Papers at the Hoover Institution Library & Archives* (Hoover Institution Press, 2019).

46 Golnar Nikpour, *The Incarcerated Modern: Prisons and Public Life in Iran* (Stanford University Press, 2024), chapter 4; see also Nikpour, "Claiming Human Rights."

47 Amnesty International cited in Matin-Asgari, *Iranian Student Opposition to the Shah*, 151; see also *US Congressional Record*, March 4, 1975; March 12, 1975; and June 18, 1975.

48 Novelists and playwrights Arthur Miller, Philip Roth, E. L. Doctorow, Ken Kesey, folk singer Joan Baez, scholars Noam Chomsky, Howard Zinn, Paul Sweezy, Erich Fromm, Kate Millet, antiwar activist David Dellinger, poets Allen Ginsberg and Lawrence Ferlinghetti; see Javier Gil Guerrero, *The Carter Administration & the Fall of Iran's Pahlavi Dynasty* (Palgrave Macmillan, 2016), 134; list of endorsees of Committee for Artistic and Intellectual freedom in Iran: Marxists Internet Archive, marxists.org; *Village Voice*, February 2, 1976; July 11, 1977; and July 18, 1977.

A few academic experts like James Bill and Richard Cottam were writing critically about Iran, while scholar-activist and former Iran Peace Corps volunteer Tom Ricks would testify before Congress that "the interest of the King is diametrically opposed to the interest of the Iranian People" and that "the last 50 years of Iran's history is a history of continuous and systematic violations of human and civil rights."[49]

By the second half of the 1970s, the shah was forced to change his attitude of arrogant denial in the face of growing critical foreign media coverage. After a 1975 ABC television interview mentioned SAVAK torture, he ordered a comprehensive public relations response. Believing that "the Jewish press in the USA is solely responsible for our poor publicity," he reached out to Israeli intelligence and hired an American consulting firm to help improve his regime's international image via the influence of Washington's "Jewish lobby."[50] The consulting firm reported that Iran's negative public image in the United States was based on the strategy of "merely having close relations with Kissinger and the State Department or handing out free caviar and party invitations to particular senators." It concluded that the Iranian government had to find new friends in Washington now that both Nixon and Kissinger were gone. Subsequently, the shah reined in Ambassador Ardeshir Zahedi, who had become infamous for handing out lavish gifts to politicians and turning the Iranian embassy into a party scene akin to the Playboy Mansion.[51] In January 1975, London's *Sunday Times* published "Torture in Iran," describing SAVAK's torture methods, including the burning of victims with a heated iron frame. The article also mentioned how the CIA restored the shah to power in 1953.[52] By 1976, mainstream US press was reporting that there were tens of thousands of political prisoners in Iran, many of whom were tortured, while *The Washington Post* published exposes of SAVAK operations against Iranian students in the United States.[53] The same year, a US congressional investigation reported: "In 1953, the CIA organized and directed the coup which overthrew Premier Mohammad

49 Matthew Shannon, "Reading Iran: American Academics and the Last Shah," *Iranian Studies* 51, no. 2 (March 2018): 289–316, 300; Thomas M. Ricks, "US Military Missions to Iran, 1943–1978: The Political Economy of Military Assistance," *Iranian Studies*, 12, no. 3/4 (summer– autumn, 1979): 163–93.

50 Alikhani, *Shah and I*, 427.

51 Ibid., 507–8, 524; Milani, *Window into Modern Iran*, document 34; on Christmas 1976 caviar presents from the royal family to the Ford, Nixon, and Johnson families, and from Zahedi to Vice President Rockefeller's family.

52 *Sunday Times*, January 19, 1975.

53 "Torture as Policy, the Network of Evil," *Time*, August 15, 1976, 31–4; "Iranian Secret Police Dirty Tricks," *Washington Post*, October 29, 1976.

Mossadegh and returned the shah to the throne. Mosaddegh had nationalized the Iranian oil industry, but after he was overthrown American companies for the first time were permitted to tap Iran's oil deposits."[54] In October 1976, the shah gave another interview to Mike Wallace on a widely watched CBS television program. During the interview, the shah admitted that SAVAK spied on Iranian students in the United States with the knowledge of the American government and that Iranian political prisoners had been tortured, a practice he claimed was stopped. At some point, Wallace quoted from a CIA psychological study describing the shah as "a brilliant but dangerous megalomaniac who is likely to pursue his own aims in disregard of US interests." The shah retorted: "Would you like me to be a stooge?" The interview was a public relations disaster, showing the shah was still acting on impulse, unable to take advice from his Israeli and American public relations advisors.[55]

The US media and Congress were now concerned not only with the shah's massive US-made arsenal but about its potential backlash affecting tens of thousands of Americans, particularly the military personnel in Iran. Between 1944 and 1979, an estimated total of eight hundred thousand to eight hundred and fifty thousand Americans had visited or lived in Iran. By the mid-1970s, approximately fifty thousand Americans lived in Iran, most of them civilians and about ten thousand working for corporations like Bell Helicopter, Lockheed, General Electric, and Rockwell International in military and intelligence-related projects. Many were "recent byproducts of the Vietnam War," relocating to Iran with their families and becoming "a particularly disruptive element in United States-Iran relations."[56] Americans lived mainly in Tehran and Esfahan, mostly in their own closed communities, but some had settled in the capital's more affluent suburbs known as "little America." There, they could grab pizza and Kentucky Fried Chicken, dance at exclusive discotheques, or relax at the Pars American Club, a huge entertainment complex with the largest swimming pool in the Middle East and a bar that could have been in any major American city. Tehran's American School enrolled thirty-five hundred students in twelve grades, offering sports events such as American football matches on weekends.[57] The

---

54 *Los Angeles Times*, February 22, 1976, part I, 25.

55 Quoted in Alikhani, *Shah and I*, 515; see excerpts of Mike Wallace interview, "The Shah on Israel, Corruption Torture and . . .," *New York Times*, October 24, 1976.

56 Bill, *Eagle and the Lion*, 381; *Newsweek*, November 20, 1978, 67; gives 41,000 in 1978; Sullivan's figures are 35,000, quote on 80, "Iran's Arsenal Raises Questions for US," *LA Times*, August 24, 1975, part 1, 5.

57 *Newsweek*, November 20, 1978, 67.

school was opened in 1954 and enrolled only Americans, teaching a curriculum that excluded Iranian history, culture, or languages. Americans lived north of a main thoroughfare that ran by the US embassy and divided the modern and affluent north Tehran from the poorer and more traditional south. They shopped at an American commissary adjacent to the US embassy, the largest department store run by the US government overseas. Each year, the commissary imported about two thousand items, including tons of American liquor, cigarettes, deodorant, pet food, and Coca-Cola, whose Iranian-made brand was not "the real thing." The great majority of Americans thus lived in a cultural and political bubble, which reinforced their detachment and prejudices vis-à-vis Iran and Iranians. According to one US resident in 1970s Iran: "Americans insisted on living here exactly as they lived in the United States. On the other hand, when Iranians go to America, they are expected to live there exactly as Americans live . . . Americans have a definite superiority complex, and Iranians know it. Many deeply resent it."[58] Another US resident in Tehran boasted: "I don't live in Iran. I live in little America." Meanwhile, at least one Iranian enjoyed life in the United States exactly as the most affluent Americans did. Crown Prince Reza Pahlavi lived in a $265,000 house in Lubbock, Texas, cruising around town in his Lincoln Continental or Jaguar. Training as a US Airforce cadet, he had piloted a supersonic F-5 fighter jet before turning eighteen. In a press interview, the crown prince mentioned Iranian student protests in the United States saying, "I want to help these people, and I don't know why, instead of coming to me, they hide themselves and put masks on their faces." Responding to him, a student leader said: "Who is he that we should talk with him? The problem is not going to be solved by this stupid baby."[59]

Until the early 1970s, the American community in Iran had lived rather peacefully with only a few cases of serious tension with the local population. A few months before the dramatic launch of their armed operations in 1971, a small guerrilla team tried to kidnap US Ambassador Douglas MacArthur II when he was returning home from a late-night meeting with Court Minister Alam. The guerrillas sprayed the ambassador's car with machine-gun bullets and tried to break into it with an axe, but the driver managed to whisk away MacArthur and his wife. Alam and MacArthur had been discussing the shah's request to purchase American naval destroyers and to train Iranian military pilots in the United

58 Bill, *Eagle and the Lion*, 378–89.
59 *Newsweek*, November 20, 1978, 66–7.

States.[60] In October 1971, Iran's Consulate General in San Francisco was bombed, following its occupation earlier that year by students protesting the twenty-five hundred years of monarchy celebrations in Iran. In January 1972, bombs detonated behind US embassy walls and at the Iran-America Society in Tehran, injuring their guards. During Nixon's May 1972 visit, the Iran-America Society and the US Information Office, as well as the corporate offices of Pepsi-Cola, General Motors, and Marine Oil were bombed, while another explosion shook the mausoleum of the shah's father just prior to Nixon's arrival. There were eight additional bombings and the guerrillas tried to gun down General Harold Price, the head of the US military mission in Iran. Nixon, who privately told the shah he would like to see student protesters executed, was greeted by rock-throwing students as his motorcade passed by University of Tehran.[61] In January 1973, US Ambassador Joseph Farland wrote back home that "perhaps the group most thoroughly opposed to the shah and his regime are students, inside and outside Iran, and the terrorists for whom they provide a fertile field for recruitment." Farland also noted "the students' one real success" was "to influence international opinion in their favour."[62] The same year, guerrillas bombed the Tehran offices of Pan American World Airways and assassinated Colonel Lewis Hawkins, the deputy chief of the US military mission. In 1974, during Kissinger's visit, they bombed the International Telephone and Telegraph's offices and sent a letter to the US embassy threatening to kill four Americans for every Iranian executed by the regime.[63] By this time, the American press was taking notice of the cycle of SAVAK repression and guerrilla violence in Iran. *Newsweek*, for example, published an October 1974 article titled "Quiet . . . SAVAK is Listening," while, in March 1975, *The New York Times* would write, "Iranians to whom all possibility of freedom of expression and cultural identity is denied have no other choice but to resort to armed resistance."[64] By 1976, even the American Peace Corps'

---

60 Ali Rahnema, *Call to Arms: Iran's Marxist Revolutionaries: Formation and Evolution of the Fada'is, 1964–1976* (Oneworld Academic, 2021), 230; Alikhani, *Shah and I*, 177.

61 Ervand Abrahamian, *The Iranian Mojahedin* (Yale University Press, 1989), 140; Alikhani, *Shah and I*, 224–5.

62 Rahnema, *Call to Arms*, 413.

63 Abrahamian, *The Iranian Mojahedin*, 141–2; Rahnema, *Call to Arms*, 474–5, 477–8.

64 "Iran Accused," *New York Times*, February 29, 1976, 5; Reza Baraheni, *Crowned Cannibals: Writings on Repression in Iran* (Vintage, 1977); "Quiet, SAVAK May Be Listening," *Chicago Tribune*, January 3, 1975, A4; Philip Jacobson, "Torture in Iran," *Sunday Times*, January 19, 1975.

relatively benign presence became a target of the guerrillas, who blew up the entrance to its Tehran office. The deadliest and most spectacular attack on Americans occurred on August 28, 1976, the anniversary of the 1953 CIA coup, when the guerrillas assassinated Donald Smith, Robert Krongard, and William Cottrell, employees of Rockwell International Corporation. The incident was vividly described by Ambassador Helms:

> A red VW pulled into the front of the car (carrying the Rockwell employees) and a minibus rammed it from the rear. Three or four men came over the wall; one went to the front and told the driver to lie down. The driver put his head up and was told to lie down again. Then the man fired through the front, killing Cottrell (one of the employees), who fell out of the car on the ground and moved his hand. One of the men came and fired point-blank into his face.
>
> After shooting the two in the back seat through the rear window somebody reached in with a pistol and shot each of them in the face. All three had powder burns in the face.
>
> One of the pistols was a stolen pistol from the United States Military Assistance Advisory Group (MAAG), the other one was believed, from the cartridge cases, to be a Browning. The people were armed with Polish submachine guns. There were about 43 rounds of expended ammunition on the ground. They escaped in a third car. The job was professional with the same modus operandi as in the past.[65]

SAVAK identified the attackers as members of an underground Marxist organization. But Helms, who was aware of this, chose to go along with the shah's insistence on attributing guerrilla operations to Iran's foreign enemies. The three Americans worked on a CIA project called IBEX, a $500,000 secret surveillance system started in 1975 in a deal with Rockwell Corporation. Fifteen CIA operatives, working undercover as employees of the United States Advisory Team in Iran, ran the highly sophisticated intelligence-gathering project. The IBEX system used airborne radar and cameras, using an extremely expensive computer network which the US government had found unreliable. The ultimate value of IBEX, therefore, remained unproven, causing the shah to angrily complain about deception by the American side.[66]

65 Bob Woodward, "IBEX: Deadly Symbol of US Arms Sales Problems," *Washington Post*, January 2, 1977.

66 Ibid.; Bill, *Eagle and the Lion*, 400–2.

Carter and the Shah: Was the Revolution Unthinkable? (1976–79)

> *Iran, because of the great leadership of the shah, is an island of stability in one of the more troubled areas of the world.*
>
> President Carter, toasting the shah in Tehran on New Year's Eve, 1978

By the second half of the 1970s, the shah's blundering response to a host of domestic and foreign challenges was destabilizing his regime. In 1974–75, the economy was spinning out of control, while the decade-long political machinations of Prime Minister Hoveyda and his New Iran Party seemed increasingly irrelevant. The explosive rise of oil income during the early 1970s, quadrupling to over $20 billion in 1973–74, had caused runaway inflation, which, along with widespread corruption, massive military expenditures, numerous wasteful infrastructure projects, including a nuclear energy grid, eroded the benefits of social welfare programs like free public health and education.[67] In addition to structural economic and political problems, a hidden destabilizing factor was the shah's 1974 diagnosis of a potentially terminal illness, forcing him to consider his departure from the scene. The combination of these factors, as well as growing tension with the United States, meant that some change was necessary. In 1975, therefore, the shah unleashed a flurry of political and economic initiatives, which proved ill-conceived and plunged his regime deeper into crisis. The fundamental flaw, as usual, was the autocratic frame of crisis management, with the shah making strategic decisions without consulting anyone. The obvious solution to managing the multifaceted crisis, and possibly securing his dynasty, would have been to restore constitutional government. This was what both religious and secular opposition, including segments of the left, were demanding and what the shah finally accepted, but too late as the entire regime was crumbling by the end of 1978.[68] During the second half of the 1970s, however, the shah consolidated autocracy instead of taking steps toward constitutional governance. In 1975 he dropped the pretense of a multi-party system and declared Iran a single-party state with himself as its spiritual, as well as political, leader. Launched in 1975, the Resurrection Party's rhetoric, organization, and goals were a bizarre mixture

67 For a well-informed contemporary account of 1970s Iran's economic meltdown, see Robert Graham, *Iran: The Illusion of Power* (St. Martin's Press, 1978).

68 Not only the Tudeh Party, but a faction of the guerrilla movement, led by Bijan Jazani, advocated a broad "anti-dictatorial" front, encompassing almost all opposition groups. Rahnema, *Call to Arms*, 306–7, 320.

of modernization theory and pseudo-Marxism. Appropriately, it was jointly led by ex-communists and graduates of American universities steeped in modernization theory.[69]

As observers like Alam feared, instead of stabilizing the political system, the Resurrection Party unleashed destabilizing ripples escalating all the way to the 1978–79 Revolution. The shah now placed his "imperial system" above both the constitution and Islam, changing the Islamic calendar to an imperial one, originating with the reign of Cyrus. Thus, in 1976, Iranians suddenly were transported from the Islamic calendar year 1355 to the imperial year 2535, the latter date adding the shah's thirty-five-year rule to the twenty-five hundred years since the founding of Cyrus's empire. Such foolhardy policies further antagonized Muslim and clerical opposition while disorienting and angering ordinary Iranians. To tame runaway inflation, land and real estate speculation was outlawed, thus preventing ordinary entrepreneurs from sharing the spoils of the oil boom, something the royal family and its cronies would enjoy without hinderance. Another blow to the business community was the price control and antiprofiteering campaign. Trying to deflect blame for economic hardships caused by his own grandiose policies, the shah declared "class war" on small and large businessman and bazaar merchants who lacked royal connections. Step-by-step, he was bringing together the multiclass coalition that would rebel against him in 1978, joining its right and left factions.[70]

Despite a deep recession and budget deficits, Iran's purchases of American military hardware continued upward. In 1975, Tehran and Washington ratified a $15 billion five-year trade deal, described by its American architect Kissinger as "the largest agreement of its kind that has been signed between two countries." In addition to $10 billion in trade and military purchases, the agreement committed the United States to building eight Iranian nuclear power plants at an initial cost of $7 billion with a multi-billion-dollar addition in the following years.[71] By the end of 1976, however, even the shah was admitting to economic failures and public dissatisfaction, telling his confidant Alam: "We're broke. Everything seems doomed to grind to a standstill." Alam bluntly responded:

69 Matin-Asgari, *Both Eastern and Western*, 233–5.

70 Ibid., 35–6.

71 "Iran Will Spend $15-Billion in US Over Five Years," *New York Times*, March 5, 1975; see also "On Curbing Freedom of Expression in Iran," *New York Times*, August 2, 1975.

> How else can I describe the way we ourselves have stirred up the people against us by our shortcomings? . . . Prolonged power-cuts right across the country, occasioning slow-down in industrial output and serious financial losses; dreadful communications; shortages of every essential foodstuff save bread; a total disregard for the public's needs; soaring inflation; the promulgation of new decrees without any preparation or waring . . . It is the government itself which deserves to be regarded as the chief agent of subversion.[72]

The shah's escalating problems in 1977 coincided with the first year in office of Jimmy Carter, followed by Iran's rapid slide into a prerevolutionary crisis in 1978 and eventually the shah's effective abdication, on Carter's recommendation, by the end of that year. As noted at the beginning of this chapter, apologists for the Pahlavi monarchy, including the shah, have blamed its fall on a US conspiracy presumably because the shah had become too independent and powerful. But, as we saw throughout this chapter, though occasionally acting erratically, the shah never deviated from Washington's strategic policy line, while his fall deprived the United States of multi-billion-dollar trade deals, destabilized the Middle East, and brought to power a regime radically hostile toward the United States. It is hard to imagine why the United States would have wanted to overthrow the shah. Conspiracy theories notwithstanding, almost all contemporary observers, as well as historians ever since, have seen the shah's relentless and misguided autocratic rule as the primary cause of his regime's structural weakness and eventual collapse. At the same time, long-term American policy priorities contributed to the shah's fall and the Iranian Revolution in a different way. For decades, successive American administrations were promoters and beneficiaries of the shah's autocracy, hence bearing significant responsibility for its rise and fall. As we see below, the Carter administration had its share of this responsibility because of its support of the shah's autocracy, neglecting Iran's deepening crisis in 1977, confusing the shah with mixed messages in 1978, and ultimately abandoning him to forge relations with Ayatollah Khomeini's camp.

In 1977 the incoming Carter administration and the shah missed their last chance to effect meaningful political change in Iran—an option that would slip away in 1978. During his presidential campaign, Carter had promised to end support for repressive American allies and to make

72 Alikhani, *Shah and I*, 535, 536–7.

respect for "human rights" the cornerstone of US foreign policy.[73] Aligning himself with the shah's critics in Congress, he specifically criticized the Nixon-Kissinger policy of unrestrained arms sales to Iran. This made the shah anxious about the future of his "special relationship" with the United States forged under the Nixon and Ford administrations. At the same time, Carter's election gave hope to Iran's liberal constitutionalist opposition that the shah might tolerate some degree of political dissent. The shah was already taking steps toward softening his regime's worst excesses, partly in response to growing criticism in the US Congress and media and in part due to his awareness of growing dissatisfaction with his failing policies at home. In early 1977, anticipating pressure from Carter, he made a few notable political gestures. Press censorship was slightly relaxed, some political prisoners were freed, torture was stopped, and international human rights organizations were allowed to visit Iranian prisons. While the 1977 emergence of moderate opposition in Iran is often attributed to Carter's election, it had started at least a year earlier, with the 1975–76 open circulation of grievance letters and petitions, by both individual dissidents and associations of lawyers and writers, all demanding constitutional government. Tolerated by the regime, this form of protest culminated in a summer 1977 open letter to the shah by three prominent National Front leaders, warning of grave consequences unless constitutional government was restored. Later that summer, Prime Minister Hoveyda stepped down, replaced by the US-educated economist Jamshid Amouzegar. Terminating Hoveyda's long tenure (1964–77) proved a hollow gesture since the shah's personal control of the political process remained intact. At this point in mid-1977, the shah had squandered the chance of compromise with the moderate opposition, paving the way for mass mobilization led by his radical opponents. By fall 1977,

---

73 Criticism of shah as a ruthless dictator was becoming more widespread. See the 1976 and 1977 articles in *The Village Voice* cited above—see, for example, "Beautiful Butchers: The Shah Serves Up Caviar and Torture," *Village Voice*, November 14, 1977. A vocal critic of the shah's regime, during the second half of the 1970s, was Reza Baraheni, a university professor and former political prisoner who had migrated to the United States in 1974. He published *God's Shadow: Prison Poems* (Indiana University Press, 1976) and *The Crowned Cannibals: Writings on Repression in Iran* (Random House, 1977), and in *Time* magazine, *The New York Times*, *The New York Review of Books*, and *The American Poetry Review*. See, for example, Reza Baraheni, "Terror in Iran," *New York Review of Books*, October 26, 1976. Baraheni joined the American branch of the International PEN, working very closely with Edward Albee, Allen Ginsberg, Richard Howard, and others at PEN's Freedom to Write Committee, sharing at the same time, with Kay Boyle, the Honorary Chair of the Committee for Artistic and Intellectual Freedom to release Iranian writers and artists from prison.

Ayatollah Khomeini was shrewdly seizing the moment, calling on his clerical followers to join the liberals' letter-writing campaign. "This is an opportunity," he said, "Do not let it slip away."[74]

Meanwhile, throughout 1977 and up to fall 1978, the Carter administration backed the shah's self-destructive autocratic course. After initially blocking the sale of advanced jetfighters and missiles to Iran, Carter personally lobbied Congress to approve a $2.5 billion package of ultra-sophisticated military hardware requested by the shah. Withholding or significantly reducing arms sales would have sent a strong message to the shah that the United States wanted a change of course. But Carter, like previous US presidents, supported the shah's autocracy until it became patently impossible in late 1978. During his first year as president, Carter in fact paid little attention to Iran, except for continuing massive weapons sales. Inexperienced and cautious in foreign policy, he remained preoccupied with brokering a peace treaty between Israel and Egypt when it came to Middle Eastern affairs. His diaries of 1977 show concern with matters such as Kissinger's approval of his foreign policy, awareness of Israel being "the most obstinate and difficult" party in Middle East peace negotiations, and the seriousness of Soviet interest in ending the nuclear arms race.[75] He barely mentions Iran, commenting once in passing that he does not care whether the shah buys advanced American weapons systems or not—something which was not true since he personally lobbied for a $10 billion Iranian arms purchase. Moreover, Carter's comments on the shah's November 1977 visit to Washington barely mention Iranian student protests, human rights, or other serious challenges the shah faced that year; nor does he say anything of substance about his own 1978 New Year's visit to Tehran, although an added footnote admits his blunder in claiming the shah's leadership had made Iran an "island of stability"; nor is Iran even mentioned among foreign policy challenges during an "extraordinary" two-day session of "self-criticism" Carter held with his top cabinet and staff in April 1978.[76]

Carter's continuation of the Nixon-Kissinger "special relationship" with the shah was clear in his instructions to William Sullivan, his new ambassador to Tehran. According to Sullivan, Carter was committed to

74 The first major open letter of protest directly addressing the shah was by Ali-Asghar Haj-Seyed-Javadi in February 1975. See Mohammad-Hossein Khosrowpanah, *Eslah ya enqelab* (Tehran: 2007), 27–30; Khomeini's letter, 411.

75 Jimmy Carter, *The White House Diary* (Farrar, Straus and Giroux, 2010), 34–5 on Kissinger, 113 on Israel, and 138 on nuclear arms race.

76 Ibid., 74–5, 185–8.

the same level of arms sales to Iran, to providing the shah with nuclear power plants, and to CIA-SAVAK cooperation, particularly in intelligence gathering and jointly running the American spy station on the Soviet border. Carter also told Sullivan to "try to persuade the shah to improve the human-rights performance of his government," something that obviously was not a priority.[77] Sullivan would play an important role as the last official US liaison to the shah, as well as the first American diplomat forging ties to the Islamist opposition that would replace the monarchy. Moreover, this last US ambassador's account of his mission to Iran provides a unique window into the shah's final perception of his relationship with the US. Sullivan had served as ambassador to Laos and the Philippines, as well as Kissinger's deputy during the Paris Peace negotiations ending the Vietnam War. Ironically, his lack of familiarity with Iran allowed him to think outside the shah-centric frame of American policy, while his experience in negotiating with the opponents of US-backed regimes in Vietnam and the Philippines enabled him to break with established American policy and communicate with the shah's opponents.[78] He was chosen for the Tehran job because of his "considerable experience in dealing with authoritarian governments" and "leaders who have forceful personalities." Once in Tehran, however, Sullivan quickly concluded that, underneath his grandiose public persona, the shah was a weak and indecisive leader, desperately seeking US advice in dealing with a fateful crisis besieging his regime. Sullivan, whose job was to deliver such advice, bitterly blames the Carter administration for its failure to develop a coherent response to the shah's predicament and to the revolution that dethroned him. During his first year in Iran and well into 1978, he dutifully toed official policy laid down by the State Department and, more recklessly, by Carter's National Security Advisor Zbigniew Brzezinski, who followed Kissinger's example. Sullivan's job was to assure the shah of the Carter administration's full support, while Washington remained oblivious to Iran's fast brewing crisis.[79]

Carter's strong assurance to the shah came with his approval of the $10 billion arms deal, followed by an invitation to the shah to visit Washington in fall 1977. During the shah's last official visit, the American public witnessed a dramatic display of opposition by thousands of Iranian students engaging in their most spectacular protest action. On

77 William H. Sullivan, *Mission to Iran* (W.W. Norton, 1981), 20–2, quoted on 22.

78 Ibid., 144–5.

79 Quoted in ibid., 16; see also ibid., chapter 4, "Shah Mohammad Reza Pahlavi," and 156–8, 167–8; see also Sullivan, *Obbligato*, 268–70.

November 15, while the shah was received at the White House, about four thousand student demonstrators broke through police lines to fight a pitched battle with a smaller crowd of shah supporters recruited by the Iranian embassy. Close to a hundred demonstrators and twenty-eight police officers were injured in what *The Wall Street Journal* called "Washington's largest and most violent street disturbance since the end of the Vietnam War." The violent confrontation, along with weepy images of Carter and the shah, stung by tear gas, appeared on the front pages of American newspapers and was broadcast on televisions across the world.[80] Though embarrassed by this event, the shah returned home confident of Carter's full support and hence determined not to compromise with the opposition. Instead, he authorized violent crackdowns by regime agents posing as civilian "patriots" on opposition gatherings, kidnapping and beating dissident leaders and bombing their homes. On December 31, 1977, Carter arrived in Tehran to celebrate New Year's Eve with the shah, issuing a declaration that became a testament to the folly of American policy. Raising a toast to the host, he said:

> Iran under the great leadership of the Shah is an island of stability in one of the more troubled areas of the world. This is a great tribute to you, Your Majesty, and to your leadership, and to the respect, admiration and love which your people give to you.[81]

Carter's Tehran declaration disabused the liberal opposition of its hopes for US support, clearing the field for the rise of a new radical opposition that would snowball in 1978. Diplomat and scholar Gary Sick, who served on the US National Security Council under Ford and Carter, claimed that on "New Year's Day 1978 there was no reason to believe that the relationship with the United States and Iran was anything but secure." However, Sick also noted that less than a year later, in September 1978, he sent a memo to Carter suggesting "Iran could be ripe for full-scale revolution."[82] This shows the extent of the Carter administration's disconnect with Iranian political reality. Other scholars have argued that the regime's collapse might have been averted had the United States pressed the shah

---

80 Matin-Asgari, *Iranian Student Opposition to the Shah*, 158–9; *Newsweek*, November, 28, 1997, reported some shah supporters admitted receiving airfare, hotel accommodations and a bonus of $100 from the Iranian government; *Wall Street Journal*, November 16, 1997, reported a total crowd size of eight thousand.

81 Bill, *Eagle and the Lion*, 233–4.

82 Sick, *All Fall Down*, 30–1, 50.

in early 1978 to call on the moderate opposition to form a government, something he did too late in January 1979.[83]

A few days after Carter's visit, a leading Tehran newspaper published an insulting personal attack on Khomeini, causing protests by clerics and seminarians in the shrine city of Qom, where the police opened fire, inflicting dozens of casualties. Thus began a chain reaction of demonstrations throughout the country, growing larger and more intense as security forces fired on crowds, killing more people, and setting off larger protests. Significantly, it was only during 1978 that the opposition's leadership, ideological makeup, and political demands radically changed. Up until 1978, the opposition was neither revolutionary nor did it have a predominantly religious character or leadership. Public protests were led by middle-class politicians, lawyers, and journalists, while street demonstrations were mostly organized by leftist university and high school students—in both cases with primarily secular demands for political liberalization.[84] Conforming to classical revolutionary patterns, the regime's failure to accommodate moderate opponents allowed the radicals to seize the political initiative and gain popular support. By mid-1978, Khomeini, who was calling for an end to monarchy, had assumed the leadership of a revolutionary mass movement. On his more secular advisors' recommendations, he declared the monarchy's successor regime a republic, which he insisted had to be first and foremost Islamic. In fall 1978, Khomeini, having moved to Paris from exile in Iraq, said:

> Republic means the same as it exists everywhere. The difference here is that our republic lies on a constitution, which is the Islamic law. That we call it an Islamic Republic relates to the fact that all conditions for the election as well as the ordinances, which rule Iran, stem from Islam.[85]

Khomeini, therefore, was clear that the political regime he proposed would be republican in form but Islamic in content. And obviously, he would define what "Islamic" meant, though he claimed the people

---

83 Luca Trenta, "The Champion of Human Rights Meets the King of Kings: Jimmy Carter, the Shah, and Iranian Illusions and Rage," *Diplomacy & Statecraft* 24, no. 3 (2013): 476–98, cited on 487.

84 Ahman Ashraf and Ali Banuazizi, "The State, Classes and Modes of Mobilization in the Iranian Revolution," *State, Culture, and Society* 1, no. 3 (1985): 3–40, cited on 26.

85 Farhang Rajaee, "A Thermidor of 'Islamic Yuppies'? Conflict and Compromise in Iran's Politics," *The Middle East Journal* 53, no. 2 (spring 1999): 217–31, Khomeini quoted on 225.

would unanimously approve his proposals. Thus, Khomeini's notion of an "Islamic Republic" was neither deceptive to his Iranian followers nor an open-ended political project, as sympathetic foreign observers like French philosopher Michel Foucault had chosen to believe.[86]

Meanwhile, the regime's confused and incoherent response, combining violent repression and political concessions, further fanned the flames of revolution. Monarchist apologists downplayed the number of protesters killed in 1977–78, while others argued that a massive bloodbath could have contained the revolution. The revolution's casualties must have reached thousands, as in just one day, on Friday, September 8, hundreds were massacred when Tehran was placed under martial law. Following the "Black Friday" massacre, Carter assured the shah of full US support, oblivious to the event most observers saw as a turning point after which compromise with the regime became impossible.[87]

Thus, even by fall 1978, the Carter administration remained dazed and confused as mass protests and strikes were spreading all over Iran. That year, in addition to Iran, US foreign policy faced several challenges, including the Camp David Egypt-Israel peace negotiations, Strategic Arms Limitation Talks (SALT II) with the Soviet Union, a smoldering revolution in Nicaragua, a communist military coup in Afghanistan, and Vietnam's occupation of Cambodia, which led to China's invasion of Vietnam. Iran, therefore, was only one moving part of a chaotic international order that seemed to be spinning out of American control. In retrospect, however, the Washington establishment seems surprisingly oblivious to the magnitude of the shah's problems. Ambassador Sullivan had left Iran on a summer vacation still confident the shah had things under control. According to Gary Sick, even by the end of October 1978, not a single high-level policy meeting in Washington was devoted to discussing the Iran crisis. In September the shah submitted a new $12 billion order for US military purchases, showing a major disconnect to his precarious situation.[88] When Sullivan came back from summer vacation, the shah asked him if the CIA was behind the unrest in Iran. "What had he done to deserve this sort of action from the United States?"

86 Responding to Foucault, eminent French scholar of Islam, Maxime Rodinson, warned about the authoritarian thrust of Khomeini's proposal of an Islamic Republic; see Janet Afary and Kevin B. Anderson, *Foucault and the Iranian Revolution: Gender and the Seduction of Islamism* (University of Chicago Press, 2005); for an unconvincing defense of Foucault's views, see Behrooz Ghamari-Tabrizi, *Foucault in Iran: Islamic Revolution after the Enlightenment* (University of Minnesota Press, 2016).

87 Sick, *All Fall Down*, 50–2.

88 Ibid., 60, 49.

the shah asked. "Had he done something? Or had we and the Soviets reached a grand design against him?" Insisting the United States was not involved in any such conspiracy, Sullivan thought the shah's desperate pleading was "pathetic."[89] Yet, the shah would go on believing the United States was not just abandoning him but had engineered his overthrow. He also blamed Iranian and foreign communists, and, by implication, the Soviet Union, accusing them of hiding behind the religious opposition. This was another baseless assertion since Khomeini was the revolution's undisputed leader by 1978, while no organized leftist group or party had a mass following. By all accounts, the Soviet Union was not involved in the anti-shah movement and did not influence the revolution's unfolding. By the time of the shah's departure in January 1979, even *Newsweek* reported that "US officials continue to insist that they have no evidence of Soviet meddling in Iran thus far."[90]

The idea of the Soviet Union, or the KGB, being behind the revolution was pushed by former CIA Director and Ambassador to Tehran Richard Helms, who, like Brzezinski and Kissinger, argued for more aggressive US support of the shah.[91] Meanwhile, a monarchist lobby in the United States was actively working to keep the shah on his throne. In May 1978, Ambassador Zahedi had asked Kermit Roosevelt to visit Iran "to discuss a repeat performance of 1953." Apparently giving up on the shah's chances of survival, Roosevelt had just published *Countercoup*, a distorted account of his role in the 1953 coup (see chapter 2). He told Zahedi that former CIA agent Miles Copeland, his chief assistant in 1953, could best assess the situation. Without informing the CIA, Copeland flew to Tehran, talked to his 1953 contacts and the shah's top generals and the chief of SAVAK, concluding that even a massive US military intervention could not save the monarchy. Since both Copeland and Roosevelt were consultants for American oil companies, the shah later claimed the CIA and big oil companies were involved in planning his downfall. But Roosevelt and Copeland were no longer with the CIA, nor is there any evidence of, or logic to, the claim of American oil companies fomenting revolution in Iran.[92]

---

89 Sullivan, *Mission to Iran*, 157. Meeting with Helms and his wife in a New York hospital, the shah again blamed the United States for intentionally causing his fall. "Why did you want to destroy what we had?" he asked. "Why did you do it?" Cynthia Helms, *An Ambassador's Wife in Iran* (Dodd, Mead & Company, 1981), 204.

90 *Newsweek*, January 8, 1979, 19.

91 *Newsweek*, December 18, 1978, 34.

92 Babak Ganji, *Politics of Confrontation: The Foreign Policy of the USA and Revolutionary Iran* (I.B. Tauris, 2012), 58–9; see also Miles Copeland, *The Game Player* (Arum Press, 1989), 249–54.

During 1978, Iran experts like James Bill and Richard Cottam had warned the Carter administration of the shah's precarious situation and the danger it posed to future Iran-US relations. All such warnings went unheeded until mid-fall 1978, when it became clear that the military government appointed by the shah was powerless in the face of countrywide protests and a general strike, spreading from the oil fields to government employees and the private sector. At this point, the shah finally admitted to major wrongdoings and acknowledged the revolution. In early November, he delivered his last address to the nation, apologizing for his regime's oppression and corruption and promising a fundamental change of course by restoring constitutional government:

> I promise that past mistakes, lawlessness, oppression and corruption, would not return . . . I promise that once order is restored, a popular government would be quickly formed to safeguard basic liberties and hold free elections, so that the Fundamental Law, purchased with blood during the Constitutional Revolution, can be fully implemented. I too heard the message of the people's revolution . . . I promise Iran's future government would be based on the constitution, social justice and popular sovereignty, and be far from despotism, oppression and corruption.[93]

The shah then began to call on National Front leaders and asked them to form a legitimate constitutional government. Possibly viable a year earlier, such moves could no longer save a regime clearly falling apart. The shah's confused and disoriented state of mind matched the collapsing state of his regime. When a former cabinet minister went to see him a week before his final departure from Iran, the shah told him: "See my head? It is not functioning anymore. Leave me alone. I want to leave. Let the army do whatever the hell it wants to on its own. There is no longer anything I can do."[94]

The Final Act: Throwing Out the Shah Like a Dead Mouse

By fall 1978, the Carter administration finally woke up to the reality of an Iranian revolution unfolding in front of it. Nor were the supposedly wily British more cognizant of the seriousness of Iran's crisis until about

---

93 Quoted in Houshang Nahavandi, *Akharin Ruzha* [The Last Days] (Sherkat-e Ketab, 2005), 267–9. Author's translation.

94 Houshang Nahavandi, interview recorded by Shahrokh Meskoob, May 14, 20, and 29, 1985; February 13, 1986; March 8 and 27, 1986; April 11, 1986, Paris, France, Iranian Oral History Collection, Harvard University, transcript 13.

the same time. British Ambassador Anthony Parsons admitted that, even by mid-1978, he thought the situation was under control, realizing how serious the crisis was only after returning to Tehran after his summer vacation. Meeting with Parsons in late September, the shah said he was not sure his regime could survive and asked him for assurance that the British were not behind the opposition. As Sullivan had said, Parsons insisted neither the British nor the Americans and not even the Soviets were behind the opposition.[95] By this time, Sullivan had become the first high-ranking American diplomat arguing the shah might not survive. The Carter White House was shocked when he suggested this in a November 9 cable, appropriately titled "Thinking the Unthinkable." Sullivan, who was already in touch with moderate opposition leaders in Tehran, suggested that Washington follow suit and draw up contingency plans for a transition of power bypassing the shah. An intense civil war then ensued within the US foreign policy establishment, with Brzezinski furiously opposing Sullivan's suggestions and trying to have him fired. Brzezinski, whose most significant connection to Iran was Zahedi, insisted the United States save the shah, which required the massive use of military force to crush all opposition. Zahedi was in touch with a few hard-line generals in Tehran, working for a repeat of the 1953 US-backed monarchist military coup. This hard-line was pushed by Kissinger, the shah's banker, Nelson and David Rockefeller, and Richard Helms, while the shah was opposed to it, saying the situation was entirely different from 1953.[96] After his fall, however, the shah would decide that the Brzezinski plan of massive repression had been the right option. He blamed Carter for undermining his regime, giving him contradictory advice, and colluding with the Khomeini camp, a policy he claimed served the interests of international communism. First articulated in the shah's *Answer to History*, this narrative became the standard monarchist explanation of the Iranian Revolution as a foreign conspiracy.[97]

In late fall, a different approach to the Iran crisis was gaining traction in Washington, soon to be adopted by the Carter administration. The outline of this approach was suggested in a policy recommendation paper drawn up by former Undersecretary of State George Ball, who had been critical of the shah's policies. Delivered in December 1978, Ball's

---

95 Anthony Parsons, *The Pride & the Fall: Iran 1974–1979* (Jonathan Cape, 1984), 67, 74.

96 Sick, *All Fall Down*, 77, 98–9. Interview with Helms in *Time*, December 18, 1978, 34. David Rockefeller took over as the shah's banker when his brother, Nelson, died in 1979.

97 "The Shah Regrets His Policy of Surrender," *Washington Post*, May 5, 1980.

report was a sobering critique of Washington's conventional wisdom about Iran. Mincing no words, Ball held the United States responsible for the shah's regime coming apart: "We made the shah what he has become. We nurtured his love for grandiose geopolitical schemes and supplied him with the hardware to indulge his fantasies."[98]

Countering Brzezinski's hard-line, Ball argued the shah's regime was "on the verge of collapse" and military repression would only lead to more instability. Instead, he called for a transfer of power from the shah to a council of notables selected by the United States and capable of appeasing the Iranian opposition. He recommended direct contact with Khomeini, concluding the United States should not become "the prisoner of a weakened leader out of touch with his own people."[99] The Ball report was a conceptual breakthrough that quickly became the administration's policy line. Since May 1978, the US embassy was already in touch with a moderate Iranian opposition faction led by Mehdi Bazargan who would become the first postrevolutionary prime minister. Bazargan had proposed a US-backed post-shah "transition government" to prevent the revolution's radicalization beyond Khomeini's control.[100] By late December, the shah too was agreeable to this option, telling Ambassador Sullivan that rather than a harsh military crackdown he preferred to install a civilian caretaker government and leave the country.[101]

According to Sick, the United States had established direct contact with Khomeini since early fall 1978, using Iran scholar Richard Cottam's liaison with Ebrahim Yazdi, who would be the first postrevolutionary foreign minister. In Washington the political pendulum was swinging further against the shah. By December Secretary of State Cyrus Vance had concluded the shah would not survive, while Brzezinski still insisted on strongly supporting him. In Tehran Sullivan and his staff regularly met with Bazargan and Ayatollah Mohammad Beheshti, chairman of Khomeini's Revolutionary Council and the powerbroker in the provisional government he would soon form. Khomeini's Revolutionary Council was set up hastily in Paris to preempt the formation in Tehran of an opposition council inclusive of secular and leftist organizations.[102]

---

98 Ball quoted in Collier, *Democracy and the Nature of American Influence in Iran*, 285.

99 Ball quoted in Guerrero, *The Carter Administration & the Fall of Iran's Pahlavi Dynasty*, 148.

100 Sullivan, *Mission to Iran*, 160–1.

101 Sick, *All Fall Down*, 126.

102 Ibid., 54–5; Sullivan, *Mission to Iran*, 200; 236–7; Ebrahim Yazdi, *Akharin talsha dar akharin ruzha* (Qalam Publishers 2000), 94–5, 276.

In addition to acting as the US liaison between the shah's regime and the Islamist opposition, Sullivan had another important job to perform. Throughout 1978 around thirty-five thousand to forty thousand Americans, including five thousand military personnel and their families, continued to live and work in Tehran, Esfahan, and Shiraz. Well into that year, Washington was not asking Americans to leave Iran, thinking this would suggest the shah had lost control. By late fall, the protests were becoming anti-American, and the residences of some US personnel were firebombed. In Esfahan demonstrators beat up an American political officer and set fire to the headquarters of Grumman Aircraft Engineering Corporation, while troops shot and killed four protesters.[103] Grumman's three hundred American employees were training Iranian pilots, crew, and maintenance personnel for F-14 fighter planes. Soon, angry crowds sacked and burned the Tehran office of Pan American World Airways, stoned the InterContinental Hotel, set fire to Pepsi-Cola trucks, and burned a Bell bus without harming its passengers. Two days before Christmas, a Texaco executive was shot and killed in the southern city of Ahwaz, and in January 1979, an ex–US Army colonel was stabbed to death in the central city of Kerman.[104] The next day, students from two high schools attacked the US embassy, shouting, "The Shah is a chained American dog" and "Death to Jimmy Carter." They threw rocks and set fire to an embassy car but stopped scaling the walls when Marine guards shot tear gas at them. Henceforth, the embassy was protected by Iranian soldiers in tanks and armored personnel carriers.[105] This incident showed the US embassy was a main target of revolutionary protests, particularly by radical students and leftist forces who managed to occupy it in February 1979 when the monarchy collapsed (see chapter 5). Some Americans blamed Carter's support of the shah for being attacked in Iran. Referring to a particularly violent protest, a Grumman employee said: "The day before all hell broke loose, Carter praised the shah as the greatest thing since sliced bread . . . Sometimes we wish he would just keep his mouth shut."[106]

A voluntary American exodus was underway by fall, although the embassy estimated around twenty thousand US citizens were still in Iran

103 *Time*, December 18, 1978, 33–4; and Christian Emery, *US Foreign Policy and the Iranian Revolution: The Cold War Dynamics of Engagement and Strategic Alliance* (Palgrave Macmillan, 2013), 106.

104 *Newsweek*, January 8, 1979, 16 and January 29, 1979, 43.

105 *Newsweek*, January 8, 1979, 16.

106 *Newsweek*, November 20, 1978, 67.

by the end of 1978. Sullivan, who was on the verge of resignation due to intense conflict with the Carter White House, claimed he stayed on his job to oversee the safe evacuation US citizens, about eight thousand of whom remained to be airlifted out of Iran after the shah's fall.[107] Despite universal rage at Carter's support of bloody repression in Iran, thousands of Americans who stayed in the country through the revolution suffered few casualties. A dramatic example of American rescue during revolutionary chaos was the case of two computer company executives who, in late 1978, were arrested and imprisoned on charges of bribery. The company's owner, Ross Perot, a billionaire who would run as a third-party presidential candidate in the 1990s, flew to Tehran, bringing a small team of former military men to free his employees. In the end, Perot's Iranian staff helped free the Americans when demonstrators attacked and opened the gates of Tehran's prisons after Khomeini's return.[108]

By January 1979, Sullivan's staff and the Bazargan-Beheshti team were coordinating plans on two shared related objectives: the shah's departure and Khomeini's return to Iran, both of which required the consent of the armed forces. According to Bazargan, in a "secret meeting" with Sullivan, an agreement was reached for transition from monarchy to an Islamic Republic, the only question being whether the shah's caretaker government or Khomeini's Revolutionary Council would hold a national referendum to that effect.[109] Sullivan was acting largely on his own, as Carter's position shifted almost daily, his cabinet still divided on how to respond to the revolution. According to Sullivan's plan, the armed forces, purged at the top but still structurally tied to the United States, would support either a caretaker government or a revolutionary regime replacing the monarchy. This plan would salvage the main pillar of US influence in Iran (that is, ties to the armed forces) while dispensing with the shah, who had become a liability. Sullivan's plan was vehemently opposed by Brzezinski but eventually accepted by Carter, apparently after his early January 1979 meeting at Guadalupe in the Caribbean with leaders of France, the UK, Germany, and Japan, who all agreed the shah's regime would not survive. Thus, upon Sullivan's suggestion, the shah agreed to leave the country presumably for medical treatment and rest while appointing Shapour Bakhtiar, a maverick National Front leader, prime minister of a caretaker government.[110] A crucial part of this transition

107 Sullivan, *Mission to Iran*, 208–9, 241, 269–70.
108 "Iran Hostage Rescue," rossperot.com/life-story/iran-hostage-rescue.
109 Mehdi Bazargan, *Enqelab-e Iran dar do Harekat* (Tehran: 1984), 71.
110 Sullivan, *Mission to Iran*, 224, 230–3.

plan was the arrival in Tehran, in early January, of General Robert E. Huyser, deputy commander of US forces in Europe, who had been to Iran many times and was familiar with the shah and his top generals. In a brazen instance of US intervention in the Iranian Revolution, Huyser would replace the shah as the acting commander in chief of the armed forces, keeping the top military brass in line behind Bakhtiar's caretaker government. Huyser was instructed to initiate a US-backed military coup or to prevent one, depending on last-minute orders from Washington.[111] In either case, the overriding objective was to keep the armed forces intact and under the command of pro-American generals, regardless of the shah's fate or the revolution's outcome. The mission would prove another American policy failure, since the armed forces were already on the verge of collapse and incapable of running the country, something Sullivan knew and Huyser quickly realized.[112] Ordered to implement martial law, army conscripts were increasingly insubordinate or defecting, some even firing on their officers when ordered to shoot demonstrators. In December, three soldiers went on a firing rampage in an army barracks near the shah's place, killing six officers and wounding ten more.[113]

Meanwhile, by the end of 1978, much of Iran was in a general strike, spearheaded in the early fall by workers in the oil industry, steel, and railways, joined by employees of newspapers, radio, and television, and eventually the entire private and public sector. The wave of strikes had developed spontaneously, beginning with economic demands that quickly turned political, aligning with Khomeini's call for the monarchy's overthrow. Arguably, the general strike made the Carter administration give up on the monarchy by January 1979 when it became clear that the military government, or even a coup by royalist generals, could not put the country back to work. Huyser's arrival was the signal for the shah to finally exit the scene. On January 16, he left Iran for Egypt, preferring to remain closer to home rather than accept Carter's invitation to the United States, which would have given the impression of taking refuge with his American benefactors. However, had the shah settled in the United States at this time, the issue of his going there for medical treatment after the revolution, which led to the hostage crisis, would not have arisen (see chapter 5). At any rate, the shah's departure on Sullivan's and Huyser's instructions must have been extremely humiliating. Referring

111 Huyser spells this out clearly in the epilogue to his *Mission to Tehran* (Harper & Row, 1987), 287; see also Sick, *All Fall Down*, 138–9.

112 Huyser, *Mission to Tehran*, 7, 18, 24, 99; Sullivan, *Mission to Iran*, 227–8, 240.

113 *Time*, December 25, 1978, 32.

to this episode, the shah quotes, without comment, one of his top generals telling the revolutionary tribunal that would order his execution, "General Huyser threw the Shah out of the country like a dead mouse."[114]

According to Huyser, the shah's four or five top generals could not agree on staging a coup, while some were secretly in touch with Khomeini's camp and ready to defect. Overall, Huyser's description of the shah's top generals is that of a lost and confused group of orphans looking up to him as a surrogate father figure. With the shah's departure, the generals fell apart emotionally, one literally crying on Huyser's shoulder, while another blurted out: "When rape is inevitable, relax and enjoy it." They all acknowledged Huyser's command, saying, "The shah told us to trust you, to listen to you, and to obey you," while he made sure they were to abandon all "foolish thoughts of military action."[115] Following the shah's exit, Carter held a press conference declaring the United States would not interfere militarily or otherwise in Iran's affairs. "We have tried this once in Vietnam. It didn't work well," he said. Meanwhile, Khomeini declared that, by the authority of his religious office and the obvious support of the Iranian people, he had formed a clandestine Revolutionary Council, presiding over Iran's transition to an Islamic Republic. He also appointed an official provisional government headed by Bazargan to replace Bakhtiar's caretaker government.[116] Still in Paris, Khomeini was receiving Carter's messages through the French government and American diplomats who regularly met with Ebrahim Yazdi. Carter had assured Khomeini of the shah's imminent departure, asking him to postpone returning to Iran so that a military coup could be avoided, allowing Bakhtiar to "restore calm."[117] Khomeini's direct response on January 27 shows the contrast between his shrewd and confident leadership style and the shah's indecisiveness:

> If Mr. Carter has good intentions, wants to restore calm, and avoid bloodshed, he should take the Shah out and stop supporting the [caretaker] government . . . I have been informed of an impending military coup, involving a huge massacre . . . A military coup would make holy jihad imperative. Neither the nation, nor the US would benefit by a military coup. If it takes place, you would be blamed for it . . . [But] If you leave Iran alone, it will follow neither communism, nor any other deviant

114 Pahlavi, *Answer to History*, 173.
115 Huyser, *Mission to Tehran*, 130–2.
116 Guerrero, *The Carter Administration & the Fall of Iran's Pahlavi Dynasty*, 175.
117 Sick, *All Fall Down*, 142–4, 146.

> path . . . I emphasize that if you want peace and calm in Iran, the only way is for the illegal monarchy to step aside, leaving the nation to itself, allowing me to appoint virtuous individuals to a Revolutionary Council effecting a transition of power to a government chosen by the nation . . . The regime and the military have been weakening for months, the military's ranks are broken and many [of them] would join us to crush a military coup, but at the price of a bloodshed that I do not want.[118]

Khomeini's confidential message to Carter soon went public, leading to allegations of collusion between the revolutionary leadership and the Carter administration. What it shows, however, is Khomeini calling Carter's bluff while reminding him that US interest lies in accepting his leadership of an already successful revolution instead of instigating a bloody but futile military coup. Significantly, Khomeini clarified that, under his leadership, the new revolutionary regime would be anti-communist and not necessarily anti-American. Moreover, the message's absence of grievance against the US left the door open to the possibility of normal relations with the US. Khomeini's prognosis was corroborated by Sullivan, who warned Washington of massive desertion from the army, correctly predicting its collapse, or defection to Khomeini, upon his arrival in Iran. This was also the consensus of the shah's top generals, who, according to Huyser, "all argued that if Khomeini returned . . . it was all over; the moment he set foot on Iranian soil, that was the end of the Shah's regime . . . The armed forces would disintegrate."[119] Huyser recommended they accept Khomeini's return unless they had a viable plan for a military coup and for managing the country afterward, which they did not.[120] The generals discussed preventing Khomeini's return by closing Tehran's airport or by diverting and even shooting down his plane. Huyser saw none of these as viable options, particularly Khomeini's assassination, which he thought would trigger a civil

118 Mahmood Toloi, *Sad ruz-e akhar* (Tehran: 1999), 217–20, quoted on 219–20. Khomeini sent the same message to the American public, via former US Attorney General Ramsey Clark who met with him in Paris. He brought back a message to the American public: "Ayatollah Khomeini said I hope the American people, the United States Congress and President Carter will respect our wishes and the United States will not interfere through the army, with American advisers, the C.I.A. or through support for Bakhtiar, and let the nation determine its own fate." Kathleen Teltsch, "Ramsey Clark Meets Khomeini and Relays a Plea to Washington," *New York Times*, January 23, 1979.

119 Huyser, *Mission to Tehran*, 160, quoted on 165.

120 Ibid., 167, 170–1.

war.[121] Since that was to be avoided, Huyser promised the military would not sabotage Khomeini's return, something a single rogue air force pilot could accomplish by downing his plane. Meanwhile, Brzezinski was still recommending drastic action to prevent Khomeini's return, but Carter sided with Sullivan, as well as CIA and State Department officials who argued a working relationship with Khomeini would be possible. In the end, Bakhtiar and the generals made careful arrangements with Bazargan and Beheshti to allow Khomeini's return and guarantee his safety upon arrival. Sullivan was even informed of Khomeini's agenda during his first days in Tehran.[122]

On the morning of February 1, Khomeini's plane carrying his close associates and over a hundred international journalists landed in Tehran, received by the revolution's largest and most emotional mass gathering. Declaring the dawn of a new political era, Khomeini's return address masterfully blended modern revolutionary rhetoric with vague references to Islam, hitting hard at US support of the shah and appealing to the military to join the revolution. The Pahlavi monarchy, he argued, was illegal and contrary to both reason and "human rights." Every generation, he proclaimed, had the right to choose its own political system instead of what it inherited. "Who said our fathers are our [political] guardians?" he asked rhetorically, and in ironic contrast to the permanent political guardianship he himself would soon impose on the nation. Finally, he invited the military leaders to join the new regime, mockingly addressing any general still holding out under Huyser's command: "Mr. General, would not you rather be your own master? Do you prefer being a lackey, Mr. General, sir? [123]

After his speech, an army helicopter airlifted Khomeini to a hospital, whence he went to a safe private residence. The generals meeting with Huyser agreed this was the end of the shah's regime.[124] Huyser, who was already the target of angry anti-American protests, was called back to Washington, leaving behind General Philip C. Gast, chief of the American

---

121 Ibid., 182, 187; Sullivan had told Huyser an Islamic Republic would be acceptable, while Huyser agreed that "if anything happened to Khomeini on his return, we would immediately have a civil war." Huyser, *Mission to Tehran*, 99–100.

122 Guerrero, *The Carter Administration & the Fall of Iran's Pahlavi Dynasty*, 179–81; Sick, *All Fall Down*, 148; Yazdi says Khomeini endorsed Beheshti's contact with military leaders. Yazdi, *Akharin talsha dar akharin ruzha*, 93, 317–18, 333, 368. See also Bazargan, *Enqelab-e Iran dar do Harekat*, 70, on the military's cooperation with the safety of Khomeini's flight.

123 Toloi, *Sad ruz-e akhar*, 427–8.

124 Huyser, *Mission to Tehran*, 230, 250–3.

Military Assistance and Advisory Group (MAAG), as US liaison with the shah's generals.[125] Within a few days, Khomeini announced the formation of a provisional Islamic government, headed by Bazargan, which became engaged in tense negotiations with Sullivan, Bakhtiar, and army generals for a transfer of power. On February 8, hundreds of military officers and conscripts joined over one million people marching in support of Bazargan's government in Tehran. The next day, armed clashes broke out between rebellious air force cadets inside their base in Tehran and units of the royalist Imperial Guard. Thousands of civilians set up barricades around the base to defend the cadets, and American military advisors trapped there had to be evacuated by helicopter and buses. Rushing to the scene to cover the fighting, American journalist Joe Alex Morris Jr. was killed by a stray bullet.[126]

During the next two days, February 9–10, military rebellion and desertion escalated as hundreds of thousands of civilians broke into army barracks in Tehran and throughout the country. On February 11, the military command declared its neutrality, effectively switching sides to the Bazargan government. Meanwhile, the US embassy in Tabriz was sacked, bullets were flying around the embassy in Tehran, and the MAAG headquarters was under heavy attack, its twenty-six personnel and General Gast trapped in a bunker below the building. Trying to call Iranian authorities to save the Americans, Sullivan was simultaneously on the phone with the emergency meeting taking place in the White House Situation Room. Responding to Brzezinski's query about the possibility of a military coup, Sullivan burst out with a short "fuck off," adding he could translate that into Polish for Brzezinski to understand if necessary. Still persisting, Brzezinski called Huyser in Europe to ask if he would return to Iran to lead a military coup. Huyser said only a full-scale military invasion with a dozen US generals and at least ten thousand troops might affect a change in Iran. At that point, Brzezinski gave up the idea of military intervention against the revolution. By early next morning, an armed convoy, led by Yazdi and Ayatollah Beheshti, delivered the freed American military personnel at the embassy.[127] Summing up this day's fateful events, an America military attaché in Tehran signed off on his report: "Army surrenders. Khomeini wins.

125 Ibid., 274, 283, 294–5; Sick, *All Fall Down*, 151–4.

126 William Branigin, "Remembering Joe Alex Morris Jr., the L.A. Times Correspondent Who Died Covering the Iranian Revolution," *Los Angeles Times*, February 18, 2019.

127 Sullivan, *Mission to Iran*, 249–54; Huyser, *Mission to Tehran*, 233–4.

Destroying all classified."[128] In response to those blaming Carter for the shah's fall, George Ball wrote:

> The reason the shah did not stand and fight was that his whole country was solidly against him and his army was beginning to disintegrate . . . It is fatuous to think that we could have kept a hated absolute monarch in power by encouraging the progressive use of military force. This was an internal revolt. What would Mr. Kissinger have done? Sent the Sixth Fleet steaming up the gulf?[129]

---

128 Sick, *All Fall Down*, 155–6.

129 Ball quoted in Barry Rubin, *Paved with Good Intentions: The American Experience in Iran* (Penguin Books, 1981), 257.

5

The Empire Strikes Back: The United States and the Islamic Republic of Iran

American Entanglement in Postrevolutionary Iran's Power Struggle

> *The long-term strategic interests of Iran dictate that Iran will wish to maintain decent relations with the United States. The military hardware Iran has bought from the United States will need to be serviced if the armed forces are to be revived. There are the seeds of a new relationship there. But they are going to have to be nurtured very slowly.*
>
> Ambassador Sullivan to President Carter, February 1979[1]

A few days after the monarchy's fall, at 10:30 a.m. on February 14, 1979, Valentine's Day, a group of armed assailants attacked and occupied the US embassy in Tehran, briefly taking Ambassador Sullivan and his staff hostage, an event that retrospectively appeared like a dress rehearsal for the embassy hostage taking that would take place later that year. Sullivan had informed Prime Minister Bazargan that the United States was going to maintain diplomatic relations with Iran, effectively recognizing Khomeini's provisional government. But the embassy had become vulnerable when its military guards left during the collapse of the shah's army on February 10–11. Anticipating an assault by hostile demonstrators, Sullivan had ordered his staff to ship all classified documents to Washington,

1 "Current Situation in Iran," cable from the situation Room to Camp David, February 19, 1979, quoted in Mohammad Ayatollahi Tabaar, *Religious Statecraft: The Politics of Islam in Iran* (Columbia University Press, 2018), 117.

keeping only what was necessary for daily operations. When the attackers broke into the embassy, he ordered its nineteen Marine guards to surrender. One Marine was injured, and two Iranians were killed as the attackers forced their way past the steel gates of the chancery building and were stopped behind its communication vault, where Sullivan, along with his staff and the general in charge of the US military mission, had taken refuge. While destroying documents and the vault's sensitive communication equipment, the Americans heard scuffle and fighting outside, realizing a rescue force had arrived. They opened the vault door and saw soon-to-be Foreign Minister Ebrahim Yazdi's armed rescue team had prevailed upon the occupiers to disengage and leave. Yazdi profusely apologized for the attack and posted armed guards to ensure the embassy's future safety. Sullivan notes that Khomeini sent a personal envoy to offer apologies, while he never received a message of support from Carter.[2]

The precise identity of the embassy's February 14 occupiers remains a mystery. Sullivan wrote that they were "about seventy-five guerrillas, armed with automatic rifles," and called them "Fedayeen," because some wore the checkered scarfs that were the trademarks of the Palestine Liberation Organization (PLO) and other Palestinian guerrilla groups. The Iranian press identified them as members of the Marxist Fada'i guerrilla organization, an allegation quickly denied by the organization's spokespersons. At the time, the Fada'i guerrillas were transitioning from an underground organization to an aboveground political group that had declared it would not oppose Khomeini's provisional government, particularly not through armed confrontations.[3] However, given their history, Fada'i guerillas were the most likely group capable of such a military operation, either directly or through their affiliate cells or "rogue" branches. In the end, the February 14 event was widely considered a leftist operation, setting a precedent that would be relevant to the American embassy's second seizure on November 4 (see below).

Following the embassy's rescue, Foreign Minister Yazdi guaranteed its safety, as well as the safety of about seven thousand Americans still waiting to be evacuated from Iran. The Valentine's Day episode showed

---

2 William H. Sullivan, *Mission to Iran* (W. W. Norton, 1981), 254–67; "Khomeini Forces Rescue US Ambassador, Staff," *Los Angeles Times*, February 15, 1979.

3 Sullivan, *Mission to Iran*, 529, 262; Anush Salehi, "*Sisant-varzi-ye cherikha-ye javan*," in GOFT-O-GO 69 (February 2015): 21–43, cited on 24; Siavush Randjbar Daemi, "*Az Mehrabad-jonobi ta daneshkadeh fanni*," in *Rahi digar* [The Road Not Taken], eds. Touraj Atabaki and Nasser Mohajer, vol. 2 (Noghteh Books, 2017), 527–53.

that, immediately after his victory, Khomeini valued diplomatic relations with the United States, allowing the operation of the US embassy, which in a few months he would denounce as a "den of spies." According to Sullivan, following this event, he warned Washington that "a move by the shah to the United States would result in the personnel of the American Embassy in Tehran being taken hostage."[4] By strange coincidence, at almost the same time on February 14, 1979, the US ambassador in Kabul, Adolph Dubs, was abducted by armed assailants and died in crossfire between them and the security forces of Afghanistan's new communist regime. In a notable contrast, Tehran's shaky revolutionary government managed to secure delicate diplomatic relations with Washington and save Ambassador Sullivan and his staff, while Kabul communists botched Ambassador Dubs's rescue, suffering a major blow to their already tense relations with the United States.[5]

A week after the embassy takeover, Sullivan met with Bazargan and Iran's new armed forces chief of staff, General Qarani, who said all weapons contracts with the United States would be honored and American military personnel could stay in Iran.[6] General Qarani, who was implicated in a 1958 coup plan tied to the United States (see chapter 3), was soon forced out of office and then assassinated, in April, by an underground group that accused the new regime of colluding with imperialism. The provisional government, however, requested that forty US military advisors remain in Iran to help with its fleet of F-14 fighter planes.[7] Sullivan also arranged for two American surveillance posts on the Soviet border to remain operational, after freeing their staff who briefly were held hostage by Iranians. In June, Sullivan was recalled to Washington, leaving ambassadorial duties to the deputy chief of the Tehran mission, Charles Naas, and chargé d'affaires, Bruce Laingen. He had been one of the most important US ambassadors to Iran, presiding over the shah's fall and the transition to the Islamic Republic, acting largely on his own and often at odds with Carter and most of his close advisors. He also had arranged an official agreement with the shah's caretaker government to

4 Sullivan, *Mission to Iran*, 277; "US Asks Iran to OK Evacuation of Americans by Air," *Los Angeles Times*, February 15, 1979.

5 Robert B. Rakove, *Day of Opportunity: The US and Afghanistan Before the Soviet Invasion* (Columbia University Press, 2023), 326–7.

6 Barry Rubin, *Paved with Good Intentions: The American Experience in Iran* (Penguin Books, 1981), 283.

7 Sullivan, *Mission to Iran*, 272; Christian Emery, *US Foreign Policy and the Iranian Revolution: The Cold War Dynamics of Engagement and Strategic Alliance* (Palgrave Macmillan, 2013), 98; *Peygham-e Emruz*, April 17, 1979.

accept liability for the cancellation of US weapons purchases Iran had already paid for. This left the United States in possession of billions of dollars of Iranian deposits, a major point of diplomatic negotiations with the Islamic Republic.[8]

The Carter administration was uncertain of its approach to revolutionary Iran, where Khomeini's provisional government was not yet a functioning state in control of the country. Conforming to classical postrevolutionary patterns, the grand coalition against the ancien régime was quickly unraveling, its various factions clashing in an intense power struggle. Soon, three factions had emerged as the main contenders: First, a group of radical clerics who formed the Islamic Republic Party, seeking to monopolize power behind Khomeini's enormous popularity; second, a loose coalition of secular and religious nationalists represented by Bazargan's provisional government; third, an incongruous grouping of secular and Islamic leftists, some enjoying popular armed support among non-Persian ethnic minorities. Most prominent among the latter were armed Kurdish parties upholding their region's virtual autonomy. Meanwhile, grassroots popular initiatives, linked to leftist groups, were spreading across the country. Factory workers, private sector and government employees, university students, and even soldiers and officers of the shah's scattered army were running their affairs through popularly elected councils (*shuras*), while landless peasants were seizing large estates and poor squatters were occupying empty urban buildings and public land. Exhorted by revolutionary promises of "free housing" and "land to the tiller," millions of urban and rural poor were asserting their agency in the absence of state power. Within two years, the inhabited area of Tehran would double as people seized and turned vast tracts of public and private land into living space. In the long run, however, the bulk of popular land seizure, in both rural and urban areas, were in public domains, the outcome being the privatization of commons, rather than the transfer of private wealth.[9] Leftist groups encouraged working-class and poor people's political initiative and economic demands, forcing the provisional government into partial compliance. With no functioning police and army, local neighborhood "committees" sprung

8 Sullivan, *Mission to Iran*, 245–7. Sullivan claims he saved the United States $4 billion.

9 Kaveh Ehsnai, "Survival through Dispossession: Privatization of Public Goods in the Islamic Republic," *Middle East Report* 250 (spring 2009): 26–33. On the workers' autonomous movement, see Asef Bayat, *Workers and Revolution in Iran: A Third World Experience of Workers Control* (Zed Books, 1987).

up everywhere to provide public order and security. The most dramatic outcome of state breakdown was the arming of ordinary citizens who had seized hundreds of thousands of guns when army barracks fell during the February 1979 uprising. A largely stateless Iran thus experienced its dream-like "Spring of Freedom," lasting from February to August 1979, when an armed populace was virtually autonomous and in charge of its own affairs. In this sense, the monarchy's fall was only the beginning of a radical revolution unfolding in the absence of state repression. Now, the main political question was whether Khomeini's Islamic Republic could contain a social revolution smoldering from below.

Among the enduring myths of the Iranian Revolution is that the Islamic Republic's formation was uncontested and supported particularly by the left. In fact, leftist intellectuals and organizations were in the forefront of opposition to Khomeini's Islamic government, some having rejected it even before the monarchy's fall. In February 1978, for example, Khosrow Shakeri, a leader of the student opposition abroad and an anti-Stalinist historian of Iran's leftist movements, published an open letter sharply criticizing Khomeini's anti-communist pronouncements as signals meant for Washington. "What you said in your recent speech," he wrote to Khomeini, "serves imperialist interests; it is carrying water for Carter."[10] In September 1978, a small Marxist organization, the Communist Unity Group, published a booklet warning an "Islamic government" was a reactionary alternative to the shah's regime:

> The "radical" religious tendency . . . opposes Iran's constitutional government . . . demanding a Koranic "Islamic government." This tendency seeks the overthrow of the Pahlavi dynasty or any form of monarchy . . . Many democratic forces, however, fail to realize this tendency opposes monarchist and constitutional government from an ultra-reactionary, rather than revolutionary, position.

In December 1978, the official organ of the same organization would write: "Khomeini believes his basic proposal of an 'Islamic government' can become a reality. This proposal means religion will seize state power."[11] On January 15, 1979, one day before the shah's final departure from Iran, Mostafa Rahimi, a democratic socialist lawyer and writer, published an open letter to Khomeini, rejecting his proposed Islamic

10 Khosrow Shakeri, *Aya berasti Khomeini democrat va zedd-e amperialist ast?* [Is Khomeini Really a Democrat and Anti-imperialist?] (Florence, 1978), quoted on 8.

11 Activists of Star and Communist Unity Group, *Az Goruh-e Setareh ta Sazman-e Vahdat-e Koministi* (Ketabe Raha, 2022), 263–9, quotes on 265–6, 269.

republic. Rahimi's letter, titled "Why I Am Against the Islamic Republic," appeared in *Ayandegan*, Tehran's widely circulating daily. It praised Khomeini's leadership of the anti-shah movement, but asked him not to assume a political role, warning that mixing religion with politics inevitably would lead to another dictatorship.[12] Outside Iran, the French Marxist scholar of Islam, Maxim Rodinson, offered the same critique of Khomeini's leadership in articles, published in December 1978 and February 1979, responding to French philosopher Michel Foucault's unabashed advocacy of Khomeini's "political spirituality."[13] The position of Iran's largest and most popular leftist organization, the People's Fada'ian Guerillas, toward Khomeini was inconsistent, reflecting their internal discord. Two days after the shah's departure, on January 17, the Fada'ian published a respectful open letter to Khomeini, offering its analysis of the revolution and rather boldly declaring:

> If your understanding of the Muslim Sharia and Islamic movement is steadfastly anti-imperialist and anti-dictatorial, we sincerely admire it . . . If, on the contrary, resorting to Islam and its teachings serves the purpose of suppressing dissenting beliefs, imprisoning ideas, reviving the apparatus of repression and censorship, bringing back the slogan of a single party, and silencing any freedom-seeking voice under the pretext of defending the Quran and Sharia, we are certain it would be condemned by all freedom-loving patriots, as well as by the people, who would recognize it as an instrument used by imperialism and reaction.

This declaration of Fada'ian's political independence was modified by the following statement in the organization's minimum program, published on February 13: "In the midst of our people's glorious revolution, we endorse Ayatollah Khomeini's righteous struggle and efforts toward overthrowing the monarchist regime, along with imperialism and its lackies, fully supporting his righteous endeavors." Here, while the adjective *righteous* made their support conditional, the Fada'ian organization strongly endorsed Khomeini's anti-shah and anti-imperialist struggle, without accepting his leadership role.[14]

12 Shaul Bakhash, *The Reign of Ayatollahs: Iran and the Islamic Revolution* (Basic Books, 1986), 71.

13 Maxime Rodinson, "Islam Resurgent?," and "Khomeini and the 'Primacy of the Spiritual,'" in Janet Afary and Kevin B. Anderson, *Foucault and the Iranian Revolution: Gender and the Seductions of Islamism* (University of Chicago Press, 2005), 223–38, 241–5.

14 Quotations in Randjbar Daemi, "*Az Mehrabad-jonobi ta daneshkadeh fanni*," 549, 552.

The first organization to openly challenge the provisional government was the leftist Democratic National Front (DNF), established on March 5, 1979, during the commemoration of former Premier Mohammad Mosaddeq's passing, attended by about one million participants. Conceived as a democratic and revolutionary version of Mosaddeq's National Front, the new organization was a liberal-left coalition that soon would openly challenge Khomeini. The DNF's core cadres included veterans of the student opposition abroad (see chapter 4), drawing on their successful experience of working in political coalitions. At the same time, a women's movement was openly defying Khomeini before the Islamic Republic was officially inaugurated. During March 8–12, 1979, tens of thousands of women came out in angry protests after Khomeini ordered mandatory veiling of government employees and abrogated existing women's rights legislation. Women's protests ended victoriously when it was announced that Khomeini had rescinded his order and veiling was not mandatory. Coinciding with International Women's Day (March 8), these protests enlisted foreign feminists who were in Iran celebrating the revolution's victory. Among them was American scholar Kate Millet, a vociferous critic of the shah, who was deported by the provisional government for giving interviews supportive of women's defiance of Khomeini. Millet's Iran interviews were later published as *Going to Iran.*[15]

Throughout spring 1979, a constitutionally undefined Islamic Republic was pushing against women's rights and press freedom, purging leftists and liberals, waging war against ethnic minorities, and summarily executing autonomy-seeking Kurds along with old regime officials. These trends, and Khomeini's unassailable status of a divinely sanctioned popular dictator, led some Iranian and foreign observers to see a protofascist movement brewing in the middle of the revolution. Warning about these trends, in April 1979 a prominent critic of the shah's regime published a sensational article titled "Hearing the Footsteps of Fascism." Soon, the leftist press was awash with accusations of the Islamic Republic's fascist behavior.[16] When independent leftist weekly *Friday Book*

15 On the Democratic National front see Afshin Matin-Asgari, "The Left's Contribution to Social Justice in Iran: A Brief Historical Overview," in *Iran's Struggle for Social Justice: Economics, Agency, Justice, Activism*, ed. Peyman Vahabzadeh (Palgrave Macmillan, 2017), 255–69, cited on 266; Negar Mottahedeh, *Whisper Tapes: Kate Millet in Iran* (Stanford University Press, 2019); Kate Millet, *Going to Iran* (Coward, McCann & Geoghegan, 1982).

16 Ali-asghar Hajj-Seyyed Javadi, "*Seda-ye pa-ye fashism*" [Hearing the Footsteps of Fascism], *Jonbesh*, April 21, 1979. "Mr. Prime Minister: Fascism Has Nested in Your Cabinet!" *Peygham-e Emruz* headline, April 24, 1979; "When Fascism Knocks on the

(Ketab-e Jom'eh) began publication in July, the lead article of its first issue was a translation of Bertolt Brecht's famous 1935 warning about the rise of fascism. *Friday Book*'s one-year run, from July 1979 to its closure in May 1980, featured hard-hitting weekly commentaries on the revolution's drift toward a new dictatorship, written by Iran's leading Marxist scholars and intellectuals. *Friday Book* was a strong advocate of democracy, as a universal norm above class or national interests, and diagnosed the US embassy hostage taking as a political coup aimed at bringing down the provisional government, beating the Marxists in anti-imperialist mobilization, and deflecting popular demands for revolutionary social change.[17] In November 1979, a small Marxist organization called Workers' Path published a series of booklets titled *Fascism: Nightmare or Reality?*, arguing the Islamic Republic would be a fascist state ruled by a clerical caste. The new regime, according to Workers' Path, was Bonapartist, meaning it appealed to contradictory social interests, rather than representing a single social class.[18] As we shall see in chapter 6, during the 1990s, dissident intellectuals and even reformist President Mohammad Khatami would criticize the Islamic Republic's fascist tendencies without acknowledging those who had identified these features as early as 1979.[19]

In addition to Khomeini's charismatic cult, classic fascist tendencies, as defined, for example, by Antonio Gramsci, were discernable in 1979 Iran. First, there was a radical mass movement, appealing mainly to society's middle strata, competing with Marxists and liberals to settle a revolutionary national crisis. Second, this movement celebrated violence and martyrdom, mobilizing its militia, along with the armed forces, for permanent war against domestic and foreign enemies. Third, while virulently anti-communist, Khomeini's followers borrowed Marxist rhetoric and agendas, claiming to serve the lower and working classes.[20] The

Door!" *Peygham-e Emruz*, April 28, 1979. *Azadi*, organ of DNF, focused on fascism either in its front-page headlines or lead articles. See *Azadi* issues of April 17, April 24, May 22, June 5, June 22, and August 12, 1979.

17 Afshin Matin-Asgari, "Marxism, Historiography and Historical Consciousness in Modern Iran: A Preliminary Study," in *Iran in the 20th Century: Historiography and Political Culture*, ed. Touraj Atabaki (I.B. Tauris, 2009): 199–231. Cited on 227–9.

18 Ibid., 230.

19 Eskandar Sadeghi-Boroujerdi, *Revolution and its Discontents: Political Thought and Reform in Iran* (Cambridge and New York: Cambridge University Press, 2019), 222–5. Akbar Ganji, *Talaqi-ye fashisti az din va hokumat* (Tehran, 2000). Khatami's warning of "religious fascism," *Iran Times*, December 11, 1998, 1.

20 Italian Marxist Antonio Gramsci listed these characteristics in his classic identification of fascism. See Antonio Gramsci, "The Revolution Against Capital" and "The Crisis of the Capitalist System," in *Italian Critics of Capitalism*, ed. and trans. by Lorella Cedroni (Lexington Books, 2010), 46–57.

new regime's militia, the Islamic Revolutionary Guard Corps (IRGC), was established in February 1979, a few days before the official declaration of the Islamic Republic. It was hastily organized as the revolution's national guard, in part responding to the left's advocacy of a people's militia to replace the shah's army. From the start, however, the IRGC was right wing, its official mandate excluding communists and Islamic leftists from membership. When this mandate was debated in the Revolutionary Council, its only left-leaning member objected, saying "if the IRGC were to be anti-communist, then it would engage in communist-killing . . . dragging us towards fascism." True to this prediction, the IRGC was immediately deployed to fight Kurdistan's Marxist-led popular militia.[21]

The 1979 debate on fascism was related to the left's understanding of the Islamic Republic's class character. Leftist groups and organizations agreed that Khomeini's movement was petty bourgeois, its core social base being in the propertied urban and rural middle strata. But the left was divided between those who thought, under Khomeini's leadership, the petty bourgeoisie was reactionary and those who, like the pro-Soviet Tudeh Party, argued it was progressive and anti-imperialist. The left was also divided between those who, led by the Democratic National Front, upheld democratic freedoms, and saw liberals as allies, and those, led by the Tudeh Party, who saw everything as secondary to anti-imperialism. As we see below, the latter issue, which effectively meant anti-Americanism, would play an important role in shaping the Islamic Republic.

Given the collapse of the shah's army, the Revolutionary Guards quickly rose in prominence, soon engaged in a war against autonomy-seeking Kurdish rebels. In spring 1979, armed Kurdish popular resistance repeatedly beat back Tehran's military campaigns, forcing the provisional government to begin negotiations on Kurdistan autonomy. Meanwhile, the IRGC was clashing with autonomy-seeking movements in the oil province of Khuzestan and the Caspian Sea region of the Turkoman Desert. To legitimize the new regime's authority, on March 30–31, a hastily organized national referendum asked Iranians to endorse the monarchy's replacement with an undefined "Islamic Republic." With the voting age lowered to sixteen, the referendum passed with a huge margin, though it was boycotted in Kurdistan and by the Fada'i guerrillas

---

21 Ali Rahnema, *The Political History of Modern Iran: Revolution, Reaction and Transformation, 1905 to the Present* (I.B. Tauris, 2023), 381–2; for a comprehensive study of the IRGC see Bayram Sinkaya, *The Revolutionary Guards in Iranian Politics* (Routledge, 2016).

and the Democratic National Front. Having obtained a blank check for a religious government, the Islamic Republic Party (IRP) now proposed a constitution that superimposed clerical control over republican institutions, giving Khomeini, as supreme juridical leader (Faqih), unlimited dictatorial powers. The IRP's push, however, faced stiff resistance not only from left and liberal groups but from senior clerics, led by Ayatollah Kazem Shariatmadari, who objected to direct clerical rule as a radical innovation in Islam. By April, hundreds of thousands of Azerbaijani supporters of Ayatollah Shariatmadari were protesting the IRP's dictatorship.[22]

Initially, even Khomeini had not called for clerical rule, repeatedly declaring in 1978 that, after the shah's departure, Iran would have a "democratic" government, in which he would serve only as a "guide," playing no political role. The first article of Khomeini's Revolutionary Council had defined its goal as "the establishment of a democratic Islamic Republic."[23] In early spring, Khomeini had endorsed a draft constitution which allowed clerics no political role except for veto power over legislation, a provision that had existed in the 1906 constitution. Khomeini recommended the draft constitution's quick adoption through a national referendum, but the provisional government and almost all secular parties opposed this, demanding instead a constituent assembly. Ironically, the call for a constituent assembly would allow the Islamic Republic Party to gain Khomeini's support for an undemocratic constitution giving the clergy far greater powers.[24] Later, Khomeini would admit to having changed his mind on this issue, saying he had erroneously assumed that nonclerics could run an Islamic government.[25]

Thus, contrary to contemporary perceptions, which echoed in scholarly studies and the American political establishment, state formation in postrevolutionary Iran had little to do with traditional Shi'i ideas of government. As a recent study puts it, "revolution came first and 'Islam' followed. Simply studying Shi'a theology would not predict or even explain the revolution . . . Islamist ideology was not used, but—more importantly—constructed and institutionalized strategically by elites in

22 *Paygham-e Emruz*, April 24, 1979.

23 Manssur Razavi, *Hashemi va enqelab* (Tehran, 2006), 167.

24 Siavush Randjbar-Daemi, *The Quest for Authority in Iran: A History of the Presidency from Revolution to Rouhani* (I.B. Tauris, 2020), 11–14.

25 For Khomeini's interviews denying clerics would rule the Islamic, see Mehdi Bazargan, *Enqelab-e Iran dar do Harekat* (Tehran, 1984), 51–5; Khomeini's admission to this being his mistake, ibid., 123–4.

response to changing opportunities and threat perceptions."[26] In fact, the arbitrary dictatorship of the Supreme Jurist resembled German jurist Carl Schmitt's notion of dictatorship arising in a political "state of exception." The Islamic Republic also conforms to Schmitt's understanding of modern sovereignty as a secularized theological concept, whereby the lawgiver's absolute power approaches divine omnipotence. Finally, and again in line with Schmitt's theory of dictatorial sovereignty, the Islamic Republic originated and remained in a state of perpetual confrontation with an existential "enemy," soon to be identified as the United States.[27]

Khomeini's August 1979 Coup Against the Revolutions' Leftist and Democratic Factions

> *We would not have had today's problems, had we acted in a revolutionary manner, banning the corrupt press, breaking their writers' pens, putting their sponsors on trial, banning all corrupt parties, and punishing their leaders, setting up public gallows to annihilate them all . . . [and] banning all parties and all fronts, allowing only one party, the party of God.*
>
> Khomeini, August 18, 1979[28]

The background to what Khomeini called Iran's "Second Revolution," launched with the seizure of the US embassy in fall 1979, was an intensifying power struggle within the revolutionary coalition, approaching a civil war in places like Kurdistan. Contemporary observers noted the linkage of Khomeini's confrontation with the United States to Iran's domestic politics, particularly the IRP's drive to monopolize power. The essentially secular character of this power struggle was soon obscured when scholarly experts, journalists, and political pundits explained the American Hostage Crisis and its aftermath in terms of Shi'i fanaticism. A recent scholarly study has revived the original understanding of the Hostage Crisis as primarily a project aimed at neutralizing and eliminating the IRP's opponents, particularly those on the left.[29] Below, we

---

26 Ayatollahi Tabaar, *Religious Statecraft*, 4.

27 Carl Schmitt, *Political Theology: Four Chapters on the Concept of Sovereignty*, trans. George Schwab (University of Chicago Press, 1985); Asghar Shirazi, *The Constitution of Iran: Politics and the State in the Islamic Republic* (I.B. Tauris, 1997), chapter 9, and 230.

28 Ruhollah Khomeini in Sahifeh Imam Khomeini, vol. 9, 282, cited in rouhollah.ir at farsi.rouhollah.ir/library/sahifeh-imam-khomeini/vol/9/page/282.

29 Ayatollahi Tabaar, *Religious Statecraft*. The original interpretation appeared, for

briefly revisit this background, as well as the Carter administration's role in events that would shape Iran-US relations for decades to come.

During the first half of 1979, leftist forces had emerged as the main contender to Khomeini, the IRP, and the provisional government. The left had expanded its prerevolutionary hegemony among the intelligentsia, primarily hundreds of thousands of high school and university students, while forging ties to politicized workers and armed autonomy-seeking populations in Kurdish, Arab, and Turkomans regions. A major challenge to Khomeini's provisional government was the country-wide movement of workers' councils, which was aligning with radical leftist organizations. During the anti-monarchist general strikes of winter 1979, millions of workers had taken control of oil and other major industries, as well as private sector factories and businesses. Defying Khomeini's back-to-work orders, revolutionary strikes and industrial action intensified during 1979, drastically declining after the US embassy takeover, and further diminishing in 1980 and 1981 as government repression intensified and workers were forced to join "Islamic councils" tied to the state.[30] At the same time, in spring and summer 1979, the left was clearly ahead of the IRP and Khomeini supporters in terms of influence among an assertive working class. On May Day 1979, for instance, the IRP's rally was the smallest of four gatherings; the other three were called by leftist groups and labor unions, together bringing out more than half a million in Tehran and tens of thousands in Azerbaijan and Kurdistan.[31] Khomeini was worried about growing leftist influence among the country's restive working classes. In July 1979, he gave a blunt speech to his industrialist and bazaari supporters, assuring the protection of their interests if they made concessions to workers to forestall a communist-inspired revolt:

> Factory-owners must make some changes in their situation . . . God-forbidding, if neglecting the workers in an Islamic country leads to an explosion among them . . . neither the clergy nor anybody else can

---

example, in the leftist weekly *Friday Book* [*Ketab-e Jom'eh*] 1, no. 31 (April 1980); and also in Bazargan in *Enqelab-e Iran dar do Harekat*, 133–42.

30 Assef Bayat, *Workers and Revolution in Iran: A Third World Experience of Workers' Control* (Zed Press, 1987). "Leftist Rhetoric Spreads in Iran Oil Fields: Newly Politicized Workers Now Talk of Union, Share in Control," *Los Angeles Times*, March 8, 1979, part I, 14–15. Practically every issue of *Peygham-e Emruz* reports on growing labor strikes, unrest, and factory takeover.

31 Ervand *Abrahamian, Khomeinism: Essays on the Islamic Republic* (University of California Press, 1993), 71–3. *Peygham-e Emruz*, May 2, 1979.

> contain it and this would endanger all of you and all of us . . . You should give a little and the workers should gain a little . . . For your own sake, and to prevent an explosion destroying the country, help them [workers] voluntarily . . . The point is to show the workers that communist and deviationist claims are not true . . . Islam recognizes legitimate proprietorship, allowing the ownership of industrial factories . . . This is not a communist country where the state can do whatever it wants; this is an Islamic country recognizing proprietorship.[32]

Meanwhile, the left was expanding its middle-class base by taking full advantage of unprecedented political freedom and a flourishing free press. Since the winter 1978 general strikes, all major newspapers were taken over and run by their employees, who mostly leaned leftward, increasingly opposing the IRP and its proposed dictatorial constitution. Tehran's independent leftist daily *Today's Message* (*Peygham-e emruz*) led the charge, fiercely defending the free press, Marxist and religious left organizations, Kurdish autonomy, and workers' councils. Along with *Today's Message*, the Democratic National Front (DNF) and other leftist groups increasingly attacked the new regime's "fascist" tendencies and its dealings with United States, demanding the cancellation of American arms contracts, the expulsion of all US military advisors, and the closure of US spying stations in Iran.[33] Khomeini had authorized Foreign Minister Yazdi to hold a meeting with the American chargé Bruce Laingen and the head of the US military mission, General Gast, in Tehran, and with US Secretary of State Cyrus Vance in New York. According to their transcripts, these meetings were tense, with US diplomats, including Vance, offering Tehran a new relationship based on mutual interests, something the Iranian side, led by Yazdi, found difficult to trust and convey to the public.[34] To mend fences with the postrevolutionary regime, the Carter administration needed to show a dramatic change of course from

32 The Persian Text of Khomeini's July 1979 speech at emam.com/posts/view/1752; see M. Stella Morgana, "Talking to Workers: From Khomeini to Ahmadinejad, How the Islamic Republic's Discourse on Labor Changed through May Day Speeches (1979–2009)," *Iranian Studies* 52, no. 1–2: 133–58.

33 See *Peygham-e Emruz* issues of April 7, 25, and 30, 1979; May 5, 13, 14, and 31, 1979; and July 4, 1979. "Bloc the Path of Fascism!" was the front-page headline of *Azadi*, organ of the Democratic National Front, April 17, 1979. Even popular weeklies, which generally were leaning to the left during the revolution, were publishing articles with headlines such as "Bazargan's Failure Will Be Followed Fascism." Article by Masud Behnud, *Tehran Mossavar*, May 3, 1979, 16–17.

34 Ebrahim Yazadi, *Shast sal Saburi va shakuri* (Tehran: 1400), vol. 5, book 2 (1400), 157–8, 163, 169–238.

decades of US policy, something that private assurance to Iranian officials could not accomplish. In fact, the provisional government's public and private interactions with the United States made it vulnerable to charges of collusions with imperialism, vociferously aired by the left and increasingly echoed in the free press.

In May 1979, the DNF held a rally, with over one hundred thousand participants, in defense of press freedom, receiving support messages from Fadaian and Mojahedin organizations.[35] It then published an open letter to Khomeini accusing him of monopolizing power, going back on his promises of freedom for all:

> You personally and directly intervene in the country's domestic foreign affairs . . . If religion and politics are intertwined and the clergy must rule, then a religious leader would manage the nation's affairs according to his divinely ordained position, as you do. In this position, his every word is a divine command that his followers must obey, or they would be opposing God . . . Is not this despotism?[36]

Today's Message criticized the provisional government's secret dealings with the United States, reporting of clandestine meeting between Bazargan and Yazdi with the American chargé Charles Nass.[37] Meanwhile, the country's leading independent daily, *Ayandegan*, angered Khomeini by reporting that the assassination of one of his closest associates was the work of an underground Islamic group and not tied to leftist groups, as Khomeini had alleged. In early August, when *Ayandegan* published an expose of clerical manipulation of elections to the assembly drafting the new constitution, it was shut down and its editorial board imprisoned. Major street clashes ensued on August 11 when hundreds of thousands responded to the DNF's call to protest new restrictive press laws and other anti-democratic measures. Backed by security forces, the Islamic Republic Party's plainclothes militia attacked the protest, causing hundreds of injuries as pitched battles raged in central Tehran.[38] These events were witnessed by leftist Iran expert Fred Halliday, who described them as the emergence of a fascist tendency from within the revolution:

35 *Azadi*, May 22, 1979.
36 *Azadi*, June 5, 1979.
37 *Peygham-e Emruz*, June 3, 1979. *Azadi*, August 12, 1979.
38 *Peygham-e Emruz*, August 14, 1979, reports hundreds of thousands.

> By chance, I was in the offices of *Ayandegan* when the revolutionary guards came to close it down. I spoke with one guard, and he told me the paper was "shit" (*goh*). When I told him that two million people read it, he replied that the two million people were *goh* too. I participated in the mass demonstration by supporters of *Ayandegan* against censorship, and visited the offices of the Fedayin and Mojahedin days before they were closed. It was at that time too that the first offensives against the Kurds were launched in the west. On leaving Iran, I realized that this had been a turning point in the revolution and that the direction and repressive capacity of the regime were to be condemned. In the *New Statesman* I published an extended report, under the title "Islam with a Fascist Face."[39]

As Halliday noted, leftist Fadaian and Mojahedin organizations were forcibly evicted from their headquarters, and, on August 18, Khomeini ordered another military offensive in Kurdistan, declaring that henceforth all parties and groups, except for his own supporters, would be crushed. Ironically, Khomeini's coup ending the revolution's brief democratic phase occurred on precisely the same calendar date, August 18–19, when the 1953 CIA coup had ended Iran's previous period of semidemocratic politics under Mosaddeq's premiership. But the military offensive in Kurdistan failed again and, by October, Khomeini opened negotiations with the Kurdish rebels to buy time and attack them from a stronger position.[40] By early fall, the DNF was openly rejecting the proposed constitution, writing in a front-page editorial:

> Supporters of the Guardianship of the Jurist promote it for their own secular interests and not to uphold God's will and the Prophet's mission . . . its approval plunges our society back into one-person rule with unexpected and unimaginable speed."[41]

Meanwhile, the left and liberal opposition found a new ally in Ayatollah Shariatmadari, who declared his opposition to the IRP and its proposed clerical constitution. With religious credentials superior to Khomeini's, and several million Azerbaijani followers, Shariatmadari challenged the claim that Iran's Shi'i population was united behind Khomeini and his

---

39 Fred Halliday, *New Left Review* 166 (1987): 29–37, quotes on 36.

40 "Kurdish Offer of Peace Turned down by Khomeini" *Los Angeles Times*, August 29, 1979, part I, p. 15. "Iran's Kurds Appear to Have Won Autonomy," *Los Angeles Times*, December 6, 1979.

41 *Azadi*, September 30, 1979.

single party. Electoral statistics for 1979–80 show a steady decline of the IRP's support and hence indirectly of Khomeini's popularity. In December 1979, sixteen million people (75 percent of the electorate) voted for the new clerical constitution, a significant drop from the more than the twenty million votes in the March 1979 referendum on the Islamic Republic. Three months later, in March–May 1980, slightly half of the eligible voters participated in the first postrevolutionary parliamentary election, in which the IRP won 85 out of 270 seats. Thus, one year into the revolution, the IRP could count on one-third of the votes cast by half of the eligible voters.[42] Significantly, during the 1980 parliamentary elections, candidates of the Marxist Fada'ian organization received nearly 10 percent of the ballots cast, about a third of IRP's votes.[43] This suggests that the Marxist left, together with the larger Mojahedin organization, could count on 20 percent of the national vote, a figure that would rise by another 10 percent if the absent ballots of provincial leftist strongholds, primarily Kurdistan, were counted.[44] With potentially 20 to 30 percent of the national vote, a united leftist front could pose a serious threat to Khomeini and the IRP, who also faced opposition by several million followers of Ayatollah Shariatmadari, as well as a growing bloc of middle-class supporters of President Bani-Sadr. Ultimately, in less than a year, the revolutionary coalition formed behind Khomeini had deeply fractured and the IRP's project of building a one-party state was on shaky grounds. In fall 1979, Khomeini and the IRP carried out a political coup allowing them to take back the initiative and first contain and then eliminate all opposition. The coup was the launch of the "second revolution" that began with the November 4 hostage taking at the US embassy. One scholar summarized this revolutionary turning point's political background and motives:

> Leftist and Islamist factions instrumentally deployed anti-Americanism to outbid one another's anti-imperialist credibility. This chain of strategic interactions culminated in the Islamists' seizure of the US embassy on November 4, 1979. The embassy occupation effectively undermined

42 Shariatmadari's challenge in Bakhash, *The Reign of Ayatollahs*, 89. The statistics on the first presidential and Majles election are in ibid., 90, 105.

43 Peyman Vahabzadeh, *A Guerrilla Odyssey: Modernization, Secularism, Democracy, and Fadai Period of National Liberation in Iran, 1971–1979* (Syracuse University Press, 2010), 67.

44 The Marxist stronghold Kurdistan, along with Sunni Baluchistan, had around 10 percent voter turnout in Iran's first presidential election in 1980, as well as in the second and third presidential elections, both in 1981. See electoral maps in Bernard Hourcade, *Atlas of Presidential Elections in the Islamic Republic of Iran: 1980–2017* (Centre de Recherche sur le Monde Iranien Paris, 2020), 8, 11, 14.

the left's cohesion, prevented the radical Islamists from defecting to the Marxist camp, and further united the loose coalition of radical and conservative Islamists behind Khomeini.[45]

The American Hostage Crisis: A Second Revolution or the Anti-imperialism of Fools

Support for the seizure of the US hostages, what I have termed "the anti-imperialism of fools," was to provide the ideal cover for Khomeini's consolidation of clerical dictatorship.

Fred Halliday[46]

The Hostage Crisis itself was in fact about outbidding the Marxists.

Former supporter of hostage taking[47]

The hostage crisis was manufactured by Khomeini and the Islamic Republic Party, but the Carter administration's misguided policy toward postrevolutionary Iran contributed to its making. Between February 1978 and November 1979, Carter had the opportunity to fundamentally change course by seriously addressing Iranian grievances against past US policies. Instead, he stayed the course of his predecessors, approaching the revolution within the Cold War frame of American economic interest and "security," backed by military linkages and covert diplomacy. During the window of opportunity from February to November 1979, Iran's provisional government was cautiously trying to mend ties with the United States, working through a private liaison with Ambassador Sullivan and his caretaker deputies Naas and Laingen. Amid a growing chorus of leftist calls for cutting all ties to the United States, Prime Minister Bazargan, Foreign Minister Yazdi, and the IRP chair, Ayatollah Beheshti, held secret meetings with American embassy officials, including CIA agents, sharing intelligence and trying to settle financial disputes over the shah's canceled military purchases. Khomeini allowed such meetings, which, after the US embassy hostage taking, he would declare treasonous. A major topic of American talks with Bazargan's government was the IBEX project and the two CIA listening posts on the Soviet border in northern Iran. Purchased by the shah, IBEX was an advanced

45 Ayatollahi Tabaar, *Religious Statecraft*, 113.
46 Fred Halliday, *New Left Review* 166 (1987): 290–37, quoted on 37.
47 Emaddein Baqi quoted in Ayatollahi Tabaar, *Religious Statecraft*, 124.

computerized intelligence-gathering system, using equipment carried on planes flying over Iranian borders (see chapter 4). The IBEX system, along with the two CIA listening posts in northern Iran, were kept in operational mode after the revolution, though their actual use required the presence of highly trained US technicians. Iran's leftist press attacked the provisional government for secretly talking with the US embassy about IBEX and the listening posts, while the embassy convinced the *Los Angeles Times* and *Washington Post* reporters not to cover the story, as it would "destroy" the shaky Iran-US relationship.[48]

Normalizing Iran-US relations hit a hurdle in May 1979 when the execution of a prominent Jewish businessman prompted the US Senate to condemn Iran's revolutionary trials. In response, Khomeini declared he would not accept a new American ambassador, while Foreign Minister Yazdi protested to Secretary Vance that the US Senate had not cared about decades of summary trials and executions under the shah. But the provisional government continued its covert meetings with chargé Laingen and CIA officers, mostly to share intelligence on the Soviet Union, Afghanistan, and Iraq. The CIA assured the Iranians that Kurdish rebels were not supported by the United States or the Soviet Union, while warning them of Iraqi preparation for an invasion of Iran. Although the latter information was perhaps exaggerated to show US support of the Islamic Republic, the fact remains that, throughout 1979, Washington was siding with Iran against Iraq, an important strategic alignment that would end with the hostage crisis.[49] The shaky relations between Washington and revolutionary Tehran collapsed when Carter decided the shah could come to the United States for medical treatment. American diplomats in Tehran had warned of a repeat of the February 1979 attack on the embassy if the shah set foot in the United States. Ignoring such warnings, Carter, in late October, gave in to intense pressure by David Rockefeller and Henry Kissinger to admit the shah, a decision without any compelling political or humanitarian reason. After deciding on the shah's admission, Carter asked his advisors what they might recommend when the Tehran embassy was taken over.[50] This blundering decision

48 Emery, *US Foreign Policy and the Iranian Revolution*, 123.

49 Mark Gasiorowski, "US Intelligence Assistance to Iran, May–October 1979," *Middle East Journal* 66, no.4 (autumn 2012): 614–27, 617–24; Emery, *US Foreign Policy and the Iranian Revolution*, 124–8.

50 Gary Sick, *All Fall Down: America's Tragic Encounter with Iran* (Random House, 1985), 179–84; William J. Daugherty, "Jimmy Carter and the 1979 Decision to Admit the Shah into the United States," *American Diplomacy*, April 2003, americandiplomacy.web.unc.edu.

was made when Carter's presidency was already sliding into crisis, his approval rating approaching Nixon's just prior to his resignation. Public dissatisfaction stemmed from an energy crisis and runaway inflation that the Carter White House was unable to control. In mid-July, Carter gave a speech admitting that after "the agony of Vietnam" and "the shock of Watergate," America faced "a crisis of confidence . . . that strikes at the very heart and soul and spirit of our national will."[51] He then reshuffled his cabinet, hoping to gain some traction in domestic politics. Nor was Carter's foreign policy more successful; his major accomplishment was an Egypt-Israel peace accord, but he had helplessly presided over the fall of a major ally in Iran and the Soviet takeover of Afghanistan, with another revolution brewing in Nicaragua. Amid these already dire circumstances, the Iran hostage crisis would doom Carter's presidency.

On the Iranian side, Khomeini would use the standoff with the United States to launch a "second revolution," harnessing the pent-up anti-imperialist charge of the first (anti-shah) revolution to consolidate his clerical dictatorship. However, as with the project of a clerically controlled government, turning the hostage crisis into a major confrontation with the United States was not something Khomeini had preplanned. An Iranian "mole" in the embassy had informed IRP leaders that US diplomats expected to be taken hostage if the shah came to the United States. This was a troubling prospect to the IRP, whose chairman Ayatollah Beheshti's secret contacts with Americans might be exposed in an embassy takeover. "If that happened," wrote a journalist who interviewed IRP leaders, "and if the leftists were able to capture documents showing the contacts between clerical leaders and the Embassy, the political ambitions of these leaders would have come to an end."[52] In this sense, American hostage taking was the IRP's preemptive move against a looming leftist threat, rather than an attempt to bring down the provisional government, which had tendered its resignation before the embassy takeover.[53]

Ironically, during the first ten days after the shah's arrival at a New York hospital, Tehran remained calm, with no major public outcries or mass protests. Even Khomeini was rather subdued, asking Foreign Minister Yazdi if the shah's wealth in the United States, and not the

51 David Fraber, *Taken Hostage: The Iran Hostage Crisis and America's First Encounter with Radical Islam* (Princeton University Press, 2005), 31–3.

52 Christos P. Ioannides, *America's Iran: Injury and Catharsis* (University Press of America, 1984), 91–3, quoted on 101–2.

53 Bazargan, *Enqelab-e Iran dar do Harekat*, 95.

deposed monarch himself, could be returned to Iran. "It's all right if he dies," Khomeini reportedly said, "but what will happen to our money?" Everything changed on November 1, the day Prime Minister Bazargan, while in Algiers to observe Algeria's Independence Day, met with Carter's National Security Advisor Brzezinski to discuss normalizing relations, a major mistake on both sides. Brzezinski had made the decision to meet Bazargan on his own, while Bazargan had not asked Khomeini's permission for such a sensitive meeting. Neither side considered the meeting's terrible timing, coming just in the wake of the shah's arrival in the United States.[54] A political firestorm broke out in Tehran, where vociferous leftist factions, joined by the IRP, vehemently condemned the meeting. Consequently, Bazargan, who had offered to resign earlier, finally stepped down from premiership. By this time, Khomeini was angrily calling on the nation, and particularly university students, to mobilize against the United States, and the IRP was organizing countrywide anti-American protests. On November 1, the IRP held a massive demonstration in front of the US embassy, rerouting it to end in a rally four miles away, thus protecting the embassy from uncontrolled attacks by leftist groups. Alarming Khomeini and the IRP, leftist groups (that is, Mojahedin, Fadaian, and the Tudeh Party) then announced plans for a joint rally in front of the embassy on November 4, "Student Day," commemorating the previous year's killing of student protesters by the military.[55] On that day, before the leftist rally could take place, five hundred "Student Followers of the Imam's Line" stormed the embassy. Some of their leaders later admitted they were trying to preempt the leftists from taking over the embassy as they were widely believed to have done in February 1979. According to one student leader, their action prevented "more violent groups" from seizing the embassy. Another student leader said, "If unchecked, (political) trends would most likely have made Mojahed and Fadai radicals more powerful . . . The embassy occupation weakened all leftists, whether Mojahedin or Fadaian."[56] The student occupiers saw their action as temporary and peaceful, some describing it as an American-style "sit-in," an occasion to air Iranian grievances against the United States. However, the event

---

54 Khomeini quoted in Ioannides, *America's Iran: Injury and Catharsis*, 119; Emery, *US Foreign Policy and the Iranian Revolution*, 138–40; Yazdi admits the meeting with Brzezinski took place without Khomeini's knowledge. *Shast sal Saburi va shakuri*, vol. 7, book 1 (Tehran, 1400), 546–52.

55 Ioannides, *America's Iran*, 120–5.

56 Ayatollahi Tabaar, *Religious Statecraft*, 115. Interview with Abbas Abadi, *Andishepouya* 4, no. 25 (May 2015), 51.

was secretly planed under the supervision of a cleric named Mohammad Khoeiniha, a student of Khomeini and close associate of his son Ahmad, who immediately endorsed the occupation, giving it official sanction. Moreover, the embassy's Iranian security guards, strengthened after its leftist takeover on February 14, offered no resistance to the November 4 occupation. Foreign Minister Yazdi claims that Khomeini was surprised by the embassy takeover, asking who the students were and telling Yazdi to "throw them out," as he had done during the leftist takeover in February. But Khomeini changed his mind later the same day, approving of the takeover and thus setting the course for a prolonged and costly confrontation with the United States.[57]

Six US embassy personnel eluded capture by taking refuge at the homes of Canadian diplomats and were secretly whisked out of Iran three months later. Of the sixty-six remaining hostages, thirteen women and African Americans were soon released, and another was freed due to illness in January 1980. The other fifty-two remained in Iran for 444 days. The hostage crisis resulted in the Islamic Republic's international isolation and was condemned by the UN Security Council, as well as the International Court of Justice at The Hague. As during the Iranian Revolution, however, Washington's response was haphazard and contradictory. Carter quickly froze $12 billion of Iran's assets, banned trade, and restricted financial transactions with Iran, labeling the Islamic Republic a "state sponsor of terrorism." Thus began the imposition of draconian US economic sanctions on Iran, effectively a state of war without direct military engagement—a situation that continues to the present. Carter soon grasped the situation's gravity, admitting, in his diary, that Iranians "have us by the balls." Privately, he expressed anger toward Kissinger's "lies and other activities," as well as Brzezinski's and the Rockefeller lobby's efforts to bring the shah to the United States.[58] Despite his hawkish posture, Brzezinski privately admitted there was little Washington could do vis-à-vis Khomeini's maneuvers. In the wake of the Tehran embassy seizure, he expressed this in a "top secret" memo to Carter:

> We are never going to be able to work with the Khomeini regime . . . The Iranian revolution was a true expression of deep-seated national will, and the anti-Americanism we are seeing is a true expression of national

---

57 Yazdi, *Shast sal Saburi va shakuri*, 18, 40; Ayatollahi Tabaar, *Religious Statecraft*, 13–33.

58 Jimmy Carter, *White House Diary* (Farrar, Straus and Giroux, 2010), 367–8, 372, 375; "They have us by the balls," quoted in Sick, *All Fall Down*, 209.

> outrage at US actions over the past 26 years . . . We are not in control of events, and we must prepare for the worst. The oil fields are what count in the final analysis.[59]

At the same time, Brzezinski was part of Washington's "Pahlavi lobby" that, spearhead by Kissinger, had worked hard to bring the shah to the US. Brzezinski had close personal ties to the Kissinger-Rockefeller clan, the shah's strongest American connection. After Nelson Rockefeller's death in January 1979, his brother David took over the family's banking empire and vast global operations. The Rockefellers' Chase Manhattan Bank held the Pahlavi family's assets and was the lead partner in a financial syndicate holding massive Iranian government deposits and loans. The freezing of Iranian assets in the United States would give Chase Manhattan and other US banks great leverage with their multi-billion-dollar Iranian portfolio. This is exactly what happened due to the hostage crisis—its final resolution dropped $4 billion into the laps of American banks, with Chase Manhattan sitting on top of the heap. In addition, Chase and other banks collected hefty interest on the Iranian holdings that Carter's freeze left in their keeping for more than a year. Some contemporary observers suspected the Rockefeller family had deliberately engineered an Iran crisis by lobbying for the shah's admission to the United States, whose consequences led to an Iranian asset freeze and a bonanza settlement for Chase Manhattan. This so-called Chase thesis was taken seriously enough to become the object of a 1981 congressional investigation, which denied its plausibility. Still, some former hostages continued to believe the Chase thesis, trying unsuccessfully to sue the Rockefeller bank for its involvement in events leading to their captivity in Iran.[60]

Back in fall 1979, the events in Tehran were sending destabilizing ripples throughout the region. On November 20, the Great Mosque in Mecca was occupied by armed militants who called for the Saudi regime's overthrow, while, the next day, the US embassy in Islamabad, Pakistan, was attacked and burned, causing two American casualties. After two weeks of fighting, the Saudi government put down the Mecca uprising by

---

59 Malcolm Byrne and Kian Byrne, *Worlds Apart: A Documentary History of US-Iran Relations, 1978–2018* (Cambridge University Press, 2022), 42.

60 On the "Chase thesis," see Bill, *Eagle and the Lion*, 340–5; see also Sasan Fayazmanesh, *The United States and Iran: Sanctions, Wars and the Policy of Dual Containment* (Routledge: 2008), 13–15; and Daniel Jackson, "Survivors of Iran Hostage Crisis Clamor to Hold Chase Bank Liable," Courthouse News Service, January 10, 2022.

killing more than a hundred rebels, later beheading dozens more. During the hostage crisis, the Islamic Republic's already tense relations with the Soviet Union further deteriorated. In contrast to Sullivan, the Soviet ambassador was received by Khomeini and was allowed regular visits with him in early 1979. Soon, Khomeini's innate anti-communism intensified in opposition to Afghanistan's Marxist regime, leading to vehement denunciation of the Soviet invasion of Afghanistan by the end of 1979. Moscow's Iran experts were concerned about the revolution's impact on millions of Soviet Muslims and, by late 1979, some commentators were calling the revolution a disaster, denouncing Khomeini as a fanatical anti-communist.[61] Less than a year into the revolution, therefore, the Islamic Republic was politically clashing with both superpowers.

The December 1979 Soviet invasion of Afghanistan was a major blunder, irreparably damaging the Soviet Union's relations with Iran and the rest of the world. This was predicted by the more seasoned Soviet diplomats who had warned against it. In March 1979, Soviet Foreign Minister Andrei Gromyko had told the Politburo that Kabul's communist regime was responsible for its own problems, warning against Soviet military intervention. He had said, "Our army, when it arrives in Afghanistan, will be the aggressor. Against whom will it fight? Against the Afghan people first of all, and it will have to shoot them . . . All the nonaligned countries will be against us." Washington, on the other hand, could see the opportunity provided by a Soviet invasion of Afghanistan. During an April 6 Special Coordinating Committee meeting, Vice President Walter Mondale said such a move "would be embarrassing to them. It would be nice for us to be seen on the other side." Predicting a Soviet invasion, Brzezinski said the United States should keep "the situation boiling, the way that they have kept it boiling for us" elsewhere in the world. He recommended covert assistance to Afghanistan's Muslim rebels, warning his colleagues, "If you don't do it, you lose an opportunity." It was decided that covert aid should be funneled through the government of Pakistan.[62] To Brzezinski and Washington hawks, the invasion of Afghanistan was proof of the Soviet Union's imperialist ambitions, as well as the perfect opportunity to entrap the Red Army in a Muslim Vietnam. Though adamantly opposed to the Soviet invasion, Khomeini did not see it as a direct threat to Iran, nor did he consider the USSR as an existential enemy on par with the United States. His view

61 Yazdi, *Shast sal Saburi va shakuri*, 22–4, 40.
62 Quotes in Rakove, *Day of Opportunity*, 329, 330, 333.

was closer to the American observers who saw the Soviet move into Afghanistan as a reckless defensive reflex, rather than part of a grand expansionist design. The Islamic Republic's different treatment of the two superpowers could be seen in January 1980, when the authorities quickly evacuated a crowd of one thousand Afghan refugees and their Iranian backers who had stormed the Soviet embassy in Tehran.[63] To bolster its anti-imperialist credentials, in early January 1980, the Islamic Republic convened a weeklong Gathering of International Liberation Movements, inviting the PLO, the Eritrean Liberation Front, the Popular Front for the Liberation of Oman, the Movement of Uruguay, the Salvadoran Movement, the Revolutionary Option in Morocco, the American Indian Movement, and the Polisario and Islamic movements opposed to the governments of Afghanistan, Iraq, Bahrain, and Saudi Arabia. Excluded from this gathering were the Iranian leftist organizations that had worked with the PLO and other Middle Eastern liberation movements during the 1970s. American Indian Movement leaders Russell C. Means and John Thomas were allowed to meet with hostage American diplomats and carry letters to the hostages' families in the United States. John Thomas visited the US embassy, where he told reporters, "I stand here as evidence of the oppression, injustice and genocide . . . of the United States against my people." The conference, however, did not endorse the Islamic Republic's opposition to both superpowers, as organizations like the PLO and the Popular Front for the Liberation of Oman, which received substantial support from the Soviet bloc, refused to condemn the Soviet Union's invasion of Afghanistan.[64] Clearly, the Islamic Republic's anti-imperialism was right wing and anti-Marxist.

Meanwhile, Khomeini prolonged the American hostage standoff, making threats and adding more demands. The hostages, he said, were to be tried as spies, while the US government had to extradite the shah and his wealth, apologize for its past Iran policies, and promise not to repeat them. Carter proposed to send the same envoys Khomeini had received in Paris to negotiate the hostages' release. But Khomeini ruled

---

63 George Kennan, an architect of the communist containment doctrine, saw the Soviet intervention in Afghanistan as "primarily defensive." "They began to meddle in Afghan politics," he wrote, "and things went wrong for them, and they got sucked into it . . . rather involuntarily." Rakove, *Day of Opportunity*, 344. Emery, *US Foreign Policy and the Iranian Revolution*, 200.

64 Mohammad Ataie, "Brothers, Comrades, and the Quest for the Islamic International," Rasmus C. Elling and Sune Haugbolle, *The Fate of Third Worldism in the Middle East: Iran, Palestine and Beyond* (Oneworld Academic, 2024), 125–9, 133–5, quoted on 129.

out negotiations, making it clear that the crisis would not be resolved until after the inauguration of Iran's new constitution and the formation of a government dominated by the Islamic Republican Party. In Washington, secret contingency plans for a rescue mission and punitive military action were prepared under Brzezinski's direction, while Carter ordered immigration screening of Iranian students, halted military spare part deliveries to Iran, and finally cut off diplomatic relations.[65] Thus, university students, the largest Iranian population in the United States suffered collective punishment solely based on their nationality, ironically as many opposed the Islamic Republic or hostage taking. Per Carter's order, all Iranian students had to report to the Immigration and Naturalization Service for the monitoring of their visa status. In the end, only 6,444 out of 54,486 students were found in violation of their visas, and 4,000 faced deportation proceedings. Nearly 15,000 Iranians, including 2,204 students, left the United States voluntarily, while thousands eventually legalized their status by various means, including political asylum seeking. In 1980, after nineteen Iranians were expelled, a US Court of Appeals stopped forced deportations. Meanwhile, the American public was consumed by anti-Iranian frenzy, as daily barrages of media coverage tied Iran and Iranians with hostage taking, terrorism, and fanatical Islam. Iranians, or Iranian-looking individuals, were physically attacked, and at least one Iranian college student in California was murdered execution-style. A week after the Tehran embassy takeover, a twenty-year-old Iranian student living in Denver, Colorado, shot three teenagers who were breaking into his apartment with baseball bats. He was found not guilty, although one of the assailants died.[66] The 444 days of hostage taking in Iran had a profoundly negative impact on the American public's perceptions of Iran, Iranians, and the Iranian Revolution. Public sympathy for the revolution, or misgivings about US support of the shah, were quickly wiped out. Beyond Iran, feelings of national humiliation and collective injury restored conservative American sentiments that were shaken in the aftermath of Vietnam. The news media saturated the country with self-righteous coverage of the hostage situation and programs such as "America Held Hostage" aired nightly

65 Babak Ganji, *Politics of Confrontation: The Foreign Policy of the USA and Revolutionary Iran* (I.B. Tauris 2012), 157–9.

66 Manijeh Moradian, *This Flame Within: Iranian Revolutionaries in the United States* (Duke University Press, 2022), 12–15. "Students Voice Khomeini Opposition," *Los Angeles Times*, December 8, 1979; Jeremy P. Meyer, "Iranian Man Who Survived '79 Attack Gets Settlement in New Case," *The Denver Post*, September 24, 2012.

on ABC. Following a trend set by the wife of a hostage, many people hoisted yellow ribbons in their front yards, while millions listened to popular songs such as "Go to Hell, Ayatollah," "Khomeiniac," and "Take Your Oil and Shove it."[67]

Back in Tehran, it turned out that the US embassy, now officially dubbed the "nest of spies," was not involved in coup plots like the one it had hatched in 1953. The classified documents seized at the embassy showed high-level Iran-US contacts but no plots to restore the shah or overthrow the Islamic Republic. Only three hostages were CIA agents, and none had spent more than a few months in Iran or spoke Persian. The CIA station chief, Thomas Ahern, would later criticize his agency's abject failure in understanding postrevolutionary Iranian politics. Per Khomeini's order, documents revealing IRP leader Ayatollah Beheshti's meeting with embassy officials were classified, although, when later released, they were not terribly incriminating. At the time, however, the mere fact of Beheshti's secret meeting with US officials would have been damaging to the IRP, which was using evidence of American meetings with its opponents, like Ayatollah Shariatmadri, to discredit them.[68]

As the hostage crisis dragged on, both Khomeini's inner circle and Carter's White House were riven by intense conflict over its resolution. Iran's first president, Abolhassan Bani-Sadr, was soon at odds with the IRP over the hostage crisis. He had won the presidency in January 1980, after Khomeini decided the job had to go to a layperson and not an IRP cleric. Winning by a large margin, Bani-Sadr opposed the IRP's prolonging of the standoff with the United States, which he saw as highly detrimental to Iran. By 1981, Bani-Sadr was vehemently opposing the IRP's power grab, claiming he would rescue the revolution from "a fistful of fascist clerics."[69] Meanwhile, Khomeini and the IRP were using the hostage crisis to crush their opponents, particularly leftists. In March 1980, Khomeini called for a "cultural revolution," beginning with a massive purge of the universities, the left's stronghold before and after the revolution. In late April, the IRP's armed militias attacked and occupied university campuses across the country, killing at least two dozen and injuring two thousand students. Close to a third of the country's faculty, staff, and students were expelled and all teaching curricula were purged

67 John Ghazvinian, *America and Iran: A History, 1720 to the Present* (Alfred A. Knopf, 2021), 336.

68 Emery, *US Foreign Policy and the Iranian Revolution*, 122–3. On Khomeini's order to protect Beheshti see Yazdi, *Shast sal Saburi va shakuri*, 255.

69 Bakhash, *The Reign of Ayatollahs*, 97.

to become "Islamic." Iranian universities remained closed for more than two years, and when they reopened, students were screened through ideological tests and women were barred from certain majors. At the same time, the Islamic Republic's misogynistic tendencies went into high gear. In 1981, veiling became mandatory while official violence against women, including punishments such as stoning to death, intensified.[70] Already, the implementation of Sharia laws had wiped out the social, political, and economic rights that Iranian women had won in decades of struggle. Meanwhile, the regime's war against Kurdish rebels and all leftist organizations, now labeled agents of US imperialism, intensified. The Tudeh Party and the "Majority" splinter faction of the Fadai'an, which supported the regime and its suppression of defiant leftists, were made exempt and temporarily allowed to function.

In April 1980, Carter ordered a hostage rescue operation, so desperately reckless that it led to Secretary of State Cyrus Vance's resignation. According to this plan, code-named Eagle Claw, six cargo transport planes and eight large helicopters would take off from an aircraft carrier in the Gulf of Oman and fly undetected to a remote Iranian desert location, whence a 106-member commando team, along with twenty-four drivers, road watchers, and translators would fly to another location closer to Tehran. The commando team would drive to Tehran, storm the embassy and the foreign ministry building, free the hostages, take them to a nearby soccer field, airlift them via helicopters, and then fly them out of Iran. A special CIA expert was dispatched to Tehran to carefully monitor the operation's various logistical parts, and the rescue team included a former SAVAK agent and two Iranian generals. Estimates predicted that half of the hostages and the rescue team would be among the operation's casualties.[71] Iranian casualties, including civilians, were estimated to be much higher because the military planes were to "hose down the streets" of Tehran around the embassy with cannons and machinegun fire. As the leader of the rescue team put it:

> When we went into that embassy, it was our aim to kill all Iranian guards—the people holding our hostages—and we weren't going to arrest them; we were going in there to shoot them right between the eyes, and to do it with vigor."[72]

70 Rahnema, *The Political History of Modern Iran*, 409–10, 414.

71 Ganji, *Politics of Confrontation*, 190; Charlie A. Beckwith and Donald Knox, *Delta Force* (New Harcourt Brace, 1983), 239–40, 260–1.

72 Bill, *Eagle and the Lion*, 301; Beckwith and Knox, *Delta Force*, 8.

But the mission was aborted after the helicopters ran into a sandstorm, two of them malfunctioned and another crashed into an airplane, killing eight commandos in the first desert landing location. On the way back to the aircraft carrier, the rescue team's leader cried, thinking "Jesus Christ, you know, what a fucking mess. We've just embarrassed our great country." Operation Eagle Flaw's failure became a major embarrassment to Carter, as it seemed to prove Khomeini's claim that the United States was powerless vis-à-vis the Islamic Republic. Brzezinski, however, remained undeterred, arguing for a second rescue mission, involving a full-scale invasion of Iran in different locations with twenty thousand troops:

> The second mission . . . involved going into the airport at Tehran, taking the airport, landing an armored mobile force, driving into the city, shooting up anything in the way, bombing anything that starts interfering, storming the embassy, taking out anybody who's alive after that process and then going back and taking off.

Brzezinski's plan was not implemented because Carter's State Department advisors opposed it.[73] In Iran, meanwhile, the threat of an all-out war with Iraq was overshadowing the possibility of military skirmishes with the United States. In both cases, Iran's military weakness was a decisive consideration, though Carter never ordered a direct military attack to rescue the hostages. During the revolution, the Iranian army had fallen apart and was then further decapitated through at least eighty-five executions and purges of close to ten thousand of its officers. In July 1980, the discovery of a major coup plot led to hundreds more arrests, 144 executions, and the purge of two to four thousand military personnel, another major blow to the armed forces two months prior to Iraq's invasion. The coup plot was hatched by an Iraqi-backed network led by some of the shah's generals and his last prime minister, Shapur Bakhtiar. The CIA knew of the plot, which Carter neither supported nor opposed, being uncertain of its effect on the hostage situation. Bakhtiar and his Iraqi backers interpreted this as a US "green light" to go ahead with the operation.[74] In the end, the Carter White House remained without a coherent Iran strategy, reacting to events rather than initiating them. Carter's memoirs show that until mid-summer 1980, he was more

73 Quoted in Ganji, *Politics of Confrontation*, 192.

74 Gasiorowski, "US Intelligence Assistance to Iran, May–October 1979," 647, 652, 657.

worried about being nominated as his party's presidential candidate than the hostage crisis thwarting his reelection chances. The shah's death, in January 1980, had resolved the question of his extradition, eliminating Khomeini's most difficult demand for Carter to accede to. The fallen monarch's passing was greeted with relief by the same American media outlets that had lavishly praised him at the peak of his power. *Newsweek*, for example, wrote condescendingly:

> As his nation's wealth increased, the Shah grew more convinced of his own infallibility. Some blamed the US for feeding his delusions. Having installed a pro-American puppet, Washington catered to his every whim and encouraged his megalomania. It shoved not only arms but whole industries into Iran, while bleeding him of the billions of dollars he paid out for his grandiose military schemes. As his image of himself grew he stopped consulting even his closest advisors.[75]

By September, secret negotiations with Tehran seemed to be edging closer to a hostage release deal whereby the United States returned the shah's wealth, unfroze Iran's assets, and pledged noninterference in its affairs. Iranian officials now openly talked about ending the standoff, some boasting it had served its political purpose. A chief Iranian negotiator, for example, said the hostages were "like a fruit from which all the juice has been squeezed out," while Khoeiniha, the leader of the embassy takeover, concurred, saying: "We have reaped all the fruits of our undertaking."[76]

It was precisely at this time that Iraq invaded Iran, after allegedly receiving a "green light" from the United States. As early as April 1980, US intelligence knew an Iraqi invasion could be imminent, but the information did not change Carter's policy.[77] The outbreak of a war was not necessarily in the United States' interest because it could complicate delicate hostage negotiations. Carter's memoirs show, in addition to the war's impact on hostage negotiations, he was worried about its destabilizing effect on the region, particularly the steady flow of oil. The war

75 "The Man Who Meant Well," *Newsweek*, August 4, 1980, 41.

76 Bakhash, *The Reign of Ayatollahs*, 149–50.

77 Allegations of US involvement in Iraq's invasion of Iran have been always circulating. For example, a memo written in April 1981 by Reagan's secretary of state, Alexander Haig, claimed Saudis had told him that Carter had given Iraq a "green light" to invade Iran. Emery, *US Foreign Policy and the Iranian Revolution*, 173–5, 181. This was denied by Carter and his officials. Gary Sick, *October Surprise: America's Hostages in Iran and the Election of Ronald Reagan* (Random House, 1991), 106–7.

quickly doubled oil prices, intensifying the US energy crisis and raising the already high rates of inflation, further threatening Carter's chances of reelection. On September 24, two days after the start of the war, he wrote:

> I conducted a National Security Council meeting. We agreed to do everything we could to terminate the Iran-Iraq conflict as soon as possible, to stay strictly neutral, to call other nations to stay out of the conflict and be neutral, and to keep open the Strait of Hormuz. My hope is that a cease-fire, with Iran still threatened, might be an inducement to them to release the hostages and repair their relations with the outside world.[78]

On October 13, he added: "We learned that [Jordan's King] Hossein had induced Saudi Arabia to give support to Iraq. In fact, Iraq is the aggressor nation and is becoming identified as such in the eyes of the world." On October 15, he wrote: "I decided that [Secretary of State] Muskie and I would declare publicly that Iraqi action against Iran was invasion or aggression, which is a fact."[79] Following Carter's instructions, Muskie informed the Iraqi foreign minister that the United States opposed the war's escalation, while Washington declared its opposition to Iran's dismemberment. Carter also intervened to prevent Iraq from using neighboring Persian Gulf countries to launch military attacks on Iran. In September 1980, the United States supported a UN Security Council resolution that called for a ceasefire, without naming Iraq as the aggressor. If White House hawks, particularly Brzezinski, had hoped for Iraqi battlefield gains pressuring Khomeini to release the hostages, they soon realized this would not be the case.[80] As the war continued under the Reagan administration, US strategy would evolve into a seemingly contradictory pattern of interventions, whose real aim was to deny victory to both sides.

The war's outbreak delayed the hostages' release deal, the so-called October surprise, which would have bolstered Carter's reelection chances. A controversial new obstacle was the purported collusion between the Islamic Republic and Ronald Reagan's election campaign officials to delay the hostages' release until Reagan's victory. Allegedly, the Islamic Republic agreed to this deal to have a fresh start with the Reagan administration, hoping it would supply Iran with badly needed US armaments.[81] This

---

78 Carter, *White House Diary*, 467.

79 Ibid., 472–4.

80 Emery, *US Foreign Policy and the Iranian Revolution*, 184–6, 189.

81 Sick, *All Fall Down*, 308–15. See *October Surprise*.

allegation was serious enough to bring about a 1993 congressional investigation, concluding that although American officials had "conducted informal, clandestine, and potentially dangerous efforts on behalf of the Reagan campaign," such efforts did not raise to the level of criminal conspiracy, nor could their effect on the outcome of the 1980 elections be determined.[82] With the approach of US presidential election date on November 4, which coincidentally marked the anniversary of the Tehran embassy seizure, Carter could see the hostages' delayed release would cost him the presidency.[83] Following his defeat by a large margin, a dejected Carter considered declaring war on Iran if hostage negotiations were to break down again. But this did not become necessary since the hostages were released precisely during Reagan's inauguration on January 20, 1980. The next day, Carter flew to Germany for an emotional meeting with the fifty-two freed Americans on their way home. He faced a few tough questions, including from the embassy's CIA station chief, Ahern, who asked why the shah was admitted to the United States in the first place.[84]

Beyond the destruction of Carter's presidency, the Iran hostage crisis profoundly affected the United States. In the wake of the Watergate scandal and defeat in Vietnam, the second half of the 1970s were exceptional years when large segments of the political elite, as well as ordinary citizens, saw America's domestic politics as deeply flawed and its foreign policy as misguided. Carter was elected promising to restore trust in domestic governance and to repair the Vietnam War's damage to America's standing in the world. An energy crisis, combined with inflation and economic recession, made him domestically unsuccessful, while the Iran hostage crisis proved his foreign policy's greatest failure. The Iran hostage crisis was arguably the most pivotal factor in wiping out the memory of America's misadventures in places like Iran and Vietnam, moving the public to embrace the Reagan presidency's self-righteous, jingoistic global posture. Already misled to blame Arab and Muslim countries for the energy crisis, Americans were further traumatized watching more than a year of daily televised images of Americans held captive, while Iranians burnt US flags and Khomeini gloated that "America can't do a damn thing!" In an even broader perspective, the Iranian Revolution and the hostage crisis marked a transition moment when the simmering right-wing global drift of the late 1970s morphed into the restoration of aggressive US global hegemony during the 1980s.

82 Quoted in Ganji, *Politics of Confrontation*, 204.
83 Carter, *White House Diary*, 476.
84 Ibid., 504, 514–16.

At the same time, the Iranian Revolution inaugurated a new geopolitical era when militant Islam, or Islamic fundamentalism, would replace communism as the chief nemesis to America's global dominance.

America's Management of the Iran-Iraq War

We just wanted them to kick the shit out of each other.
CIA operative on the US position during the Iran-Iraq War[85]

The settlement of the hostage crisis satisfied none of Khomeini's demands. The shah of course was dead and gone, while his assets in America were not returned and the Islamic Republic forfeited to arbitration more than half of its $12 billion frozen holdings in the United States. Nor did the United States apologize for its past interventions or guarantee future noninterference in Iran. By this time, the war with Iraq had replaced the hostage crisis as the Islamic Republic's existential preoccupation, simultaneously threatening and strengthening the regime, while fundamentally shaping its state-building project. The war was the predictable outcome of escalating conflict between the two regimes, and not, as Khomeini claimed, simply imposed on Iran by Saddam Hussein acting as an American proxy. Iraq of course had invaded Iran, but the Islamic Republic had recklessly escalated tensions and increased the risk of war while relying on a decimated army and internationally isolated because of the hostage crisis. Saddam Hussein, who became Iraq's dictator in 1979, initially had welcomed the shah's overthrow, proposing friendly relations with Iran's provisional government. In summer 1979, Saddam invited Prime Minister Bazargan to visit Baghdad, while Foreign Minister Yazdi met with Saddam and invited him to Tehran.[86] Khomeini, however, was adamantly opposed to normal relations with Saddam, whose regime he blamed for the treatment of Iraq's Shi'i opposition movement and the execution of its leader, Ayatollah Baqer Sadr. Saddam considered this interference in Iraq's domestic affairs, and hostile propaganda and border skirmishes between the two countries intensified in fall 1979. In 1980, the chances of war increased as Khomeini repeatedly called for Saddam's overthrow, while the hostage crisis and confrontation with the United States placed Iran in an increasingly weaker position. At the same time,

85 Quoted in Ghazvinian, *America and Iran*, 369.
86 Ganji, *Politics of Confrontation*, 125–8.

Iran's relations with the Soviet Union had deteriorated over its invasion of Afghanistan, while Iran's Arab neighbors felt threatened by the Islamic Republic's attempts at exporting its revolution. Saddam seized this seemingly perfect opportunity to launch an invasion, hoping to inflict a quick defeat on Iran, either overthrowing the Islamic Republic or forcing it to accept Iraq's peace terms. Thus, on September 22, 1980, Iraqi columns rolled across the border and its air force hit military targets across Iran.[87]

Though impaired, Iran's air force was able to contain the Iraqi aerial attack, but Iraq's ground offensive advanced steadily toward its main target, the oil-exporting port of Abadan. But Iran's regular army, along with the Revolutionary Guard (IRGC) and its civilian militia forces, were putting up a stiff resistance, though it would take them a few months to halt Iraqi advances. On September 28, the UN Security Council called for a ceasefire, which Saddam accepted but Iran rejected because it did not name an aggressor or require Iraq to pull back to prewar borders. Clearly, no Security Council member, not the least the United States, sympathized with the Islamic Republic. When Iraq failed to achieve a quick victory, a long, drawn-out war of attrition ensued in which Iran's human resources (that is, the three times larger and more politically motivated population) would prove a decisive advantage. At the same time, while no other country, except for Syria, supported Iran's war effort, Iraq's war expenses were underwritten by Kuwait and Saudi Arabia, and it received significant technical and military support from many countries, including the United States. The war would last eight years at tremendous human, financial, and political cost to both countries. Iraq had started the war, but Iran was responsible for prolonging it for six agonizing years, inflicting massive carnage, suffering, and deprivation, mostly on its own population. After Iran took back its lost territory in 1982, Khomeini and IRP leaders decided to carry the war into Iraq and overthrow Saddam, rejecting ceasefire proposals involving significant financial compensation. For the next six years, Iran was fighting a war of aggression, which Khomeini and official propaganda insisted was the "sacred defense" of Iran and Islam against American imperialism. As we see below, this narrative was belied by revelations about the Islamic Republic secretly receiving arms shipments from Israel and the United States.

As with the hostage crisis, the Islamic Republic would continue the war as long it served its domestic agenda of state building and regime

87 Rob Johnson, *The Iran-Iraq War* (Palgrave Macmillan, 2011), 42–5.

consolidation.[88] During the war's first year, all opposition was violently crushed, and henceforth not even loyal dissent was tolerated. Casting the war as an existential confrontation with the United States, Khomeini blamed domestic opposition and all other problems as instigations of the "Great Satan." This narrative thus defined the basic ideological stance of the Islamic Republic, lasting all the way to the present. The year 1981 was truly fateful as the Iraqi invasion and an armed insurrection by domestic opposition put the regime's survival to the test. When the war began, almost all the regime's opponents, including the religious and secular left, rallied to its support, while armed rebellion continued in Kurdistan, where the Kurdish Democratic Party accepted Iraqi support. In the course of 1981, the Islamic leftist Mojahedin organization, with tens of thousands of dedicated followers, finally broke with the Islamic Republic, having endured two years of increasingly violent repression. By this time, the Mojahedin were lining up behind President Bani-Sadr, who had emerged as the leader of resistance to the IRP's monopolization of power. In June 1981, after Bani-Sadr's removal from the presidency, the Mojahedin and some smaller leftist groups launched a desperate armed insurrection. The regime responded with extreme violence, including the summary execution of street protesters, whether armed or not. The Mojahedin struck back with a bombing campaign that killed Bani-Sadr's replacement as president, the prime minister, IRP chairman Beheshti and his replacement, and dozens of IRP cabinet ministers and Majles deputies. Badly shaken, the regime held together and unleashed a bloody reign of terror unprecedented in modern Iranian history. Between June 1981 and the end of mass killings in June 1985, the regime had massacred 12,250 political dissidents, 75 percent of whom were executed; the rest died in armed clashes. This far surpassed the most repressive period of the shah's rule in the 1970s when less than one hundred political executions were recorded.[89] In 1983, the Tudeh Party, which had supported the regime's brutal suppression of other leftists, was smashed as its leaders were forced to make public recantations and confess to spying for the Soviet Union. The party's suppression was a foregone conclusion, although information provided by a Soviet defector, allegedly

88 Kaveh Ehsani, "War and Resentment: Critical Reflections on the Legacies of the Iran-Iraq War," *Middle East Critique*, 26 no. 1 (2017): 5–24, cited on 6. Hossein Seyfzadeh, "Revolution, Ideology, and War," in *The Iran-Iraq War: The Politics of Aggression*, ed. Farhang Rajaee (University Press of Florida, 1993): 90–103.

89 Bakhash, *The Reign of Ayatollahs*, 219–21; Matin-Asgari, "Twentieth-Century Iran's Political Prisoners," *Middle Eastern Studies* 42, no.5 (September 2006): 689–707, 701.

shared with Tehran by the CIA and the MI6, helped seal its doom.[90] Thus, within four years, the Islamic Republic had physically decimated two generations of Iranian leftists, a task that the shah's regime had failed to accomplish in four decades.

As well as justification to crush all opposition and dissent, war making shaped the Islamic Republic's broad political orientation and postrevolutionary social agenda. Sociologist Charles Tilly's famous dictum, "War makes states and states make war," found yet another application in the case of Iran. Tilly noted how perpetual warfare fundamentally shaped modern European states, forcing them to provide their subjects with limited rights and rudimentary welfare in exchange for their wartime loyalty and enormous sacrifice.[91] The Islamic Republic too needed to build a social base by responding to at least some revolutionary demands, while asking for the public's extraordinary loyalty and sacrifice in a decade of war and domestic strife. During the 1980s, the regime levied a "blood tax" on the nation, especially on the urban and rural poor and working classes, who were asked to bracket their revolutionary aspirations and sacrifice everything to build a new state amidst a seemingly endless war. Borrowing leftist rhetoric, Khomeini constantly reached out to the nation's "oppressed," promising them the revolution's material and spiritual rewards. The Islamic Republic's 1979 constitution had guaranteed free education and welfare, as well as the elimination of poverty. In its anti-imperialist posture during the hostage crisis, the Revolutionary Council tilted to the left, decreeing laws in favor of labor, controlling the urban housing market, and breaking up large estates in the countryside. Within a few years, however, all these decrees were rescinded or amended to conform to traditional Islamic precepts respecting private property.[92] Still, a prolonged war necessitated social and economic policies that would shape the Islamic Republic into a "Martyrs' Welfare State." The regime's welfare policies built on foundations laid by the shah, who, during the 1970s, relied on the rising oil income to offer Iranians free education, health care, and social security.

---

90 Dmitry Asinovskiy, "'A Priest Does Not Consider the Toppling of the Shah As an Option' The KGB and the Revolution in Iran," *Iranian Studies* 55 (2022): 929–51, 944–7; see also Vladimir Kuzichkin, *Inside the KGB: My Life in Soviet Espionage* (Pantheon Books, 1990).

91 Charles Tilly, *Coercion, Capital and European States, A.D. 990–1992* (Wiley-Blackwell, 1992). For the application of Tilly's analysis to the Islamic Republic, see Ehsani, "War and Resentment," 3.

92 Bakhash, *The Reign of Ayatollahs*, 211–14; Abrahamian, "Why the Islamic Republic Has Survived," *Middle East Report* 250 (spring 2009).

Despite its positive results, the monarchist welfare state was limited in coverage, particularly in rural areas, regions the Islamic Republic would reach to build its social base and recruit for the war. Through sustained efforts, mostly via the IRGC-affiliated Construction Jihad, the regime brought tangible improvements in health, education, electrification, and transportation, mainly in rural and provincial regions, a policy that would also sharpen class stratification and demands for political inclusion.[93] In the end, as one scholar put it succinctly: "State elites created and relied upon a set of welfare institutions that channeled the *popular mobilization* of the 1979 revolution and the eight-year war with Iraq into a *warfare-welfare complex*."[94]

The Islamic Republic rewarded loyalty, primarily benefitting veterans and the families of war martyrs and militias, turning millions of poor citizens into potential regime supporters, counterbalancing dissatisfaction among the rest of the population. During the 1980s, the Martyrs Foundation gave about $4,000 annual stipends to immediate family members of the war dead, a hefty subsidy at a time when everyone, and especially the poor, suffered food shortages and the rationing of necessities. Military servicemen received an annual grant of $24,000, while martyrs' and veterans' families received preferential treatment in employment, university admission, and car ownership.[95] The regime's discriminatory welfare policies contributed to its longevity, although in time these policies' beneficiaries, and particularly their children, would join the ranks of dissidents.[96] The war also laid the foundations of the Islamic Republic's political economy. War mobilization required massive state intervention in the economy, including wage and price regulation, food subsidies, rationing of basic commodities, nationalization of foreign trade, tight control of banking and monetary policies, and state confiscation of private sector businesses and factories that were taken over by their workers and employees. Contrary to regime rhetoric, reflected in contemporary academic studies, this was not a leftist turn, but the kind of war-induced state-planned economy whose variants had existed since the First World War. At the same time, the new regime was setting up intertwined paramilitary and

93 Eric Hooglund, "Thirty Years of Islamic Revolution in Iran," *Middle East Report* 250 (spring 2009): 34–9.

94 Kevan Harris, *A Social Revolution: Politics and the Welfare State in Iran* (University of California Press, 2017), 14. The term "martyrs' welfare state" was used earlier by Ervand Abrahamian, *The Iranian Mojahedin* (Yale University Press, 1989), 70.

95 Johnson, *The Iran-Iraq War*, 62.

96 This is the main argument of Harris, *A Social Revolution*, outlined in the book's introduction.

parastate institutions that would define its long-term political, social, and economic character. The Islamic Republic's political economy took shape and continued to function as if in a permanent state of war, with the regime confiscating private assets and public goods such as land, pastures, forests, water, and mineral resources. The Islamic Republic's constitution defined confiscated economic assets as *anfal*, literally meaning "spoils of war," referring to a Koranic surah of the same name. The first of these anfal institutions was born in March 1979, when Khomeini set up the Foundation of the Oppressed, a vast conglomerate holding confiscated factories, businesses, banks, hotels, and trading companies owned by the Pahlavi Foundation, members of the royal family and the economic elite with ties to the old regime. Ostensibly to serve the poor, the Foundation of the Oppressed and similar anfal foundations would grow into economic powerhouses, controlled by Khomeini, and exempt from taxation and government purview. During the war, the IRGC and Basij Militia grew exponentially and were economically linked to conglomerates such as the Foundation of the Oppressed, Martyrs' Foundation, Housing Foundation, and the Imam's Aid Committee. The Foundation of the Oppressed quickly became Iran's second largest economic entity after the National Iranian Oil Company. By 1989, it covered over one thousand factories, farms, mines, construction, and other companies whose total assets added up to nearly $20 billion. Anfal institutions also include the enormously wealthy Imam Reza Endowment in Mashhad and the Khatam al-Anbiya Foundation, the construction and engineering arm of the IRGC. Eventually, around 60 percent of the Iranian economy would come under anfal institutions and foundations, geared to profit making and capital accumulation, but in a "predatory" manner, superimposed above the operational realm of private or state-owned capital.[97] Anfal thus forms the economic foundation of Iran's unelected "deep state" or parastate, politically unaccountable to citizens and commanding larger assets than both the state and private sectors. The deep state also relies on the permanent militarization of politics, connecting anfal assets to the growing economic, social, and political clout of the Revolutionary Guard and Basij militia.

The Basij quickly enlisted 2.5 million members, mobilizing a half-million militia of men and boys to fight the war.[98] Khomeini had called the

97 Mehrdad Vahabi, *Destructive Coordination, Anfal and Islamic Political Capitalism: A New Reading of Contemporary Iran* (Palgrave Macmillan, 2023), xi–xiv, epilogue; see also Mehrdad Vahabi, *The Political Economy of Destructive Power* (Edward Elgar Publishing, 2004); *The Political Economy of Predation: Manhunting and the Economics of Escape* (Cambridge University Press, 2004).

98 Johnson, *The Iran-Iraq War*, 121–2.

war a "blessing," and state-controlled mass media relentlessly saturated public space with the regime's narrative of the war as "scared defense" of Iran and Islam against a panoply of "world-devouring" enemies led by the United States. Child soldiers recruited into Basij militia were used as cannon fodder for tasks such as walking across minefields to clear them for advancing Iranian troops. A fifth of Iran's total war fatalities, about thirty-seven thousand, were teenagers, while tens of thousands more children were seriously wounded or spent years in Iraq as war prisoners.[99] The war unfolded in two distinct phases, corresponding to shifts, and at time radical reversals, in US policy toward the Islamic Republic. The first phase began with Iraq's September 1980 invasion and lasted until summer 1982, when Iran had taken back its lost territory and was pushing into Iraq. During this phase, the United States was officially "neutral," while effectively supporting Iraq, refusing to name it as the aggressor and backing Saudi Arabia and Kuwait to underwrite Baghdad's war effort. In 1980–82, when Iraq was the aggressor, more than 20 percent of its weapons were purchased from France and close to 70 percent from the Soviet Union and Eastern European countries, the latter figure remaining steady to the end of the war. By the war's end, the Soviets had sold Iraq $20 billion worth of armaments. Meanwhile, 70 percent of arms sold to Iran during the war were Chinese and North Korean, while China sold arms to Iraq as well. Syria was the only Middle Eastern country openly providing armaments and material support to Iran, while Israel was secretly sending arms shipments to Tehran as early as 1980. By fall 1982, the war's second phase began as the Islamic Republic launched its relentless push into Iraqi territory, making ceasefire conditional on regime change in Baghdad and the payment of hundreds of billions of dollars in reparations. The UN issued several resolutions during the war, but Iran rejected all of them because they failed to name Iraq as the aggressor or address Iranian demands for reparations. The Islamic Republic complained the superpowers had turned the UN and the international community against it, ignoring its own defiance of international norms during the hostage crisis and intransigence in accepting peace terms during the war. The UN, however, was indeed biased against Iran, as it failed, for example, to act against Iraq's use of chemical weapons.[100]

Sources differ on the exact figures of the war's casualties and economic cost. When Iran went on the offensive in 1982, an estimated one

99 Abbas Amanat, *Iran: A Modern History* (New Haven and London: Yale University Press, 2017), 790, Ehsani, "War and Resentment," 8–9.

100 Johnson, *The Iran-Iraq War*, 96–7, 103–6.

hundred twenty thousand Iranians and sixty thousand Iraqis had already died, whereas by the war's end, in 1988, the total tally of casualties (killed or injured) surpassed one million, 60 percent of them Iranian. Tens of thousands were taken prisoner and millions were made homeless or displaced in both countries. Iraq counted two hundred thousand dead, four hundred thousand wounded, and seventy thousand taken prisoner, while Iranian casualties were two hundred twenty thousand dead and four hundred thousand injured. The economic cost of the war was staggering, estimated at a minimum of $200 billion and possibly more than one trillion dollars, counting indirect expenses. At about $260 billion, Iran's minimum war expenses were several times larger than its total revenue from eighty years of oil income. By 1988, the war was swallowing two-thirds of Iran's national income. In sum, during this war, Iran and Iraq had inflicted incalculable costs and suffering on their people, while financially mortgaging their future.[101]

As with the hostage crisis, the Islamic Republic ended the war without achieving any of its declared objectives, suggesting that in both cases the ultimate motivation was the domestic consolidation of power. This was noted by contemporary observers including former Prime Minister Bazargan, who cautiously had noted that continuing the war, after taking back all lost territory, would serve the IRP's monopolization of power and the interests of Iran's enemies.[102] The war indeed served US and Israeli foreign policy interests, but not in the way the Islamic Republic claimed. During Carter's last months in office, Israel had asked the United States to allow it to sell arms to Tehran, which would violate the American ban on arms sales to Iran. A few months after Reagan took office, the United States cleared Israel's arms shipments to Iran, which amounted to several billion dollars each year during the early 1980s.[103] According to a former CIA analyst, "Israel was the only consistent source of spare parts for the Iranian air force's US-built jets throughout the war. Israeli leaders, notably Yitzhak Rabin and Shimon Peres, brought considerable pressure on Washington, and the Iran-Contra affair was in many ways their idea."[104] The Israelis argued their backdoor arms sales could help the release of American hostages, while opening a secret line of

101 Amanat, *Iran: A Modern History*, 840; Ehsani, "War and Resentment," 2, 6–7; Johnson, *The Iran-Iraq War*, 175–6, 193.

102 Bazargan, *Enqelab-e Iran dar do harekat*, 157–8, 162.

103 Seymour Hersh, "The Iran Pipeline: A Hidden Chapter/A Special Report: US Said to Have Allowed Israel to Sell Arms to Iran," *New York Times*, December 8, 1991.

104 Former CIA analyst, Bruce Riedel quoted in Ayatollahi Tabaar, *Religious Statecraft*, 156.

communication and influence with the Islamic Republic, the same rationale used by the Reagan administration when its own secret dealing with Iran were exposed. In both cases, the more strategic consideration was to see Iran and Iraq remain at war with each other, with Israeli and American intervention preventing the outright victory of either side. The strategy was summed up by Kissinger, who said he hoped "mutual exhaustion might rid the Middle East of the aggressive regimes of *both* Ayatollah Khomeini and Saddam Hossein." In his testimony to Congress, Robert McFarlane, Reagan's point man in arms shipments to Tehran, claimed he had told the Iranians that "we were not prepared to give them the level of arms which would allow them to win the war." As a CIA operative put it bluntly: "We just wanted them to kick the shit out of each other."[105] In June 1981, Israel militarily intervened on Iran's side when, after a green light from Washington, its air force bombed and destroyed the Osirak nuclear reactor near Baghdad, finishing a task that the Islamic Republic had tried but failed to accomplish.[106] According to an Israeli historian:

> Ideally, the Israelis would have liked both sides to lose this war. The second-best scenario was for Iran and Iraq to demolish one another in a long, drawn-out war of attrition. The supply of arms to Iran, which had been under a strict American embargo since the revolution, was one way of fueling the war and sustaining the stalemate.[107]

Once Iran went on the offensive in 1982, the United States began to openly side with Iraq. Washington removed Iraq from the list of countries supporting terrorism, and in 1983 provided it with $2 billion credit for nonmilitary purchases. By 1984, diplomatic relations with Baghdad were restored, while the United States provided Iraq with military intelligence through means such as Saudi-based AWACS (Airborne Warning and Control System) planes flown by American pilots. The same year, the United States started supporting Iraq's procurement of chemical and biological weapons, selling Baghdad material that could be used for their manufacture and facilitating the sale of such material by German and British private and government sources. In 1984, the US delegation at

105 Quotes in Ghazvinian, *America and Iran*, 369. See Fayazmanesh, *The United States and Iran*, 24–7, for US policy of managing the Iran-Iraq War to the detriment of both sides.

106 Sick, *October Surprise*, 196–200, 207.

107 Quoted in Fayazmanesh, *The United States and Iran*, 57.

the UN helped defeat a Tehran-sponsored resolution condemning Iraq's use of chemical warfare.[108] In January 1987, *The New York Times* published a report on how "American intelligence agencies provided Iran and Iraq with deliberately distorted or inaccurate intelligence data in recent years." Distorted "information," the article went on to say, "had been shared in an effort to prevent either Iran or Iraq from prevailing in their conflict."[109]

Like the Carter White House, the Reagan administration was sharply divided on its Iran policy, with the State Department, after 1982 headed by George Shultz, advocating a pro-Iraqi position. Officially, the administration was committed to Operation Staunch, which aimed to block the flow of arms to Iran. However, during Reagan's second term, CIA Director William Casey and National Security Advisor Robert McFarlane became more involved with the Israeli arms pipeline to Tehran. In July 1985, the Israeli foreign ministry told McFarlane that the Islamic Republic had offered to help free American hostages, held in Lebanon by the Shi'i militia Hezbollah, in exchange for arms delivered directly from the United States. Though his secretaries of state and defense opposed it, Reagan approved the deal. As Israel delivered more weapons, Hezbollah freed a few American hostages. In May 1986, a delegation consisting of McFarlane, who had resigned as national security advisor, two CIA Iran experts, Lieutenant Colonel Oliver North, and an Israeli intelligence officer flew to Tehran to negotiate a broader arms-for-hostages deal and establish direct contact with Islamic Republic leaders. North was simultaneously in charge of another illegal operation, diverting the funds from the Iran arms sales to the US-sponsored "Contras" fighting Nicaragua's leftist regime. To show his personal endorsement of the mission, Reagan had sent Khomeini a Bible adorned with his handwritten favorite verse and signature. No senior Iranian official met with McFarlane's delegation, though Iran's second-most-powerful man, Parliament Speaker Hashemi-Rafsanjani, was overseeing the American deal, as was Khomeini. As both sides tried to increase their leverage, the Islamic Republic revealed a list of new American captives in Lebanon, while CIA Director Casey and Vice President George H. W. Bush increased US pressure by urging Iraq to intensify its bombing campaign deep inside Iranian territory. But everything collapsed in October 1986 when a rogue agent, attached to the Revolutionary Guard, exposed the news of the Islamic Republic's

108 Ibid., 29–33.

109 *The New York Times*, quoted in Fayazmanesh, *The United States and Iran*, 45.

secret dealings with the United States, a sensational story first published in a Lebanese magazine that quickly reached the United States, causing a political firestorm that almost destroyed Reagan's presidency.[110]

Responding to the public's confusion and anger, Reagan accepted responsibility for the affair without admitting his personal authorization of the doubly illegal missions of McFarlane and North, emphasizing instead his goal of freeing American hostages. Media attention and a congressional investigation focused on the illegal funding of the Nicaraguan Contras, something that was not traceable to Reagan because his national security advisor, John Poindexter, had destroyed relevant documents and accepted all responsibility. Subsequently, Poindexter was convicted of lying to the congressional investigation of the Iran-Contra cover-up, but his convictions were later overturned. Of the key figures accused in the cover-up, Defense Secretary Caspar Weinberger was indicted, McFarlane convicted with a probation sentence, and North's conviction was overturned on technicality. Vice President George Bush, himself a prime cover-up suspect, pardoned them all when he replaced Reagan as president, while an independent investigating council declared the case closed, without adding any new findings.[111]

Iranian style cover-up was cruder and more efficient, dispensing with American political theatrics. A few weeks after the secret meetings' disclosure, Khomeini predictably declared the whole affair a victory "greater than all our [previous] victories." He explained: "Those who broke relations with Iran have come back—presenting themselves meekly and humbly at the door of the nation, wishing to establish relations and making apologies."[112] No further discussion of the affair was allowed, and the man who had exposed the Islamic Republic's secret dealings with the United States was executed on unrelated charges. To cover their tracks, both governments intensified their propaganda war, while the United States became more openly involved in supporting Iraq. By 1987, as Iran and Iraq were attacking each other's oil shipments in the Persian Gulf, the United States let Kuwaiti ships sail under its flag, providing direct military protection to Iraq's major ally. At the same time, Iran's tensions with Saudi Arabia reached a new height in summer 1987, when more than four hundred pilgrims, mostly Iranian, were killed

110 Murray Wass and Caring Unger, "In the Loop: Bush's Secret Mission," *New Yorker*, November 2, 1992, 64–83; Seyyed Hossein Mousavian, *Iran and the United States* (New Bloomsbury, 2014), 93–5.

111 Sick, *October Surprise*, 223.

112 Ghazvinian, *America and Iran*, 369.

in clashes with Saudi security forces during Hajj processions. The Saudis claimed Iranian pilgrims were using the hajj to make political statements, and Khomeini angrily denounced King Fahd as an "infidel."[113] By 1988, the largest American fleet since the Vietnam War was assembled in the Persian Gulf, where growing skirmishes with the Iranian navy signaled Washington's readiness for all-out military confrontation. In April 1988, Iranian mines laid in the Gulf almost sank an American naval ship protecting reflagged Kuwaiti oil tankers. No lives were lost but the United States retaliated strongly by sinking three Iranian warships, as well as destroying two fighter jets, several armed boats and two Iranian oil platforms. Two US servicemen died when their helicopter crashed in the Gulf.[114]

At the same time, the Islamic Republic's leaders had concluded the war was unwinnable, while Iran's human and economic resources were dangerously depleted. Up to a point, the war had politically strengthened the regime, but its continuation was now a danger to its survival. Moreover, it was clear that the United States had moved beyond preventing an Iranian victory to aggressively, and perhaps militarily, intervene against the Islamic Republic. Further proof of this came on July 3, 1988, when USS *Vincennes* shot down an Iranian passenger plane over the Persian Gulf, killing its 290 crew and passengers, including sixty children. Though the US government would later express "regret" over the incident and pay compensation, Iranians saw it as a signal of extreme American hostility, and within two weeks, the regime's inner circle prevailed upon Khomeini to accept a ceasefire.[115]

Almost immediately after the ceasefire, Khomeini ordered a special commission to finalize the status of Iran's political prisoners, freeing those who would repent and cooperate with the regime and executing all the rest. Within a few months, an estimated five to twelve thousand prisoners were secretly murdered.[116] Given that many of the prisoners had served their terms and none posed any threat to the regime, this was an unprecedented act of brutality even by the Islamic Republic's standards. Faced with crushing failures in a decade of war and confrontation with the world's hegemonic superpower, the regime was turning its murderous rage on imprisoned opponents. Khomeini would die within

---

113 *New York Times*, August 29, 1987.

114 Johnson, *The Iran-Iraq War*, 17–4.

115 Mousavian, *Iran and the United States*, 101–4. For a richly detailed firsthand observation and commentary on both sides of the war, see Robert Fisk, *The Great War for Civilization* (Vintage Books, 2005), chapters 5–8.

116 Matin-Asgari. "Twentieth Century Iran's Political Prisoners," 703.

a year of the war's end, in June 1989, but not before making yet another global grandstand to divert attention from the wreckages he was leaving behind in Iran. Once again defying international norms, he issued a fatwa condemning to death Indian-born British author Salman Rushdie, whose novel *The Satanic Verses* had disparaged the prophet Muhammad. Technically in accord with sharia laws, the fatwa was a deliberate political provocation, creating a major obstacle in Iran's postwar efforts at diplomatic rapprochement with the UK and other European countries.

The United States and the Iranian Revolution's Thermidor (1990s)

> *As President Clinton has said, the United States must bear its fair share of responsibility for the problems that have arisen in US-Iranian relations.*
> Secretary of State Madeleine Albright, 2000

About six months before the war's end, in January 1988, Khomeini issued one of his most important decrees concerning the authority of the Islamic state. He claimed the Islamic state's authority was absolute, derived from absolute divine authority, bestowed by God upon the prophet Muhammad and passed through him to the Shi'i imams and jurists. State ordinances therefore could suspend even the most essential pillars of Islam, such as prayers. Khomeini thus bequeathed absolute political authority to his heir, proposing a theory of government clearly at variance, if not at odds, with the historical tradition of Islam.[117] Following his death the same year, a small circle of his closest associates quickly agreed on his replacement, as supreme religious leader, by Ali Khamenei, who was not the most high-ranking candidate for the office. This was in-line with Khomeini's recommendation that his replacement should personify the state's absolute political authority, overriding any religious credentials. In practice, political leadership was collective, albeit within a very small circle, in which Majles speaker Rafsanjani appeared equally powerful as the new supreme religious leader. Soon, however, Khamenei was going to claim and exercise the full powers of his office. He had been Khomeini's student and a member of his trusted inner circle, serving as Iran's president from 1981 to 1989. As a young political cleric, he had mingled with 1970s Iran's secular-leftist intellectuals, adopting

117 Shirazi, *The Constitution of Iran*, 229–31; Mehdi Moslem, "Ayatollah Khomeini's Role in the Rationalization of the Islamic Government," *Critique* 14 (spring 1999): 75–92.

their perception of the United States as an imperialist power. Thus, he emphatically ruled out diplomatic negotiations with the United States, a position he would modify during Obama's second term, though he never trusted the result of negotiations with the United States.[118] In 1987, he took his first and only trip to the United States to attend the UN General Assembly as Iran's president. In the United States, Khamenei faced protests and demonstrations by the Iranian community, including the self-immolation of a young political activist in Los Angeles.[119]

In 1989, Rafsanjani became president, initiating an era of "reconstruction" in postwar domestic and foreign policy. During the political chaos and war of the 1980s, Iran's GDP per capita fell to about half of what it was immediately before the revolution, taking fifteen years to climb back to that level. The 1990s would be a decade of economic growth, when significant oil price increases allowed major reconstruction projects. Expanding the 1980s warfare-welfare state, the Islamic Republic provided basic education and health care to the rural and urban poor, who also received subsidies in food, fuel, and medicine, as well as additional help through charity institutions. Though poverty was significantly reduced, structural economic inequality remained the same as prerevolutionary levels.[120] Iran's 1990s changes coincided with shifts in global balance of political and economic power. The Soviet bloc had collapsed, the Cold War had ended, and the neoliberal model of American capitalism was globally triumphant. American pundits declared "the end of history," when capitalism, liberal democracy, and "Western" culture would dominate the entire world indefinitely. President George H. W. Bush announced a "New World Order," where the United States was the only superpower, using military intervention to police the planet, as it did in the case of Saddam Hussein's invasion of Kuwait. Iran's economy gradually adapted to the global trends of privatization and structural adjustments, although the commanding role of parastate foundations grew stronger. Privatization meant selling state-owned factories, businesses, and land to well-connected speculators. The sale of urban space and skylines created a real estate boom in Tehran and across the country, starting an inflationary cycle in housing prices that has continued

118 Akbar Ganji, "Who is Khamenei? The Mind of Iran's Supreme Leader," *Foreign Affairs* 92. No. 5 (September–October 2013): 24–48; Mousavian, *Iran and the United States*, 109.

119 Laurie Becklund, "Iranian Who Set Himself Afire Surprised Friends, Kin," *Los Angeles Times*, September 22, 1987.

120 Javad Salehi-Isfahani, "Poverty, Inequality, and Populist Politics in Iran," *Journal of Economic Inequality* 7 (2009): 5–28, cited on 8, 16–19.

annually to the present.[121] While the private sector was active in real estate, housing, and construction, the most lucrative contracts and projects would go to entrepreneurs with the strongest state connections. The parastate conglomerates, mainly the IRGC, the Foundation of the Oppressed, Basij Militia, Rural Development and Construction Jihad, and the Imam Khomeini Relief Committee, would gradually own or control hundreds of companies, banks, investment firms, welfare institutions, and pension funds. They employed millions and provided welfare to millions more poor citizens, operating outside the government's taxation and regulatory frame, under the supreme leader's office. As in post-Soviet economic transformations, the Islamic Republic's massive state-owned assets were gradually transferred to a new oligarchy connected to the parastate. The private sector remained active as a broker and subcontractor for projects and investments that domineering parastate organizations handed down to it.[122]

Dealing with US-trade sanctions remained a major challenge to Iran's postwar economic reconstruction. The sanctions began with Carter and continued unabated with varying degrees of intensity. President Rafsanjani tried to reduce tensions with the United States by quietly helping the release of American hostages held by Lebanon's Shi'i Hezbollah militia. His administration brokered the release of five American hostages, without reciprocation from the American side.[123] Rafsanjani was more successful at normalizing relations with Europe, where the Islamic Republic literally could get away with murder. In 1991, agents of the Islamic Republic assassinated the shah's last premier, Shapur Bakhtiar, in Paris, and, the next year, they murdered three Kurdish opposition leaders in Berlin. German investigators eventually issued an arrest warrant for the head of Iran's intelligence ministry and implicated both the supreme leader and Rafsanjani. But neither case affected Tehran's relations with France or Germany. Meanwhile, Rafsanjani was pursuing a quiet détente with the United States, cooperating with the

---

121 Kaveh Ehsani, "The Politics of Property in the Islamic Republic of Iran," in *The Rule of Law, Islam, and Constitutional Politics in Egypt and Iran*, eds. Said Amir Arjomand and Nathan J. Brown (SUNY Press, 2013): 153–78, cited 160–3.

122 Kevan Harris, "The Rise of the Subcontractor State: Politics of Pseudo Privatization in the Islamic Republic of Iran," *International Journal of Middle East Studies* 45, no. 1 (2013): 45–70, cited on 46–50; see also Mehrdad Vahabi and Nasser Mohajer, "A Critical Reflection on Neoliberalism," *Critique* 48, no. 4 (2020): 461–503.

123 Mousavian, *Iran and the United States*, 112–17, 121, 126–32. Mousavian, who was Iran's ambassador to Germany when the murders took place, denies any connection to them. Since 2009, he has been visiting research scholar at Princeton University's Woodrow Wilson School of Public and International Affairs.

Bush administration's punishing war against Iraq, and remaining flexible toward the 1991 US-sponsored peace negotiations between Israel and Arab regimes. By this time, Israel was taking a sharp anti-Iranian turn, soon becoming the decisive factor shaping US policy toward the Islamic Republic. After Iraq's 1991 containment by the United States, Israel was virtually at peace with all Arab countries and no longer able to claim it faced an existential threat. Tel Aviv needed a new nemesis, and the Islamic Republic was willing to assume that role, as it too needed an existential threat to justify its perpetual state of intelligence and military alert. George H. W. Bush was the last American president who set conditions on Israeli demands of US military and financial support. Under President Bill Clinton, Congress took tight control of Israel policy, basically handing it over to the powerful Israel lobby, spearheaded by the American Israel Public Affairs Committee (AIPAC). The Israel lobby concocted the policy of dual containment, designating Iran, along with Iraq, as enemy states the United States needed to contain through sanction and military intervention. Iraq was already contained, but the Islamic Republic remained defiant, allegedly in pursuit of nuclear weapons, supporting terrorism, and opposing the Arab-Israeli peace process.[124] In 1995, the Israel lobby scored a major victory by defeating the Islamic Republic's efforts at normalizing economic relations with the United States. Tehran had signed a $1 billion contract with the US company Conoco to develop a major Iranian oil field. Pushed by AIPAC, President Clinton issued executive orders canceling the Conoco deal and placing an embargo on American companies investing in Iran's energy sector. The same year, the AIPAC sponsored Iran-Libya Sanctions Act (ILSA) passed the US Senate overwhelmingly and the House of Representatives with 415 to 0 votes. ILSA expanded Clinton's ban on US corporations to foreign companies dealing with Iran's energy sector. At the same time, Congress added $18 million to the CIA's budget allocated for overthrowing the Islamic Republic.[125] *The Washington Post* reported:

> The campaign against Iran has been strongly supported by the American Israel Public Affairs Committee, the chief pro-Israel lobbying organization. AIPAC has aggressively lobbied for the new sanctions legislation,

124 On AIPAC's clout in Washington, see John J. Mearsheimer and Stephen M. Walt, *The Israel Lobby and US Foreign Policy* (Farrar, Straus and Giroux, 2007).

125 Steven Hurst, *The United States and the Iranian Nuclear Programme: A Critical History* (Edinburgh University Press, 2018), 100–3.

> which would impose penalties on foreign corporations, banks and lending institutions that make major investments in Iran's oil and gas industries, the countries principal source of revenue.[126]

The Israeli allegation with most traction in the United States focused on Iran's development of nuclear weapons capability and long-range ballistic missile technology. During the 1990s, the Islamic Republic had restarted the shah's nuclear energy program, though the supreme leader had reiterated Khomeini's ban on nuclear weapons, which were deemed anti-Islamic. Nevertheless, Iran's buildup of nuclear technology infrastructure, including uranium enrichment, were bringing it closer to the "breakout" capability of nuclear weapons production. Moreover, even without nuclear warheads, Iran's increasingly far-reaching ballistic missiles could inflict serious damage on Israel. Another source of tension was the military presence in Lebanon, Iraq, and Syria of the Quds Force, the Islamic Revolutionary Guards Corps' foreign operations unit. The IRGC had not directly confronted Israel and later would cooperate with the United States against the Islamic State (ISIS) in Iraq and Syria, yet it was placed on the US list of terrorist organizations, its foreign activities becoming a major excuse for sanctioning Iran. The Islamic Republic refused to scale back the Quds Force's presence in Iraq or Syria, arguing it was invited there by friendly governments. The Tehran regime generally adhered to the letter of international law and UN conventions, but its defiance of American and Israeli demands led to the piling up of new sanctions on top of the existing ones. In the long run, decades of onerous sanctions would place crushing burdens on Iran's ordinary citizens, who had no say on whether Iran needed a nuclear energy program, ballistic missiles, or military presence in other countries.[127]

During Clinton's second presidential term, it seemed a Iran-US détente might be possible. By the mid-1990s, Iran's economy was in its worst shape since the war years, with high inflation and unemployment, currency devaluation, sharp decline in oil revenue, and US sanctions taking a heavy toll. Iran was also the world's largest host country to refugees, taking in about 1.5 million Afghans fleeing the Taliban regime. Narcotics addiction was a national concern, and the Islamic Republic was engaged

126 Quoted in Fayazmanesh, *The United States and Iran*, 77; see ibid., 73–8.

127 Narges Bajoghli, Vali Nasr, Djavad Salehi-Isfahani, and Ali Vaez, *How Sanctions Work Sanctions: Iran and the Impact of Economic Warfare* (Stanford University Press, 2024), 56–60.

in a major campaign against drug trafficking from Afghanistan.[128] Iran's mostly young population was more educated and less traumatized than the aging revolutionary generation, expecting a better life and more political participation. At the same time, the country's political elite was fracturing into new factions, some advocating political reform and greater engagement with the outside world. The 1997 presidential election thus became a contest between a regime stalwart, Ali Akbar Nategh-Nouri, standing for conservative continuity, and Mohammad Khatami, a relatively young cleric with a "liberal" political and cultural reputation. Khatami's landslide victory, with 70 percent of the vote in an 88 percent voter turnout election, was proof that a great majority of Iranians wanted change. Khatami was a highly educated intellectual whose writings and career record showed liberal inclinations, albeit within the constraints of the Islamic Republic. In foreign policy, he famously advocated a "dialogue of civilizations," the title of a book he had published in response to American political scientist Samuel Huntington's "clash of civilizations" thesis. While Huntington had focused on Islam as the main adversary of a US-led post–Cold War global order, Khatami presented Islam as heir to a rich and diverse civilizational tradition, compatible with the liberal democratic values of "Western" civilization. He also talked about the United States differently, expressing his appreciation of "American civilization" and "the great American people," while shifting the dialogue with the US government from hostility toward respectful disagreement. He would argue, for instance:

> [American] civilization is best described by the renowned French sociologist Alexis de Tocqueville . . . In his view, the significance of this civilization is in the fact that liberty found religion as a cradle for its growth, and religion found protection of liberty as its divine call. Therefore, liberty and faith never clashed. And we see, even today, Americans are a religious people . . . I believe that if humanity is looking for happiness, it should combine religious spirituality with the virtues of liberty . . . And it is for this reason that I say I respect the American nation because of their great civilization.[129]

Khatami's message was that Islam, like Christianity, could be compatible with liberty, and therefore, despite their differences, Iran and the United States had a lot in common. This was an idealistic reading of both

128 *New York Times*, September 20, 1998.

129 Khatami quoted in Ghazvinian, *America and Iran*, 406.

Islamic and American history, but the tone and content of Khatami's discourse were refreshingly conciliatory and eventually effective in reducing tensions with Washington. In an interview with CNN, Khatami called for a "crack in this wall of mistrust" between the two countries, and he expressed "regret" about the 1979 hostage crisis and acknowledged it had been hurtful to Americans. He proposed a "people-to-people" détente, building bridges between Iranian and American academics, writers, artists, journalists, athletes, and tourists.[130] Though diplomatic relations were not restored, there was a breakthrough in Iranian-American cultural exchange, most notably in sports diplomacy. Iran had been absent from international sports events, having boycotted the 1980 Moscow and 1984 Los Angeles Olympics. The Iranian "athlete" familiar to many Americans was the "Iron Sheikh," a villainous character in staged wrestling matches widely watched on television. In 1996, real Iranian wrestlers began visiting the United States, and two years later, as part of Khatami's people-to-people diplomacy, American wrestlers were invited to Tehran, where they were well received by official hosts and the public. The same year, Iranian and American national soccer teams met at the World Cup match in Lyons, France. This was the two countries' most high-profile encounter in decades, recognized as such by President Clinton, who issued a statement saying he hoped the match would be a "step toward ending the estrangement between our two nations," and later congratulated Iran on its victory. In 2000, Iranian and American national soccer teams met in Pasadena, California, finishing with a happy draw in front of over fifty thousand mostly Iranian American fans.[131] Khatami's peak moment of international recognition came the same year, when the United Nations declared 2001 to be the "Year of Dialogue Among Civilizations." The UN Secretary-General thanked Khatami for proposing that year's designation to the General Assembly.[132] Within two years of Khatami's election, Iran appeared to be shedding its two-decade long image of a pariah country.

Khatami's charm offensive coincided with Clinton's second term, when a powerful American corporate lobby slowed the momentum of Iran sanctions legislation, pushed by Israel and AIPAC. Ultimately, however, the sanctions remained in place, showing how a single foreign

130 *The Economist*, January 10, 1988, 37.

131 H. E. Chehabi, "Sport Diplomacy between the United States and Iran," *Diplomacy and Statecraft* 12:1 (2001); 89–16, cited on 94, 96, 98, Clinton quote on 99.

132 United Nations, "United Nations Year of Dialogue Among Civilizations, 2001 Launched with Round Table Discussion," news release, September 5, 2000, press.un.org.

government (that is, the state of Israel) could undermine the multi-billion-dollar interests of major American corporations. Throughout the 1990s, major corporations, mostly in oil, aerospace, and agriculture, had intensely lobbied against Iran sanctions. They included Chevron, Halliburton, Conoco, Amoco, Unocal, Mobil, Caterpillar, Motorola, and at least eight agriculture groups, including the National Association of Wheat Growers. This corporate lobby funded policy institutes and hired high-profile figures, including former National Security Advisors Brzezinski and Brent Scowcroft, as well as former Secretaries of Defense and State Richard Cheney and James Baker. The lobby was joined by the American Iranian Council (AIC), established in 1990 to advance "dialogue and understanding between the United States and Iran." The AIC founder and president, Hooshang Amirahmadi, was a Rutgers University professor with ties to the Iranian government and American oil companies. Brzezinski, whose hawkish views had softened after the fall of the Soviet Union, was now an oil industry consultant, insisting that engagement with Iran served American business interests. In 1997, he wrote:

> The policy of unilateral US sanctions against Iran has been ineffectual, and the attempt to coerce others into following America's lead has been a mistake . . . One negative consequence of current policy is the damage inflicted on America's interest in gaining greater access to energy sources . . . Another area of common interest is the resuscitation of US-Iranian commercial relations. To this end, Washington should be open-minded regarding the resumption of activity by American oil companies in Iran.

Along with the oil industry, American agribusiness heavily lobbied Washington for access to Iranian markets, sponsoring its own advocacy groups such as the Center for Strategic and International Studies, whose board of trustees enlisted Brzezinski and Scowcroft and Iranian American academic experts such as Shireen Hunter. Overlapping with the above lobby groups was a new organization, USA Engage, set up in 1997 by oil, aerospace, and agribusiness giants, including Mobil, Texaco, and Boeing, and enlisting influential congressmen and former President Carter, who now opposed unilateral US sanctions against Iran.[133] In-line with this corporate push, in 1998, Secretary of State Madeleine Albright gave a speech inviting the Islamic Republic to join the United States in sketching "a road map leading to normal relations." In January 1999,

133 Fayazmanesh, *The United States and Iran*, 84–91, Brzezinski quoted on 87.

Carter's secretary of state, Cyrus Vance, the honorary chairman of AIC, gave a lecture urging the restoration of diplomatic relations with Iran. Clinton then eased the sanctions policy, allowing the sale of food and medical supplies to Iran. Changing his bellicose tone, he talked about "reconciliation with a country that had suffered at the hands of the West," admitting that "sometimes it's quite important to tell people, look, you have the right to be angry at something my country or my culture or others that are generally allied with us today did to you 50 or 60 or 100 or 150 years ago."[134]

In March 2000, the Clinton administration gave its clearest response to Khatami in a speech by Madeleine Albright to the American Iranian Council. Despite its mixed messaging, including the criticism of "unelected hands" repressing Iran's reform movement, Albright acknowledged the most important Iranian grievances vis-à-vis the United States:

> In 1953 the United States played a significant role in orchestrating the overthrow of Iran's popular Prime Minister, Mohammed Mossadegh. The Eisenhower Administration believed its actions were justified for strategic reasons; but the coup was clearly a setback for Iran's political development. And it is easy to see now why many Iranians continue to resent this intervention by America in their internal affairs. Moreover, during the next quarter century, the United States and the West gave sustained backing to the Shah's regime. Although it did much to develop the country economically, the Shah's government also brutally repressed political dissent. As President Clinton has said, the United States must bear its fair share of responsibility for the problems that have arisen in US-Iranian relations. Even in more recent years, aspects of US policy towards Iraq, during its conflict with Iran appear now to have been regrettably shortsighted, especially in light our subsequent experiences with Saddam Hussein.

Angered by Albright's reference to the Islamic Republic's repressive "unelected hands," Supreme Leader Khamenei dismissed the importance of her speech, saying, "The confessions of American crimes are of no use to the Iranian nation," and claimed also that Clinton's offer of negotiations was a "deceitful" ploy "to set the stage for more enmities and to regain its former interests in Iran." Khamenei may have missed a major opportunity, but the fact remained that the Clinton administration

134 Fayazmanesh, *The United States and Iran*, 92–3.

made no major concessions to Iran, making exemptions only of pistachios and carpets and medical items in its sanctions list. As Khatami's foreign minister noted, Clinton had offered nothing that could placate hard-line Iranian opposition to a breakthrough with the United States.[135]

During his second year in office, Khatami was being challenged by the "unelected hands" that were pushing back against a grassroots reform movement gathering momentum under his administration. Led by university students, the postrevolutionary generation coming of age by the late 1990s was testing the limits of the Islamic Republic's political tolerance. During the two postrevolutionary decades, Iran's literacy rate had risen from slightly under 50 percent to almost 80 percent. Whereas in the mid-1970s only 2 percent of the population had university degrees, by the time of Khatami's election in 1997, around three million Iranians were university graduates or were enrolled in higher education, more than 51 percent of that year's university graduates being women. Meanwhile, Iran's book publication and reading public had experienced a phenomenal growth. In 1976, slightly over sixteen hundred book titles were published, a figure that in 1997 had grown almost tenfold to over fifteen thousand, with almost eighty million titles being in circulation.[136] Aligned with Khatami, the postrevolutionary generation was in tune with the 1990s global discourses of civil society, human rights, women's rights, and freedom of expression, articulated in a panoply of newspapers and periodicals pushing against censorship. According to one estimate, between 1992 and 1998, the number of periodicals published in Iran had doubled, from 513 to 1,250, while millions followed global cultural and political trends via satellite television, the internet, and email.

In late 1998 and early 1999, a turning point was reached when the defiant press helped expose the ministry of intelligence's involvement in the serial murder of prominent dissidents. Khatami took a stand for bringing the culprits to justice, a campaign that, despite limited success, delivered a major blow to the deep state's impunity. The hard-liners retaliated by closing one reformist newspaper after another, eventually passing a draconian new press law. In July 1999, student-led protests against the new repressive press law were crushed in Tehran and other cities, while two dozen senior Revolutionary Guard officers issued a public statement, threatening "direct action"—effectively a military coup—unless

135 Byrne and Byrne, *Worlds Apart*, 167; Albright's speech, 167–71, quoted on 170; Khamenei's response to Albright in Hurst, *The United States and the Iranian Nuclear Programme*, 117.

136 Sadeghi-Boroujerdi, *Revolution and its Discontents*, 45.

Khatami changed course. This he did, as he followed the supreme leader in condemning people taking to the streets in support of student protests. Several students and other protesters were killed, hundreds injured, and more than fifteen hundred arrested and jailed.[137] In 2000, Khatami's reformist camp had a major victory in parliamentary elections, but it was already in disarray, having shed its radical faction and offering no path forward to the rest of its disillusioned followers. The deep state was once again in full control, successfully muzzling the press and unleashing violence on reformers who dared cross its red lines, something that would be repeated on a more massive scale in 2009.[138]

137 Randjbar-Daemi, *The Quest for Authority in Iran*, 138–40; Ali Akbar Mahdi, "The Student Movement in the Islamic Republic of Iran," *Journal of Iranian Research and Analysis* 15, no. 2 (November 1999): 5–32.

138 *Middle East Report*, 29, no. 3 (fall 1999), special issue on "Pushing the Limits: Iran's Islamic Revolution at Twenty."

6

From a Nuclear Deal to War: Iran, the United States, and Israel

Israel Pushes the Islamic Republic into the Axis of Evil

> *We got a leader in Iran who has announced that he wants to destroy Israel. So . . . if you're interested in avoiding World War 3, it seems like you ought to be interested in preventing [the Iranians] from having the knowledge necessary to make a nuclear weapon.*
>
> President George W. Bush, 2007[1]

As we saw in the previous chapter, during the 1990s, Tehran's nuclear energy program became a major point of contention with Washington. The program originated in the late 1950s, when the United States signed an agreement to help Iran with the peaceful development of nuclear energy, providing technical assistance and enriched uranium for a small light-water reactor, set up by an American company in 1967. A year later, Iran signed the Treaty on the Non-Proliferation of Nuclear Weapons (NPT), and, in 1974, the shah declared Iran would build twenty nuclear power plants to produce electricity. He allocated an annual budget of $1 billion to buy nuclear fuel and technology from German and French companies. President Nixon was supportive of the shah's ambition for acquiring nuclear weapons, but Congress pressured his successor, Gerard Ford, to announce a moratorium on the US export of nuclear technology to Iran. In 1977, President Carter told the shah that the United States would

1 Quoted in Steven Hurst, *The United States and the Iranian Nuclear Programme: A Critical History* (Edinburgh University Press, 2018), 172.

not agree to Iranian control of the nuclear fuel processing cycle, and, by 1978, the country's nuclear program was suspended as an assertive opposition movement deemed it wasteful. As would be the case with the Islamic Republic, the shah had tried to maximize Iranian control of the nuclear fuel processing cycle, the prerequisite to building atomic bombs, something the United States had initially supported but opposed by the late 1970s.[2] Thus, there was some continuity in the American response to Iran's nuclear program before and after the revolution, though there were also major differences.

During the 1980s war with Iraq, the Islamic Republic had asked the International Atomic Energy Agency (IAEA) for assistance in restarting its nuclear energy program. The IAEA is the UN agency monitoring its member countries to make sure their nuclear energy program does not go toward building nuclear bombs. But Tehran's plans made no progress since the Reagan administration pushed for a global ban on the transfer of nuclear material and technology to Iran. During its 1990s postwar economic reconstruction, the Islamic Republic declared it would build ten nuclear power plants to produce 20 percent of Iran's electricity. The Islamic Republic signed contracts with China and Russia to help build a nuclear infrastructure and bought uranium and sensitive technology from them and on the black market. Tehran informed the IAEA of its nuclear activities, though without full transparency, presumably for protection from possible Israeli or American military strikes against them. By the end of the 1990s, Iran had mastered the nuclear fuel processing cycle, moving closer to the "breakout" capability of building nuclear weapons.[3] At the same time, and as under the shah, the Islamic Republic had no compelling case for its enormously costly and dangerous nuclear energy program, since Iran had abundant solar energy in addition to its vast reservoirs of oil and natural gas. But the Islamic Republic was making nuclear energy a political issue, central to its narrative of defying global adversaries, and hence a question beyond public discussion. The American response to Iran's nuclear energy program was equally contradictory and cynical. In 2005, Henry Kissinger, then an elderly statesman, chimed in, arguing that nuclear energy was a waste of resources for a major oil-producing country like Iran. Thirty years earlier, serving as President Ford's secretary of state, Kissinger had endorsed the shah's

2 Ibid., 23–54; on the history of nuclear nonproliferation see Susan Watkins, "The Nuclear Non-Protestation Treaty," *New Left Review* 54 (November–December 2008): 5–16.

3 Hurst, *The United States and the Iranian Nuclear Programme*, 73–5, 93–4.

nuclear ambitions, saying "nuclear power will both provide for the growing needs of Iran's economy and free remaining oil reserves for export or conversion to petrochemicals."[4]

Despite Washington's objections, during the 1990s, Russia and China remained engaged with Iran's nuclear program, while European countries bypassed US sanctions on Iran's energy sector. The French company TOTAL signed a $2 billion contract to develop the country's natural gas fields, while IAEA inspections of Iran reported no nuclear weapons-related activities. By the late 1990s, under President Mohammad Khatami, a Tehran-Washington diplomatic breakthrough, including some agreement on Iran's nuclear energy program, seemed possible, but eventually failed to materialize.[5] As we saw in chapter 5, the major obstacle to a Iran-US rapprochement was Washington's powerful Israel lobby, whose impact grew exponentially under President George W. Bush and his neoconservative foreign policy team. Led by Vice President Richard Cheney and Defense Secretary Donald Rumsfeld, the neoconservatives were linked to the Project for a New American Century, a political lobby group advocating for US global hegemony imposed via military intervention. Despite setbacks, just before the September 11, 2001, attacks, Iran-US relations were improving, as secret negotiations in Europe coordinated the two countries' joint military action against the Taliban government in Afghanistan. In 1998, Iran almost had gone to war with Afghanistan after the Taliban regime massacred hundreds of its Shi'i subjects and murdered Iranian diplomats. Even after the September 11 attacks, Iran and the United States were initially on the same side, both facing off against the Taliban government and Osama bin Laden's Al-Qaeda network as their common enemy. Through 2001, Iranian and American diplomats were meeting in Germany, where Afghanistan's neighbors negotiated to find ways of ending that country's civil war. Following the September 11 attacks, the Islamic Republic offered close cooperation with the US military invasion of Afghanistan. Quietly, Tehran had become a tactical ally in America's global war against Al-Qaeda and its Taliban backers.

But everything changed when Tel Aviv delivered a masterstroke, accusing the Islamic Republic of sponsoring international terrorism. On

---

4 Mohammad Javad Zarif, "Tackling the Iran-US Crisis: The Need for a Paradigm Shift," *Journal of International Affairs* 60, 2 (spring–summer 2007): 73–94, Kissinger quoted on 81.

5 Hurst, *The United States and the Iranian Nuclear Programme*, 106–8, 124–15; Holly Ellyat, "Oil Giant Total has Pulled Out of Iran and Giant Gas Project, Report Says," CNBC, August 20, 2018.

January 3, 2002, Israel declared it had seized a ship loaded with Iranian-made weapons sailing on the Red Sea for delivery to the Palestinian Authority. This Israeli "smoking gun" evidence would kill a Iran-US rapprochement, on the verge of turning into an effective political-military alliance. At a time when Tehran was delicately mending fences with Washington, sending a shipload of Iranian weapons on open sea toward Israel's impenetrable coastline made no sense. But the Islamic Republic's protests about the whole thing being a fabrication had no traction in the Bush White House. On January 29, 2002, President Bush delivered a State of the Union speech declaring Iran, along with Iraq and North Korea, had formed an "axis of evil, arming to threaten the peace of the world." Israel had prevented a possible grand bargain between Tehran and Washington, managing to place Iran on top of the enemy list in America's War on Terror.[6]

The Islamic Republic nevertheless continued to assist the US occupation of Afghanistan and even offered cooperation when Iraq emerged as the next target of an American invasion in 2002. In need of a more compelling argument, the Israel-neoconservative lobby now focused on the accusation that, in addition to sponsoring terrorism, Tehran was secretly building a nuclear weapon. According to Tel Aviv, the Islamic Republic was doing this in two nuclear facilities whose activities were not reported to the UN monitoring agency. The evidence was an intelligence "dossier," allegedly provided by Mojahedin-e-Khalq, an Iranian exile group based in Iraq and armed by Saddam Hussein to carry out military operations against Iran. The Mojahedin, known in the United States as the MEK, was listed as a terrorist organization by the Clinton administration, but, after forging links to Israel, it found support in US Congress. The "MEK dossier" included intelligence data, such as satellite photography of Iran's secret nuclear facilities, that an exile group based in Iraq could not have obtained or produced. Soon, American investigative journalist Seymour Hersh and others traced the "MEK dossier" back to Israel. The MEK's role as an instrument of Washington and Tel Aviv became more apparent after the 2003 US occupation of Iraq, when its bases came under American control. At that point, Washington's neocons and the Israel lobby insisted the MEK, presumably still a terrorist organization, should keep

6 Trita Parsi, *Treacherous Alliance: The Secret Dealings of Israel, Iran, and the United States* (Yale University Press, 2007), 226–37. Bush quoted in Malcom Byrne and Kian Byrne, *Worlds Apart: A Documentary History of US-Iran Relations, 1978–2018* (Cambridge University Press, 2022), 175.

its arms to fight the Islamic Republic.[7] As one of their congressional supporters put it:

> OK, so the [MEK] is a terrorist organization based in Iraq, which is a terrorist state. They are fighting Iran, which is another terrorist state. I say let's help them fight each other as much as they want. Once they all are destroyed, I can celebrate twice over.[8]

Despite the dubiousness of Israeli allegations, the Islamic Republic's nuclear program became the main bone of contention between Iran and the United States. Whether or not Iran's nuclear energy program, or its weaponization, were justifiable, American objections to them were biased and hypocritical. The United States was the only country that had used atomic bombs and then rejected a 1946 UN plan to ban their further manufacture.[9] Later, the United States did not oppose Israel's building a nuclear arsenal and looked the other way when Pakistan developed its nuclear bomb, both in defiance of the UN and international law. Iran's nuclear energy program had developed largely, though not entirely, under UN inspections. In 2003, Hassan Rouhani, then secretary of Iran's national security council, admitted that the Islamic Republic had "concealed part of its legal nuclear activities" because of the "illegal sanctions against it." Iran's foreign minister Javad Zarif also would admit the program's partial "concealment" for security reasons, while insisting its goals always remained peaceful.[10]

In 2003, under the threat of UN Security Council sanctions, Tehran agreed to suspend uranium enrichment and allow full and regular IAEA inspection of its nuclear facilities. For the next three years, the Islamic Republic negotiated with the European Union and Russia to find a diplomatic solution to its nuclear imbroglios, while the Bush administration tried to take Iran's case to the UN Security Council. The US position grew weaker as its occupation of Iraq and Afghanistan ran into major difficulties, ironically leading to Iran's influence growing in both countries. In 2005, with mounting threats of Israeli military action, the Bush administration produced an Iran Action Plan, aimed at "regime

---

7 Sasan Fayazmanesh, *The United States and Iran: Sanctions, Wars and the Policy of Dual Containment* (Routledge, 2008), 121–3.

8 Gary Ackerman quoted in Fayazmanesh, *The United States and Iran*, 85.

9 Larry G. Gerber, "The Baruch Plan and the Origins of the Cold War," *Diplomatic History* 6, no. 1 (1982): 69–95.

10 Rouhani quoted in Fayazmanesh, *The United States and Iran*, 146; see Zarif, "Tackling the Iran-US Crisis," 84.

change" in Tehran by sponsoring opposition groups and massive "pro-democracy" propaganda through the *Voice of America* and *Radio Free Europe* broadcasts. The US-backed "democratic" alternatives to the Islamic Republic were the MEK and Iranian monarchists, led by Reza Pahlavi, the shah's son, both being small exile factions lacking significant support inside the country.[11] Meanwhile, Iran's domestic politics were shifting after Mahmoud Ahmadinejad won the 2005 presidential election, with the reformist camp in disarray after Khatami's two presidential terms were blocked from delivering any fundamental change. Ahmadinejad promised a return to 1980s "populist" policies by making poor Iranians direct beneficiaries of the country's oil income, which was experiencing a boom due to major price rises. He proposed the transfer of billions of dollars of public and state assets, called "Justice Shares," to the lower-income half of the country's population. Though the actual worth of Justice Shares was dubious, their millions of recipients could, at least for a time, be enlisted as regime supporters and a voting bloc for Ahmadinejad.[12] With the supreme leader's approval, the political and economic clout of the Islamic Revolutionary Guard Corps (IRGC) would also grow under Ahmadinejad. Nineteen former Revolutionary Guard members served in Ahmadinejad's cabinet, while the IRGC and its affiliate Basij militia opened their own banks and expanded their economic activities. The IRGC's construction and engineering branch, the Khatam al-Anbiaya station, received billions of dollars of no-bid contracts in dams, housing, highways, shipping, oil, and gas projects. The IRGC's growing political presence was linked to its role in what the supreme leader called the "Resistance Economy." As sanctions disrupted Iran's normal trade, banking, and financial system, the IRGC would step in to set up a "shadow economy," clandestinely managing financial transactions and moving goods and services across the borders. In addition to the windfall reaped from running the "shadow economy," the IRGC derived enormous riches from its central role in Iran's burgeoning telecommunications, defense, and nuclear energy industries. These activities made a great leap forward during Ahmadinejad's first term, coinciding with the peak of a growth cycle in oil income, the price

11 Hurst, *The United States and the Iranian Nuclear Programme*, 155–6; Parsi, *Treacherous Alliance*, 253–5; Seymour M. Hersh, "The Coming Wars," *New Yorker*, January, 5, 2005.

12 Kevan Harris, *A Social Revolution: Politics and the Welfare State in Iran* (University of California Press, 2017), 55–6; Kaveh Ehsani, "Survival Through Dispossession: Privatization of Public Goods in the Islamic Republic," *MERIP* 39, no. 250 (spring 2009): 26–33.

per barrel of crude oil rising from $33 to almost $200 between 2001 and 2010.[13]

In foreign relations, Ahmadinejad continued wrangling with the United States over the nuclear issue while making outlandish empty threats against Israel. In October 2005, he gave a speech repeating Khomeini's famous statement that "the Quds [Jerusalem] occupation regime must disappear from the pages of time." A distorted translation of this sentence immediately appeared as a *New York Times* headline: "Iran's President Says Israel Must Be 'Wiped off the Map.'" The US House of Representatives then passed a resolution condemning Ahmadinejad's alleged call for the destruction of the Jewish State, while Israel and its American lobby compared him to Hitler and demanded the Islamic Republic's expulsion from the United Nations. As Iran experts pointed out, Ahmadinejad's statement was deliberately mistranslated, but the US media and political establishment never corrected the false attribution.[14] Ironically, while the threat of Israel's destruction was wrongly attributed to Ahmadinejad, senior American politicians would make similar threats against Iran with impunity. In April 2008, Hillary Clinton, competing against Barack Obama for the Democratic Party's presidential nomination, declared that, if she were president, the United States could "totally obliterate" Iran in retaliation for a nuclear strike against Israel. "That's a terrible thing to say but those people who run Iran need to understand that, because that perhaps will deter them from doing something that would be reckless, foolish and tragic," Clinton clarified. Obama rejected Clinton's rhetoric as "saber rattling."[15] In 2019, President Donald Trump would repeat the same threat, declaring that a war with the United States would be "the official end of Iran."[16]

Meanwhile, when the Islamic Republic ended its two-year suspension of uranium enrichment in 2006, the Bush administration pressed the IAEA to declare Iran in violation of the NPT, managing to refer its case to the UN Security Council. Pushing back against US pressure, IAEA director Mohamed ElBaradei had said the world should not "jump the gun" with erroneous information, as with the 2003 US-led invasion of Iraq, or drive Iran into defiance as North Korea was in response to international

13 Ali Rahnema, *The Political History of Modern Iran: Revolution, Reaction and Transformation, 1905 to the Present* (I.B. Tauris, 2023), 557–8; "Crude Oil Prices (1946–2025)," Macrotrends, accessed March 12, 2024, macrotrends.net.

14 Fayazmanesh, *The United States and Iran: Sanctions*, 174–6; Juan Cole, "Bill Scher Importance of Cole v. Hitchens," May 4, 2006, juancole.com.

15 David Morgan, "Clinton Says US Could 'Totally Obliterate Iran,' Reuters, April 22, 2008.

16 NIAC, accessed July 19, 2022, niacouncil.org.

sanctions. As with the lead-up to the US invasion of Iraq, ElBaradei's opposition to sanctions and war threats on Iran made him clash with the Bush administration, which unsuccessfully tried to remove him as IAEA director. But the United States convinced Russia and China not to veto UN resolutions imposing further sanctions on Iran in 2006–7, a move that made the Islamic Republic end its voluntary cooperation with the IAEA. By 2007, the United States barred its banks from doing business with Iran and pushed European governments to do the same, a move that seriously disrupted Iran's access to global financial transactions.[17] Then, in December 2007, while Israel pressed for American military action to stop Iran's alleged nuclear bomb building, the US National Intelligence Estimate declared that Iran had halted all nuclear weapons–related activities since 2003. The previous year, a *New Yorker* magazine article had claimed: "The CIA found no conclusive evidence, as yet, of a secret Iranian nuclear weapons program." The author, Seymour Hersh, suspected the Bush administration was trying "to prevent the CIA assessment from being incorporated into a forthcoming National Intelligence Estimate on Iranian nuclear capabilities" because the finding went against "the administration's planning for a military attack against Iran."[18] But the 2007 National Intelligence Estimate did incorporate the CIA report, putting a dent in the urgency of Israel's case for military action. Nevertheless, the Islamic Republic's refusal to follow IAEA recommendations led to more UN sanctions. Bush's second term thus ended in a stalemate with Iran, whereby American threats of regime change and growing punitive sanctions failed to make the Islamic Republic change course, while the Iranian people had to endure the crushing burden of their government's defiance.[19]

Obama's Iran Deal Prevails Over the Israel Lobby

> *You change, and we shall change as well.*
>
> Supreme Leader Khamenei, responding to President Obama, 2009[20]

During the 2008 American presidential campaign, signs of a possible change of course were appearing on both sides of the Iran-US divide.

17 Fayazmanesh, *The United States and Iran: Sanctions*, 193, 183–4, 209, 234–355.

18 Seymour Hersh, "The Next Act," *New Yorker*, November 27, 2007; Hersh is quoted in Zarif, "Tackling the Iran-US Crisis," 77.

19 Hurst, *The United States and the Iranian Nuclear Programme*, 172–6.

20 Khamenei's speech in Byrne and Byrne, *Worlds Apart*, 245.

In a September 2008 panel discussion featuring former US secretaries of state, even Kissinger recommended resolving the conflict over Iran's nuclear program through diplomatic negotiations.[21] Endorsing this approach, Obama called for engagement with Iran during his campaign and, when elected president, sent a confidential letter to Supreme Leader Ali Khamenei, proposing talks and assuring him that the United States did not seek regime change in Iran. Khamenei's response showed flexibility and his confidential correspondence with Obama continued. A cautious appreciation of Obama's overture could be noted in Khamenei's open declarations; for example, a March 2009 speech in which, after repeating his familiar grievances against the United States, he directly addressed Obama:

> Please pay attention. If you go on with the slogan of discussion and pressure, saying you will negotiate with Iran, and at the same time impose pressure, threats, and changes, then our nation will not like such words. We do not have any experience with the new US President and Government. We shall see and judge. You change, and we shall change as well.[22]

However, this important breakthrough in relations, for the first time involving direct communication between a US president and the Islamic Republic's supreme leader, was paused when Iran plunged into a massive domestic upheaval. In June 2009, millions of Iranians were taking to the streets denouncing Ahmadinejad's winning a second presidential term as fraudulent. Named after the color in display during the anti-Ahmadinejad campaign, this was the Green Movement, Iran's largest mass political protest since the early years of the revolution. Ahmadinejad had been facing strong contenders, most notably Mir-Hossein Mousavi, who was prime minister during the 1980s war years and subsequently a quiet dissident for two decades. During televised debates, Mousvai and other candidates sharply criticized Ahmadinejad's government for record-high inflation, unemployment, and poverty, as well as a reckless foreign policy. Ahmadinejad responded with personal attacks; for example, questioning the academic credentials of Mousvai's spouse, Zahra Rahnavard, a university professor and women's rights advocate whose recognition had significantly boosted her husband's campaign.

21 Daily Dash, "Kissinger on Engaging Iran," *The Atlantic*, September 26, 2008.

22 Khamenei's speech in Byrne and Byrne, *Worlds Apart*, 245. Khamenei answered all of Obama's messages. See "Hame-ye namehay-e Obama be ayatollah Khamenei," bbc.com.

A preelection survey, conducted by an American pollster through telephone calls to 1,001 Iranians, showed Ahmadinejad's support as 34 percent and Mousavi's 14 percent, with half of the electorate being undecided. But, even if accurate, this survey put Ahmadinejad ahead at the start of a rapidly shifting campaign, whose actual result could give Mousavi and the other two candidates a larger portion of the undecided votes.[23] Coincidentally, Ahmadinejad's 34 percent support in the American survey matched his 35 percent approval rating in an Iranian poll of 2006, when his supporters were defeated in countrywide municipal elections. By 2009, even segments of the ruling elite appeared dissatisfied with Ahmadinejad, whose economic policies were criticized in right-wing newspapers and by more than half of Majles deputies.[24]

A few hours after the polls closed, Ahmadinejad was declared the winner with 65 percent of the vote, Mousavi finishing second with 33 percent. The result was immediately challenged by Mousavi and the other two candidates, who each were reported with less than 2 percent of the votes, despite being nationally known figures. Many observers believed the real results would have sent the 2009 election into a second round, something the political establishment deemed risky since it might lead to Ahmadinejad's defeat.[25] When Mousavi and another candidate called on their supporters to come out in protest, Tehran and many parts of the country saw demonstrations as massive as those during the peak of the revolution. Tehran's protest procession was five miles long, suggesting at least one million participants—the city's mayor estimated three million demonstrators.[26] Ahmadinejad responded by mobilizing smaller counterdemonstrations, while everyone waited for the Supreme Leader's verdict. Within a few days, Khamenei endorsed the election results, ominously warning that further demonstrations would not be tolerated. Still, hundreds of thousands defied him as protests continued across the country. As Khamenei had warned, the regime unleashed its security

---

23 The same American poll showed 80 percent of respondents wanted the supreme leader to be publicly elected; 77 percent wanted better relations with the United States; and 70 percent thought the UN should have more access to Iran's nuclear facilities. See Ervand Abrahamian, "I Am Not a Speck of Dirt, I Am a Retired Teacher," in *The People Reloaded: The Green Movement and the Struggle for Iran's Future*, eds. Nader Hashemi and Danny Postel, (Melville House, 2010): 59–69, cited on 61–2.

24 Jahangir Amuzegar, "The Ahmadinejad Era: Preparing for The Apocalypse," *Journal of International Affairs* 60, 2 (spring–summer 2007): 35–53, cited 43, 47, 50.

25 Bernard Hourcade, *Atlas of Presidential Elections in the Islamic Republic of Iran: 1980–2017* (Centre de Recherche sur le Monde Iranien Paris, 2020), 49.

26 *Time*, June 9, 2009, reported 2–3 million. Robert Fisk, who was in Thran, reported one million protesters. *Independent*, June 16, 2009, 4–5.

forces and the Basij militia, who broke up the protests by shooting into crowds and driving cars and motorbikes in their midst. Foreign journalists, who had globally broadcast the first week of peaceful protests, were now expelled. For several weeks, however, scenes of defiant protests and their brutal suppression were captured by cell phones and posted on social media for the world to see. By this time, around twenty-three million people, close to 40 percent of Iran's adult population, were internet users, while more than 50 percent of all Middle East internet users were Iranians. Protesters used cell phones, Facebook, email, YouTube, and SMS messages to showcase their movement in cyberspace, where they received the support of the Iranian diaspora, especially Iranian Americans. Within two years, the new tactic of using cyberspace to organize leaderless grassroots protests would be used by millions of young Tunisians and Egyptians during the "Arab Spring" of 2011.[27]

Iran's election protests continued into fall 2009, with dozens of demonstrators killed and thousands injured or jailed, many prisoners reportedly being tortured. Mousavi, Rahnavard, and another candidate contesting Ahmadinejad's election were placed under house arrest, while the leaderless spontaneous opposition eventually dwindled down in the face of brutal repression.[28] In the end, ten years after the crushing of countrywide 1999 protests (see chapter 5), another popular attempt at peacefully reforming the Islamic Republic was violently contained. In Washington, Obama was in the difficult position of outwardly expressing support for Iranian dissidents while continuing secret negotiations with the regime that was suppressing them. The situation was further complicated because the Islamic Republic blamed the United States for the protests, even though Mousavi and other opposition leaders were aligned with the regime's foreign policy, being "nuclear nationalist" and supporting Iran's nuclear energy program. Meanwhile, Obama's outreach to Iran was facing stiff opposition from Congress and Israel, with Secretary of State Hillary Clinton and her Israeli counterpart advocating more "crippling" Iran sanctions. Consequently, Obama gave the Islamic Republic an ultimatum to halt uranium enrichment by the end of 2009

27 Arash Reisinezhad, "The Iranian Green Movement: Fragmented Collective Action and Fragile Collective Identity," *Iranian Studies* 48, 2 (March 2015): 193–222, cited on 200–2; Siavush Ranjbar-Daemi, *The Quest for Authority in Iran: A History of the Presidency from Revolution to Rouhani* (I.B. Tauris, 2018), 222–9.

28 Peter Rothberg, "Protests in Iran," *Nation*, February 4, 2010. *The Guardian* reported eighty dead, and hundreds injured by the end of July 2009; *The Guardian*, July 29, 2009. Ranjbar-Daemi, *The Quest for Authority in Iran*, 216–29.

while continuing verbal support of Iranian protesters.[29] In fall 2009, representatives of the Islamic Republic and the of P5+1 (that is, the five permanent members of the UN Security Council: China, Russia, France, the UK, and the United States, plus Germany) met in Geneva for a new round of negotiations. But, when the talks stalled over technical issues, the American delegation walked out, declaring Washington was opting for more sanctions. By January 2010, the US Congress overwhelmingly had passed "crippling" new sanctions, banning the sale of gasoline to Iran, and placing secondary sanctions on European and Asian companies doing business with the Islamic Republic. The Israel lobby had won the day, bringing Obama completely in step with its agenda. In June 2010, punitive American sanctions expanded to Iran's central bank, effectively forcing the country out of global financial networks. Already in 2009, the UN Security Council had yielded to US-Israeli pressure and replaced ElBaradei, the independent-minded head of the IAEA, with Yukiya Amano, who would side with the Washington-Tel Aviv axis. Throughout 2010, therefore, the UN imposed embargos on Iran's arms sales, banking, and technology transfers related to its ballistic missile program, while freezing the assets of the IRGC and Iran's national shipping line. In addition, the United States and Israel waged sophisticated cyber warfare against Iran, inflicting considerable damage to its nuclear energy facilities with various computer viruses. Going further, Israel used its local agents to assassinate four Iranian nuclear scientists as well as the head of Iran's ballistic missile program and the commander of its cyber warfare headquarters.[30] In November 2010, *The New York Times*, relying on evidence including WikiLeaks disclosures, gave the following summation of Obama's contradictory Iran policy: "In essence, the administration expected its outreach to fail, but believed that it had to make a bona fide attempt in order to build support for tougher measures."[31]

Soon, the crippling global sanctions took their toll on the Iranian economy. Access to international banking was disrupted, oil exports were halved, the currency crashed, and unemployment and inflation rose sharply. The economy sank into a deep recession and GDP growth came to a halt. By one estimate, canceled foreign contracts amounted to

29 Hurst, *The United States and the Iranian Nuclear Programme*, 190–5. Sasan Fayazmanesh, *Containing Iran: Obama's Policy of Tough Diplomacy* (New York: Cambridge Scholars Publishing, 2013), 136–42.

30 Hurst, *The United States and the Iranian Nuclear Programme*, 207.

31 Fayazmanesh, *Containing Iran*, 149–50; John Ghazvinian, *America and Iran: A History, 1720 to the Present* (Alfred A. Knopf, 2021) 494–507; *New York Times* quoted in ibid., 507.

$60 billion and Iran's energy sector shrank 15 to 20 percent. Given such staggering costs, Iranian leaders were hard-pressed to justify the nuclear energy program's meager benefits. By 2013, Iran's single nuclear reactor in Bushehr, which had cost $11 billion, produced no more than 2 percent of the country's energy needs. Another major loss, related to sanctions pressure, was the flight of "human capital." Iran has experienced one of the world's highest rates of "brain drain," which, according to government estimates, cost the country close to $40 billion annually.[32] Still, none of these enormous setbacks affected the Islamic Republic's resolve to steadily raise its nuclear fuel enrichment to levels above what was required for peaceful use. Several polls showed the Iranian public was generally supportive of the nuclear program and apparently willing to put up with its punishing consequences. At the same time, even government officials were admitting Iran's economic problems were partly caused by "mismanagement" and not entirely by foreign sanctions.[33] Ultimately, however, by the end of Obama's first term, what Israeli and American hawks had hoped for (that is, crippling sanctions causing a successful popular push for regime change in Iran) did not happen, just as it had not happened in other countries under long-term US sanctions. Moreover, international support for comprehensive Iran sanctions, which took an economic toll on Europe, Russia, and China, was faltering. Finally, being forced out of UN controls, the Islamic Republic was moving closer to weapons-grade nuclear enrichment, making the threat of an Israeli military strike more real. Barely out of the 2008 economic recession, the Obama administration could not afford being dragged into an Israeli war with Iran, a conflict certainly with more disastrous consequences than America's failed ventures in Iraq and Afghanistan. Thus, Obama began to push back against Israeli Prime Minister Benjamin Netanyahu's relentless pressure for US military action or support of Israeli strikes against Iran's nuclear facilities. By 2012, Obama's personal relations with Netanyahu were openly strained, while Congress backed Netanyahu and both American and Israeli military and intelligence establishments opposed war with Iran.[34]

Obama's second term began with the replacement of hawkish Secretary of State Hillary Clinton by John Kerry, who advocated diplomatic engagement with the Islamic Republic. As chair of the Senate Foreign

---

32 Thomas Juneau and Sam Razavi, "Costly Gains: A Cost-Benefit Assessment of Iran's Nuclear Program," *The Nonproliferation Review* 25, 1–2 (2018): 69–86, 76–7.

33 Hurst, *The United States and the Iranian Nuclear Programme*, 212–13.

34 Ibid., 212–6; Parsi, *Treacherous Alliance*, 150–4.

Relations Committee during Obama's first term, Kerry was already involved in quiet diplomacy with Tehran. Kerry's back-channel contacts began with a 2009 incident when Iranian border guards seized three young American hikers who had crossed from Iraqi Kurdistan into Iranian territory. The hikers, Joshua Fattal, Sarah Shroud, and Shane Bauer, were jailed on charges of espionage. But they were soon released when Sultan Qaboos bin Said of Oman quietly mediated a deal swapping them with three Iranians imprisoned by the US government. Ironically, Sultan Qaboos, who had stayed on his throne since the 1970s, when the shah had supported him militarily, enjoyed high-level confidence in the Islamic Republic. When he offered to open a confidential channel of communication with Iran's supreme leader, Obama decided to explore the option. In 2011, Kerry visited the Sultan in Muscat, Oman, where the first clandestine meeting of American and Iranian diplomats would take place in 2012. Beginning his second term, Obama was no longer concerned with reelection and felt less restrained by Israel and its congressional lobby. He had reached the conclusion that the Islamic Republic would not buckle or fall under the most onerous US sanction, and that war with Iran unacceptable. Moreover, international support for Iran sanctions was faltering and could not be sustained indefinitely. The only realistic option was to lower tensions by accepting Iran's right to have a peaceful nuclear program under strict IAEA supervision. As Obama put it, "They have a right to peaceful nuclear power and to enrichment in that purpose. But they don't have a right, obviously, to be outside of the other restraints of IAEA and the nonproliferation agreement." He also conceded, "Even the so-called moderates and reformists inside of Iran would not be able to simply say, we will cave and do exactly what the United States and Israelis say. They are going to have a path in which they feel that there is a dignified resolution to this issue." Thus, when Iranian and American delegations held their second meeting in Muscat nine months later, the high-level US diplomatic team carried Obama's dealmaking offer of conceding Iranian enrichment with exacting conditions.[35]

Meanwhile, Iran's negotiations with European powers were making progress after the June 2013 election of Hassan Rouhani as president. A regime insider and experienced nuclear negotiator, Rouhani had promised to resolve the standoff with the United States and won with

35 Parsi, *Treacherous Alliance*, 161–79; Hurst, *The United States and the Iranian Nuclear Programme*, 213–17, Obama quoted on 214; text of Obama's letter to Qabous in Byrne and Byrne, *Worlds Apart*, 267–9.

slightly over 50 percent of the vote. His pick for foreign minister was the US-educated Javad Zarif, who proved to be the Islamic Republic's most polished and successful diplomat. While secret negotiations with Washington continued, Rouhani and his team emphasized flexibility at the UN and in the Geneva negotiations with the P5+1 group. Now, even the supreme leader signaled a different tune, declaring the Islamic Republic would assume a posture of "valiant flexibility" in dealing with its adversaries. While Netanyahu and the Israel lobby insisted the Islamic Republic's new approach was a mere deception, numerous antiwar advocacy groups, including the National Iranian American Council (NIAC), the Ploughshares, the Arms Control Association, Americans for Peace Now, Win Without War, and the liberal Jewish lobby J Street called for negotiations with Iran. Sponsored by NIAC, twenty-nine senior American diplomats and military officials signed a letter urging Obama to seize the opportunity provided by the Rouhani presidency. At the same time, an open letter advocating the removal of Iran sanctions was signed by 131 members of the US House of Representatives. The momentum was shifting away from the Israel lobby, while Netanyahu's open acrimony toward Obama and his brazen overreach into American politics was backfiring.[36]

By January 2014, it was announced that an interim "Joint Plan of Action," between Iran and the P5+1 group, would be ready within months, though the actual Joint Comprehensive Plan of Action (JCPOA) was completed in July 2015. According to this agreement, Iran would keep uranium enrichment strictly within the limits allowed for peaceful use, cut down the number of its centrifuges, abandon all advanced nuclear research and allow regular and total IAEA inspection of its nuclear facilities. In return, the P5+1 group would roll back its sanctions in a step-by-step manner, reversible any time the Islamic Republic was found in violation of its obligations. Significantly, the agreement would end only the sanctions related to Iran's nuclear program and oil exports, leaving in place those against Iran's ballistic missile program, human rights violations, trade, and banking.[37] Moreover, the JCPOA was not a treaty and could be overturned by the US Congress. Therefore, its opponents, led by the American Israel Public Affairs Committee (AIPAC), launched a massive campaign to kill it through congressional resolutions, which Obama promised to veto. On the other side, a coalition of

36 Parsi, *Treacherous Alliance*, 213–16.

37 Text of JPAC in Byrne and Byrne, *Worlds Apart*, 272–6; Mahmood Monshipouri, *In the Shadow of Mistrust: The Geopolitics and Diplomacy of US-Iran Relations* (Oxford University Press, 2021), 57–8.

eighty-five liberal and antiwar organizations supported Obama's initiative. The coalition was led by the antinuclear Ploughshares Fund and the National Iranian American Council, while cyber-activist groups, like MoveOn.org, mobilized millions in its support. Their campaign circulated the endorsement of a former IAEA director and a letter by twenty-nine top US scientists, including five Nobel Prize laureates, all supporting Obama's Iran deal. During the summer of 2015, the campaign made one hundred fifty thousand phone calls to US Congress, sent 307,700 emails, gathered 1.1 million signatures on petitions, published 199 newspaper editorials and 442 op-eds, and sent over two hundred letters to editors of local newspapers.[38]

In a conference call with ten thousand campaign activists, Obama acknowledged their contribution, saying: "In the absence of your voices, you're going to see the same array of forces that got us into the Iraq war, leading into a situation where we forego this historic opportunity and we are back on the path of potential military conflict." NIAC also circulated a letter signed by eighty leading Middle East scholars endorsing the deal, and finally, *The New York Times* published an add by two dozen leaders of American Jewish organizations, including a former AIPAC director, saying, "The deal is the best available option to halt Iran's nuclear weapons program." Polls showed that 60 percent of American Jews, compared to 56 percent of the American public, supported the Obama deal, a clear victory for liberal Jewish organizations like J Street, over the arch-Zionist AIPAC. As J Street put it: "The overwhelming majority of Jewish Americans identify more with Barack Hossein Obama and what he stands for than they do with the leadership of AIPAC."[39] In the end, Congress did not vote on the deal, whose supporters had lined up enough votes to prevent a legislative override of Obama's veto. This was AIPAC's greatest defeat to date and a major setback for its congressional Republican allies, but the long-term battle was not over. As an open letter from a group of Republican Senators put it, the deal was "nothing more than an executive agreement between President Obama and Ayatollah Khamenei. The next President could revoke such an executive agreement with the stroke of a pen"—an accurate prediction of what would happen under President Donald Trump.[40] Nevertheless, the 2015 agreement showed two things:

38 Hurst, *The United States and the Iranian Nuclear Programme*, 223; Parsi, *Treacherous Alliance*, 327–8.

39 Parsi, *Treacherous Alliance*, 336–7, 342; Hurst, *The United States and the Iranian Nuclear Programme*, 226.

40 Hurst, *The United States and the Iranian Nuclear Programme*, 225.

First, US policy toward the Islamic Republic could change from the path of military intervention and regime change; and, second, given proper inducement, the Islamic Republic's leaders, including Supreme Leader Khamenei, could be accommodating to the United States.

The JCPOA, or the so-called Obama deal, had a highly positive reception in Iran; at its official announcement thousands came out to celebrate in the streets, while the supreme leader declared it a great victory.[41] As in the United States, however, Iran's political establishment was sharply divided on the Obama deal, some hard-line factions rejecting any compromise with the United States. Aggressively pushing back against these factions, a confident President Rouhani publicly declared the deal's opponents could "go to hell."[42] Still, Rouhani could not roll back the Iranian economy's militarization and securitization, structurally adapted to decades of US sanctions and war threats. After the Obama deal, Rouhani made cautious moves to curtail the IRGC's economic clout, which included over $25 billion just in oil and gas contracts bypassing the sanctions. In a veiled 2014 reference to the IRGC, Rouhani had complained, "If intelligence, arms, money, newspapers, and other instruments of power are concentrated in one entity . . . it would become corrupt." In the end, however, there was nothing he could do while the IRGC's economic clout was tightly protected by the supreme leader.[43]

Like Rouhani, Obama had to push back against right-wing resistance to JCPOA. Doing this, he would go further than any US president in acknowledging Iranian grievances against the United States. In 2015 he stated:

> I do think that you have to have the capacity to put yourself occasionally in their shoes, and if you look at Iranian history, the fact is that we had some involvement with overthrowing a democratically elected regime in Iran. We have had in the past supported Saddam Hussein when we know he used chemical weapons in the war between Iran and Iraq, and so, as a consequence, they have their own security concerns, their own narrative.[44]

---

41 Parsi, *Treacherous Alliance*, 334; *The Guardian*, July 14, 2015, E10.

42 "Rouhani Says 'To Hell' with Nuclear Critics," Al-Monitor, accessed July 18, 2022, al-monitor.com.

43 Hesam Forozan and Afshin Shahi, "The Military and the State in Iran: The Economic Rise of the Revolutionary Guards," *The Middle East Journal* 71, 1 (winter 2017): 67–86, 77–9, Rouhani quoted on 83.

44 Thomas L. Friedman, "Obama Makes His Case on Iran Nuclear Deal," *New York Times*, July 14, 2015.

In an interview published a year later, Obama further explained why automatically siding with Arab regimes, and implicitly with Israel, against Iran was not a wise US strategy:

> An approach that said to our friends "You are right, Iran is the source of all problems, and we will support you in dealing with Iran" would essentially mean that as these sectarian conflicts continue to rage and our Gulf partners, our traditional friends, do not have the ability to put out the flames on their own or decisively win on their own, and would mean that we have to start coming in and using our military power to settle scores. And that would be in the interest neither of the United States nor of the Middle East.[45]

Despite his avoidance of military confrontation with Iran, Obama, who had received the Nobel Peace Prize in 2009, was far from a global peacemaker. He did not hesitate to throw US military weight around, ordering, for example, hundreds of drone strikes in Pakistan and Yemen, killing an estimated 3,797 people, including 324 civilians.[46] During his last years in office, Obama earmarked the expenditure of $400 billion on nuclear weapons buildup during 2017–26, a 15 percent increase over the preceding decade. He also approved a massive modernization of the nuclear stockpile projected to cost over $1 trillion over thirty years.[47] His deal-making with Iran was the intelligent handling of a tenacious adversary that no US administration had been able to contain.

As we saw above, an organized segment of the Iranian American community lobbied on behalf of the 2015 Obama deal to reduce the burden of US sanctions on the people of Iran. On the other side, and allied with the Israel lobby, right-wing and monarchist Iranian diaspora factions vehemently worked toward maintaining and even increasing the Iran sanctions. Despite their media overrepresentation, monarchists are a marginal presence in the Iranian diaspora's broad political spectrum. Their main source of influence is a well-funded network of right-wing television and radio programs reaching millions in Iran. These include the *Voice of America* (Persian) and *Radio Farda*, both funded by the US

45 Jeffrey Goldberg, "The Obama Doctrine," *The Atlantic*, April 2016, quoted in Monshipouri, *In the Shadow of Mistrust*, 173.

46 Micah Zenko, "Obama's Final Drone Strike Data," *Council on Foreign Relations* (blog), January 20, 2017, cfr.org.

47 Kingston Reif, "Trump Continues Obama Nuclear Funding," Arms Control Association, July/August 2017, armscontrol.org; David Sanger, *Confront and Conceal: Obama's Secret Wars and Surprising Use of American Power* (Crown, 2012).

government, Iran International television network, funded by Saudi doners linked to bin Salman, and Manoto television, a purportedly private station broadcasting via satellite to Iran from 2010 to 2024 and thereafter on Instagram, YouTube, and Facebook.[48] Mostly based in the United States, but also spread out across Canada, Europe, and Asia, the Iranian diaspora and its politics remain an understudied subject. The term "Iranian diaspora" in the United States is of recent coinage, referring to communities formerly known as Iranian immigrants, Iranian Americans, or people of (mixed) Iranian decent. Counting all these people as members of an "Iranian diaspora" could be misleading because those generically called "Iranian" or "Persian" often self-identify primarily in more specific ethnonational terms, such as Kurds or Azeris, or by religious affiliation, such as Jewish or Armenian. In 2015, the annual American Community Survey estimated 486,994 Iranians lived in the United States, about two-thirds of whom were born in Iran and the rest in the United States. This population had grown four times from its 122,000 baseline in the 1989 census.[49] US census data probably underestimates the size of the Iranian diasporic community, which according to various other sources could approach one million. About half of this population lives in California, while most of the rest reside in New York, New Jersey, Connecticut, Washington, DC, and Maryland, Virginia, and Texas. This is a highly educated community, partly because large segments of it are the offspring of tens of thousands of Iranians who studied in the United States in the 1960s–70s. Iranian Americans are also among the country's most successful professional and entrepreneurial immigrant communities. About 10 percent of them are high-earning physicians and lawyers, another 10 percent are engineers, teachers, and professors, and most of the rest are white-collar workers.[50] According to a 2008–9 survey, Iranian Americans range politically from small right-wing monarchists to cultural or ideological leftist minorities, with a large majority somewhere

48 See the websites of Radio Farda, *Voice of America* (Persian), and Manoto; for Iran International see Saeed Kamali Dehghan, "Concern Over UK-Based Iranian TV Channel's Links to Saudi Arabia," *Guardian*, October 31, 2018.

49 Mehdi Bozorgmehr and Eric Ketcham, "Adult Children of Professional and Entrepreneurial Immigrants: Second-Generation Iranians in the United States," in *The Iranian Diaspora: Challenges, Negotiations, and Transformations*, ed. Mohsen Mostafavi Mobasher (University of Texas Press, 2018): 25–49, cited on 26–8. The recent Iran-US histories are Ghazvinian, *America and Iran* and Firoozeh Kashani-Sabet, *Heroes to Hostages: America and Iran, 1800–1988* (Cambridge University Press, 2023).

50 Ibid., 37–9, 41–3. The geographic spread and educational level of Iranian Americans conforms to the broad patterns of Americas' recent immigration population. See "More than Half of Foreign-Born People in the United States Live in Just Four States," *Los Angeles Times*, April 14, 2024.

in between. Other data estimate about half of Iranian Americans to be Democrats, while 10 to 15 percent are Republicans. About two-thirds believe Iran-US relations should focus on the promotion of democracy and human rights, pursued through diplomacy. Almost all Iranian Americans surveyed oppose any US military move against Iran.[51]

The Iranian community in the United States quickly grew during the 1980s. In the revolution's immediate aftermath, particularly during the hostage crisis, Iranians living in the United States experienced widespread hostility, something the second generation of the Iranian diaspora also encountered, albeit to a lesser extent, in the post-9/11 backlash against Middle Eastern people. Meanwhile, the 1980s Iranian community, initially consisting of recent immigrants and refugees, gradually acquired permanent diasporic features, struggling to assimilate into mainstream American culture. Clustering mainly in California, Iranians were developing their own brand of "exilic culture," preoccupied with postrevolutionary angst and dreams of returning home. This was a rather conservative subculture, sharply in contrast to the leftist orientation of the anti-shah student movement in the United States during the 1960s–70s. During the 1980s, Iranian exilic culture was disseminated largely through Los Angeles–based private television networks, recycling prerevolutionary popular culture and media celebrities. It also produced new music, television shows, and feature films dealing with the cultural pain and confusion of newly arriving immigrants.[52] Distancing themselves from the Islamic Republic, many immigrants embraced the Pahlavi era's "Persian imperial identity," basking in fantasies of pre-Islamic Iran's imperial glory and its supposedly Aryan racial lineage. Still, a minority, especially among former student activists, held fast to their leftist ideals, passing them to a second Iranian diaspora generation who would adopt the values and mores of America's cultural left.[53]

By the turn of the twenty-first century, the Iranian American community moved toward assimilation, while some of its second-generation

---

51 *Public Opinion Survey of Iranian Americans Commissioned by: Public Affairs Alliance of Iranian Americans (PAAIA) & conducted by Zogby International* (Public Affairs Alliance of Iranian Americans 2008) and *Public Opinion Survey of Iranian Americans* 2009.

52 Hamid Nafici, *The Making of Exilic Cultures: Iranian Television in Los Angeles* (University of Minnesota Press, 1993).

53 Manijeh Moradian, *This Flame Within: Iranian Revolutionaries in the United States* (Duke University Press, 2023), 23. Based in part on interviews with former student activists, this book surveys the 1960s–70s Iranian student movement's contribution to America's internationalist left milieu, the "affects of solidarity" this interaction produced, and its persistence among former student activists.

cohorts pushed back to craft a distinct diasporic identity. Cumulatively, the cultural and intellectual output of Iranian American scholars, academic experts, journalist, artists, and fiction writers has partially remedied widespread American misunderstandings of Iran and Iranians. Studies of the Iranian diaspora and its traits have moved along two distinct but overlapping tracks. The first relies largely on census and demographic data to categorize Iranians in terms of their education, employment, socioeconomic status, and voting patterns.[54] The second, informed by anthropological and cultural studies, looks at Iranians mainly through their literary and artistic self-reflections, digital social media, and interactions with American racial and gender trends.[55] A possible third approach focuses on this population's interactions with Iran, through political activity, travel, business dealings, satellite television, and social media.[56] Meanwhile, a litany of memoirs, autobiographies, fiction, and accounts of sojourn to Iran marks the Iranian diaspora's

54 For examples of this kind of research, see Mehdi Bozorgmehr, "Internal Ethnicity: Iranians in Los Angeles," *Sociological Perspectives* 40, 3 (1997): 387–408; Mehdi Bozorgmehr and Daniel Douglas, "Success(Ion): Second-Generation Iranian Americans," *Iranian Studies* 44 (2011): 3–24; Mehdi Bozorgmehr and Maryam Moeini Meybodi, "The Persian Paradox: Language Use and Maintenance Among Iranian Americans," *International Journal of the Sociology of Language* (2016): 99–118; Bozorgmehr and Ketcham, "Adult Children of Professional and Entrepreneurial Immigrants"; Mohsen M. Mobasher, *Iranians in Texas: Migration, Politics, and Ethnic Identity* (University of Texas Press, 2012).

55 This approach seems to have produced the largest body of studies. See Daniel Grassian, *Iranian and Diasporic Literature in the 21st Century: A Critical Study* (McFarland, 2013); Farzaneh Hemmasi, *Tehrangeles Dreaming: Intimacy and Imagination in Southern California's Iranian Pop Music* (Duke University Press, 2020); Persis M. Karim and Mohammad Mehdi Khorrami, eds., *A World Between: Poems, Short Stories, and Essays by Iranian Americans* (George Braziller, 1999); Persis M. Karim, ed., *Let Me Tell You Where I've Been: New Writing by Women of the Iranian Diaspora* (University of Arkansas Press, 2006); Neda Maghbouleh, *The Limits of Whiteness: Iranian Americans and the Everyday Politics of Race* (Stanford University Press. 2017); Nilou Mostofi, "Who We Are: The Perplexity of Iranian-American Identity," *The Sociological Quarterly* 44, 4 (2003): 681–703; Amy Malek, "Public Performances of Identity Negotiation in the Iranian Diaspora: The New York Persian Day Parade," *Comparative Studies of South Asia, Africa and the Middle East* 31, 2 (2011): 388–410; Maria D. Wagenknecht, *Constructing Identity in Iranian-American Self-Narrative* (Palgrave, 2015).

56 Azadeh Moaveni, *Lipstick Jihad: A Memoir of Growing Up Iranian in America and American in Iran* (PublicAffairs, 2005); Sam Fayyaz and Roozbeh Shirazi. "Good Iranian, Bad Iranian: Representations of Iran and Iranians in 'Time' and 'Newsweek' (1998–2009)," *Iranian Studies* 46, no. 1 (2013): 53–72; Donya Alinejad, *The Internet and Formations of Iranian American-ness: Next Generation Diaspora* (Palgrave Macmillian, 2017); Arash Davari, "Like 1979 All Over Again: Resisting Left Liberalism among Iranian Émigrés," in *With Stones in Our Hands: Writings on Muslims, Racism, and Empire*, eds. Daulatzai Sohail and Rana Junaid (University of Minnesota Press, 2018).

footprint in mainstream American culture. This body of work finds a minor companion in the writings of Americans who lived and worked in Iran before the revolution. As noted in previous chapters, many US Peace Corps volunteers developed deep links to Iran, later writing scholarly works, memoirs and personal accounts based on this connection. Even deeper levels of personal dedication to Iran, however, could be found among a small number of Americans who spent prison time under the shah due to their involvement with the Iranian student movement.[57]

Killing the Obama Deal and Iran's Domestic Dissent

> *The Islamic Republic is sitting on a volcano of amassed discontent . . . The system has remained in power by ever-more ruthlessly repressing the recurring cycles of violent uprising.*
>
> A history textbook written before the outbreak of Iran's 2022 mass protests[58]

The Obama administration's limited removal of sanctions had immediate tangible effects on the Iranian economy, which grew 13 percent in 2016 and another 7 percent in 2017, as oil exports rose to the pre-sanction levels of two million barrels per day. Still, Iran's accesses to international banking faced major obstacles, while European companies remained hesitant about investing in Iran due to the Obama deal's murky regulations and uncertain future. More importantly, the Iranian economy's improvement did not reverse the declining trend in ordinary people's living standards. Between 2011 and 2019, close to nine million people (that is, more than 10–15 percent of the population) sank into the ranks of the poor.[59] By the end of 2017, pent-up public anger was boiling over

57 Moradian, *This Flame Within*, 196–7, 264–5. A young lawyer, Nancy Hormachea, became involved with a Maoist Iranian student faction in Texas and went to Iran during the revolution, where she was arrested on political charges in 1981 and served almost a year in prison; In 1971, another young American woman, Sharon La Bere, also involved with the student opposition, was sentenced to three years imprisonment while visiting Iran, though she was soon released. *Christian Science Monitor*, December 2, 1971.

58 Ali Rahnema, *The Political History of Modern Iran*, 620.

59 Narges Bajoghli, Vali Nasr, Djavad Salehi-Isfahani, and Ali Vaez, *How Sanctions Work: Iran and the Impact of Economic Warfare* (Stanford University Press, 2024), 79, 99. See also Moosa Anbari and Sedigheh Piri, "Poverty and Deprivation Problems in Post-Revolutionary Iran," *Middle East Critique*, 32, no. 4 (2023): 463–71. This study

into violent riots. For ten days, from late December 2017 through early January 2018, protest demonstrations erupted in more than one hundred cities. About half of the protests turned violent as crowds chanted antiregime slogans and attacked banks, government offices, Basij and police stations, and seminary schools. Between twenty-five to fifty people were reported killed, several hundred injured, and four to five thousand arrested before the protests could be put down. The crowds were mostly from poor and lower-middle-class backgrounds, and, unlike the 2009 Green Movement's reformist demands, they called for the regime's overthrow. These protests were not an isolated eruption, as they occurred in the wake of rolling strikes by industrial workers throughout 2017, followed by 2018–19 countrywide agitation and protests by teachers demanding higher pay and job security.[60] Apart from the impact of foreign sanctions, labor unrest was related to the economy's structural transformation, particularly what one scholar has called "the unmaking of the Iranian working class." According to official statistics, whereas in 1990 only 6 percent of the workforce had temporary contracts, by 2014 the figure had reached 90 percent. This was a devastating blow to the job security and bargaining power of Iranian workers and wage earners in general.[61]

Meanwhile, the election of Donald Trump reversed the limited easing of Iran-US tensions, delivering a heavy blow to ordinary Iranians' prospects for relief from crushing economic burdens. In January 2017, Trump issued an executive order banning travel to the United States by citizens of Iran and several other Muslim countries, exempting only individuals with US citizenship or permanent residency. In May 2018, strongly pressured by Israel, Saudi Arabia, and United Arab Emirates, and despite objections from his secretaries of the state and defense, Trump withdrew from the JCOPA. Though Iran was in full compliance with the Obama deal, Trump claimed he could force a "better deal" on Tehran, something that none of America's European allies believed was possible and, of course, never happened. Later that year, Secretary of State Mike Pompeo set twelve conditions for negotiating with Tehran, including Iran's acceptance of total UN inspections and ending its uranium enrichment, ballistic missiles program, and support of Lebanese Hezbollah,

---

tends to blame growing poverty on US sanctions, offering only muted criticism of the Islamic Republic's own failures in poverty reduction.

60 Rahnema, *The Political History of Modern Iran*, 606–7.

61 Mohammad Maljoo, "The Unmaking of the Iranian Working Class since the 1990s," in *Iran's Struggle for Social Justice: Economics, Agency, Justice, Activism*, ed. Peyman Vahabzadeh (Palgrave Macmillan, 2017): 47–64.

Palestinian resistance, and Shi'i militias in Syria and Iraq. Pompeo also demanded the Islamic Republic's observance of human rights to the Trump administration's satisfaction. Obviously, these conditions were set to ensure talks would fail, since accepting them would leave nothing for Tehran to negotiate.[62] As the European Union's foreign policy chief pointed out, Washington's allies disapproved of Trump's scrapping of the Iran deal:

> Secretary Pompeo's speech has not demonstrated how walking away from the JCPOA has made or will make the region safer from the threat of nuclear proliferation or how it puts us in a better position to influence Iran's conduct in areas outside the scope of the JCPOA. There is no alternative to the JCPOA.[63]

At the same time, Pompeo and other Trump administration officials ratchetted up the rhetoric of US support for Iranian democracy and the country's middle class.[64] This flew in the face of evidence showing comprehensive US sanctions, of the kind imposed on Iran and previously on Iraq, devastated these countries' middle classes and destroyed their democratic prospects. This was sometimes acknowledged by US official, for example in a 1996 interview with Madeleine Albright, then US ambassador to the UN, who was asked about the effects of US sanctions on the Iraqi people. "We have heard that half a million [Iraqi] children have died. I mean, that is more children than died in Hiroshima," said the interviewer. "And, you know, is the price worth it?" Albright promptly answered, "We think, the price is worth it."[65]

At times, American officials were equally sanguine about economic sanctions being designed to hurt ordinary Iranians. In 2010, referring to Iran sanctions, California Democratic Congressman and Israel lobbyist Brad Sherman wrote, "Critics [complain] that these measures will hurt the Iranian people . . . Quite frankly, we need to do just that." Responding to concerns that sanctions "would hurt the Iranian people," Sherman's

---

62 Noah Annan, "Pompeo Adds Human Rights to Twelve Demands to Iran," *Atlantic Council* (blog), October 23, 2018; Monshipouri, *In the Shadow of Mistrust*, 190, 192–3.

63 Quoted in Monshipouri, *In the Shadow of Mistrust*, 193.

64 Palladino R (2019) Secretary Pompeo's meeting with Iranian women's rights activist Masih Alinejad. US Virtual Embassy, Iran. https://IR.usembassy.gov/secretary-pompeos-meeting-with-IRanian-womens-rights-activist-masihalinejad/

65 Ahmed Twaij, "Let's Remember Madeleine Albright For Who She Really Was," *Al Jazeera*, March 25, 2022.

Republican colleague, Representative Mark Kirk, said bluntly: "It is that actual pain that I think has to be imposed."[66]

As in the case of Iraq, however, decades of onerous US sanctions severely punished ordinary people without leading to regime change by forcing the Islamic Republic to change its behavior or improving Iran's democratic prospects. Under Trump's maximum pressure sanctions regime, Iran's economy contracted by more than 10 percent, while poverty rose by about the same percentage. Inflation got out of control, food prices rose by 200 percent and health care costs by 125 percent. All available data show that, during the last decade, the living standards of middle- and lower-class Iranians have significantly declined.[67] US sanctions have certainly contributed to this, even if they are not its only cause. At the same time, instead of improving democratic prospects, US sanctions have pushed the Islamic Republic to become more tenaciously repressive. Khamenei and regime hard-liners see the sanctions as a war waged by the United States and Israel to weaken the Islamic Republic and bring about its overthrow through a domestic uprising supported by their intervention. This is a hybrid war, combining onerous sanctions with the assassination of Iran's military personnel and scientists, sophisticated cyberattacks on its economic and military infrastructure, ceaseless political propaganda, and the sponsorship of right-wing Iranian diaspora opposition. The Islamic Republic has used this narrative, which has elements of truth, to falsely claim antiregime protests are caused by the United States and Israel and hence must be repressed at any cost.

Regardless of the regime's claims, Iran's popular discontent has grown more intense and frequent, caused by the economy's downward spiral and the state's socially and culturally repressive policies. In November 2019, angry demonstrators once again took to the streets when gasoline prices suddenly increased after the removal of government subsidies. Some two hundred thousand people took part in protests across the country, attacking and setting fire to hundreds of government offices and banks, while the regime deployed machine guns, tanks, and helicopters to put them down. The extent of violence unleashed against unarmed protesters was unprecedented in the history of the Islamic Republic. Amnesty International estimated that there were more than three hundred killed, and Reuters reported fifteen hundred casualties. Thousands were arrested, there was a news blackout, and the internet

66 Sherman and Kirk quoted in Ghazvinian, *America and Iran*, 522.

67 Bajoghli et al., *How Sanctions Work*, 128; Monshipouri, *In the Shadow of Mistrust*, 91.

was shut down for a week. The government admitted to massive casualties, claiming hundreds were police and security personnel.[68] As many observers noted, however, the crushing of the 2017–19 protests did not mean the end of explosive dissent. A 2020 academic study, for example, concluded:

> The country has seen various violent and non-violent protests over the last 40 years. However, the two major protests in December 2017 and November 2019 suggest that the prevailing dynamics of political protest in Iran are changing. There is an increasing sense of radicalization among protesters, while the state is prepared to resort to extreme violence to maintain control . . . The concentration of power in unelected factions of the state guarded by the iron fist of the armed and security forces, the dismal economic situation, the paralyzing corruption at every level and the lack of accountability have increased the already existing crisis of legitimacy for a revolutionary regime which came to power to be on the side of "the poor."[69]

The suppression of the 2019 protests repeated a cycle of deadly violence the Islamic Republic has unleashed regularly, almost at the end of every decade, against thousands of political prisoners in 1988, vis-à-vis tens of thousands of students and other dissidents in 1999, against millions during the Green Movement of 2009, and against thousands of poor and working-class demonstrators in 2017–19. Widely anticipated by various observers, the next outbreak of the cycle would not take another decade but only three years to arrive. The 2022 protests took place in the wake of further economic deterioration, the COVID-19 pandemic, the installation of a reactionary and incompetent president, and the escalation of tensions with the United States and Israel. In 2019, after the Islamic Republic shot down a US surveillance drone, Trump ordered a direct military retaliation but called it off the last minute.[70] Later that year, an American was killed when Iranian missiles hit an Iraqi airbase. The United States retaliated by hitting Tehran's Iraqi militia allies, who

---

68 Eskandar Sadeghi-Boroujerdi, "Iran's Uprisings for 'Women, Life, Freedom': Overdetermination, Crisis, and the Lineages of Revolt," *Politics* 43, 3 (2023): 404–38, cited 431. Afshin Shahi and Ehsan Abdoh-Tabrizi, "Iran's 2019–2020 Demonstrations: The Changing Dynamics of Political Protests in Iran," *Asian Affairs* (February 2020): 1–41, cited, 1–2.

69 Quoted in ibid., 2.

70 Sanctions 135–7; "Strikes on Iran Approved by Trump, Then Abruptly Pulled Back," *New York Times*, June 20, 2019.

in turn laid siege to the US embassy in Baghdad. On January 3, 2020, Trump ordered the assassination in Iraq of General Qasem Soleimani, commander of the Quds Force, the IRGC's branch outside Iran. A few years earlier, Soleimani had coordinated Quds Force operations with the US forces fighting the Islamic State in Iraq and Syria. This was admitted by General McKenzie, leader of the US military's Central Command, who claimed Soleimani was responsible for killing hundreds of Americans, having survived Israeli attempts on his life. Soleimani was recognized as a shrewd and effective adversary by the Obama administration and plans for his assassination were on the table when Trump finally authorized them. As was his wont, Trump wrongly assumed that killing Soleimani would bring the Islamic Republic to the negotiating table.[71] One day after Soleimani's assassination, Trump threatened to strike more than fifty targets inside Iran, including nonmilitary sites and cultural landmarks. Four days later, the Islamic Republic fired a dozen ballistic missiles at an Iraqi military base stationing fifteen hundred American troops but sent advanced warning to prevent casualties and an even larger US retaliation. A few hours later, the IRGC shot down a Ukrainian airliner taking off from Tehran, killing all its 176 passengers, mostly Iranians residing in Canada. The IRGC later admitted the plane was mistaken for an incoming US cruise missile. This blunder led to angry demonstrations in Tehran and other cities, countering public expressions of sympathy for IRGC commander Soleimani's murder. Meanwhile, Israel ratcheted up its brazen attacks on Iran. In July 2020, it triggered an explosion at the Natanz uranium enrichment plant, causing major damage and setting back Iran's nuclear enrichment program by several months. In November, Tel Aviv further embarrassed Tehran's security establishment and the IRGC when it used long-distance satellite targeting to assassinate a leading Iranian nuclear scientist traveling in his car near Tehran.[72]

Suffering devastating blows by its foreign enemies, Iran became one of the first countries hit hard by the COVID-19 pandemic in 2020. In response, the United States loosened its financial transactions ban to allow Iran's purchase of urgent medical necessities. But Khamenei turned down the American offer of COVID assistance, dismissing it as an empty gesture. Going further, he banned the import of vaccines from the United States and Britain, arguing they could not be trusted, and that Iran would develop its own vaccine. Six months later, as the pandemic

71 Kenneth F. McKenzie Jr., "I Carried Out the Strike that Killed Soleimani. America Doesn't Understand the Lesson of his Death," *The Atlantic*, May 24, 2024.

72 Rahnema, *The Political History of Modern Iran*, 592, 615–17.

was ravaging the country, he quietly approved the use of European and American vaccines. Nothing changed when Joe Biden was elected president and kept all of Trump's more than fifteen hundred sanctions in place, making Iran the most sanctioned country in the world.[73] The Biden team wanted Iran to further restrict uranium enrichment and curtail its missile defense, terms that the Islamic Republic, under a new hard-line government, would not accept. Thus, a semblance of diplomatic engagement and negotiations resumed, without producing any results. Meanwhile, the Islamic Republic was tightening political screws at home. The 2021 presidential election purged the candidates associated with the 2015 nuclear deal, leading to the virtually uncontested election of Ebrahim Raisi, a cleric involved in the 1988 massacre of thousands of political prisoners. Only 48 percent of the electorate had participated in this election, a sharp drop from the 73 percent taking part in Rouhani's 2017 election. Even by the regime's own standards, the Raisi government represented a minority of the electorate. In a new political configuration, the regime seemed not to care about the appearance of political participation, to which the public responded by staying away from the polls.[74] These tense conditions set the stage for Iran's most severe and sustained protest cycle since the revolution, breaking out just as the country was emerging from the COVID-19 pandemic in fall 2022.

In addition to its intensity, the countrywide 2022–23 uprising was different from all previous antiregime mass movements in several important ways. Protests began in September 2022 in response to the death of twenty-two-year-old Jina Mahsa Amini in police custody, a Kurdish woman arrested for improper veiling in Tehran. The leading role of young women, many discarding or burning their headscarf in public, was the first distinctive feature of this protest cycle. Second, arriving in the wake of ongoing vigils, demonstrations, and strikes by workers, teachers, and government pensioners, the 2022–23 protests united middle-class and working-class Iranians around economic grievance. Third, unlike all previous protests, the radical epicenter of the 2022–23 uprising was not Tehran but the provinces, particularly Kurdistan and Balochistan, regions that suffered the double burden of official Persian chauvinism and Shi'i prejudice in addition to exceptional economic neglect and underdevelopment. Though spontaneous and leaderless, countryside

73 Bajoghli et al., *How Sanctions Work*, 70–2; Rahnema, *The Political History of Modern Iran*, 616–17.

74 Mohammad Ayatollahi Tabaar, "Iran's War within: Ebrahim Raisi and the Triumph of Hardliners," *Foreign Affairs* 100, no. 5 (September–October 2021): 155–68.

protests showed remarkable synergy and unity, the participants using digital technology to connect, coordinate and reinforce their action. The Sunni provinces of Kurdistan and Baluchistan had specific ethnic and religious grievances, but they stayed in sync with the rest of the country, showing the uprising's national unanimity. This also showcased the new protest cycle's fourth outstanding feature, namely its strikingly secular and at times anticlerical character. Significantly too, the regime's rhetoric against the protests was mainly secular, claiming they were a political conspiracy hatched by the United States and Israel. Arguably, therefore, the 2022–23 protests marked the end of an era, highlighting that religious politics had effectively run its course in Iran.[75] This brings us to the protest's fifth outstanding feature, namely its political demands. Here, although the overall thrust of the uprising was clearly antiregime, its shared positive demands, or proposed alternative to the Islamic Republic, was less clear.

The uprising continued into winter 2023, while the regime kept up its violent suppression, inflicting hundreds of casualties, half of them in Kurdish and Baloch regions. By the end of winter 2023, protests had largely subsided, leaving behind more than five hundred dead, many more casualties and twenty thousand arrested. Though initially seen as a winning strategy, in the long run, the protests movement's lack of common leadership, organization, and political demands proved a major liability.[76] The leader of the 2009 Green Movement, Hossein Mousavi, called for peaceful regime change through a national referendum, while former President Mohammad Khatami more cautiously mentioned the possibility of constitutional change. An agitated Iranian diaspora enthusiastically supported the uprising, its right-wing monarchist faction claiming to speak for the protests, which had expressed almost no monarchist sympathies. The diaspora's most notable action was an October 2022 rally in Berlin, bringing together eighty thousand people in the largest opposition gathering ever held outside Iran. This event was unique in uniting the diaspora's divergent political factions, allowing every group and organization to participate with its own flag and slogans. But this fragile unity collapsed quickly as US-based monarchists tried to force their leadership on the diaspora opposition. For years, the monarchists were able to reach millions in Iran through

---

75 Afshin Matin-Asgari, "The Iranian Protests are the Latest Phase in a Long Cycle of Popular Protests," *Jacobin*, December 1, 2022.

76 "Iran's Supreme Leader Pardons 'Tens of Thousands' of Prisoners," *Al Jazeera*, February 5, 2023.

satellite television stations funded directly or indirectly by US government and Saudi money. Instead of direct monarchist propaganda, right-wing media outlets waged more subtle cultural warfare, saturating the airwaves with nostalgic fantasies of a prerevolutionary golden age, implying it could be restored through the Islamic Republic's overthrow by American or Israeli military intervention. Although the 2022–23 protests featured almost no monarchist sympathies, the pretender to the crown, Reza Pahlavi, declared himself the head of a coalition ostensibly leading the Iranian uprising from his base in Washington, DC. He then conducted an online "referendum," asking for a personal mandate to represent the Iranian nation from abroad. This effort became a fiasco when his campaign admitted receiving about four hundred thousand votes from a nation of about ninety million. When his leadership council quickly unraveled, Reza Pahlavi rushed to Tel Aviv, where Prime Minister Benjamin Netanyahu anointed him, repeating Israel's official threat of military action against Iran. This kind of right-wing diaspora politics is welcomed in Tehran, as it lends credence to the Islamic Republic's claims about domestic opposition being sponsored by American and Israeli conspiracies.[77]

In the end, neither the left nor the right wing of the Iranian American diaspora had much influence on the protest cycles unfolding in Iran during the first Trump and then Biden presidential terms. By early 2023, the Islamic Republic had put down the protest movement, even though mass discontent and civil unrest continued. At the peak of the 2022–23 protests, even regime spokespeople had conceded the need for "new governmentality," but nothing changed once tight control was reestablished. Nor was there any attempt to address the underlying causes of unrest. A main contention of the 2022–23 protests, mandatory hijab, was the most visible symbol of the regime's impositions on half the population. Its defiance by a growing number of young women therefore is a political act, amounting to public rejection of state authority. This is one area where the 2022–23 protests have been relatively successful, since the regime was not able to enforce full compliance with mandatory hijab. At the same time, waves of strikes by workers, teachers, and government employees continued in tandem with the economy's downward spiral, while the most rebellious provinces, Kurdistan and Balochistan, remain

77 Afshin Matin-Asgari, "Iran's Rulers Have Contained the Protest Movement, But the System Is Far from Stable," *Jacobin*, July 7, 2023. Even monarchist sympathizers admitted to their movement's abject failure. See Arash Azizi, "The Fiasco of Iranian Diaspora Politics," *New Lines Magazine*, April 22, 2024.

under military and security siege. An egregious instance of exceptional state violence is the case of Kurdish *kolbers*, impoverished laborers who work like pack animals, carrying goods on their back across the Iran-Iraq border. Kolbers are routinely shot to death by the Islamic Republic's security forces, who consider them bandits and smugglers. According to some estimates, in 2020–21, around 170,000 Kurdish men and women made their living as kolbers, 370 of whom suffered death or injury inflicted by the Iranian military.[78]

The Islamic Republic observed its forty-fifth anniversary in 2024, more politically bruised and unpopular than ever, but nowhere near the verge of collapse. It had contained yet another wave of popular protest while proving it could survive and adapt to decades of US enmity and onerous economic warfare. The unelected "deep state," with Supreme Leader Khamenei at the helm, was now openly in charge, its decisions being rubber-stamped by the handpicked "elected" government of President Raisi and the Majles. That year's parliamentary elections marked the lowest turnout of any national election since the beginning of the revolution, with 60 percent of the electorate staying away, a figure that reached 90 percent in Tehran. Politics was openly militarized with the Islamic Revolutionary Guard Corps (IRGC) being the backbone of the "Resistance Economy," fashioned in defiance of US sanctions. The IRGC was now estimated to control between 10 to 30 percent of the economy, including its most sensitive and lucrative sectors in defense, energy, and construction, as well as in advanced technology and electronic business. While American digital giants, like Amazon, YouTube, and Google are barred from Iran, their domestic counterparts have been set up in connection to the IRGC, which runs Iran's Mobile Telecommunication Company serving over forty-three million subscribers. By 2021, more than two-thirds of Iranian households had internet service, provided mainly by the government, its intelligence organizations, and the IRCG. At the same time, the Islamic Republic has switched its foreign trade from European countries to Russia, China, India, Turkey, and its Persian Gulf neighbors, while diversifying the sources of foreign exchange from oil to nonoil exports. From 1979 to 2018, the share of oil and gas in Iran's total exports fell from 96 percent to 60 percent, while the value of nonoil exports increased from $753 million to $37 billion.[79]

78 Sadeghi-Boroujerdi, "Iran's Uprisings for 'Women, Life, Freedom,'" 420–1.

79 Nasr, 267; Dario Laudati & Mohammad Hashem Pesaran, "Identifying the Effects of Sanctions on the Iranian Economy Using Newspaper Coverage," *Journal of Applied Econometrics* 38, no. 3 (2023): 271–94, 292–3, 275.

China has become Iran's most important trade partner, in 2021 signing a reportedly $400 billion accord stipulating long-term economic, military, and security cooperation with the Islamic Republic. Mainly in exchange for discounted oil imports, China has committed to massive investment in Iran's oil, gas, and petrochemical industries. The China deal also involves the upgrading of Iran's transportation and manufacturing infrastructure, linking them to the Belt and Road Initiative, an ambitious plan of global economic integration sustained by Chinese capital and leadership.[80] Though the full extent and features of the China deal are not transparent, it clearly signifies Iran's strategic exist from the US-dominated global order and integration into an alternative political and economic grid led by China. Most likely irreversible, the Islamic Republic's Asia-centric strategic realignment means almost half a century of relentless American economic and political pressure has failed to bring Iran back into the American orbit. In fact, the Islamic Republic's defiance of the United States grew bolder over time, as the regime moved militarily closer to Russia, selling Moscow drones to use in its war with Ukraine. As events would show, however, the Islamic Republic had harbored illusions about strategic support from Russia and China, whose alignment with Iran would not go beyond mutually beneficial economic and political transactions.

Meanwhile, at the start of negotiations with the Biden administration in 2021, the Islamic Republic had abandoned JCPOA restrictions in order to enrich uranium closer to the point where building nuclear bombs could happen in a matter of months. All the while, Tehran declared it would not make atomic weapons, something that, according to Khamenei, was forbidden in Islam. This strategy of bringing the country to the threshold of nuclear bomb making while denying any intent of building a bomb was a dangerous risk and a huge burden on an economy already stretched to breaking limits. Apparently, Iran's leaders thought this gambit could strengthen their hand in negotiating with the United States, ignoring the fact that it appeared to confirm Israel's narrative about Iran's bomb-making intentions. Nor did the strategy of threat escalation work to soften the American position on Iran, which Washington increasingly saw as a more dangerous adversary. This was recognized in the 2024 Annual Threat Assessment to the United States, based on "the collective insight of the intelligence community." The document

80 Maziar Motamedi, "Iran Says 25-year China-Iran Agreement Enters Implementation Stage," *Al Jazeera*, January 15, 2022.

named Iran as the third country, after China and Russia, "challenging longstanding rules of the international system as well as United States primacy within it."[81] According to this report, after the dismantling of JCPOA, Iran was closer to being able "to produce a nuclear device, if it chooses to do so." The report admitted the ineffectiveness of sanctions and military strikes, noting the Islamic Republic would move to nuclear bomb–making capacity "in response to additional sanctions, attacks, or censure against its nuclear program."[82]

Iran, the United States, and the post-October 2023 Israeli Onslaught[83]

About a month before the October 2023 Hamas attack on Israel, Iran-US negotiations appeared to have made some progress as each side freed five detainees in a larger deal whereby the United States allowed the return to Iran of $5 billion held in South Korea. This breakthrough in negotiations with the United States was the immediate background to Iran's cautious response to the October 7 events and Khamenei's denial of Iranian involvement in or even knowledge of Hamas's operation. Israel, of course, claimed Tehran was behind the attack and, on April 1, 2024, carried out an airstrike on Iran's embassy in Damascus, killing several military commanders of the Quds Force, the IRGC's branch of foreign operations. Having endured years of Israeli killings of its military and civilian personnel inside and outside its territory, the Islamic Republic finally decided on direct retaliation. Two weeks later, Tehran launched Operation True Promise, unleashing hundreds of drones, as well as cruise and ballistic missiles toward military targets inside Israel, while giving advance notice to Washington. Assisted by the United States, Jordan, France, and the UK, Israel shot down almost all incoming Iranian drones and missiles, although a few breached its defense, inflicting some military damage. Iran and Israel were now at war. On April 19, Israel delivered its first direct military strike on Iran, hitting military targets near nuclear facilities deep inside the country.[84] Exactly one month later, on May 19,

81 *Annual Threat Assessment of the US Intelligence Community* (Office of the Director of National Intelligence, February 5, 2024), 5.

82 Ibid., 19.

83 Robert O. Keohane and Joseph S. Nye, Jr., "The End of the Long American Century: Trump and the Sources of US Power," *Foreign Affairs*, July/August 2025.

84 Mohsen M. Milani, *Iran's Rise and Rivalry with the US in the Middle East* (Oneworld, 2025), 236–8.

2024, Iranians heard the shocking news that President Raisi, along with the country's foreign minister, had died when their helicopter crashed due to bad weather. Rumors quickly circulated about the involvement of foreign enemies or even foul play by the regime itself to get rid of a highly unpopular figure. The latter suspicion gained ground as a hastily conducted election led to the presidency of Masoud Pezeshkian, a candidate aligned with the regime's purged reformist faction. The new president could claim no popular mandate, as 60 percent of the electorate had stayed away during the first round of elections, while he had received slightly over 50 percent of the tally during a second run in which only half the eligible voters participated. In another setback for the ruling elite, the only clerical presidential candidate in 2024 received less than 1 percent of the votes, while the percentage of clerics elected to the Majles that year had dropped to 6 percent, a drastic decline from its 60 percent peak during the revolution's early years.[85]

On July 31, 2024, Israel raised the stakes by assassinating Hamas's political leader, Ismail Haniyeh, who was in Tehran attending Pezeshkian's presidential inauguration. The Islamic Republic's response to this brazen strike on its capital, as well as to Israel's assassination of Hezbollah leader Hassan Nasrallah in Lebanon along with another Iranian military commander, came on October 1, 2024. This was Operation True Promise II, whereby about two hundred ballistic missiles were fired at targets in Israel, once again almost all of them intercepted by Israel's Iron Dome, the US Navy, and Jordanian air defense. Though more effective than Iran's first strike, True Promise II did not significantly damage military targets, and it caused two civilian casualties, one of them a Palestinian. On October 26, 2024, Israel retaliated with three waves of strikes against twenty locations in Iran, targeting air defense batteries and ballistic missile production sites. The attack involved more than one hundred Israeli aircraft, some penetrating Iran's air space, and all returning unscathed. Iran reported insignificant damage and four military casualties. Evidently, the damage was serious, aimed at softening Iran's air defense in preparation for the major invasion that was to follow in 2025.

Escalating military confrontation with Israel coincided with moves toward flexibility in Iran's foreign policy. Early during Pezeshkian's term, the shift toward diplomatic engagement with the United States became more pronounced as the Islamic Republic suddenly lost "the strategic depth" it had cultivated in the region at great cost. During 2024, Israel's

85 bbc.com/persian/articles/ceqd8dgj35jo.

deadly blows against Lebanon's Hezbollah and the collapse of the Assad regime in Syria had broken the so-called Axis of Resistance, the network of political-military alliances Iran had helped construct around Israel at great cost. Hamas, Hezbollah, the Assad regime, and Yemen's Houthi government had their own agendas, but the alliances forged with them were supposed to be the Islamic Republic's forward defense outside its borders and a deterrence against Israel's direct military attack on Iran. Israel saw the Axis of Resistance as the tentacles of an Iranian octopus reaching out to strangle the Zionist state. Whether the Axis of Resistance served as deterrence or provocation in Iran's shadow war with Israel and the United States, its dismantling during 2024 left Iran considerably weaker and more vulnerable.[86] The Islamic Republic's strategic weakening was noted in the 2025 Annual Threat Assessment of the US intelligence community, which amended its 2024 ranking of Iran as the third major challenger, after China and Russia, to US global hegemony. The 2025 assessment noted Tehran's more cautious stance and desire to avoid conflict with the United States, given the changed circumstances of the previous year:

> Regional and domestic challenges, most immediately tensions with Israel, are seriously testing Iran's ambitions and capabilities. A degraded Hizballah, the demise of the Assad regime in Syria, and Iran's own failure to deter Israel have led leaders in Tehran to raise fundamental questions regarding Iran's approach. Iran's consistently underperforming economy and societal grievances will also continue to test the regime domestically . . . Supreme Leader Ali Khamenei continues to desire to avoid embroiling Iran in an expanded, direct conflict with the United States and its allies.[87]

In the wake of Raisi's convenient departure, the Pezeshkian administration was making important, though not strategic, changes in both domestic and foreign policy. Given the failure of the Raisi years' policy of total intransigence, the regime now intensified diplomatic engagement with the United States and quietly made concessions to some of

86 Eskandar Sadeghi-Boroujedri, "Iran and the 'Axis of Resistance': A Brief History," *Jadaliyya*, May 19, 2025. According to one scholar, between 2011 and 2020, Iran had spent $20–30 billion in Syria alone. Milani, *Iran's Rise and Rivalry with the US in the Middle East*, 247.

87 "The 2025 Annual Threat Assessment of the US Intelligence Community," Office of the Director of National Intelligence (March 2025), 22, odni.gov.

the demands of the 2022–23 protests. The most obvious domestic policy concession was the nonenforcement of mandatory veiling (hijab) laws, while in foreign policy, Tehran signaled eagerness to settle differences with either Biden or Trump in the White House. Trump's reelection, with a blatantly protofascist agenda, had complex causes, including Biden's demented sleepwalking campaign, his last-minute replacement by Vice President Kamala Harris, and the Democratic Party's steadfast backing of Israel's genocide of Palestinians. The Islamic Republic's reaction to Trump's victory was a mix of confusion and wishful thinking about the possibility of "making a deal" with him. In March 2025, Trump sent a letter to Khamenei proposing negotiations, setting a two-month deadline for reaching a new nuclear deal. Tehran responded positively, and formal talks began, once again facilitated by the government of Oman and focused on Iran's nuclear program, whose uranium enrichment was almost at the threshold of bomb building. Trump kept sending mixed messages, threatening military action and dangling the prospect of normal relations sweetened by massive US investment in Iran. Israeli Prime Minister Netanyahu vehemently opposed Iran-US talks, arguing Iran's entire nuclear energy infrastructure had to be forcibly dismantled rather than curtailed. Considering what soon transpired, the Islamic Republic walked into a trap, entering negotiations earnestly and without taking proactive measures such as slowing or halting uranium enrichment or long-range ballistic missile production. Such measures would have underlined Iran's flexibility, even if they made no difference to Netanyahu's warmongering resolve.

On June 13, one day past Trump's deadline for reaching a deal, Israel unleashed a massive aerial bombardment of Iran, targeting sensitive military sites and nuclear infrastructure and assassinating dozens of high-ranking military and intelligence leaders and scientists working in the nuclear program. The assassinations involved precision strikes from inside of Iran, suggesting Israel's significant operational capabilities on the ground as well as its deep penetration into Iran's security and intelligence establishment. In addition to nuclear facilities and missile sites, Israel bombed civilian targets such as Iran's energy infrastructure, hospitals, residential neighborhoods, the state broadcasting building, and the notorious Evin Prison, where several dozen detainees, including political prisoners, were killed. Close to five thousand casualties were reported on the Iranian side, with over one thousand deaths, including hundreds of civilians. Hundreds of thousands of Iranians were displaced and millions tried to flee Tehran when Trump threatened to "burn" the capital. The Islamic Republic responded by sending barrages of ballistic missiles and drones toward Israel, most of which were intercepted while some passed through Israel's Iron Dome to hit military targets and inflict hundreds of casualties and a few dozen deaths, mostly among civilians. Some international observers, and many Iranian sources, claimed Netanyahu had intervened to prevent Trump's closing of a deal with Iran. But, even before directly joining the bombing of Iran on June 22, Trump openly and fully backed the Israeli invasion, which obviously was planned and executed with American involvement and logistical support. In the end, the twelve-day war on Iran was a joint American-Israeli venture, with the United States carrying out a highly complex long-range aerial bombardment, dropping twelve thirty thousand–pound "bunker-buster" bombs on three Iranian nuclear sites, including the deeply buried Fordo enrichment plant.[88] Trump had gone to war without securing the legally necessary congressional approval, something US presidents had habitually done, and he got away with it more easily than his predecessors.

An uneasy ceasefire began to take hold on June 24, after Trump reportedly told Netanyahu to order Israeli jets to return during an ongoing mission. While all sides declared victory, Iran was the party suffering by far the heaviest damage militarily and to its nuclear infrastructure, as well as in terms of human casualties. At the same time, the Islamic Republic had survived a devastating war in which all its neighbors had sided with the United States and Israel, while it had received no significant material assistance from anyone, Iran's powerful "friends" (that is, Russia and China) offering only token diplomatic support. Right-wing pundits and Iran's monarchist diaspora were disappointed since no "regime change" took place with the Iranian people rising to topple the Islamic Republic while being bombed by foreign enemies. But the Islamic Republic's "victory" was pyrrhic, since the war's material and political damages had shaken the regime to its core, leaving it standing but without a clear path of dealing with the war's aftermath or its likely resumption.

The extent of damage the Islamic Republic inflicted on Israel remains a matter of dispute, but it is undeniable that Israel exercised total control of Iranian skies and unleashed devastating cyberattacks on the ground, showing it could assassinate the regime's top political and military leaders and, if it so chose, even Khamenei himself. Two broad narratives

88 Sasan Fayazmaneh, "The Madmen Behind the Israel/US-Iran War," *CounterPunch*, July 4, 2025.

on Iran's possible response emerged in the war's immediate aftermath. The first, advanced mainly by observers outside Iran and ranging from realist international relations scholars like John Mearsheimer to some on the anti-imperialist left, argues the war proved the Islamic Republic's resilience and hence the regime should continue to build up its military capabilities, possibly even going nuclear. The second line of argument, discernable mainly inside Iran through statements by reformists, civil society activists, and some regime factions, sees unflinching military defiance as an unbearable burden on the people of Iran, forced to continue an unwinnable war with the United States and Israel. These different takes on foreign policy have divergent implications for the Islamic Republic's domestic politics. Those suggesting military defiance vis-à-vis the United States and Israel tend to downplay the regime's domestic instability and unpopularity, while the critics of this line argue a combination of military defiance and domestic repression would bring the regime to implosion, its internal vulnerabilities amplified by relentless United States and Israeli military attacks. Critics of staying the present course advocate concessions on Iran's nuclear program and military posture, coupled with the easing of domestic repression. A plethora of public statements and open letters by scholars, human rights and civil society activists, lawyers, former and current political prisoners, trade unionists, women's organizations, repressed ethnic and national groups, and purged loyal oppositionists demand what a group of one hundred eighty dissident economists calls a necessary "paradigm change in the ruling system." These statements converge on demanding the freedom of political prisoners, parties, and associations, ending state control of the media, transfer to the government of massive economic assets controlled by the supreme leader and unelected institutions, and ending the involvement of military institutions, primarily the IRGC, in economic affairs. All statements condemn the US-Israeli invasion of Iran and reject "regime change" through foreign intervention or violent uprising.[89] While a reaction to the twelve-day war, these statements build on an ongoing momentum for political change, made more urgent by the anticipation of the eighty-six-year-old and ailing supreme leader's departure from the scene. One year short of matching the shah's thirty-seven years of rule, Khamenei's departure would be a major destabilizing factor, as

89 See, for example, "More than 800 Iranian figures supported Mir Hossein Mousavi's proposal to form a Constituent Assembly and change the constitution," BBC Persian, July 16, 2025, and "Statement by a number of political and civil activists: We are concerned about the fate of Iran," BBC Persian, July 18, 2025.

his unique place, as the decades-long commander of postrevolutionary politics, is unlikely to be filled by any successor.

From the revolution's early years under Khomeini to the present, the Islamic Republic has survived a host of seemingly existential crises, almost all of them overdetermined by Iran's conflict with the United States. The present crisis, however, dwarfs all previous ones, as the regime domestically confronts an increasingly restive public clamoring for political change, while the United States and Israel have broken through the gates, determined to effect regime change via military intervention. It remains to be seen whether the Islamic Republic chooses structural transformation to survive or stays the present course trying to endure by resisting fundamental changes.

Conclusion: The Uncharted Future of Iran-US Relations

At the end of this book, it is appropriate to ask whether the multitude of events and episodes chronicled in its chapters might cohere in a big storyline, a grand narrative of Iran-US history. Though intellectually hazardous, broad historical interpretations inevitably impose themselves, even when historians imagine their work to be merely descriptive. The book's introduction noted how academic accounts of Iran-US history involve implicit or explicit narrative assumptions, such as the myth of auspicious beginnings, tropes of cultural misunderstanding, unfortunate Cold War myopia, Iranian xenophobia, or overreaction to American impositions. A recurrent metanarrative is one of tragedy, with historians lamenting present irreconcilable conflicts and war between the two countries, pondering exactly what might have gone wrong in the past. This book turns that question around, arguing that not much was going right between Iran and the United States in the first place—if we look soberly at state actors (that is, primarily successive American administrations since the Second World War, and secondarily the Pahlavi monarchy and the Islamic Republic).

As we saw in chapter 1, the first century of Iran-US relations (1830s–1930s) looks qualitatively different because it is defined mainly by interactions between individual Americans and Iranians, rather than their governments. The American actors in this period are mostly Protestant missionaries who failed in their evangelical mission but brought modern education and health care to tens of thousands of Iranians, most of them poor people of the provinces. While burdened by cultural biases and occasionally political tensions, on balance, the American missionary impact on Iran left behind a positive legacy unmatched by anything during the second century of Iran-US relations. It is important to remember that the missionaries, as well as well-regarded individual Americans, like Howard Baskerville and Morgan Shuster, did not represent the US government. By the early 1920s, however, the structure of relations was changing as American oil companies sought concessions in Iran, where the American high commissioner of finance, Arthur Millspaugh, lobbied on their behalf. Millspaugh, unlike Baskerville and Shuster, was no supporter of Iran's democratic aspirations, siding instead with the State Department and US business interests and hence aligning with the emerging Pahlavi dictatorship.

US involvement with Iran went into high gear after Washington joined the Allied occupation of the country during the Second World War. Franklin Roosevelt's ideas about a postwar Iran were irritating to Churchill as they implied the extension of the American open door into the British Empire's lucrative backyard, threatening its oil monopoly. From this point onward, access to oil became a primary American interest in Iran, part of a global open-door framework sustained by US military preponderance, requiring growing ties to the Iranian armed forces and to Mohammad Reza Shah, their commander in chief. America's pivotal Cold War intervention in Iran, the 1953 coup, would not have been possible without the decade-long structural links between the United States and the Iranian military. Nor was it a coincidence that US companies received a share equal to their British counterpart in the consortium that would run Iran's nationalized oil industry after the coup. By mid-century, Washington had joined Tehran to its Middle Eastern military satrapies, in CENTO, while getting deeply involved with Iran's economic development by providing loans and planning blueprints. The 1960s became the transition point for Iran's close alignment with American-style social and economic modernization, a project that worked best with autocratic regimes, such as what the shah was building. Though not a mere puppet, the shah led Iran into a vortex of economic and military entanglements with the United States, a dependent relationship that peaked under Nixon and Kissinger, who cynically encouraged the shah's megalomania, supporting him to become a despot at home and the world's leading customer of American armaments. The post-Nixon crisis of US foreign policy destabilized relations with Iran, where the flaws of US-dependent economic development were already showing, and the shah's one-man rule faced growing opposition.

The Carter administration failed to recognize the seriousness of the shah's problems until his regime reached the verge of collapse in late 1978. At that point, the structural weakness of America's game plan in Iran became apparent as a checkmated Carter dropped the king while Iranian revolutionary pieces moved toward the vizier position. Beyond sacrificing the shah, the Carter administration showed further incompetence in dealing with revolutionary Iran. Instead of any fundamental policy change, the United States focused on rebuilding military and security ties with a shaky provisional government out of touch with an unfolding revolution. Khomeini then used the 1979–80 standoff with the United States, the so-called hostage crisis, to divert the revolution's anti-imperialist momentum toward building a clerical dictatorship. Fabricating an existential confrontation with the United States allowed the Islamic Republic to suppress grassroots demands for revolutionary social transformation and crush all dissent, particularly from a defiant left. The hostage crisis doomed Carter's presidency and served Khomeini's state-building purposes at the enormous cost of an effective state of war with the United States, lasting for almost half a century. Iraq's Saddam Hussein used the opportunity to invade Iran and settle scores for Khomeini's interference against his regime and the shah's previous impositions on Iraq. Though Khomeini was responsible for prolonging the Iran-Iraq War, the United States, following Israel, decisively intervened to make sure neither side could prevail. This involved the secret shipment of American arms to Tehran, known as the Iran-Contra Affair, whose exposure almost destroyed Ronald Reagan's presidency. In part to whitewash this embarrassment, the United States escalated its support of Iraq to the point of direct military confrontation with a warworn Islamic Republic, eventually forcing Khomeini to accept a ceasefire in 1988.

The post-Khomeini era in Iran coincided with the collapse of the Soviet Union, leaving the United States as the world's sole superpower. In 1991 President George H. W. Bush declared a "New World Order," defined by uncontested American political, economic, and military hegemony. Devastated by eight years of war, the Islamic Republic then entered its postrevolutionary Thermidor, adapting to a global environment where US domination was more entrenched than ever. Washington's punishment of Saddam Hussein's invasion of Kuwait provided some relief to Tehran, though US economic sanctions and the effective state of belligerence persisted under the Clinton administration. By the end of the 1990s, especially after the election of Mohammad Khatami as president, tensions eased with a de facto Iran-US détente seemingly emerging. This path, however, was blocked by the powerful Zionist lobby in the United States that had identified Iran as the existential threat Israel needed after containing all adversaries. Though the Islamic Republic was quietly cooperating with the United States against the Al-Qaeda network and Afghanistan's Taliban regime, the Israel-neocon lobby managed to place Iran among the "axis of evil" countries targeted by President George W. Bush's global war on terror. Israel's most ominous allegation was that the Islamic Republic diverted its nuclear energy program toward atomic bomb making. But Iran's nuclear program was monitored by the UN, and eventually even the CIA and other US intelligence organizations reported no bomb-making activities by Tehran. Still, Bush added more Iran sanctions, a policy that Barak Obama continued during his first presidential term. A breakthrough occurred during Obama's second term, when he reached out to Iran's supreme leader, arranging for high-level diplomatic negotiations that led to a 2015 formal agreement for tight international control of Iran's nuclear program in exchange for partial but significant US sanction reduction. In 2018, President Trump withdrew the United States from the "Obama deal," piling up unprecedented levels of sanctions on Iran, which had remained in compliance with its commitments to the 2015 agreement. Trump also pushed the ongoing economic war into a military phase by ordering the assassination of high-ranking Iranian military personnel in Iraq. After Trump's departure, President Biden engaged Tehran in direct and indirect talks and rolled back some of Trump's sanctions, but the basic structure of comprehensive US sanctions remained in place.[1]

Starting in 1979, the state of belligerence with the United States has affected Iran's domestic politics, as the Islamic Republic has blamed Iraq's invasion, domestic political dissent, and growing popular disaffection on American machinations. US economic sanctions were meant to make life unbearably difficult for ordinary Iranians, particularly the poor and working classes, who were then expected to turn against their own government in desperation and overthrow it. However, as with other countries targeted by US economic warfare, the Islamic Republic survived the challenge to remain tenacious and defiant vis-à-vis both the

1 For a recent treatment of Iran sanctions, in comparative global context, see Muhammad Sahimi, "A Century of Economic Blackmail, Sanctions and War against Iran," in *Sanctions as War: Anti-Imperialist Perspectives on American Geo-Economic Strategy*, eds. Stuart H, Davis and Emmanuel Ness (Brill, 2022): 165–89; see also Narges Bajoghli, Vali Nasr, Djavad Salehi-Isfahani, and Ali Vaez, *How Sanctions Work: Iran and the Impact of Economic Warfare* (Stanford University Press, 2024).

United States and a battered Iranian populace. Through a "resistance economy," it became more self-reliant, while replacing the United States and European countries with Middle Eastern and Asian trade partners and drawing close to Russia and China. At the same time, and partly in response to foreign sanctions, Iran's economy was increasingly militarized and securitized, allowing powerful but unchecked foundations and organizations, particularly the Revolutionary Guards, a pivotal role in massive underground trade and financial black markets, escalating structural corruption and cronyism.

In sum, instead of weakening and pushing back the Islamic Republic at home and abroad, decades of US sanctions helped make it tenaciously self-reliant, more repressive domestically, and more defiant in foreign relations. The Iranian regime has managed to contain and crush massive waves of popular protest, starting in 1999 and recurring with more intensity in 2009, 2017–18, and most recently in 2022–23.[2] Ultimately, neither the American government nor a growing Iranian diaspora in the United States were able to significantly influence opposition to the Islamic Republic. In the very different circumstances of the 1970s, a mostly US-based Iranian student opposition movement played a crucial role in turning international public opinion against the shah's regime. But a much larger and more resourceful Iranian American diaspora active in the early twenty-first century has produced no viable political agenda or alternative to the Islamic Republic, its main intervention being the sponsorship of satellite television programs saturated with monarchist messages aligned with US government propaganda, thus undermining its own credibility.

At this writing, the Iran-US state of belligerence has moved into a new phase of military confrontation, with President Trump not only backing but joining Israel's invasion of Iran, though in a limited capacity. Trump had lured the Islamic Republic into diplomatic negotiations only to subvert the whole effort by giving Israel the green light for an all-out military attack on Iran and then ordering the massive bombardment of the country's nuclear facilities. The war broke out in the wake of limited air strike and missile attacks between Tehran and Tel Aviv, while the "Axis of Resistance" network of Iran's military allies was dismantled by Israel's invasion of Lebanon and the fall of the Assad regime in Syria. During the twelve-day war of June 2025, the Islamic Republic received

2 Afshin Matin-Asgari, "The Iranian Protests Are the Latest Phase in a Long Cycle of Popular Protests," *Jacobin*, December 1, 2022; Matin-Asgari, "Iran's Rulers Have Contained the Protest Movement, but the System is Far from Stable," *Jacobin*, July 7, 2023.

no material support from any country, all its neighbors effectively siding with the United States and Israel. Despite Israel's devastating blows to its military capabilities and systematic killing of its leading personnel and civilian population, the Islamic Republic did not buckle, managing to inflict considerable damage deep within Israel. Nor did the "regime change" scenario, in which the Iranian people were expected to rise and overthrow the Islamic Republic under attack by foreign enemies, materialize. Clearly, Israel alone cannot bring down the Islamic Republic through warfare, unless the United States joins an all-out invasion of Iran, an unlikely scenario given its catastrophically destabilizing economic and political consequences for the whole region. Now, a battered but defiant Islamic Republic must decide how to respond to the likely resumption of US-Israeli military attacks, while also answering the demands of a restive Iranian public that stood by the regime in the face of foreign aggression but is increasingly pressing for meaningful political participation. The regime is still open to diplomatic negotiation with the United States, willing to make concessions without giving up its right to a peaceful nuclear program under international monitoring. It may also accept restrictions on its ballistic missile defense, which, in addition to a demilitarized nuclear program, could make possible a deal with Trump, but not with Netanyahu. One might argue the Islamic Republic could emerge stronger from the current crisis by making at least tactical concessions on two fronts, vis-à-vis foreign enemies and the people of Iran. That would require a delicate recalibration of intertwined foreign and domestic policy, a task made more urgent by the anticipated crisis of Supreme Leader Khamenei's succession. Regardless of what the United States and Israel might do, the Islamic Republic must accept responsibility for its own contribution to the present impasse and take the initiative to chart a new course, instead of following the worn-out strategy of merely reacting to what its enemies impose. This would be a tall order of major foreign and domestic policy changes, which, even if pursued, will not yield results unless the United States reciprocates by modifying its Iran policy of crushing sanctions and threats of war, while reining in Israel's reckless belligerence toward Iran.

Index